Marketing Communications Stra

The Marketing Series is one of the most comprehensive c̲_̲_̲_̲_̲_̲_̲_̲_̲ _̲_̲ _̲_̲_̲_̲_̲_̲_̲_̲_̲_̲_̲
and sales available from the UK today.

Published by Butterworth-Heinemann on behalf of the Chartered Institute of Marketing, the series is divided into three distinct groups: *Student* (fulfilling the needs of those taking the Institute's certificate and diploma qualifications); *Professional Development* (for those on formal or self-study vocational training programmes); and *Practitioner* (presented in a more informal, motivating and highly practical manner for the busy marketer).

Formed in 1911, the Chartered Institute of Marketing is now the largest professional marketing management body in Europe with over 24,000 members and 28,000 students located worldwide. Its primary objectives are focused on the development of awareness and understanding of marketing throughout UK industry and commerce and in the raising of standards of professionalism in the education, training and practice of this key business discipline.

The CIM Student Workbook Series: Marketing

Business Communication
Misiura

Effective Management for Marketing
Hatton and Worsam

International Marketing Strategy
Fifield and Lewis

Management Information for Sales and Marketing
Hines

Marketing Communications Strategy
Yeshin

Marketing Fundamentals
Lancaster and Withey

Marketing Operations
Worsam

Promotional Practice
Ace

Sales and Marketing Environment
Oldroyd

Strategic Marketing Management
Fifield and Gilligan

Understanding Customers
Lea-Greenwood

Marketing Communications Strategy

Tony Yeshin

*Published on behalf of
the Chartered Institute of Marketing*

Butterworth-Heinemann Ltd
Linacre House, Jordan Hill, Oxford OX2 8DP

ℛ A member of the Reed Elsevier plc group

OXFORD   LONDON   BOSTON
MUNICH   NEW DELHI   SINGAPORE   SYDNEY
TOKYO   TORONTO   WELLINGTON

First published 1995

British Library Cataloguing in Publication Data
A catalogue record for this book is available from the British Library

ISBN 0 7506 1989 9

Printed and bound in Great Britain by
Martins the Printers Ltd, Berwick upon Tweed

Contents

Preface

Welcome to the workbook for the new CIM Diploma paper on Marketing Communications Strategy. A number of important changes have been made to the content of the paper to ensure that it covers the area of strategy more fully. The practitioner area is now substantially covered in the Advanced Certificate Paper on Promotional Practice. As a result, the examiner assumes that you have either taken this paper already, or possess the practitioner knowledge which will be appropriate to your understanding of the strategic issues.

This workbook has been carefully constructed to provide you with the necessary information to tackle the examination with confidence, and in some cases will serve to remind you of the practitioner issues of which you should be aware. To help guide you in your studies, the new syllabus for the Marketing Communications Strategy paper is described below, together with the weighting of the various sections.

As you work through this book, however, you will be aware that there are important structural differences between the contents and the structure of the syllabus. These changes have been made to ensure that you gain a comprehensive understanding of all the important areas of marketing communications, and that you are able to meet the Chief Examiner's overriding requirement – to be able to demonstrate the ability to *develop integrated marketing communications programmes*.

Read through the syllabus carefully to familiarize yourself with the areas which you will be required to cover in the examination. If you apply yourself diligently and work through each of the units carefully, your knowledge of the area will improve substantially.

Good luck with your study programme, and with the examination itself.

Note: the terms *promotional* and *marketing communications* are used interchangeably both here and throughout this workbook.

Tony Yeshin

Acknowledgements

This workbook is dedicated to the patience, forbearance and understanding shown by my family during the period that I slaved over a hot computer keyboard.

How to use your CIM workbook

The authors have been careful to structure your book with the exams in mind. Each unit, therefore, covers an essential part of the syllabus. You need to work through the complete workbook systematically to ensure that you have covered everything you need to know.

This workbook is divided into fifteen units each containing the following standard elements:

Objectives   tell you what part of the syllabus you will be covering and what you will be expected to know having read the unit.

Study guides   tell you how long the unit is and how long its activities take to do.

Questions   are designed to give you practice – they will be similar to those you get in the exam.

Answers   give you a suggested format for answering exam questions. *Remember* there is no such thing as a model answer – you should use these examples only as guidelines.

Activities   give you the chance to put what you have learnt into practice.

Exam hints   are tips from the senior examiner or examiner which are designed to help you avoid common mistakes made by previous candidates.

Definitions   are used for words you must know to pass the exam.

Extending activity sections   are designed to help you use your time most effectively. It is not possible for the workbook to cover *everything* you need to know to pass. What you read here needs to be supplemented by your classes, practical experience at work and day-to-day reading.

Summaries   cover what you should have picked up from reading the unit.

A quick word from the Chief Examiner

I am delighted to recommend to you the new series of CIM workbooks. All of these have been written by either the senior examiner or examiners responsible for marking and setting the papers.

Preparing for the CIM exams is hard work. These workbooks are designed to make that work as interesting and illuminating as possible, as well as providing you with the knowledge you need to pass. I wish you success.

Trevor Watkins
CIM Chief Examiner,
Deputy Vice Chancellor,
South Bank University

The nature of marketing communications

In this introductory unit you will:

- Consider the background to marketing communications.
- Consider the relationship between marketing and marketing communications.
- Review the process and components of marketing communications.
- Look at the nature of perception and the influences on it.
- Examine the dimensions of market segmentation.

By the end of this unit you will:

- Understand the role of marketing communications and the relationship with other components of the marketing mix.
- Appreciate the components of marketing communications.
- Understand the process of communications.
- Be able to apply the principles of market segmentation.

STUDY GUIDE

This first unit of this Marketing Communications Strategy workbook is designed to establish a broad base for the study of marketing communications. Many of you will have completed the CIM Advanced Certificate in Marketing or will have an understanding of the practical issues of marketing communications through your other studies.

This unit will re-aquaint you with the broad area of marketing communications and examine its role within the context of the marketing mix. The material has been designed to be straightforward and easy to use, and provides the foundation for your study of the subsequent material.

We would expect you to take about 3–4 hours to work through this first unit and suggest that you allow a further 4 hours to work through the suggested activities.

Organize your material carefully and systematically from the beginning of your course.

- Ideally, keep all of your material together in a single file.
- Use file dividers to keep broad topic areas indexed and the relevant materials with the pertinent notes.
- Look out for appropriate articles and current examples which will be useful to illustrate your examination answers.

The background to marketing communications

As consumers, we are exposed to a vast amount of information on a daily basis – everything from news reports on television, radio and in the press, to weather forecasts, traffic information, store signs, product packaging, in-store point-of-sale material, and so on. Advertising is just one of the elements with which the consumer must deal every day.

Recent years have seen an explosion in all forms of media. Apart from the four land-based television channels (BBC1, BBC2, ITV and Channel 4) we have an increasing number of satellite and cable stations, and the number will continue to grow as the technology improves. We have radio on FM, medium wave and long wave and, apart from the national and local BBC stations, we have three national commercial stations (Classic FM; Virgin 1215 on AM; and Atlantic on long wave) and more than 150 regional and local commercial radio stations. There are national and regional, morning and evening, daily, weekly and Sunday newspapers. There over 3500 magazines, covering every form of interest area imaginable. There is a wide range of outdoor media, not just fixed poster sites, but also posters on the sides of buses and taxi cabs, on the underground and at railway stations. And many of us have become walking advertisements for the brands we wear, with our clothes bearing logos for all to see.

In 1993, according to the Advertising Association (*Advertising Statistics Yearbook*, Advertising Association/NTC Publications, 1994), some £9155 million was spent on advertising, representing slightly under 1.7 per cent of our gross domestic product. This is slightly above the levels recorded throughout most of the rest of Europe, although it is below that of both Spain and the USA. The lowest percentages of GDP spent on advertising are recorded for Belgium (0.61%), Italy (0.62%) and Japan (0.80%).

Of the UK total, approximately one-third was in the form of press display advertising (£3022 million); 28 per cent was on television (£2065 million); and 23 per cent was in the form of classified advertisements (£2105 million). Other media represented much lower levels of expenditure. Some £300 million was spent on outdoor poster and transport advertising; £194 million on radio and £49 million in the cinema. It is estimated that a total of £904 million was spent on direct mail. Although there has been some slow down in this area, direct mail now represents around 10 per cent of all marketing communications expenditure.

Marketing and marketing communications

Marketing communications is an essential part of the marketing mix – sometimes described as the 'four Ps' (see Figure 1.1). It is important to understand that each of the elements interacts with each of the others. Thus, the nature of the product – and its appeal to the end consumer – will be influenced by the price which is charged. Similarly, the availability of the product at specific retail outlets may influence consumers' perception of the quality of the product. And marketing communications – the fourth P – affects all the other components of the marketing mix.

The attitudes of the consumer towards a particular brand will, to a substantial extent, be a reflection of the nature of the marketing communications elements that are used to support a brand. The task of marketing communications is to present the product or service in the most appropriate manner. In that respect, it must be considered a logical extension of the fundamental principles of marketing itself.

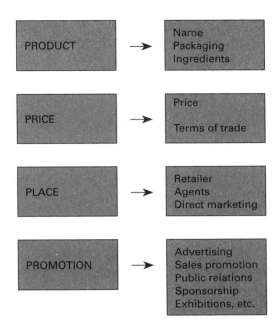

Figure 1.1 From: *Advertising Statistics Yearbook* (Advertising Association/NTC Publications, 1994)

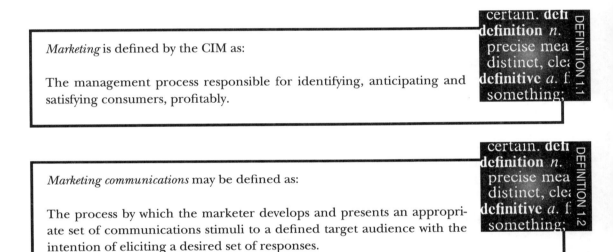

The words *defined target audience* need to encompass more than simply the consumer. The process of communications must be effective to the internal company audience as much as it is with external audiences. And the nature of the external audience will, often, be much broader than potential end users of the product or service.

In order to achieve the desired marketing and marketing communications objectives, a company may well have to communicate with: governmental agencies (to influence existing or potential legislation); the city, financial institutions and shareholders (in order to raise the necessary funds to pursue its marketing programmes); distributors and retailers (to encourage them to stock the product); the media and other opinion formers (to ensure that they think and write positively about the product); the community at large; and its own employees.

The components of marketing communications

Conventionally, marketing communications may be said to include several distinct elements which are used either individually or in combination to achieve the defined objectives. The elements which go to make up the marketing communications mix are advertising, public relations, sales promotion, direct marketing and personal selling. The strategic role and function of each of these elements will be developed in the chapters which follow, but it will be useful at this stage to provide some definitions to aid the understanding of the part they play:

- *Advertising* is any form of paid for media (television, press, radio, cinema, outdoor) used by the marketer to communicate with his or her desired target audience(s).
- *Public relations* consists of all forms of planned communication between any organization and its publics with the objective of establishing and maintaining mutual understanding. It is important to note, however, that public relations is *not* publicity, nor is it free advertising.
- *Sales promotion* is the use of short-term, often tactical, techniques (money-off, coupon offers, gifts, contests) to achieve specific sales objectives.
- *Direct marketing* is an interactive system of marketing which uses one or more advertising media to effect a measurable response and/or transaction at any location (British Direct Marketing Association).
- *Personal selling* is the process by which a salesperson communicates with one or more prospective purchasers for the purpose of making sales.

ACTIVITY 1.1

- Identify an example of each of the marketing mix components.
- Define the task that each has been designed to fulfil and decide whether it is likely to achieve its primary goals.

The promotions mix is the use of any or all of the above-described elements in a unified and cohesive manner designed to achieve specifically defined and measurable promotions objectives. It is important to understand at this stage that these are the tools used in all forms of marketing communication, whether they be for packaged consumer goods, consumer durables, industrial products or services. In terms of marketing communications planning, the nature of the product or service which is to be promoted makes little difference – the same communications tools will be employed. Each component of the marketing communications mix will, however, have a specific task to achieve and it is the deployment of the tools to achieve the objectives which will be an important part of the overall understanding of the subject.

ACTIVITY 1.2

- Identify a product (this may be something from a supermarket or chemist) and a service (such as banking or dry cleaning).
- Write down the elements of marketing communications which are used by the company to achieve their presumed strategic objectives.

Obviously, each component of the marketing communications mix can be used on its own. In fact, though, this is rarely the case. Most companies use some combination of the marketing communications tools in order to achieve their objectives. Most advertising campaigns will be supported with sales promotions activities, or public relations or both. A direct mail campaign may follow media activity designed to stimulate interest in the product. Most companies use point-of-sale material to remind the consumer of their advertising message at the point of purchase, and so on.

What is important, and vitally so, is that each element of the communications mix should integrate with the other tools in the mix in order to achieve the communication of a single and unified message. Clearly, the impact of the message will be enhanced if it is reinforced by other parts of the mix, and the campaign objectives will be achieved in a more cost-effective manner.

The communications process

It is not surprising that with all this 'noise' surrounding us, the task of marketing communications has become increasingly difficult. For any message to get through, it must break through the surrounding noise and grab hold of the potential consumers' attention. To understand the complex process of marketing communications, we have to recognize that each and every one of us has to use some form of filtering system, in order to extract the information we need from everything that surrounds it.

How do we decide what information to absorb, and which to ignore?

We can look at a simple model which describes the various stages. At its simplest level, we can describe the model as having three elements. The first is the sender of the message. The second is the message itself, and the third is the recipient of the message. This could be depicted as shown in Figure 1.2. Unfortunately, this model oversimplifies the nature of the process. It makes no allowance for the fact that the message may not be understood by the recipient; nor does it take into consideration the means by which the message is transmitted to the receiver.

Figure 1.2

A better understanding of the process is provided by the more detailed model shown in Figure 1.3. A number of new elements have been introduced which illustrate the more complex nature of communications. In order to convey any message, we need to encode it into some form of symbolic representation, This may take the form of words or pictures or both. Advertising is usually a combination of both words and pictures which combine to convey a desired impression of the product or service to the consumer. The message to be transmitted will need to be placed into some form of medium or carrier which the sender believes will be seen or heard by the intended receiver. This may be the conventional media, such as television, the press, radio, or posters, but may also include point-of-sale material and the packaging of the product. Later on in the text, we will explain how the medium itself may play an important part in assisting or changing the intended message.

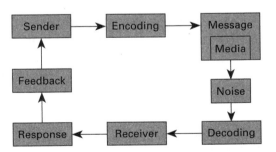

Figure 1.3

Importantly, we must recognize that the message is only one of many which the intended receiver will be required to deal with. To understand that, think of yourself reading a colour magazine. The advertiser who wants to tell you something about his product must compete for your attention not only with the variety of other advertisements included in that issue, but also the diversity of articles for which you bought the publication in the first place. The resultant noise may well interfere with the effective communication of the message. The reader may not spend enough time reading the advertisement, and may only glean enough information to form an impression of the intended message. This is an important aspect of the process of communications which we will return to in later units. And, of course, there is all the 'surrounding noise' with which we have to deal. Few of us have the opportunity to consider an advertisement in splendid isolation. Invariably there will be a whole variety of things going on around us which may detract from our ability to concentrate and to extract the full message being sent by the advertiser. The decoding process may, therefore, be incomplete or confused. In any case it will be influenced by the recipient's preconceptions of the sender. If he or she regards the company as being reliable and trustworthy, then it is likely that the message will be interpreted in that light. However, if the individual has previously had some form of bad experience with another product or service from the same company then it is less likely that the message will be interpreted in a positive manner.

The response which the receiver makes will vary according to the nature of the message and these extraneous factors. Some advertisements simply convey information, others contain some form of injunction to purchase. The response of the receiver to the specific message will be of great importance to the sender, who will need to build in some form of feedback mechanism in order better to understand the nature of the response and, if appropriate, be in a position to change the message if that response is negative.

The decision-making process

Depending on the nature of the product or service that we are intending to buy, we tend to follow a series of distinct 'steps' which form the decision-making process. Commonly, we recognize five stages in the decision-making process, although it must be noted that not every purchase decision involves each of the stages, nor can we say that the consumer always begins the process at the beginning and ends at the end! A model of the purchase decision-making process is shown in Figure 1.4.

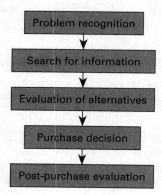

Figure 1.4

Problem recognition

The starting point in the purchasing process is the identification of a problem or unfulfilled need on the part of the consumer. In some instances, these will be basic human needs relating to, say, hunger or thirst. In other instances, the stimulus to problem recognition may be derived from some external source – the comment of a friend or relative, seeing a television commercial or press advertisement, and so on. In all cases, the consumer recognizes that there is a difference between the actual state and the desired state, and that in order to resolve the imbalance, a purchase may need to be made.

EXAM TIP

It is beneficial to be able to illustrate your answers to exam questions with examples from contemporary marketing and marketing communications experience. To help yourself in this process:

- Make sure you regularly read relevant newspapers and professional journals.
- Keep cuttings of relevant articles.

The search for information

In many purchase decisions, there is little time between the identification of the problem and the purchase of the product to fulfil the need. Impulse purchase decisions typically illustrate this type of decision making. The consumer may, for example, pass a confectionery outlet and feel slight pangs of hunger. He or she will enter the outlet and select a product, say a bar of chocolate, to satisfy that hunger. We will see, shortly, that this is indicative of what is known as *routine problem solving*. Indeed, many purchase decisions, particularly of fast-moving consumer goods, are of this nature. In essence, the consumer has previously stored sufficient information about the product category in order to make an appropriate brand selection without any need for additional information.

In more complex purchasing decisions, such as the decision to buy an expensive item such as a hi-fi, television or car, such spontaneity is impossible to contemplate. Even if the consumer recognizes that their existing hi-fi no longer performs in the desired manner, it is extremely unlikely that he or she would simply go down to the nearest electrical retailer and purchase the appropriate equipment. Prior to embarking on the purchase, the consumer will seek as much information as possible to aid the purchasing decision.

Some of this 'information' may come from friends and relatives, who may describe their personal experiences with a particular make or model. Further information might be obtained from independent sources, such as consumer evaluation magazines – *Which?* or *What Hi-fi*, etc. And, in many instances, the consumer will consult specialist retailers for advice. Needless to say, the latter is less than likely to be totally unbiased, but will nonetheless contribute to the sum of knowledge that the consumer is building up about products that might be appropriate. Marketing communications, in the form of advertising, public relations and sales promotion will also play a significant part in this information-building process.

Evaluation of alternatives

The third stage of the process will be a consideration of the alternatives available to satisfy the need. Some of the criteria will be self-referenced. For example, the purchase may be restricted by the availability of funds. Accordingly, products which are too expensive to be affordable will be discarded. Other criteria might be the performance of the product. What output does it have? Will the look and appearance fit in with my existing decor? The scope of the equipment – does it, for example, play records, tapes and CDs? And so on.

Here again, marketing communications makes an important contribution to the evaluation process. As we will see later, some advertising is specifically designed to identify appropriate criteria on behalf of the consumer. Indeed, much advertising for expensive consumer durables is of this nature in which comparisons are made between the advertiser's product and those of his competitors in order to assist the consumer in the purchase selection.

Only when the consumer has gathered sufficient information and evaluated the various alternatives against the established criteria, will the consumer pass to the next stage – the decision to purchase.

What are the factors which, in your opinion, influence the evaluation of alternatives? Relate this question to a recent purchase of an infrequent-purchase item which you have made.

QUESTION 1.2

Purchase decision

Even having passed through the previous stages, it would be naive to assume that the process invariably ends with a decision to purchase. Personal or other considerations may dictate that the consumer either defers the decision or abandons it completely.

If, as was suggested earlier, the consumer has insufficient money to purchase the 'best' equipment at that time, they may feel that cheaper items lack some of the desired features. Accordingly, the decision might be made to delay the purchase until such time as the desired product is affordable.

Alternatively, the consumer might feel that none of the available alternatives really satisfies the need. Perhaps the improvement sought represents too great an investment and it would be better to remain with the existing equipment, at least for the time being.

However, it is equally reasonable to assume that many consumers reaching this stage of the decision-making process end it by making a purchase selection.

Post-purchase evaluation

Once the consumer has returned home with the selected item, a stage known as 'post-purchase evaluation' begins. We have already seen that the consumer has built up an idealized image of the desired purchase during the earlier stages of the process, resulting from a variety of internal and external influences. Inevitably, they will make comparisons of the performance of the product with those criteria.

Where the consumer is satisfied that the product meets the level of expectations, then we have consumer satisfaction. Obviously, this may well impinge on the purchase decisions of other consumers, since the purchaser will, in this instance, comment favourably on the performance and other attributes of his or her purchase to others seeking advice and input.

However, where the consumer feels that the product does not live up to expectations, he or she is said to experience 'dissonance' or 'post-purchase dissatisfaction'. The latter may be brought about, for example, by an advertising message which overclaims for the product. Or there may be an imbalance between the true needs and the product delivery. In either case this post-purchase dissatisfaction is an important element to understand. Consumers who have this response will comment unfavourably on the product, perhaps undermining the impact of marketing communications campaigns. They may write letters of complaint to the manufacturer or, in extreme cases, begin their own programme of publicity by writing to newspapers, specialist publications, and so on. Certainly it is extremely unlikely that they would purchase the same brand again on another purchase occasion.

QUESTION 1.3

- Why is a consideration of post-purchase satisfaction so important in the context of marketing communications?
- What does this suggest for the creation of marketing communications messages?

The nature of purchasing

We have already seen that purchase decisions will be made more or less spontaneously, depending on the nature of the purchase. We can distinguish between three types of decision according to the nature of the 'problem solving' in which the consumer is involved:

- Routine problem solving.
- Limited problem solving.
- Extensive problem solving.

Routine problem solving

As we have already seen, many purchases, especially those involved with low-priced, fast-moving consumer goods, are of this type. In many cases, because the consumer has prior experience of the product category and the variety of brands that are available, little information seeking is involved in the process. Moreover, where the price of the item is comparatively low, little risk is involved in the purchase decision. Hence the decision will tend to be taken quite quickly and in a routine and automatic way.

Limited problem solving

Sometimes, when a consumer is considering the purchase of a new or unfamiliar brand, even when it is within a familiar product category, there may be a limited amount of information seeking, and the consumer will tend to spend slightly more time before making a purchase decision. This is also associated with slightly more expensive purchases, where the cost involves a slightly more detailed consideration or where there is a degree of risk in the purchase. The selection, for example, of over-the-counter medicines is likely to involve some careful consideration of the ingredients, the identity of the manufacturer and so on, before the decision to purchase is made.

Extensive problem solving

The consumer will become involved in a more detailed search for information and the evaluation of alternatives in those instances where the product category is unfamiliar or where a purchase is made on a very infrequent basis.

Obviously, purchases which involve a high capital outlay on the part of the consumer (durable items, cars, houses) or a high degree of personal commitment (life insurance, membership of clubs and societies) will be of the extended problem solving variety.

Identify four examples of:

- A routine purchase.
- A purchase involving limited problem solving.
- An extended problem solving purchase.

Communications strategy

An understanding of the consumers' decision-making process is a vital ingredient in the determination of an appropriate promotional (and marketing) strategy. Although we will explore this in more detail in later units, some examples will be given at this stage by way of illustration.

In the instance of impulse purchase decisions, marketing communications will tend to stress brand name and single attributes, in order to ensure the build up of familiarity. Since the consumer will spend relatively little time considering the available alternatives, manufacturers will need to ensure that appropriate trigger mechanisms are delivered to yield the desired response. Accordingly, a great deal of attention will be paid to aspects such as packaging design, branding, and similar, to provide the necessary levels of familiarity and reassurance which the consumer will require.

At the other end of the spectrum, marketing communications for purchases with a high degree of consumer involvement and those which require extensive problem solving will, necessarily, require to be more informative and detailed in their content. The aim may be to establish a series of criteria for the evaluation of alternatives within the category, and position the product as having the most desirable attributes against those criteria.

- Describe the rational and emotional decisions involved in the purchase of a can of Coca Cola.
- How do these differ from the purchase of a second-hand car?

The nature of perception

The process of decoding a message, whether it be from an advertiser or simply in the form of an article which interests us, will be substantially influenced by a number of perceptual factors. All of us, whether we think about it consciously or not, are influenced by a number of factors in our perception of a situation. And, as we will see in later units, perception itself is a key factor in the field of marketing communications.

Often, the consumer will possess only limited information on which to base a purchase decision. Some of that information, gleaned from other sources, will be incomplete. Value judgements will be based on that limited understanding since, for the individual involved, their perceptions are reality. It is irrelevant that what they understand about the nature of a product or service is lacking or even wrong. In the field of marketing communications we must deal with those perceptual values and either play to them or seek to change them if that be the appropriate course of action.

How does an understanding of consumer behaviour assist in the development of marketing communications strategy?

Our background, family values, the society in which we live and the culture to which we belong all exert a significant impact on our own decision-making process. A product which is wholly acceptable in one society might be taboo in another because of social, religious or moral values. Even the colour of the packaging may mean something different in different markets. And the advertiser must be conscious of these factors when developing the communications campaign. Let us consider these influences on perception in more detail.

Social class

The social class to which we belong will have an important bearing on the way in which we interpret messages, whether they come from the area of marketing communications or elsewhere. All societies operate some form of class system which establishes clear sets of values in the minds of the members of the class. In very real terms, classes differ in their occupations, lifestyles, their way of speaking, their educational expectations, their possessions, and so on. Most individuals perceive that different classes within society have differing amounts of status, privilege and power.

Most importantly, class will impinge on people's behavioural patterns. It will affect such things as the clothes they wear, the food they eat and the newspapers they read. From the perspective of marketing and marketing communications, we need to be concerned with such issues as how the buying patterns of the social classes differ from each other since they inherently represent a major opportunity for market segmentation.

Age and sex

These are two further variables which will affect our attitudes towards products and services. Again, such areas as clothing and foods will have different appeals to people of different age and sex. Both the nature of the clothes worn and, importantly, the brands which are perceived to have desirable attributes, will be affected by the age of the individual.

Clothing products bearing the names of manufacturers such as Chipie, Benetton and the various designer labels have a particular appeal to young or more affluent consumers. Others, like Jaeger and Burberry, will tend to have greater appeal to a somewhat older audience. Older consumers tend to be more 'traditional' in their food consumption patterns. Snack foods and convenience meals have a far greater acceptance amongst the young than the old, for example.

Again, these factors will be important considerations in the process of market segmentation, which we will examine in more detail later.

Family

The influences of the family on patterns of consumption are important to understand. Products which were consumed as part of childhood and growing up tend to continue to be purchased even after the individual has become independent and left home.

Race and religion

All races and religions have fundamental beliefs which impact upon purchasing decisions. This may occur either because they are included within accepted doctrines, or simply because of familiarity.

Income

This is an obvious consideration in the process of segmentation. The ability to purchase products and services is an important factor. Whilst it is obviously desirable that all products should be aspirations of their target audiences, aspiration will not of itself sell products. The consumer must have sufficient disposable income to be able to at least consider purchasing a product offered to them.

Roles

All of us occupy different roles at different times. The same person may be an employer, a son, a father, a husband, a member of a club, and so on. Importantly, these roles will affect our purchasing decisions since, even within the same category, different products may be considered more or less appropriate to the role being fulfilled.

If a man was, for example, contemplating buying flowers, the purchase decision would be substantially influenced by the role and environment in which those flowers would be seen. Thus, the flowers selected for his office would very likely be different from those bought as a gift for his wife.

Reference groups

All of us, similarly, relate to reference groups within society. As with roles, it will be important to the individual to adopt the style and traits of the reference group to which they belong or wish to belong. An immediate example would be the style of clothing. Whilst in the office, a person would be likely to wear formal clothing in keeping with other employees. That same person might wear more casual clothing at home or for leisure, but equally might buy specific clothes similar to those worn by other members of, say, a sports club or other membership group.

Family life cycle

The nature of the products purchased will be influenced to a substantial degree by the stage which the individual occupies within the overall family life cycle. Typically, family life cycles may be divided into several distinct stages, as shown in Figure 1.5.

Figure 1.5

The *dependent* individual is typically under 18 years old and living at home with his or her parents. At a very early age, all purchasing decisions are made on his or her behalf, although as the individual becomes older there may be an increased level of consultation. Even very young people may exert a considerable influence on purchasing decisions, especially in terms of the selection of brands.

As age increases, so too does the level of independence, even within the family environment. The break up of the nuclear family has resulted in, on occasion, separate meal times and a consequent personal selection of the foods to be consumed.

The *bachelorhood* stage is that of a young single adult living away from parents. The individual may be employed or unemployed and this will have a substantial bearing on the nature of products and services consumed. There will, however, be strong evidence of family influence on purchasing decisions, typically in the areas of which familiar brands of fast-moving consumer goods will continue to be purchased. At the same time, the individual will be seeking to stress his or her independence, and some purchase decisions will be specifically made to enhance this feeling.

This stage will most commonly be followed by the *honeymoon* period. Whether the couple are married or living together, the key features are the enhanced wealth – derived from two income earners – and the relative lack of commitments. This affords a more indulgent lifestyle and the consumption of luxury products. This may evolve into the nest-building stage in which consumption patterns will be dictated by the expenses involved in setting up a permanent home.

The period of *parenthood* will be typified by the diversion of income to the problems of bringing up children. Financial resources will often be stretched considerably and former purchases will sometimes be deferred. The purchase of a new car, for example, may be given lower priority in the context of feeding and clothing one or more children. Here again, the period will embrace a number of significant changes. Income will tend to increase over the period. However, as the children become older their needs will change, resulting in a diversion of income to other expenditure areas, such as education.

The penultimate stage is that of *post-parenthood*. Here the children have left home, leaving the parents with a relatively high disposable income. Most of the household needs will have been purchased previously and, except for replacement, monies can be spent on a new form of indulgence – travel and holidays, leisure pursuits, and so on.

The final stage is that of the *survivor*. This stage occurs with the death of one spouse. Here, again, purchase patterns will change. There will be an increased tendency to purchase packaged convenience food products, and in many cases the pursuit of a more economical lifestyle.

A proper understanding of the family life cycle is an important facet in the determination of marketing communications strategies. The appropriate positioning of products and services to individual life-cycle groups will be an important ingredient in the successful communication of the supporting message.

ACTIVITY 1.5

Identify six products which might have special appeal for each of the life-cycle stages described above.

Personality

How the individual responds to his or her environment will impinge upon product and service purchase decisions. The products and services purchased will tend to be those which are considered to be consistent with the individual's personality traits. More extrovert individuals will tend to buy more flamboyant clothing, wear more intrusive perfumes and so on. Conversely, introverted individuals will tend to be recessive in terms of their purchasing behaviour patterns.

QUESTION 1.5

How do marketers set about changing consumer attitudes?

Attitudes

Attitudes are an expression of an individual's feelings towards a person or object, and reflect whether they are favourably or otherwise disposed towards that person or object. Attitudes are not directly observable, but can be inferred either from behavioural patterns or by some form of interrogation, typically using market-research methods.

Attitudes towards products and services are an important dimension, since they will affect the individual's propensity to purchase. Products for which favourable attitudes are held are far more likely to be purchased than are those which create negative attitudes.

Lifestyle

Research amongst consumers has shown that specific lifestyle factors in terms of shared beliefs, attitudes, activities and behavioural patterns often transcend other forms of differentiation. Lifestyle segmentation tends to group people on the basis of their interests, activities and opinions and, as such, provides a much fuller picture of consumers than does conventional demographic segmentation.

Lifestyle segmentation measures three key facets of the individual:

- *Activities* – how they spend their time.
- *Interests* – the dimensions of personal interest in their surroundings.
- *Opinions* – the factors which are important to them.

Several attempts have been made to group people according to lifestyle characteristics. Typical of these is the work done by the Stanford Research Institute in the USA known as VALS. This divides the population into groupings according to their self-orientation – whether they are *actualizers* (successful and sophisticated individuals with high self-esteem and high resources who seek to develop and express themselves in a variety of ways) or *strugglers* (who tend to be of poor health and of low income and who represent relatively limited markets for most consumer goods and services). The VALS typology depicts eight separate groupings:

- *Actualizers.*
- *Fulfilleds*   Mature, satisfied and comfortable individuals who tend to seek knowledge concerning their surroundings. They tend to be less concerned with images than functionality and value for money.
- *Believers*   A group with comparatively conservative beliefs, with a strong attachment to tradition and the community. As such, they are relatively slow to change their purchasing patterns and rely on familiar brands.
- *Achievers*   Tend to be successful in their careers and are in control of both themselves and their lives. Their purchases tend to reflect this in terms of those items which display their success to others.
- *Strivers*   These are very image conscious and tend to emulate those whom they perceive as having done well. Although their income will tend to be limited, they spend their money in ways which, they hope, will secure the approval of those they wish to be like.
- *Experiencers*   Tend to be young and impulsive. They are very much the followers of fashion and, whilst rejecting conformity, tend to be avid trialists of new products and experiences.
- *Makers*   These are practical individuals who have a belief in their own skills. They tend to be absorbed in the home and family and enjoy participation in practical hobbies such as DIY, wine making, gardening, and so on.
- *Strugglers.*

Why do marketers use techniques other than basic demographics to develop a better understanding of market segment opportunities?

QUESTION 1.6

The above discussion shows that there are a wide variety of opportunities to engage in *market segmentation*. In essence, manufacturers are continuously examining ways in which consumers can be grouped together in different ways in order to present their product or service in a unique light. The key to these important dimensions of market segmentation is, predominantly, market research (which we will explore in more detail in Unit 6).

There can be no single prescription for the process of market segmentation. What is important is that companies have a deep understanding of their potential consumers and their needs and respond to them with an appropriate array of products and services specifically designed to meet those needs.

How do the major manufacturers in the soaps and detergent markets differentiate their products from those of their competitors?

In this unit we have:

- Begun the process of understanding the nature of marketing communications and its role within the marketing mix.
- Seen some of the difficulties which marketing communications messages must confront in an increasingly crowded media environment and the various stages through which the message must pass on its way to the recipient.
- Begun an examination of some of the important constructs of consumer behaviour which have an important bearing on the development of both marketing and marketing communications strategies.
- Looked at the consumers' decision-making processes and their different needs depending on the nature of their intended purchase (the more complex the purchase, the greater the amount of information they will require), and how this will affect the construction of the message and its content.
- Seen that we must remember that the consumer cannot be considered in isolation, waiting readily to hear what we have to say. They are subject to a great number of influences on their opinions and attitudes which will impact on the final purchase decisions.
- Seen how markets can be segmented according to a number of different dimensions to provide an organization with the ability to direct its message not to potential consumers as a whole, but rather to separate segments of the market whose needs may differ and to whom a more targeted proposition can be made.

In the chapters which follow, we will explore the important dimensions of marketing communications strategy and develop in more detail the underlying principles which govern the practical implementation of marketing communications programmes.

- Write out the segments of the beverage market. Consider all the various options available (e.g. hot, cold, alcoholic, non-alcoholic).
- Taking any one segment, consider the additional segmentation possibilities.

Examination hints and specimen questions

Below are two specimen questions taken from recent CIM papers. Although much of the material to answer the questions will be derived from this unit, it is important to understand that you will only have a complete grasp of the topic once you have completed all the *remaining units of study*. Nonetheless, it is important that you begin to *practise tackling examination questions* of this type, and there is no better time to start than now! It will probably be worth while returning to these questions once you have completed the other units. It will demonstrate the other learning that has taken place since your first attempt.

Both questions are taken from the second part of the paper in which you are required to answer a total of three questions. Several questions will be available from which you can choose the ones you prefer to attempt. This second section is worth 50 per cent of the total marks allocated to the paper, and you should allocate your time accordingly. Since the paper, in total, is of 3 hours duration, no more than one and a half hours should be allocated to part 2, which represents 30 minutes per question tackled.

- *Time allocation* is an important aspect of exam technique.
- Remember the law of *diminishing returns.*
- After a certain amount of time, the amount of *new information* that you will provide to the examiner is limited.
- You are far better moving on to the next question than spending more than the allocated time on the question you are answering!

Central to the definition of marketing communications is the concept that all marketing mix variables, and not just the promotional variables alone, communicate with customers. You have been asked to submit notes for a talk to business people. The talk is intended to describe the ways in which any organization should go about developing a completely integrated marketing communications campaign.

(June 1992)

According to research carried out by Mintel, children are aware and sophisticated consumers who influence parents when it comes to buying food, environmentally friendly products and the latest fashions in clothes and footwear. Identify the factors which have influenced this situation and assess the implications in developing effective communications strategies for manufacturers of these products.

(December 1992)

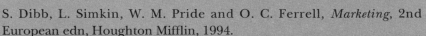
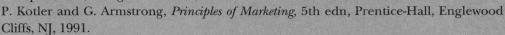

EXTENDING KNOWLEDGE

To gain a fuller grasp of marketing concepts, it is recommended that you refer to:

S. Dibb, L. Simkin, W. M. Pride and O. C. Ferrell, *Marketing*, 2nd European edn, Houghton Mifflin, 1994.
P. Kotler and G. Armstrong, *Principles of Marketing*, 5th edn, Prentice-Hall, Englewood Cliffs, NJ, 1991.

For a deeper understanding of marketing communications concepts:

J. F. Engel, M. R., Warshaw and T. C. Kinnear, *Promotional Strategy*, 8th edn, Irwin, 1994.
P. R. Smith, *Marketing Communications – An Integrated Approach*, Kogan Page, 1993.
J. Wilmshurst, *Fundamentals of Advertising*, 3rd edn, Butterworth-Heinemann, Oxford, 1991.

To gain more knowledge in the area of consumer behaviour:

H. Assael, *Consumer Behaviour and Marketing Action*, 4th edn, Brooks/Cole, 1992.
J. C. Mowen, *Consumer Behaviour*, 2nd edn, Maxwell Macmillan, 1990.
L. G. Schiffman and L. Kanuk, *Consumer Behaviour*, 12th edn, Prentice-Hall, Englewood Cliffs, NJ, 1990.
K. Williams, *Behavioural Aspects of Marketing*, 2nd edn, Butterworth-Heinemann, Oxford, 1991.

Marketing communications strategy – an overview

In this unit you will:

- Study the nature of marketing communications strategy.
- Consider the task of establishing communications objectives.
- Examine the need for integrating marketing communications.
- Look at the external factors that affect marketing communications.
- Explore the dynamics of relationship marketing.

By the end of this unit you will:

- Understand the importance of strategy in the context of marketing communications.
- Be able to set guidelines for the establishment and measurement of communications objectives.
- Appreciate the strategic importance of integrated marketing communications.
- Be aware of the forces that affect marketing communications strategy.

STUDY GUIDE

This unit is concerned primarily with providing a comprehensive understanding of the strategic implications of marketing communications and, especially, the dynamics of integrated activities.

This is a particularly important unit, since it establishes key principles which will affect your understanding of the further processes involved in the discipline.

In order to work through this unit, you should allocate about 3–4 hours to study and a further 4 hours to complete the various activities.

STUDY TIP

- Create a new file for this section of study.
- Make concise and detailed notes on the various topics covered by this unit.
- Collect any relevant articles and examples from marketing and advertising journals. Since the topics are all of major importance, there will be many to collect and read.

Almost everyone involved with marketing communications has a direct interest in the measurement of results. Not unreasonably, any company spending money in the area of marketing communications is keen to determine the level of return on its investment and the impact of its expenditure.

By the same token, advertising agencies, public relations, sales promotion and direct marketing consultancies as well as specialist media agencies, are keen to demonstrate that their campaigns have a meaningful impact both on the consumers and the trade alike. The various media, through which the specific message is communicated, wish to demonstrate their efficiency and effectiveness in the targeting of chosen groups.

Although considerable progress has been achieved in the measurement of results, with new techniques being developed, it has to be recognized that some aspects of the marketing communications process remain unclear. Frequent attempts are made, for example, to determine the precise way in which advertising works. In a recent book by Colin McDonald (*How Advertising Works, A Review of Current Thinking*, The Advertising Association/NTC Publications, 1992), some 150 pages are devoted to an examination of current theories and, although the author makes some valid recommendations, there is no definitive answer to the question of how advertising works. Indeed, since its publication in 1992, several new theories have been propounded, which add to the debate but fail to resolve it.

Thus, although it is clear that the techniques of marketing communications are capable of delivering a chosen message to a desired audience, the precise working of these messages is less clearly understood. Marketing communications remains a comparatively imprecise science. This does not mean that we should abandon the search for truth, or the development of a more systematized approach to the process. Far from it. We need to become progressively more sophisticated and analytical in our approach to the management of marketing communications, if we are to build confidence in the techniques.

If we don't understand how advertising works, how can we justify spending our money in that area?

As we will see (Unit 6), much time and effort has been expended on the development of measurement techniques designed to ensure that, as far as possible, the results of our actions can be determined with a reasonable degree of accuracy before the event rather than after it.

A starting point for the process is the *determination of objectives.* To begin with, it is vital that we discriminate and distinguish the aims of marketing communications from those of marketing in general.

Marketing communications objectives are specific communications tasks to be achieved amongst a defined audience to a defined extent and within a specific time frame. To this might be added the words 'within a predefined budget'.

In many instances, the objectives outlined for marketing communications remain imprecise and vague, or are confused with the overall marketing objectives. Objectives written as:

- To increase our share of market.
- To encourage more young users to purchase the brand.
- To ensure a wider level of distribution.

are all areas in which the process of marketing communications can make a contribution. However, they are properly the province of marketing rather than marketing communications itself. Moreover, they lack the necessary precision which will enable us to monitor whether, after the completion of marketing activities, these objectives have been met adequately and cost effectively.

By the same token, statements written as:

- To improve the company image.
- To develop favourable attitudes towards the brand.
- To establish the product as a leader in its field.

whilst more properly the province of marketing communications, are similarly vague and imprecise. It is imperative that all marketing communications objectives are clearly defined and understood.

Setting marketing communications objectives

It is important that, in establishing marketing communications objectives, certain 'rules' are followed. These are not hard and fast rules, but are intended to provide guidelines for the establishment of realistic objectives which can be agreed upon, adhered to and monitored.

A marketing communications objective is a succinct statement of the specific communications tasks within the overall marketing plan

As we have already seen, it is vitally important that the tasks of marketing communications are distinguished from those of marketing. As such, they must state the specific tasks that marketing communications techniques are uniquely qualified to perform and should not encompass aims that require the use of other marketing techniques. Moreover, since marketing communications is a relatively abstract area, it is even more important to have clearly defined objectives in order to provide real substance to any debate.

Marketing communications should be written down in finite and measurable terms

It is not sufficient to define marketing communications objectives simply as, for example: 'To increase awareness, to build loyalty, to encourage trial'. Such statements fail to establish the necessary targets which are required to be met and, perhaps more importantly, do not allow for the proper evaluation of the campaign upon completion. If the level of awareness has increased by, say, 10 per cent or we have 15 per cent more loyal users, can we agree that the campaign has worked? It is important to include these levels at the outset in order both that the appropriate strategy can be determined and that the outcome of the campaign can be properly tested and evaluated.

It is important that marketing communications objectives are agreed upon by everyone involved in the process

From the management to the creative team, all the people involved in the process of marketing communications must agree, at the outset, what the specific objectives are. By ensuring this level of agreement, everyone involved knows precisely what is required and, equally important, has a benchmark against which to assess recommendations.

Are the techniques recommended capable of achieving the objectives? Does the proposition communicate the desired position to the target audience?, etc. The absence of agreed objectives can result in considerable wastage of both time and effort, since the parties involved do not hold a unified view of what is to be achieved. Moreover, the objectives themselves will provide a focus for debate and the means of resolving differences of opinion.

There is little doubt that people can achieve more when they are given a precise statement as to what they must achieve. This is increasingly important as the costs of marketing communications multiply, and the need to avoid waste becomes more pressing.

The statement of objectives should not conflict with the creative process. Whilst it remains true that we are always looking for the 'big idea', it is more likely that we will find it if the work is properly focused. Clearly defined objectives assist the process of creative thought. By establishing a precise definition of what it is that we wish to communicate, the creative team can concentrate their efforts on deciding how best to say it. In the absence of clear and definite objectives, there is a tendency towards 'compromise'. By being precise, the tasks can be more readily achieved.

The process of planning must be separated from that of implementation

As much time must be spent on determining what needs to be said and to whom, as how to say it. The fundamental requirement is to ensure that the delivered message is consistent with consumer needs and wants. It follows that determining which segment of the overall audience represents the target for a marketing communications campaign, and precisely what it is that they require of the product category, are essential prerequisites to the creation of a campaign designed to communicate that proposition. Similarly, the planning process must be based on an intimate knowledge of the markets and consumer buying behaviour.

Markets, and consumers within them, have become increasingly volatile. Few people can claim to have a precise understanding of the particular requirements at any moment of time without accessing additional information.

The introduction of new products, with new properties and attributes will serve to change expectations of how an existing product should perform. And, as we will see, we need to be concerned as much with perceptions as with the reality of product performance and delivery. What the consumer *believes* about a product is far more important than the reality.

If we want to know where we are going, it is important first to know where we are

Some realistic assessment of the current state needs to be made in order to establish a series of benchmarks against which objectives can be set.

Objectives, in order to be realistic, must take account of the current position of the product or service. If a brand already has a high level of awareness, for example, then it is unlikely that expenditures in this area will achieve much. If the brand is failing to make progress, then it can be assumed that it is in some other area that there are shortcomings. These need to be determined before campaign objectives can be set.

At the same time, the task of taking awareness levels from, say, 20 to 50 per cent will be markedly different from that of improving to, say, beyond 80 per cent. There will be significant implications for target definition, media selection and so on, which we will consider in later units.

Monitoring and control are vital ingredients and must be built in in advance

It is important that agreement is achieved in advance as to the methods to be employed for evaluation and control. Again, as we shall see, there are a wide variety of measurement techniques pertinent to the area of marketing communications. However, the different techniques are themselves designed to monitor different aspects of marketing communications. It is important that the relevant approaches are employed to monitor performance, since the use of the wrong technique may fail to assess performance within the desired areas.

It is important to establish that monitoring is not an end in itself. The purpose of using techniques such as market research is to aid the process of learning and understanding, and to enable the accurate assessment of the cost-effectiveness of the techniques employed.

ACTIVITY 2.2

- Identify three examples of markets where the physical product differences are minimal.
- What are the differences that marketing communications seeks to communicate in those markets?

QUESTION 2.3

Without referring to the previous section, outline the important requirements when defining marketing communications objectives.

Integrated marketing communications

A major contemporary issue in the field of marketing communications is the drive towards integrated activity. There are a number of reasons for this fundamental change in thinking which need to be examined.

Key to the issue is the fact that the consumer does not see advertising, public relations, sales promotion and other marketing communications techniques as separate and divisible components. As the receivers of a variety of messages from an equally wide range of sources (see Unit 1) consumers build up an image – either favourable or unfavourable – of a company, its brands and its services. As far as they are concerned, the source of the message is unimportant. What they will be concerned with is the content of the message.

A parallel consideration is the fact that the communicator desires to achieve a sense of cohesion in the messages which he or she communicates. If, for example, advertising is saying one thing about a brand and sales promotion something different, a sense of dissonance may be created with the consumer left in some doubt as to what the brand is really trying to say.

There is little doubt that marketing communications funds spent on a single communications message will achieve a far greater impact than when a series of different or contradictory messages are being sent out by the brand. With the pressure on funds, marketers desire to ensure that they a presenting a clear and precise picture of their products and services to the end consumer. This is particularly true in those instances where a company with a comparatively small budget seeks to take on competitors with significantly larger levels of expenditure.

Ian Linton in his new book *Integrated Marketing*, cites the example of Sally Line, the cross-channel ferry company. The Sally Line could not match the expenditure levels of P&O or Sealink in the context of mainstream media. However, by developing an integrated communications campaign that reinforced their theme in direct mail, videos and brochures, together with limited above-the-line expenditure, the company can ensure that it delivers a single and consistent message to its potential customers.

Few companies are specifically concerned with issues of whether to spend their money on advertising, sales promotion, public relations, or elsewhere. They are concerned with ensuring that they develop a cohesive marketing communications programme which most effectively communicates their proposition to the end consumer. The specific route of communication is far less important than the impact of the message. In budgetary terms, companies need to consider where their expenditure will best achieve their defined objectives. The previous notions of separate and distinct advertising, sales promotion, public relations, and other budgets fail to appreciate that the considerations of the marketing communications budget need to be addressed as a matter of priority.

But, at the heart of the debate is the recognition that the consumer must be the focus of all marketing communications activity. If we return to the CIM definition of marketing (Unit 1, Definition 1.1), we can see that the primary need is the anticipation and satisfaction of consumer wants and needs. It is the development of an understanding of the consumer and his or her wants and needs that will ensure that marketing communications works effectively to achieve the objectives defined for it. This represents a fundamental change of focus. A shift from the functional activity of creating marketing communications campaigns to an attitudinal focus in which the consumers' needs are at the heart of all marketing communications planning. And, with it, a change from a focus on the product itself to the ultimate satisfaction of the end consumer. Of course, there are functional implications.

The task of developing and implementing marketing communications campaigns is becoming increasingly divergent. No longer is the task in one pair of hands. As the specialist functions develop further, the marketer must seek and co-ordinate the input from a number of different sources. Many organizations will retain an advertising agency, a public relations consultancy, a sales promotion company and, perhaps, even a media specialist. Ensuring that all of these contributors work to the same set of objectives and deliver a cohesive message to the consumer is a task which is an increasingly challenging one.

Above all else, there is an increasing recognition that companies need to identify what position their product or service occupies in the minds of the consumer relative to that of other products or services. Only when they have gained that knowledge can they begin the process of planning marketing communications either to alter or enhance that position.

Find two examples of an integrated marketing communications programme. Describe the variety of communications techniques used, and how they are integrated with each other.

ACTIVITY 2.3

The impact of external factors on marketing communications

External and environmental factors have forced marketers to undertake a fundamental re-think both of marketing strategies and of the positioning of products, and this in turn must impact on the process of marketing communications.

Information overload

As noted in Unit 1, the consumer is continuously bombarded with vast quantities of information. Whether the information is orchestrated by the marketer or the media in general is less relevant than the fact that there is simply too much information for the average consumer to process effectively. The inevitable consequence is that much of the material is simply screened out and discarded. The result is that the consumer may make purchasing decisions based on limited knowledge, or even a misunderstanding of the real facts. The individual is far less concerned with the average advertising message, which makes the task of ensuring appropriate communications with the target audience an event more daunting prospect.

An important dimension of the screening process is what I have described elsewhere as the 'submarine mentality'. In essence, since none of us can absorb all of the information around us, we establish personal defence mechanisms to screen out unwanted or irrelevant information. The analogy would be that of a submarine which goes underwater and hence avoids the surface bombardment. At periodic intervals, the submarine lifts its periscope to examine particular aspects of the world around it. And when it has finished gathering the new information, it descends again – oblivious to any changes which might be taking place.

As consumers, our awareness of specific advertising messages is treated in a similar way. Some form of trigger mechanism is usually required to encourage us to pay attention to the variety of marketing communications messages. Usually, this is an internal recognition of an unfulfilled need which heightens the levels of awareness of pertinent advertising and other information. The principle can be commonly observed. If, for example, you have recently purchased a new car, your awareness of the marque will be enhanced and you will immediately become aware of similar vehicles all around you.

However, in the process of attempting to find better and more effective ways of communicating, we have also gained a greater appreciation of the nature of marketing communications itself. Much work has been done in the area of model construction and theoretical examination (as we will see in Unit 3) which has helped us to enhance areas of implementation.

The discerning consumer

The 1990s have seen the progressive improvement in levels of education which, in turn, has made consumers both more demanding with regard to the information they receive and more discerning in their acceptance of it. Marketing communications propositions developed in the 1950s and 1960s would be treated with disdain by today's more aware consumers. Specious technical claims and pseudo-scientific jargon which were once at the heart of many product claims are no longer given quite the same credence.

A contradiction

The above two factors, however, combine to create a new dynamic for marketing communications. The inability to store and process new information, coupled with the demand for a greater focus in marketing communications messages, has resulted in the consumer relying more on perceptual values than on factual information. All consumers build up a set of 'values' which they associate with a company or a brand. Some of these values will be based on personal experience, or the experience of others. Many of their values will, however, be based on a set of 'short-handed conclusions' based on overheard opinions, the evaluation of third-party organizations, or even the misinterpretation of information.

However these thought processes are developed, and however the information is received, is less important than the fact that for the individual their views represent the truth. A product which is perceived to be inferior (even though there is factual evidence to contradict this view) is unlikely to be chosen in a normal competitive environment. The imperative, therefore, is to understand the process of perceptual encoding and relate it to the task of marketing communications. A simple example will suffice.

Most consumers are responsive to a 'bargain' proposition. Certain assumptions are made, particularly in relation to well-known and familiar brands. If a potential consumer sees a product on sale in a market environment, there is some expectation that the price will be lower than, say, in the normal retail environment. If the brand name is well established, then it is likely that they will be able to draw from it the confidence and reassurance which will be necessary to the making of a purchase decision. Indeed, there is considerable evidence that these perceptual factors, influenced by the environment, will for some consumers induce them to make a purchase, even though they might have been able to purchase the same product at a lower price elsewhere.

Many retailers have recognized this situation and have adopted a positioning relative to their competitors of low price. By marking down the prices of a narrow range of products, they encourage the consumer to believe that all products are similarly discounted. The result is that the consumer will decide to make all of his or her purchases at that outlet, based on the perceptions derived from a limited comparison of those brands upon which the retailer has focused marketing communications activity. Since few consumers are in a position to make objective comparisons across a wide range of comparable outlets, these perceptions are accepted and become the reality.

The situation is compounded by the fact that price is only one consideration in a purchase decision. Most people have an ideal view of a price and quality combination. Needless to say, such a view is highly personal and subjective, but becomes the basis of making subsequent purchase decisions for that individual. Thus reputation, both for retailers and brands, will be an important consideration in the purchase selection (as we will explore in Unit 4).

ACTIVITY 2.4

Consider the apparent positionings for three different products in the same market category. What are the consumer segments to which each product seeks to appeal?

22

Changes in family composition

The notion of the family comprising two adults and 2.4 children is long gone. In all countries, the notion of family itself has different meanings. Some communities perceive the family as a small integrated unit, others adopt a model of the extended family with the elder children having responsibility for ageing members of the family – either parents or grandparents. The increasing levels of divorce and the growing acceptance, by some, that marriage is not a norm to which they wish to comply, has resulted in growing numbers of single-parent families. In all these situations, the needs and expectations of different families will be substantially different from each other, and effective marketing communications needs to recognize and respond to these underlying changes in society.

The ageing population

In many countries, improved standards of living and better health care have resulted in two parallel changes. On the one hand, in order to sustain living standards, people are deferring having children or are having fewer of them. On the other hand, life expectancy is improving as medical care is enhanced. These forces have resulted in a progressively ageing population in most developed markets, and with it a change in the values, needs and wants which consumers exhibit with regard to products and services.

The green imperative

Increasing numbers of consumers are concerned with the environmental impact of the products and services they consume. The abandonment of chlorofluorocarbons (CFCs), the reduction in the volume of packaging waste, the consumption of scarce and irreplaceable resources and similar factors have all impacted on consumers' perceptions of desirable products and services. No longer is the single focus of their attention the efficacy or otherwise of the products they might buy. They require reassurance that, not only do the products perform in the way that they expect, but that they also contribute to a better environment.

The growth of narrow casting

The advent of an increased number of media channels – land based, cable and satellite television, an increasing number of radio networks, and a mammoth explosion in the number of 'specialist' magazine titles – have resulted in a fundamental shift in terms of media planning. Where once the advertiser had to recognize that the use of a chosen medium might, whilst providing excellent coverage of the desired target audience, carry with it a substantial wastage factor, the situation has now changed somewhat.

Consumer groups can be targeted with a far higher level of precision. A specific message can be developed to appeal to a subgroup of users accessed by the nature of the television programmes they watch or the magazines they read. The increasing use of direct marketing techniques has resulted in the possibility of one-to-one marketing – where the proposition can be tailored specifically to respond to the individual needs of the single consumer.

The growth of global marketing

The changes brought about largely by mass communications have, to some degree, encouraged the movement towards global marketing. With the recognition that national and cultural differences are growing ever fewer, major manufacturers have seized upon the opportunity to 'standardize' their marketing across different markets.

It is now possible to purchase an ostensibly similar product with the same name, same identity and similar product ingredients in many different markets. From the ubiquitous Coca Cola, now available in almost every country, to products like the Mars Bar, manufacturers are seizing the opportunity to ensure a parity of branding throughout all the markets they serve, and to extend the territories in which they operate. There are few markets (although the product contents may well be different) which would not recognize the Nescafé coffee label or what it stands for. 'M' means McDonalds in any language, and Gillette run the same copy platform for its Series range of male shaving preparations in many different countries. We will examine the international dimensions of marketing communications in more detail in Unit 13.

Non-verbal communications

We have already seen that the emergence of new media has enabled a more precise focus on target groups of consumers. But it has also demanded a new approach to the execution of marketing communications propositions, particularly on television. Increasingly, satellite channels are unrestricted in their availability. The same programmes can be watched simultaneously in France and Finland, Germany and Greece. And, if that is true of the programming, it is equally true of the advertising contained within.

Whilst programmers have the opportunity to overcome language and other barriers to communication within their formats, the same is not so readily true for the advertiser. The response has been a growth in the recognition that visual communication has a vital role to play in the overall process. Increasing numbers of television commercials are being made with a pan-European or global audience in mind. The emphasis is less on the words being used than on the impact of the visual treatments employed.

Currently, a constant visual treatment is being used by Gillette to support their Series range of products across diverse markets. Here, the voiceover is modified to verbalize the proposition in each market place. Other companies have gone considerably further. The verbal component of the proposition has been minimized, with the storyline being developed entirely, or almost entirely, in visual form. Current television commercials for Dunlop, Levi's and Perrier are examples of this approach.

ACTIVITY 2.5

Find three examples of advertising using non-verbal methods to communicate their propositions. Write down your interpretations of their messages.

Speed of information access

Not only has the growth of information technology meant that information can be processed more rapidly, it has also meant that access to information can be made far more speedily than at any time in the past. This is of significant importance for the marketer.

Census information which was previously tabulated by hand, or on comparatively slow computers – and which was substantially out of date by the time it was made available – is now available within a relatively short period of time. Marketers can determine with far greater precision than at any time in the past the likely audience for their propositions, and can more readily segment markets into groups of users, rather than communicating with them as an aggregation.

QUESTION 2.4

Describe the factors which have brought about a change in our approach to marketing communications.

The impact on marketing communications

We have already seen that marketing communications needs to focus on the end user rather than on the nature of the product or service provided. But, it is suggested, marketing communications needs to move rapidly to respond to these underlying changes in the social and environmental framework.

In their important book on integrated marketing communications, Shultz et al. have suggested that it is time to abandon the principles of the four Ps (see Unit 1) for the four Cs:

* Forget *product*. Study *consumer* wants and needs. You can no longer sell whatever you make. You can only sell something that someone specifically wants to buy.

- Forget *price*. Understand the consumer's *cost* to satisfy that want or need.
- Forget *place*. Think *convenience* to buy.
- Forget *promotions*. The word in the 1990s is *communications*.

If marketing communications is to be effective, it is vitally important that we move from a situation of specialization – in which marketers are experts in one area of marketing communications – to people who are trained in all marketing communications disciplines. At the same time, as we have already seen, the process of change requires us to look at focused marketing approaches rather than adopt the litany of the 1960s – that of mass marketing.

With the recognition that all consumers are different and hence have different needs and wants – even of the same product or service – there is the need to ensure that we are able to communicate with them as individuals rather than as a homogenous unit. The increasing concern is the desire to communicate with ever smaller segments of the global market and, in an ideal world, reach a position where we can communicate with them individually. This desire manifests itself in the increasing drive towards direct marketing techniques (see Unit 8), the most rapidly growing sector of the marketing communications industry.

How will the role of marketing communications differ in the case of a fast moving consumer good product as compared with a consumer durable product?

Relationship marketing

A development of the marketing communications process, as it moves through the 1990s, is the area known as relationship marketing. With the ability to reach consumers on a highly segmented or even one-to-one basis has come the recognition that the process itself can become two way. Hitherto, marketing communications primarily concerned itself with the process of communicating *to* the end consumer. By encouraging the process of feedback, we can now communicate *with* the consumer.

Increasingly, companies such as Nestlé and Heinz have announced moves into club formats which enable the establishment of a direct relationship between the manufacturer and the consumer. Many loyalty programmes, such as the Frequent Flyer and Frequent Stayer programmes now run by most international airlines and hotel groups, have a similar objective of establishing a relationship with the consumer, to their mutual benefit.

The encouragement of a 'feedback' loop is a facet of marketing communications which is destined to grow apace over the next few years and, as companies perceive the benefits of encouraging a positive relationship with their customers, their consumers, their suppliers and others, so we will witness the growth of developed two-way marketing communications programmes.

Why is there a growing trend towards relationship marketing? What are the benefits to the company? What are the benefits to the consumer?

It has to be recognized that contemporary marketing is more complex than at any time in the past. No longer is it sufficient to rely on the traditional marketing mix variables to achieve differentiation between manufacturers. Areas such as product design and development, pricing policies, and distribution are, in themselves, no longer capable of delivering the long-term differentiation required.

With an increasing level of convergent technologies, product innovation may be going on in parallel between rival manufacturers, even without their knowing what the other is doing. And, even where this is not the case, any new feature can rapidly be copied by the competition. Where once a new feature, ingredient, or other product attribute would enable a manufacturer to achieve a unique stance for an extended period, this is no longer the case. One has only to look at the area of the rapid innovation within the soap powder and detergent markets to see just how speedily rival manufacturers catch up with each other.

With the concentration of distribution into relatively few hands, the opportunities for achieving solus distribution of brands is minimized. Indeed, the retailers themselves represent an increasing threat to the manufacturers' brands as their packaging moves ever closer to that of the manufacturers' own.

Pricing, once a major area of differentiation, similarly provides less scope. The pressure on margins brought about by the increasingly competitive nature of retailers' own products has restricted the scope to use price to differentiate effectively. Clearly, this is particularly true of fast-moving consumer goods where price dissimilarity can only operate over a very narrow range. Other products, such as perfumes and toiletries, and luxury goods ranging from hi-fi to cars still have more flexibility in the area of price.

We are left, therefore, with only one of the four marketing mix variables which can be utilized to achieve effective brand discrimination – marketing communications. Shultz et al. argue that the area of marketing communications will, through the 1990s, be the only opportunity of achieving sustainable competitive advantage. If all other things are equal – or at least more or less so – then it is what people think, feel and believe about a product and its competitors which will be important. Since products in many areas will achieve parity or comparability in purely functional terms, it will be the perceptual differences which consumers will use to discriminate between rival brands. Only through the use of sustained and integrated marketing communications campaigns will manufacturers be able to achieve the differentiation they require.

To appreciate the impact of this statement, it is worth looking at a market which replicates many of the features described above. In the bottled-water market, several brands coexist, each with unique positionings in the mind of the consumer. Yet, in repeated blind tastings, few consumers can identify any functional characteristics which could be used as the basis for brand discrimination.

SUMMARY

In this unit we have seen that:

- There is a need to differentiate clearly between marketing objectives and those for marketing communications.
- It is important that the latter are clearly defined and specific tasks for the communications programme, are designed to communicate to a defined audience to a defined degree, within a specific time frame and against a predefined budget.
- There are key guidelines for the setting of marketing communications objectives, which need to be clearly defined, specific, and measurable, in a succinct, written form, agreed by all those involved in the communications process. We need to establish realistic benchmarks prior to the programme in order that monitoring and control can take place.
- There are benefits obtained by creating an integrated marketing communications programme to ensure the cohesive unification of all components in order to deliver a single consistent message to our defined target market or markets.
- There is a variety of external factors which have, and will continue to have, an impact on the marketing communications process.
- There is an emergence of relationship marketing, which is designed to ensure a feedback mechanism between the manufacturer and the consumer, to their mutual benefit.

These are all key principles of the marketing communications process and it is important that they are fully understood, since they will provide the basis for further studies in the area.

Examination hints and specimen questions

Two further questions, taken from recent CIM papers, are reproduced below. These, like those in Unit 1, are taken from Part 2 of the paper, in which you are invited to choose the answers you wish to attempt. This unit, together with your additional reading, should provide you with sufficient material to be able to tackle these questions with confidence. Here again, you should allow no more than 30 minutes for each question.

Integrated Marketing Communications is a concept of planning that recognizes the added value of a comprehensive plan and which evaluates the strategic roles of a variety of communications disciplines. These disciplines are integrated to provide consistency and maximum communications effectiveness. Write notes on why you think this concept is increasingly important and also set out ways in which this integration might be planned and implemented.

(June 1994)

Central to the definition of marketing communications is the concept that all marketing mix variables, and not just the promotional variables alone, communicate with customers. You have been asked to submit notes for a talk to business people. The talk is intended to describe the ways in which any organization should go about developing a completely integrated marketing communications campaign.

(December 1993)

Reference has been made in this unit to a book on integrated marketing communications by Shultz et al. It provides a 'new perspective' on many aspects of marketing communications and it is strongly recommended that you should read it:

D. Shultz, S. Tannenbaum and R. Lauterborn, *Integrated Marketing Communications*, NTC Business Books, 1992.

A more general text which is also a good source of additional material is:

P. R. Smith, *Marketing Communications – An Integrated Approach*, Kogan Page, 1993.

A text in a similar vein is:

J. F. Engel, M. R. Warshaw and T. C. Kinnear, *Promotional Strategy*, 8th edn, Irwin, 1994.

A new text which provides a detailed examination of the important operations issues relating to integrated marketing communications is:

I. Linton, *Integrated Marketing Communications*, Butterworth-Heinemann, 1995.

The theoretical background to marketing communications

This unit is designed to build on your understanding of marketing communications developed in the previous units. It will help you:

- Develop an understanding of the implications of the working of the marketplace on the development of marketing communications strategy.
- Appreciate the contribution that marketing communications makes to the four Ps of marketing.
- Understand the strategic roles of marketing communications.
- Explore the models which have been developed to explain the workings of the communications process.

By the end of this unit you will:

- Be able to relate your understanding of marketing communications to the dimensions of price, product and place.
- Be able to demonstrate an understanding of the key thinking in the field.
- Be able to illustrate the development of the models in the area of marketing communications.
- Be able to apply the principles of the models to real-world issues in communications.

There are a number of important issues covered this unit and, in many respects, they will underpin your ability to deal with the topics contained in the units that follow. Try to go over each of the topics carefully and, if necessary, re-read them to make sure that you have grasped all the points that are raised.

Under the new Diploma syllabus, it is quite likely that you will be called upon either to discuss the various models described in this unit, or to apply the principles of these models in order to demonstrate an understanding of the relevance of theory to practical applications. For this reason, it is important that you should develop a clear understanding of the individual aspects of each of the models described. Think about why they have been developed and their relationship to the 'real' world.

Allow about 4–5 hours to cover the unit, and make sure that you practise dealing with the models.

Marketing communications, by its very nature, exists in a dynamic environment. All around us things are changing constantly. The underlying reasons for the purchasing of a product or service are affected by a variety of important factors. The economic environment will play a substantial part in forming people's attitudes to their patterns of expenditure. What is considered 'essential' at some times, will be regarded as something of a luxury when family income is under pressure, either because of the broad economic circumstances, or individual factors such as continuity of employment or the 'feel-good factor'.

Attitudes in general reflect changing patterns over time. The activities of pressure groups, peer groups and others will make some purchases more desirable, whilst others are less so. One only has to look at the growth in the awareness of environmental issues to see how brands have had to respond. Product ingredients which were once widely accepted can now no longer be included if the brand is to enjoy wide acceptance. Fashion exerts a similar influence. Once popular brands are now scorned by consumers as being unfashionable, whilst others have grown from limited acceptance to broad popularity as fashion dictates their purchase.

For any product or service to enjoy continued success, it must understand and reflect these factors in terms of the marketing communications which support it. In the course of working through this study text, you will examine the implications of the dynamic marketplace for the appropriate determination of marketing communications strategy.

It must be clear that, from the outset, the imperative will be how best to communicate with the marketplace and ensure that we have a full understanding of their needs and wants, so that the propositions which support our brand will best reflect their requirements.

As we have already seen, the definition of marketing as used by the CIM (Unit 1, Definition 1.1) represents a good starting point for the determination of communications strategy. Marketing communications is inextricably linked with the marketing concept. To ensure its effectiveness, the communications strategy must reflect the marketing concept. It must serve to identify consumer needs and must integrate all the activities of the company which are designed to satisfy these needs. Marketing communications must retain consistency with all the other aspects of the marketing mix in order to present a cohesive proposition to the target consumer.

How does marketing communications relate to the marketing concept? Give examples of communications campaigns which underpin the relationship between the two.

We have at our disposal a variety of techniques which will play an important part in the identification of consumer needs and wants, and, most importantly, ensure that our communications tools are used effectively and with impact to inform consumers of the ability to satisfy these needs. We will explore these in much more detail in Unit 6, which discusses the role and contribution of market research. Whilst it can be assumed that all candidates are aware of the four Ps of marketing (product, price, place and promotion), it is important that they are re-examined in the context of their role within marketing communications. The first three are considered below, whilst the whole of this workbook deals with promotion.

Product

All products are multi-dimensional in their nature. At the most basic level there are a series of functional features designed to meet the essential requirements of the target consumers. Sometimes referred to as the 'core product', this consists of the assembly of ingredients which provide the basic character of the product. Thus a car consists of an engine, a passenger compartment and four wheels; a washing powder is a collection of ingredients designed to ensure that clothes are washed clean; and so on. Clearly, however, these describe only the basic characteristics. At this level, many consumers are unable to distinguish between competing products within the same category.

An example of this differential perception is given in *Creating Powerful Brands*, by C. De Chernatony and M. McDonald (Butterworth-Heinemann, 1993). In a blind taste test of the two leading carbonated diet beverages, when the brand identity was concealed 51 per cent of those sampled preferred Diet Pepsi, 44 per cent preferred Diet Coke, and 5 per cent said that they were the same or that they couldn't tell the difference. When the products were sampled in an open test, with the brand identities revealed, only 23 per cent indicated that they preferred Diet Pepsi, with 65 per cent preferring Diet Coke, and 12 per cent saying that they were equal or didn't know. The key differentiating factor was the brand identity, which provided additional values to the consumer, overriding the physical characteristics of the products.

ACTIVITY 3.1

Consider the recent launch of Pepsi Max. What has the manufacturer sought to achieve in terms of marketing communications?

A recent blind taste test carried out by students at the University of Greenwich demonstrated that only 8 per cent could discriminate between tap and bottled water!

Manufacturers invest vast sums of money into the development of other facets of the product which are designed to assist the consumer in their identification of a brand in a crowded marketplace. The brand name and the packaging all serve to add other dimensions to the core product. Again, at a basic level, these facets may only be there to provide a clear identification of the product on the supermarket or chemist shelf. However, in most cases, they go much further and invest the core product with a series of intangible values which, to a much greater degree, serve to assist in the discrimination of one manufacturer's product from that of a competitor. Names, logos and pack designs and colours all provide the consumer with the ability to recognize a particular manufacturer's product and determine whether or not it is likely to meet their specific needs and wants.

Much more important in the overall purchasing decision are the intangible aspects of a product – the image dimensions and perceptual factors which are the real discriminators in brand purchase. It is here that marketing communications plays a key role. The key brand dimensions relating to awareness, image, brand values, etc., are, for the most part, the direct result of the work done within marketing communications.

Brand images are not fixed in time. Powerful marketing communications activity can serve to alter, amend or even change totally the perceptual values of an individual brand. It must be recognized that this is not an easy task and will often require considerable investment in advertising. Lucozade was, for many years, sold on the platform of recovery from illness. Today it is a energy-giving drink. Kellogg's All Bran was a brand in decline, and seen by consumers as old-fashioned. Advertising served to reposition the brand and reverse the decline. For a full explanation of how the campaign for Kelloggs All Bran was developed, see *How Advertising Works 7*, edited by Chris Baker (Institute of Practitioners in Advertising/ NTC Publications, 1994).

Price

As with product, price is an important dimension of the overall proposition to the consumer, and will have important implications from the perspective of marketing communications. In a purely marketing context, pricing decisions will be considered as a distinct element of the marketing strategy. However, it is important to remember that all pricing decisions will have an impact on consumers' perceptions of the product or service. In this context, therefore, pricing can be seen to have a promotional dimension which we will consider below.

It may be a cliché, but many consumers relate price to quality expectations. Thus, a more expensive product is innately assumed to be of higher quality, whilst a cheaper one may be perceived as being of lesser quality. It is important, here, however, to distinguish between perceptions of value for money. All consumers make a fundamental equation between price, performance and value for money. Economic circumstances may dictate that a cheaper product is purchased, but many consumers continue to separate this decision from overall product performance.

In many instances, price is an important discriminator between private label products and those produced by major manufacturers. Advertising is often used to reinforce the values associated with manufacturers' brands to ensure that, despite the higher price charged, the product still represents superior value for money. Advertising for Fairy Liquid has stressed the product quality and longevity of use against cheaper rival brands, for example.

Price positioning may have other important implications for the successful promotion of a brand. At its inception, Brut, a male aftershave manufactured by Fabergé was positioned at the premium end of the market. A significant price reduction, accompanied by a change in the pattern of distribution, and supported by a major communications campaign served to reposition the brand in the minds of consumers – with a considerable impact on the value of sales generated.

The price of a product will often be used as a reference point by consumers. If, in a given market, brands are segmented by price, then the price of a product will serve to identify the relative position of an unknown brand. In, say, the market for compact disc players, some manufacturers will charge £75, others around £150, and yet others at prices in excess of £500. A new product entering the market at a price of £175 will immediately be perceived as a contender in the middle range in the first instance.

Of course, as consumers learn more about the various competitors and their respective product offerings, the absolute price may recede in importance. However, it is important to remember that in many instances, particularly where the consumer lacks sufficient information to compare all the available brands on the basis of the features which they offer, price will be an important guide.

In some instances, a high price can reinforce the prestige image of a brand. If the price of a product is well known, then ownership of the particular product can reinforce the social prestige. This is particularly true of premium priced jewellery and watches, but may also relate to the use of perfumes and items of clothing.

Where the price differential between competing brands is small, a marginal premium may give the potential consumer a sense of reassurance. Important in this respect is the theoretical work done by Ernst Weber in the area of 'just noticeable difference', or JND, often referred to as 'Weber's law'. Although developed in the late nineteenth century, Weber's law has important ramifications for promotional strategy.

Place

Where the product is sold may, similarly, have a considerable impact on consumer perceptions of a brand. The nature of the outlet which stocks a particular brand may transfer certain dimensions of image to the brand itself and make it more or less desirable as a purchase. Products which are uniquely stocked by high-quality outlets tend to be perceived as high quality, whilst those stocked by discount stores may have the image of those outlets transferred to the brand and encourage consumers to perceive those brands as being of lower quality. The presentations of the major perfume houses stressed this aspect of their marketing activity to the Monopolies and Mergers Commission to prevent their prices from being discounted in 'cheap price' outlets.

The retail environment may play a significant part in establishing credibility for a product within its category. In the case of many ethical pharmaceutical products, manufacturers can choose the nature of their distribution. On the one hand, they can achieve a wider reach of the marketplace by encouraging the major supermarket chains to stock their products. On the other, they can restrict their distribution to specialist chemist outlets. With the latter, however, there is the clear transference of the professional authority of chemists to these products. In some respects, this may be regarded by the consumer as a professional endorsement of the efficacy of the product, which is clearly not derived from other outlets. Thus, a clear choice must be made between the reference value of the stockist and the wider distribution gained through a broader range of outlets.

Many manufacturers deliberately restrict the nature of distribution to ensure the projection of a desired image for a brand – watches, jewellery, hi-fi. It can be seen, therefore, that marketing and marketing communications are inextricably linked. And, for this reason, the strategic approach of one area must equally be applied to the others.

QUESTION 3.2

Define the contribution of marketing communications to each of the four Ps.

Marketing planning

All marketing planning must be consistent with the overall objectives established by the senior management of a company or organization. These, in turn, will be shaped and influenced by a consideration of the broader environmental factors – both internal and external. A consideration of the political, economic, social, technological and environmental and competitive issues must, therefore, be conducted both in the context of basic marketing planning as well as in relation to the development of marketing communications strategy. But there will be a number of other factors which will shape the development of communications strategy.

Management philosophy

Even where, as is often the case in contemporary marketing, there is little to differentiate between the products of rival manufacturers, the approach which they adopt in terms both of their overall marketing efforts and the construction of their marketing communications plans will be substantially influenced by their respective management philosophies. Contrast, for example, the various manufacturers in the European car market. Their very different philosophies can be discerned from the positioning of their products in the marketplace.

Strategic goals

A wide variety of models have been developed to identify the various strategic options available to marketers. Much of this work will be covered in other areas of the CIM Diploma course, and will be an essential part of your overall studies. It will be important to understand, among others, the workings of the Ansoff matrix, Porter's five forces, the Boston matrix and the GE screen.

DEFINITION 3.1

O' Shaughnessy (*Competitive Marketing – A Strategic Approach*, Allen & Unwin, 1984) defines *corporate strategy* as the broad conception of how the firm's strengths are to be deployed to overcome resistance to the achievement of objectives.

The importance of these models in the context of our current studies is the fact that the strategic direction of the company will have a significant impact on the strategic planning of the marketing communications programme.

Taking recent examples of marketing communications (use current television commercials and press advertisements), contrast the relative positionings adopted by Mercedes, Audi, Renault, Fiat and Rover.

The relationship between strategy and marketing communications

It has been argued that marketing communications fulfils four basic roles:

- Want conception.
- Want development.
- Want focus.
- Want satisfaction.

Want conception

In many instances, consumers have a series of latent wants which need to be activated before the purchasing process can begin. The role of marketing communications, in this context, is to assist the prospective consumer to conceive the want and to recognize the product's or service's potential for satisfying that want.

The role of want conception is especially important in the context of new product development, since the consumer may be unaware both of the existence of the product and the need that it is intended to satisfy. Clearly, the primary aim of such marketing communications activity will be to attract customers to the product by encouraging trial. When Sony introduced the Walkman, the first task of the support activity was to identify the latent need for a portable communications device. Once the consumer began to appreciate the potential benefits of 'music on the move', trial of the new product could be encouraged.

Want development

In order to extend the use of an existing product, the manufacturer may seek to identify new uses for that product and to communicate them to potential consumers. The role of marketing communications will be to present alternative uses of the product and to stimulate the usage of the product in new ways.

Frequently, manufacturers of food products employ food hygienists and nutritionists to develop new recipes which, they believe, will encourage new usage of an existing product in different ways. Promotion will often be in the form of some recipe device contained in advertising, public relations, or sales promotion.

What are the goals of marketing communications in the context of want development?

Want focus

Marketing communications is often used as the vehicle to identify the parity between the product offered and the consumer need. In some instances, marketing communications will seek to establish a particular product attribute or benefit as the basis of the consumer's subsequent choice criteria. The purpose of such activity is to ensure that, at the very least, the consumer includes the promoted product within the list of brands to be evaluated and, by suggesting that the attribute should be used as the basis of comparison, guide the consumer to a specific purchase decision.

This approach is often used in the field of high technology. Advertising for computers, hi-fi, in-car entertainment and similar categories seeks to position a particular attribute as being highly desirable. Sometimes, although not always, comparisons will be included in advertising which attempt to complete the information search for the consumer.

Want satisfaction

Once a consumer has completed a purchase, advertising and other forms of marketing communications may be used to reassure the consumer that the purchase made was the correct one. Often, especially in the case of the purchase of expensive consumer durable items, external factors (such as the comments of relatives and friends) may indicate that the purchase decision was unsound or undesirable. Marketing communications in various forms will be used to reinforce the purchase decision and, in some instances, to provide the purchaser with information to allay the doubts of others.

It is commonly accepted, for example, that many consumers only read the product brochure for a new car *after* they have bought the vehicle. The information contained in the brochure – performance, fuel economy characteristics, luggage space, etc. – will be used by the purchaser to justify the particular purchase to others.

ACTIVITY 3.3

Find three examples of advertising which work at the want satisfaction stage.

How does marketing communications work?

The shortest answer to this question is that we don't really know! Although a great many theories have been put forward to explain the mechanical operation of marketing communications, many of them have either been too simplistic or have simply not stood up to empirical examination.

For a considerable period of time, the most widely used theory was that known as the **'black box' effect** (Figure 3.1). Expressed simply, the model states that if you were prepared to spend sufficient money and targeted the correct group of people, in time enough of them would buy your product to make the investment worthwhile! Needless to say, the premise was fairly basic and it certainly does not aid our understanding of the mechanical process of communications effectiveness.

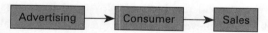

Figure 3.1   The 'black box' effect

A somewhat more realistic model, and certainly one which held sway for a number of years, is that known as **'AIDA'** (Figure 3.2). Originally proposed at the turn of the century to explain the process of personal selling, it was rapidly adopted as a model to explain the process of communications in advertising. The basic tenet was that, in order to have effect, the first task of any campaign was to gain the *attention* of the viewer or reader. From the outset, it was recognized that a fundamental aim of communication was to cut through the surrounding clutter and arrest the attention of the potential purchaser. Moreover, it suggested that the process of communications required the audience to pass through a series of sequential steps, and that each step was a logical consequence of what had gone before. The principle of sequential activity or learning is used commonly in many marketing models, and is often referred to as a *hierarchy of effects*. It is clear that the attention phase is key to the process, since whatever follows will be of little value if the attention of the audience has not been achieved.

The second stage is the stimulation of an *interest* in the proposition. In most cases, it would be reasonable to assume that if the first requirement – attention – had been met, the second would follow on almost automatically. Indeed, if the communications message has been properly constructed, this will be true. However, in some instances, particularly where an irrelevant attention-getting device has been employed, the potential consumer does not pass fully to the second stage.

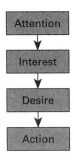

Figure 3.2 The AIDA model

The third stage is to create a *desire* for the product or service being promoted. Often, this will take the form of a 'problem–solution' execution in which the advertiser seeks to position the product as the answer to a problem which has previously been identified.

Soap powder advertisements often follow this sequence of events, although many other examples can be found from contemporary marketing activity. Personal care, hair care, and DIY products are other areas where this approach is currently employed.

Identify at least three examples of current advertising (not including the markets mentioned above) where the problem–solution approach is currently employed.

ACTIVITY 3.4

The fourth and final stage of the AIDA model is the stimulation of some form of response on the part of the audience – the *action* stage. Most advertisements have a specific call to action, and many are linked with promotional offers designed to induce a purchase of the product or some other desired end result.

An alternative, and more recent, model of marketing communications is referred to by the acronym **DAGMAR** (Figure 3.3). In the early 1960s, Russell Colley proposed a new approach to advertising planning entitled 'Defining Advertising Goals for Measured Advertising Results'. Unlike some previous models, the DAGMAR approach proposed a precise method for the selection and quantification of communications tasks which, in turn, could be used as the basis for measuring performance. As with the AIDA model, the suggestion is that there is a series of specific steps which effective marketing communications must follow.

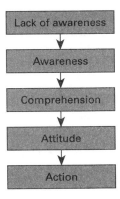

Figure 3.3 The DAGMAR process

This model postulates a pre-stage, in which there is the need to move the potential consumer from a state in which he or she is *unaware* of the product or its proposition, to a positive *awareness* of the brand's existence in the marketplace.

Only once a basic level of awareness has been created can the task of improving understanding or *comprehension* of the brand properties and attributes begin. It is important to recognize that, whilst some of the attributes will be physical – a better product, more for the same money, etc. – many will be associated with intangible aspects of the brand, the most important of which is image.

The *attitude* stage described by the model is that part of the process in which the consumer is persuaded as to the merits of purchasing the product, or the reinforcement of existing positive views.

The final stage, as with AIDA, is the promotion of a specific course of *action* on the part of the consumer. This may be to encourage the trial of a new product, motivate repeat purchase, providing a means of obtaining additional information on which a purchase decision may be made, or the taking of some other step desired by the advertiser.

Unlike AIDA, however, Colley proposed a specific procedure to ensure that the goals established for advertising were precisely formulated and capable of being monitored. An imperative of the approach was to ensure that the objectives established were capable of unbiased measurement. This is not simply a question of, for example, quantifying levels of awareness, or of trial, but rather of defining precise levels to be achieved for specific aspects of comprehension of the message. At the same time, Colley suggested that precise time-scales be determined for the achievement of the objectives set.

In order to enable such measurements, it was suggested that a series of benchmarks should be identified. Apart from the obvious benefit of providing the base against which subsequent achievements could be measured, the benchmarking process has a far more important role in the process of strategy determination. It provides a major contribution to the overall planning process, by indicating areas in which marketing communications activity might be appropriate. Importantly, the proponents of the DAGMAR approach argue that benchmarking is an *essential prerequisite* of the planning process.

QUESTION 3.4

What marketing communications tools would you use to achieve each of the goals described in the DAGMAR process?

Targeting is a further dimension of DAGMAR, whereby a detailed understanding would first be developed regarding the target audience(s). Again, it is argued that, without such knowledge, the impact of the message is likely to be weakened. By understanding exactly who (age, sex, class, usership patterns, lifestyle factors, etc.) represents the best prospect for the proposition, not only can they be targeted more effectively by careful media selection but, similarly, the message can be made to appeal directly to them, rather than potential users as a whole.

Needless to say, Colley recommended the adoption of a written approach to the procedure, partly to impose discipline on the process – the need to express thoughts clearly and precisely in written form demands more care and attention to the meaning given than does the verbal expression of an idea – and partly to ensure that all participants to the process are both aware of, and committed to, the task.

Although the DAGMAR model is widely used, it is often criticized for implying that consumers are essentially *passive* in the marketing communications process. The inference of this and the AIDA model is that consumers are moved by advertising rather than making choices as to which advertising to respond to.

QUESTION 3.5

To what extent does the application of the principles of DAGMAR conflict with the notion of developing creative advertising?

The response has been the development of a series of *active* models which seek to include more emotional elements into the process of communications. These draw heavily on the body of work in the field of human psychology and consumer behaviour. Several recent attempts have been made to explain the consumer's response to advertising in a more active sense. Although these models all suffer from some limitations, what they share in common is the view that advertising – and for that matter all of marketing communications – is not a linear process in which the consumer passes sequentially from one stage to the next. Rather, the communications process is more complicated and circuitous; recognizing that the consumer may enter the cycle at different points and that each action may feed back to influence other stages in the overall process.

One such model is that developed by **Joyce** (*Models of the Advertising Process. How Advertising Works and How Promotions Work*, ESOMAR, 1991) (Figure 3.4). Although comparatively complex at first glance, this model attempts to weld the process into a cohesive whole. It suggests that there are three dynamic areas which need to be considered:

- Advertising.
- Purchasing behaviour.
- Consumer attitudes.

Each area interacts with the others to produce an outcome.

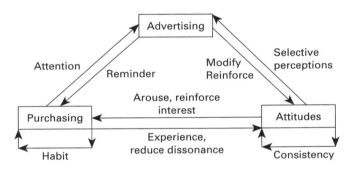

Figure 3.4   From: T. Joyce, *Models of the Advertising Process. How Advertising Works and How Promotions Work* (ESOMAR, 1991)

As we have seen elsewhere, the consumer holds a series of *attitudes*, some of which may relate to the brand and the purchasing decision. Although most of these attitudes will be formed by external factors – age, sex, class, the influence of relatives, friends and peer groups, cultural factors and so on – some are the direct result of the impact of an advertising message. In some instances, the *advertising* will serve to reinforce existing beliefs; in others, it will modify existing attitudes. If the consumer already believes that a well-balanced diet is essential to good health, then a product which promotes itself with this proposition is likely to be well received. The advertising will reinforce held beliefs and attitudes and strengthen the perception of the brand. In some instances, the advertising message may modify attitudes, perhaps by presenting a potential solution to a problem which the consumer previously felt could not be resolved.

It is important to recognize that attitudes are not easy to change. Most consumers adopt fairly consistent behavioural patterns which can only be changed over time. If the consumer is of the view, for example, that all drink is evil, then no amount of advertising for alcoholic beverages is likely to alter that attitude.

Identify examples of advertising which:

- Seeks to change existing beliefs.
- Seeks to reinforce beliefs.

However, we have to recognize that the consumer will not necessarily take in all of the advertising message, or may modify the content of the message to suit their existing views.

Advertising promoting health-care insurance will be irrelevant if the consumer believes that they are too young, for example, to be likely to fall seriously ill.

In turn, these attitudes will influence the *purchasing* decision. In some instances, held beliefs will arouse interest in a product category or a brand. Exposure to a specific advertising message may induce the consumer to go and buy the product. It is important to recognize that this is a two-way process. If the consumer is dissatisfied with the purchase, or feels that it does not live up to the promises of the advertising, then a process of dissonance will take place. Their attitudes towards the brand will be modified to reflect this lack of satisfaction and the advertising message will be viewed in a different light.

Some purchases are the result of habitual behaviour – consumers buying the same brand on repeated occasions. This may the result of perceived family preferences – breakfast cereals are often purchased because the rest of the family 'like the brand' – or simply the result of inertia. In some instances, advertising can seek to change the pattern by alerting the consumer to a new proposition. In others it will serve to reinforce existing purchasing patterns by reminding and reassuring the consumer of the wisdom of their purchase decision. Sometimes, the process of purchasing itself, however, will cause the consumer to respond to an advertising message. Having, perhaps, seen a product in store, they will become more aware of the brand's advertising proposition. Unlike the previous models, Joyce's model suggests a continuous cycle of events, with each component of the model influencing other parts of the behavioural pattern.

QUESTION 3.6

If a consumer's initial experience with a product is poor, how can the manufacturer use marketing communications to overcome the resistance to repeat purchasing with the introduction of a new formulation of the product?

A similar, if slightly more complex, model of the influences on buying behaviour is that developed by **Franzen** (*Advertising Effectiveness*, NTC Publications, 1994). This model suggests that there are seven key variables, or effects, each of which interacts with each other to describe the overall buying process. The starting point for his model is *exposure*. In order for any message to impact upon the target audience, it must first receive some form of exposure. Following this, and incorporating some aspects of previous models, Franzen suggests that the influences on advertising processing and buying behaviour are as follows:

- Attention.
- Advertising processing.
- Brand awareness.
- Brand associations.
- Brand positioning.
- Brand evaluation and attitude.
- Brand behaviour and product experience.

The interactions between these various components are depicted in Figure 3.5. It is worth examining each of these dimensions individually.

Attention, as suggested by other models, is an essential prerequisite of the other levels of the process. If the attention of the potential consumer is not secured by the marketing communications message, then it is impossible to communicate salient aspects of that message. In some respects, attention is determined by the consumer's attitudes towards the product category and the brand within it. If there is little interest in the product category, then gaining attention will be a difficult task. By the same token, however, if the consumer has become interested in the particular category (heightened awareness) for some reason, then significantly more attention will be devoted to the advertisement and its contents. This may come about, for example, because the consumer has decided to purchase a new car. Following that emotional decision, advertisements for cars, particularly those in the area of interest and relevance, will be more readily perceived.

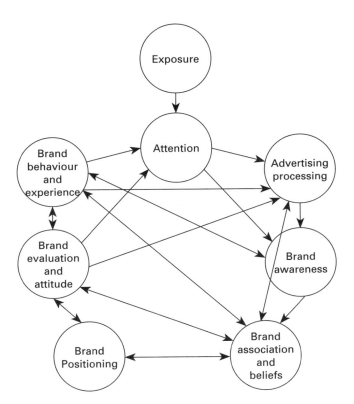

Figure 3.5 From Giap Franzen (1992)

QUESTION 3.7

Gaining the attention of the prospective consumer is a major require-ment of all the models of advertising effectiveness. What techniques can be used to achieve this objective?

Advertising processing is the process whereby the viewer or reader 'translates' the informa-tion provided into a form which is consistent with existing attitudes and beliefs. It will be very much influenced by prior awareness of the product category and personal attitudes and experiences with the particular product. Information which confirms existing views will tend to be more readily accepted than that which contradicts them.

Brand awareness is an important dimension of the process, and one to which marketing communications makes an important contribution. The 'aura' or associations which the advertising creates with the brand will be an important dimension of image (we will exam-ine this in more detail in Unit 4). Except for 'new to the world' products, the consumer is likely to have some level of brand awareness, either through previous personal experience or because of the experiences of others.

Brand associations are the result of product usage and advertising processing. Sometimes, for example, the consumer will have existing awareness of related brands, the values of which may be transferred to the product being considered. This might be the case with 'family' brands which seek to communicate common values and attributes – such as the Fairy range of soaps, detergents and washing-up liquids. In other instances, the strength or otherwise of the manufacturer will add to or detract from the credibility of the brand. If, for example, the consumer believes that Nestlé makes high-quality products, then a new cereal range bearing that name will be more favourably received. It has been suggested that these brand associations 'colour' the interpretation of an advertising message. Advertising for 'liked' brands tends to be regarded as better than that for other products.

Positioning is the process by which consumers compare brands with one another. The process of *perceptual mapping* is an important one for the determination of marketing com-munications strategy. It involves the identification of the key attributes which are desired by the consumer of a particular product category (both physical and emotional) and assessing the relative performance of the competing products against those dimensions. This will be examined in greater depth in Unit 6.

Brand attitude is the result of the other dimensions. Clearly, factors such as awareness, brand associations, previous experience, and the consumer's perception of the positioning of the brand relative to its competitors will determine attitudes towards the brand. A product which has been sampled previously but has fallen short of expectations will hold a negative attitude. Marketing communications designed to alter or amend such attitudes represents a much greater degree of difficulty than does that designed for areas where the consumer is already favourably disposed.

In turn, *buying behaviour* and usage experience are influenced by brand awareness. But several authors have suggested that, in some purchase situations, purchasing occurs before the other stages of the process.

QUESTION 3.8 Some consumers purchase products spontaneously. What role does marketing communications play in this context?

If, for example, the consumer's attention is grabbed by the appearance of a product in store, they may be prepared to purchase it immediately and learn more at a later date. In this case, particularly with a favourable usage experience, the consumer will be more inclined to be receptive to subsequent advertising messages and view them in a more positive light. As noted earlier, however, the reverse is also true. A poor experience with a product will result in the consumer disregarding or rejecting any advertising proposition being made for the product.

The importance of the model, as can be seen, is the interaction which exists between the various dimensions. In some instances, a variable can be seen to have a 'one-way' impact on another, such as that between exposure and attention, or advertising processing and brand awareness. Elsewhere, there is a 'two-way' or 'feedback' effect, as between advertising processing and brand associations and beliefs.

Although many other models have been developed to explain the consumer interaction with advertising and the processing of advertising messages, the **heightened appreciation model** is a valuable tool for explaining some of the mechanics of the advertising message and, importantly, assists in determining advertising strategy (Figure 3.6). What the model suggests is that, by identifying a desirable attribute of a product (through the use of consumer research) and linking it directly with the brand, the consumer is both made more aware of that, attribute and associates it with the brand. The direct result of this activity is to create a more positive awareness of the product or service, which results in more frequent usage and the building of a better image.

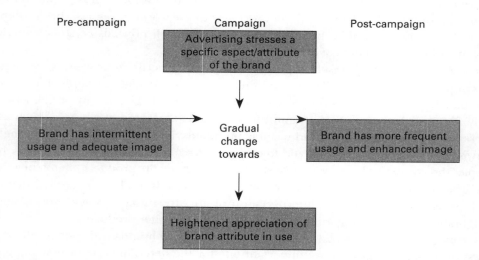

Figure 3.6 From: T. Yeshin (ed.), *Inside Advertising* (Institute of the Practitioners of Advertising, 1993)

The model described above stresses heightened appreciation. Find examples of marketing communications campaigns which attempt to heighten the consumer's awareness of a specific attribute of a product or service.

As with all models, it is important to stress that it is not the model itself which is important. Indeed, as has been noted, the very complexity of consumer behaviour, and the process of purchasing decisions and the influence of marketing communications on them, makes many of these models somewhat imprecise. Nonetheless, they add considerably to our understanding of the elements which make up the process, and assist us by indicating a more precise thrust to effective marketing communications strategy. They are also important tools as a contribution to learning.

If the various models of marketing communications are incomplete, how can they assist us in the development of effective marketing communications campaigns?

In the course of this unit we have:

- Considered some more important dimensions of the theoretical background to marketing communications and examined some of the work which has been done in the field.
- Considered the relationship between the marketing concept and marketing communications, and seen the role played by the latter in the context of the four Ps.
- Seen that there is a fundamental relationship between the determination of marketing strategy and the establishment of marketing communications objectives.
- Seen that, whilst we continue to recognize that our understanding of the workings of marketing communications remains somewhat ambiguous, we are progressively gaining more knowledge of the process.
- Seen that various models that have been developed in the past, and which continue to be developed, add to our understanding of the mechanics of communications. And, whilst marketing communications remains an imprecise area, study of the models helps us develop more effective communications approaches.

Examination hints

This is a new area for the Diploma paper and, as such, there are no past questions for you to experiment with. It is for this reason that a large number of questions have been built into the text.

It is important that you attempt to develop answers to each of the questions in order that you build up your ability to tackle questions in this area. As a general rule, and to help you focus on the issues raised in this unit, it is a good idea to try to relate your understanding of the theoretical concepts to their practical application.

Constantly be on the look out for examples from contemporary marketing which you can use to illustrate your answers.

Many of the basic marketing texts will provide a good insight into the theoretical aspects of marketing communications. It cannot be stressed enough that you should develop a relationship with at least one of these texts, for example:

S. Dibb, L. Simkin, W. M. Pride and O. C. Ferrell, *Marketing*, 2nd European edn, Houghton Mifflin, 1994.
P. Kotler and G. Armstrong, *Principles of Marketing*, 5th edn, Prentice-Hall, 1991.

In addition, you should become familiar with the texts on consumer behaviour:

H. Assael, *Consumer Behaviour and Marketing Action*, 4th edn, Brooks/Cole, 1992.
J. C. Mowen, *Consumer Behaviour*, 2nd edn, Maxwell Macmillan, 1990.
L. G. Schiffman, and L. Kanuk, *Consumer Behaviour*, 12th edn, Prentice-Hall, 1990.
K. Williams, *Behavioural Aspects of Marketing*, 2nd edn, Butterworth-Heinemann, 1991.

You should also consult the IPA series *Advertising Works*, Vols 1–7, Institute of Practitioners in Advertising (IPA)/NTC Publications.

The brand personality

This unit is designed to cover very important issues relating to the brand and brand personality. These are key aspects of your understanding in the field of marketing communications, since the brand is the focus of all activity. In this unit we will:

* Examine the valuation of brands.
* Examine the role of brands and brand image.
* Examine issues relating to branding strategy.
* Examine the building of brand values.
* Explore the positioning of brands using perceptual maps, and questions relating to the alteration of brand images.
* Explore two important aspects of contemporary marketing communications – the issue of brand look-alikes and international branding.

By the end of the unit, you will:

* Have a clear understanding of the importance of brands, both in the marketing context and that of marketing communications.
* Be able to apply the principles to a wide range of communications issues.

STUDY GUIDE

Branding is the core of all marketing communications activity, and it is very important that you develop a deep understanding of the issues raised in this unit. You will all have a high degree of familiarity with many brands – both domestic and international – which will underpin your studies in this area.

As with other areas, it is important that you practise applying the principles to real branding issues, and the unit provides a number of key questions and activities to enable you to do that. Make sure that, by the time of the exam, you have identified your own examples with which to illustrate your answers.

STUDY TIPS

Although you need to approach each of the units in this workbook as an independent aspect of your studies, you will soon begin to see how each of the units relates to each of the others. The further you get, the greater your understanding of the whole topic of marketing communications, and the better your ability will be to provide clear and concise answers to the examiners' questions.

However, it is not a good idea to try to do too much in one go. Spread your workload out over a number of days. This has two important benefits. Firstly, the tasks will not appear so daunting; and, secondly, it will give you time to consolidate the work in your mind.

Allow about 3–4 hours to complete this unit, but spread the workload over a number of days

One of the key issues in contemporary marketing communications is that of the brand personality. Although the value of branding has been long understood, it was brought into sharp focus with the valuation of the brand name of Guinness on the balance sheet during the Distillers takeover battle. The practice has been followed by others, ensuring that the valuation of brands is given close consideration, since the value placed upon them may exceed the value of the tangible assets of a company. In 1988, for example, Rank Hovis McDougall identified more than 50 brands on its balance sheet with a combined value of £678 million. Thus, the goodwill represented by these brands was worth almost 60 per cent of the total value of the company.

DEFINITION 4.1

A *brand* is defined as a name, term, design, symbol, or any other feature that identifies one seller's goods or services from those of other sellers. A *brand name* may identify one item, a family of items, or all items of that seller.

(P. D. Bennett (ed.), *Dictionary of Marketing Terms*, American Marketing Association, 1988)

Aside from the financial implications of brand valuation, the topic is an important one in marketing terms for other reasons.

QUESTION 4.1

What are the benefits to a company of assigning a financial valuation to a brand?

Consumers buy brands. Thus, the loyalty which the brand identity can create in the marketplace is fundamental to the ability of a company to offset competitive activities. If the positive values associated with a brand are sufficiently strong, it will enable the owner to overcome major problems with product quality. Both in the UK and elsewhere, major brands have suffered from such things as contaminants which have required the company to withdraw temporarily from the market.

Early in 1990, some bottles of Perrier were found to contain benzene. Despite its dominant presence, and the obvious implications of its decision, the company determined to remove all stocks of its products from the shelves of supermarkets and other outlets. Advertising and public relations were used to inform the public of the action the company had taken and, following exhaustive research to eliminate the problem, the brand was relaunched. The fact that Perrier was able to regain much of its market share is a testament both to the strength of the brand name and to the positive approach taken by the company in dealing with the issue.

In the USA, Tylenol suffered similar problems when a dangerous chemical was introduced into a few containers on retailers' shelves. A similar response in dealing with the problem enabled the brand to return to the market with many of the values associated with the name intact.

This issue is one which, unfortunately (in the context of what it says about society), needs to be addressed by marketers. In the very recent past, several products have been removed from supermarket shelves following the disclosure of tampering with the product contents, sometimes with disastrous consequences for the purchaser.

What role does branding and packaging play in identifying a product to the consumer?

Branding and packaging are the overt and tangible aspects of a product, and serve to distinguish one manufacturer's product from that of their competitors. In the crowded retail environment, it is these aspects of the product which help the brand to stand out from the crowd. Most brand names are made up of letters and numbers, and in some instances may also include an additional graphic design which is unique to that product. In most instances, manufacturers will register these logo designs to ensure legal protection of their mark, and to avoid the risks of 'passing off'. It is important to remember, however, that in most cases a brand name will only be protected within the specific category of trading, and thus other manufacturers will, potentially, be free to use the same name in another category. In the 1960s, Granada, which had registered the name in the context of television production, rental and associated areas, attempted to preclude its use by Ford in the automotive industry. The legal case decided in favour of Ford and they were able to retain the use of the name for a range of cars. The issue of brand protection is an important one, both in a domestic and an international context, and we will return to the topic throughout this unit.

We have already seen (Unit 3) that the core product offered by a manufacturer may, in most instances, be indistinguishable from that of their competitors. Indeed, given the nature of technology, the specific product advantages which one manufacturer has over their competitors will often be readily and rapidly duplicated by them. In countless blind tests, many consumers are unable to distinguish between different manufacturers' products. The key factor, and an area in which marketing communications plays a key role, is the association of other values with the brand name to ensure that the perceptions of the potential consumer may be altered to create a favourable impression of the brand.

Brand image

certain. defi
definition n.
precise mea
distinct, clea
definitive a. f
something;

DEFINITION 4.2

Brand image is the total impression created in the consumer's mind by a brand and all its associations, functional and non-functional.

(J. Walter Thompson, *Directory of Market Research Terminology.*)

If, for one moment, we strip away the brand marks of Levi, Kellogg's, Cadbury's, Mercedes, and Johnson and Johnson, to name but a few, we are left with commodity products shorn of all of the brand values which are associated with those names. All the investment made by those companies over many years into creating image values through the use of marketing communications is lost. It is the latter area which establishes in the minds of consumers a series of defined images and values which are instantly recalled on exposure to the brand name. The brand values are equally important to the company in terms of its longer term extension of activities. Many brand names have positive values associated with them which extend beyond the particular product with which the name is identified. These intangible values can be used by the company to extend its portfolio into other areas.

Within the soap and detergent markets, two brands stand out as examples of the positive values of branding. Fairy and Persil have both been used as brands which have taken their owners into extended categories by the association of new products with the positive values built up around those names. Mars demonstrated the power of their brands with the moves into the ice-cream market. Despite the fact that the company had no prior representation within the sector, the values associated with the names of Mars, Bounty and others gave an immediate identity to the ice-cream products which bore these logos.

Brand names and identities may also be used in other ways. Once a brand has built up a high level of recognition among consumers, it may be sold or leased to other manufacturers to provide them with an immediate entrée into another sector of the market.

Taking any major consumer brand of which you are aware, identify the components which differentiate it from its competitors, based on the dimensions of the Chernatony and McDonald chart.

The dimensions of a brand can be visually depicted on a Chernatony and McDonald chart (L. de Chernatony and M. McDonald, *Creating Powerful Brands*, Butterworth-Heinemann, Oxford, 1992) (Figure 4.1). It must be remembered, of course, that not all of the listed dimensions apply to all products and services. In some instances, the tangible aspects of the proposition will be more important; in others, differentiation may be achieved as a result of the quality of the services – before, during and after sale, guarantees, etc. – which are provided; in yet other instances, it will be the brand image and identity which will assume the greatest level of importance.

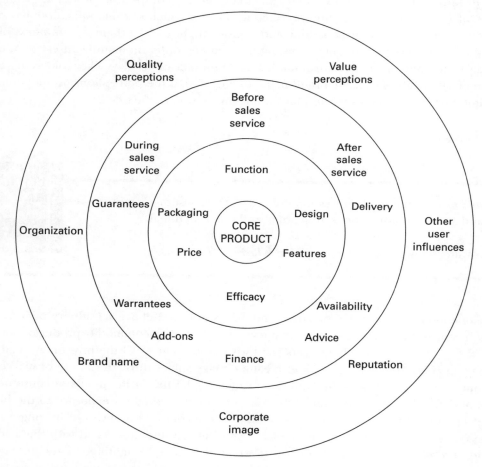

Figure 4.1

Branding strategy

We can discriminate between a series of very different branding strategies adopted by companies (Figure 4.2).

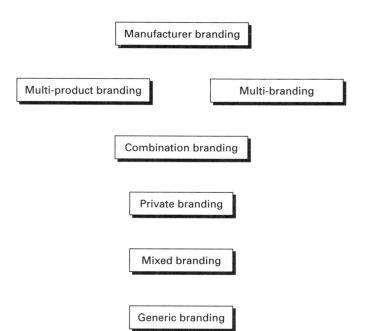

Figure 4.2

- Why do manufacturers adopt different branding strategies?
- What benefits do each of the different branding strategies described in this unit provide?

Manufacturer branding

A key decision to be taken by all manufacturers is the branding policy towards the products which they introduce to the market. In some instances, the manufacturer will choose to adopt a *multi-product* branding strategy. Here, the manufacturer uses the strength of the parent name to communicate a series of common values which 'endorse' all the products which bear that name. Sony and JVC, for example, have both established strong reputations within various sectors of the consumer electronics market. Whether the consumer is intending to purchase a television, a compact disc player, or a video recorder, the endorsement and reputation of the parent company singles out the appropriate product as being worthy of consideration. The name of Kellogg's is synonymous with breakfast cereals and Colgate with dental care. The same principle is equally true within the service sector. Products such as 'Liquid Gold' benefit from the endorsement of the parent company – the Leeds Building Society. Similarly, the standing of the Automobile Association lends credibility to its offering of car and other insurance facilities.

Usually, although not always, manufacturers restrict such activity to directly related markets, since it can be reasonably expected that the products all have common values and attributes. If, for example, the consumer perceives the names of Black & Decker and Bosch as being those of manufacturers of quality power tools, those names can reasonably be expected to carry a similar weight within the broader DIY markets. Both those companies have moved into gardening tools, for example.

In many instances, manufacturers maintain several brand names which are used to endorse separate market categories, but the names are kept distinct from each other to avoid the creation of confusion in the minds of the consumer. For example, Gillette maintains its name for the personal care market, but uses the Braun brand for the related electrical appliances market, embracing dry shaving, electric hair dryers, toothbrushes, etc.

Multi-branding is a strategy adopted by those manufacturers who choose to keep the parent name subservient to the end user. For example, the name of Proctor and Gamble is little known by consumers, although the brands they produce are all major players in their respective markets. Proctor and Gamble manufacture a variety of brands including, among many others, Ariel and Daz in the detergents market, Oil of Ulay (Olay), Vicks, Pampers and Pantène.

In some instances, the benefit of a multi-branding approach is that it enables the parent manufacturer to have competing products within the same sector of the market. This principle can be seen from the example of Proctor and Gamble above, as well as Kraft, Jacobs, Suchard (itself a subsidiary of Philip Morris), which maintains several brands of coffee including Maxwell House, Kenco, Jacobs and Gevalia which variously compete with each other in different markets.

This same principle is adopted in the retail environment where, for example, Thorn EMI are the owners of several competitors in the rental market, including Radio Rentals and DER, whilst the British Shoe Company has multiple retail trading names in the high street. An important dimension of multiple branding which deserves mention, is the use of third-party endorsement. Increasingly, manufacturers are recognizing the importance, as underpins to the product message, of names which may be only distantly related to the product category. When Proctor and Gamble acquired the name of Vidal Sassoon, it was used to establish major credibility in the hair-care sector, for example. By the same token, the addition of names like Chanel and other couture houses has added a valuable dimension to products which might otherwise not have been distinguishable from their competitors.

In certain instances, typified by the approach of Nestlé, a *combination* approach is taken, where the parent name is used to endorse some products – directly or indirectly – but where others are left to stand alone. In the instant-coffee market, for example, the brand name for their main product is a derivation of that of the parent company – Nescafé; Gold Blend, their premium quality product, is endorsed with the Nescafé logo; in the cereals, confectionery and other markets, the Nestlé symbol is used alongside that of brand names such as Cheerios and Kit Kat; whilst in the bottled water market, the name of Perrier is left to stand alone.

Within the retail sector, operators are becoming increasingly concerned with issues relating to branding. For many years they were content to use their operating name on the products which were manufactured on their behalf and sold by them. Consumers derived their perceptions from the support activity which surrounded the store identity. Retailers such as Sainsbury's, Safeway and others developed distinctive positionings within the marketplace in relation to quality, value for money and other dimensions, and the products which bore their logos reflected those values. In recent years, however, the retailers have seen the need to elevate their own (private label) products to brand status. Sainsbury's introduced Novon (a range of washing powder and liquid products) and Gio (a competitor in the soft drinks market) with a distinctive identity. More recently, Tesco have announced a brand called 'Unbelievable' to compete with Unilever's 'I Can't Believe It's Not Butter'. Safeway maintain a comprehensive range of products with distinctive packaging and identities to compete with manufacturers' brands. We will consider other aspects of 'lookalike' brands later in this unit.

Mixed branding

Several manufacturers adopt a *mixed branding* approach to distinguish between products which they manufacture under their own brand names and identities, and those which are supplied to retailers and packaged with their retail identities. Although several manufacturers (including Kellogg's and Heinz) refuse to supply products to private labels, and indeed have used advertising to communicate that fact, others such as Allied Bakeries, United Biscuits, Dalgety and Britvic, to name just a few, simultaneously sell products under their own brand names to compete on-shelf with retail competitors which they have supplied.

Generic branding

In some instances, manufacturers or retailers have been content to sell their products under generic or 'no brand' identities. Often this stance is taken to emphasize dimensions such as value for money. The notion of the 'white pack' originated in France to provide consumers with a range of 'no frills' products at considerable discounts against conventional brands. The approach has been met with mixed success, although there is little doubt that many of those consumers who purchased the products packaged in this way expressed satisfaction and rated them highly in terms of value for money.

Why do you think that generic branding has not achieved the anticipated impact on consumers?

Brands and consumer perceptions

Brands continue to maintain a considerable price premium, despite expressions to the contrary. It was anticipated that pressure on disposable income during the recession would force consumers progressively towards cheaper products. A recent sample pricing comparison between major brands and those bearing the Tesco name was carried out by Leo Burnett and reported in *Marketing Magazine* (7 April 1994). It revealed a differential of some 87 per cent in favour of branded goods.

The same study, using Infoscan NMRA data, across market categories, revealed that the brand leader average price was some 45 per cent above that of private label products. Significantly, they also enjoyed a premium of around 10 per cent against secondary brands.

Importantly, whilst there has been much talk in the trade press concerning the erosion of the position of brands, there is no evidence to support these assertions. Indeed, the reverse is true. Despite the recessionary pressures of 1992–1993, the average brand leader still occupies over 34 per cent of the retail value of a category. This would support the belief that, although many consumers suggest there is little to choose between branded and private label products, the perceptual values continue to be vitally important.

We have already seen (Unit 3) that consumer perceptions are influenced by a variety of internal and external factors. However, we have also seen that marketing communications plays an important role in influencing those perceptions and creating images which go far beyond the normal functional factors and may affect the choice of a brand. There are, of course, some areas where these added values may indeed be real and tangible. Virgin Airlines are currently stressing several key dimensions of their service delivery in their Club Class advertising – additional seating room, provision of in-air 'lounge facilities', choice of movies, car pick up at destination, and so on.

In most cases, however, especially with low involvement products – which include the vast majority of fast-moving consumer goods – it is the combination of the physical attributes of a brand together with the values created by marketing communications, which are important to the creation of perceptual values.

Find examples of advertising which stress:

- The tangible benefits offered by a brand.
- The emotional benefits offered by a brand.

How are these appeals different?

In a recent article in *Campaign* (5 August 1994), Max Burt, Senior Account Planner at Abbott Mead Vickers BBDO, argued that it is the brand personality which is the key to sparking consumer desire. We need to consider the impressions of the brand that are left, beyond the actual message being communicated. He cites, amongst others, Tango, John Smith's, Courage Best and Fosters as examples where the personality created by advertising is a major contributor to the consumers' propensity to purchase the brand.

In many instances, the consumer may be more concerned with the intangible benefits delivered by the brand than the physical performance of the product itself. The reputation and lifestyle factors involved in, say, owning a Rolex watch, or wearing a Pierre Cardin suit, have little to do with direct performance comparisons with other watch brands or other clothing manufacturers.

Identifying and building brand values

QUESTION 4.5

Why is it important to identify the brand values *before* the process of developing marketing communications begins?

The process of identifying and building brand values is interactive with that of marketing communications. As we have already seen, the environment of the message which is communicated to the potential consumer is as important as the nature of the message itself. The values and expectations that consumers have of a brand must be clearly identified *before* work on marketing communications can commence. The whole issue of positioning is one of great significance, but it starts with the consumer, rather than ending with them. The key to a proper understanding of the brand in the context of consumer expectations is *market research* (see Unit 6).

QUESTION 4.6

Why is an understanding of consumer perceptions important to the identification of brand values?

However, it is not possible simply to ask consumers what they think about a brand, or at least, not if the purpose is to identify the *underlying* characteristics which make up a brand image. In response to a question 'What do you think product X is like?', answers are likely to be physical and tangible – for example, it tastes good, it lasts a long time, and so on. One approach to the problem is to use a series of *projective techniques,* which enable the respondent to use a series of other stimuli in order to make some form of meaningful response.

The simplest technique is to ask consumers (and potential consumers) to identify the sorts of people that they think use the product. This will allow us to access the important dimension of user image. If consumers identify brand users as being substantially different from themselves, it is apparent that there is some form of dissonance between them and the offering. Where consumers identify more closely with the product being investigated, they will tend to describe users as 'people like me'. Identifying such dissonance may be a key dimension in rectifying an image problem, especially if the 'real' product delivery is felt to be appropriate to users who perceive themselves in a different light.

QUESTION 4.7

How can a manufacturer overcome dissonance towards a brand and its proposition?

For example, in the UK, non-users of cruises tend to identify users of cruises as being older (perhaps retired), fairly sedentary (what is there to do on board a ship?), wealthy (cruising is expensive), and so on. However, if exposed to the product, many non-users tend to find it attractive and rapidly become converts. Accordingly, companies like Royal Caribbean and P&O have sought to associate other values with their proposition to make it more appropriate to a younger audience.

ACTIVITY 4.3

Try this out for yourself. How would you describe the users of a specific product which you do not use yourself?

An alternative research approach is to ask respondents to imagine what sort of personality the product would have if it were human. Some interesting results emerge which are directly applicable to the identification of brand personality. A product might be seen as young or old, male or female, passive or aggressive, wealthy or impoverished. All of these, and many other dimensions, will provide important clues as to how the individual perceives a product or service.

ACTIVITY 4.4

Again, carry out this exercise for yourself. It won't take long and may reveal some interesting dimensions of how you see different products from the same category. Describe some brands as if they possessed human characteristics.

Other techniques involve getting the consumers, often in a group discussion format, to use visual elements – providing them with illustrations taken from newspapers and magazines – and inviting them to prepare a collage of their impressions of a product or service.

The key factor in all these exercises is that we identify what it is that makes a product 'behave' in the way that it does, in order that we can then determine whether the image is close to the one desired, or whether we will have to take action to change it.

An important way of depicting brand positionings is with the use of a *perceptual map*. Using the techniques outlined above, it is possible to build up a typology for all the brands which compete in a market category. By identifying the key considerations in the minds of the consumer (to isolate the important dimensions of a desired brand) and placing them on a matrix we can illustrate the relative positions of the competing brands within a market. The resultant 'map' relates all brands to each other, and allows for exploration of their relationship to an ideal position to occupy. Sometimes, it will be necessary to build up multiple maps, where the market is segmented and where the desired values of each segment differ from those of the others. A hypothetical example of such a market map is shown in Figure 4.3, which describes some of the competitors in the UK car market. You might wish to add some more car marques to this map to make it more complete.

ACTIVITY 4.5

Attempt to develop a perceptual map for any market with which you are familiar.

- Identify what values are sought from brands in the category.
- Decide how the various brand offerings match up to these criteria.
- Check whether your map identifies any gaps in the market for a new product.

Altering brand images

It is important to understand that brand images are not fixed. They can be amended or changed completely by the appropriate use of marketing communications tools. In my youth, Lucozade was a product which I drank when I was ill. Today, marketing communications has transformed it into a product which is seen by its young audience as a trendy and refreshing beverage. Another example is provided by Hellman's, who have transformed salad dressing from an old fashioned to a modern and desirable accompaniment to food.

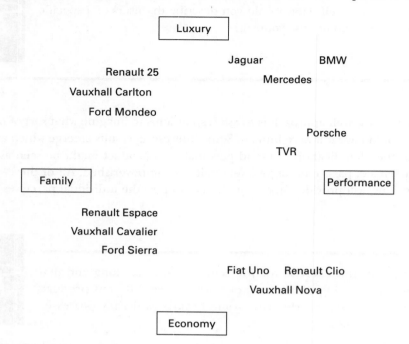

Figure 4.3

QUESTION 4.7

- How easy is it to alter brand images?
- Describe the process involved in changing consumers' perceptions of a brand.

The role of marketing communications

David Ogilvy in his book *Ogilvy on Advertising* says: 'Every advertisement should be thought of as a contribution to the brand image. It follows that your advertising should project the same image, year after year'. In the context of current thinking, the analogy should be taken to include more than just advertising. It is vitally important that all communications messages on behalf of the brand communicate a single and consistent image.

We have seen that the consumer may be unaware of the source of the message, in specific terms. Often, he or she will be unable to determine whether the impressions were created by advertising, public relations, packaging or any other dimension of the brand activity. Nor, for that matter, does the source really matter, providing that the impression that the consumer receives is a favourable and positive one. But it does demand that the marketer examine all aspects of the communications message to ensure that the elements are consistent with each other, and that the consumer does not receive contradictory impressions of the brand. There are a number of important facets to consider.

Is the advertising proposition consistently applied?

Some of the most effective advertising campaigns, in terms of brand development, are those which have developed an enduring message. PG Tips, in the UK tea market, have used the executional treatment since the 1960s – the chimps are synonymous with the brand; Cadbury's Flake advertising has conveyed the same message with essentially the same story-line in its commercials over much of the same timescale; the mnemonics employed by Proctor and Gamble continue several decades after they were first used; the values contained in the Levi's jeans commercials have been constant over the past decade. These, and many other examples, illustrate the importance of consistency in advertising. The specific treatment and the executional content may change, be refreshed and updated, but the underlying proposition about the brand remains the same – with the benefit that each advertising message delivered serves to reinforce all of those which have been received in the past.

This should not be taken to imply, however, that advertising, like all the other aspects of marketing communications, should not be subject to frequent review. Even long-running advertising campaigns may reach a point where the message needs to change. Both British Telecom and Perrier are examples of long running and successful advertising campaigns, both of which have won numerous awards, where the advertising strategies have been changed in response to underlying changes in the competitive environment. The advertising strategy should be re-examined and the executions monitored to ensure that the approach continues to be appropriate.

QUESTION 4.8

> If consistency is a key factor in the development of brand image, why do marketers insist in changing advertising executions so often?

Does sales promotion underpin the brand image?

Here, we are not talking about the short-term use of sales promotion techniques designed to achieve specific objectives. Rather we must consider the longer term sales promotion strategy. If certain techniques are used frequently, they will combine to build up an image of the brand. If, for example, a sequence of reduced-price offers and money-off discounts are used to achieve short-term offtake, the likelihood is that consumers will build up an expectation of the reduced price as being the norm. This may be in direct conflict with the positioning of the brand as a high-quality, premium-priced brand. By the same token, the offering of inferior quality free gifts and other merchandise, or the inconsistent presentation of the brand at the point of purchase may undermine the imagery of the brand which advertising and other activity has sought to build.

Are sponsorships and other involvements relevant and consistent?

As manufacturers become increasingly involved with other organizations to promote their brands, the question must be asked as to whether the visibility gained reflects favourably on the brand. Providing an appropriate synergy exists between the brand and the sponsored activity, it is likely that favourable impressions will be created for both parties to the sponsorship.

Swatch sought to reinforce its youthful imagery with the sponsorship of the television programme 'The Word'; Stone's Bitter sponsors football programmes in the Midlands; the Prudential has long been involved with sponsorship of various of the arts, and so on. Guinness claim that their recent sponsorship of the Irish football team in the 1994 World Cup helped to boost the company's profits.

The converse, however, may equally be true. The choice of the wrong party, or the sponsorship of activity with the wrong image and franchise, may act detrimentally to the brand.

Do spokespersons for the brand reflect similar values?

In some instances, the brand uses a 'personality' either to endorse the product, or to act as its spokesperson. This may have a positive impact on consumer perceptions of the brand if the image associated with the personality is a positive one. In the recent advertising for Quorn, a meat-alternative product based on soya beans, advertising has featured famous athletes including Sally Gunnell and Will Carling. Their sporting prowess and achievements underpin the product as a contribution to healthy eating.

However, the involvement of the veteran actor Tony Curtis with an anti-smoking campaign had to be terminated when it was revealed that he smoked cannabis, whilst Pepsi Cola were forced to terminate their use of Michael Jackson when alleged scandals arose concerning his private life.

Do public relations activities reinforce the brand message?

Whilst the intention of public relations is to promote the values of the brand, it is important to ensure that the messages are consistent with those of other areas of marketing communications. Providing a common communications strategy is adopted, public relations will support the other aspects of the brand effort, but it has to be remembered that public relations is the least controllable of the communications tools and, on some occasions, the intended message will be revised by the recipients before being passed on to the intended audience.

Is packaging reassessed to ensure consistency with the desired image?

Packaging is the consummate form of branding. It is the tangible representation of all dimensions of the brand to the consumer. When used well, the dimensions of packaging – the nature of the container, the colour of the label, the typeface, and other elements – can project and reinforce a desired image for the brand. However, it has to be remembered that image dimensions may change and, more importantly, so will consumer expectations of the brand. Whether the desire is to project traditional values, or stress modernity, packaging makes a vital contribution. If the nature of the pack proposition is not considered regularly, a danger exists that this final presentation to the consumer may lag behind other communications dimensions.

The importance of packaging and pack design should not be underestimated. Although some products and services are supported by considerable marketing communications budgets, the vast majority receive minimal expenditure behind, them, and many receive none at all. The weight of communicating the values of the brand in these circumstances rests entirely with their presentation to the consumer. Not only must the packaging provide a positive guide to the contents and their uses, it must also identify the benefits of the product. And, in the absence of media or other support, the packaging must also supply the emotional values which contribute to a brand's value.

A good example of the way in which packaging can contribute in this way is provided by several competitors within the bottled-water market. The on-shelf aspirational values which high-quality packaging provides, contribute to the various brands' ability to secure a considerable price premium over many of their competitors. Several packs are archetypal examples of the positive contribution that pack design makes to consumer recognition and differentiation: the box and jar (now plastic) that instantly communicate Vicks Vapour Rub; the instantly recognizable Heinz Tomato Ketchup and HP Sauce bottles; the gold packaging for Benson & Hedges cigarettes.

It should be remembered that the principles of 'packaging' apply equally to the retail environment. Few could fail to recognize a McDonalds outlet the world over. The selection of the style and colours of the decor for these and other fast-food outlets assist the consumer to identify 'freshness' and 'modernity', amongst other values.

Brand lookalikes

The role played by packaging in communicating brand values is receiving considerable attention in another context. The increased number of retail products which take on the visual appearance of the brand leader is focusing attention on the subject of 'lookalikes'.

As we have seen, in many instances, particularly in a crowded retail environment, the consumer devotes little time to brand selection. The decision to purchase is made on the basis of a series of visual cues as to the identity of the brand. Until comparatively recently, such cues as the pack shape, its colour, the style of the typeface, and similar visual hints were a ready guide to the brand identity of the product purchased. Today, however, the situation is far less clear.

Consumers could be forgiven for mistaking the identity of a product, given the number of packs which have been specifically designed to emulate the appearance of another. Retailers have, similarly, recognized the importance of packaging design and the contribution that it can make, not only to their profits but, importantly, to their overall image.

Find several examples where a retailer has developed product packaging which is similar to that of the brand leader. What is the objective of such activity?

International branding considerations

We will examine many of the important issues relating to international marketing communications in Unit 13. However, in this unit we will consider some of the aspects which relate to international branding.

In the development of companies, many find themselves forced to seek further opportunities to continue the process of brand expansion. In many cases, these opportunities exist by expanding into new countries. The benefits which can be derived from the economies of production and the apparent similarity of the markets in other countries has attracted some brands to expand beyond their original marketplaces.

The process of developing *international* brands is very similar to that adopted for *national* brands, although inevitably the former is both more complex and time consuming – especially if the underlying desire is to achieve parity of brand image in all of the markets in which the product is sold. A series of fundamental questions must first be asked about how products in the category are expected to perform in different markets. The functional areas of a product may be different from country to country. The fact that many consumers in different countries all drink instant coffee, for example, should not suggest that their expectations of product performance are the same. Almost all the Latin countries, for example, tend to drink their coffee much stronger than, say, in the UK. Offering the same blend to all markets might lead to acceptance in some, but would find rejection in most. The evaluation of the performance of washing powders might be the same in most markets – How white do they get my clothes? – but factors such as the way in which the product is used may have an important bearing. Is the penetration of automatic washing machines similar, or do many consumers in some markets still wash by hand?

Understanding the brand personality is, arguably, even more important in the international context. We have seen that the dimensions of brand personality are largely perceptual. They relate to the images which have been created over time by the various aspects of marketing communications. Equally important, however, they relate to elements of consumer behaviour in the different markets.

In some markets, the use or possession of a particular product may have no meaning beyond its functional purposes. In others, it may be regarded as a symbol of success or affluence. Setting what for some is an aspirational product in a mundane environment (a wholly appropriate setting for others) for advertising purposes is likely to undermine the values associated with the brand. It is important to ensure that there is an adequate 'fit' between the positioning of the brand and the perceptions of the consumers in all of the markets in which it is to be sold. Ultimately, of course, it may be possible to alter the underlying perceptions and reach a point at which all markets share a common view of the brand. Until that time is reached, however, it is important that the brand continues to deliver against the expectations of the consumers who purchase it.

Why do some brands (like Coca Cola) achieve global status, whilst others continue to be sold in different forms to different markets, even if they share the same brand identity?

In this unit we have:

- Examined the important role of brands and the dimensions of branding.
- Seen that, increasingly, there are few physical differences which serve to enable the consumer to discriminate between competing brands. Many rely on the differences in positioning, image, lifestyle values, and so on, to provide a reason why the consumer should select one brand in preference to another.
- Examined the various branding strategies that may be adopted by companies to assist in this process.
- Looked at a variety of techniques, especially that of perceptual mapping, which are used by manufacturers to identify unique positionings for their products.
- Seen that the process of altering brand images, whilst not an impossible task, requires a great deal of investment on the part of the brand owner and is one in which marketing communications plays a vital role. The important strategic issues and the contribution of the various marketing communications tools have all been examined.
- Considered the issue of brand personality which is attracting increasing attention with the introduction of brand 'lookalikes', and begun to consider the international dimensions of branding.

By studying this unit, you should have built up a clearer understanding of the importance of brands and the role they play in the determination of marketing and marketing communications strategies.

Examination hints and specimen question

In recent years, a number of questions have related to this important area, especially in the context of the case study question. In June 1993, for example, the compulsory case question dealt with issues relating to the Nescafé brand. In many ways, an understanding of brands underpins much of what we attempt to achieve within the field of marketing communications since, of course, the brand is at the centre of all such activity.

The short questions which have been provided within the unit will help you to develop an understanding of the important issues and to relate them to your exam answers.

The following question was taken from Part 2 of the exam paper, and will give you the opportunity of tackling a specific question set by the examiner.

In the last decade, the power of national manufacturers of consumer goods has declined relative to the power of multiple retailers. The manufacturers' brands have suffered increasing competition from 'own label' or retailers' brands. You are the marketing manager of a manufacturer of a nationally branded food product. In a memorandum to your managing director set out the guidelines for changes in your future marketing communications strategy brought about by changes in the power of retailers. In particular, show how you intend to work more effectively with retailers.

(June 1992)

EXTENDING KNOWLEDGE

As we have seen, the issues relating to branding are important to ensuring a full understanding of the role of marketing communications. It is important, therefore, that you read widely around the subject. Reference to periodicals including *Marketing*, *Marketing Week* and *Campaign* will provide you with many contemporary examples of effective branding activity. Several texts will provide you with invaluable reference and an array of practical examples with which to illustrate your examination answers. It is not necessary to read all the titles below, but they are provided as alternatives to enable you to choose those with which you feel most comfortable.

L. De Chernatony and M. McDonald, *Creating Powerful Brands*, Butterworth-Heinemann, Oxford, 1993.

D. Cowley (ed.), *Understanding Brands – By 10 People Who Do*, Kogan Page, 1991.

G. Hankinson and P. Cowking, *Branding in Action*, McGraw-Hill, New York, 1993.

C. Macrae, *World Class Brands*, Addison-Wesley, New York, 1991.

In the Far East, a title which will relate the theory to the practice, using many examples with which you will be familiar, is:

S. Subroto, *Brand Positioning*, Tata/McGraw-Hill, New York, 1994.

Managing the marketing communications process

In this unit you will:

- Discover a framework for the development of a marketing communications plan.
- Go through the important stages which must be followed in the planning process, and undertake practice exercises that will enable you to apply your learning to real situations.
- Consider the structuring of a company to deal with the important aspects of marketing communications, and the appointment of agencies and consultancies which will assist you in the development of effective and integrated marketing communications plans.

By the end of this unit you will:

- Have developed a thorough understanding of the role of planning.
- Know what contribution planning makes to the development of a cohesive message to various audiences.
- Understand the use of external agencies.

The development of a carefully structured marketing communications plan is a critical facet of the communications process. If there is any lack of clarity in the planning phase, this will have significant consequences for the activity which follows. It is therefore important to ensure that your understanding of the topic is comprehensive.

You must carry out the various exercises contained in this unit which have been specifically designed to reinforce your learning, and answer the short questions which have been included for the same reason.

Allow about 3 hours to read through the unit, and about 4 hours to carry out the exercises.

Two sample questions taken from recent CIM papers are included at the end of the unit, which you might like to try.

With each of the units in this workbook, you must be careful to ensure that you have absorbed the relevant information before you move on. Some of the issues will be amplified in more detail as you progress, but if you haven't established a solid base of understanding before you reach them, they will be much more difficult.

The old adage 'practice makes perfect' applies here. Practise writing out your answers to the questions in the text – without reference to the material contained in the unit – to see for yourself how much you have absorbed. It is always better to build knowledge slowly and carefully, rather than rush through it.

The development of a cohesive and integrated marketing communications plan demands the adoption of a systematic process to ensure that all dimensions of the plan are carefully and thoroughly considered. There is no such thing as the 'ideal' planning format. Each plan must be adapted to meet the specific circumstances which need to be addressed.

What follows is an outline format (which has served the author well in many years of developing marketing communications programmes). Inevitably, the format follows a series of individual stages, each of which serves to identify specific aspects of the performance – or lack of it – of the company, its competitors, and the marketplace.

In some instances, information will be readily accessible. In others, the task of collecting relevant data will be more difficult. In all cases, the need to conduct specific programmes of market research will be important to identify key consumer issues.

It is unlikely that the examiner will ask you to examine all of the elements which are contained in the plan shown in Figure 5.1. However, it is important that you understand the process of creating a comprehensive plan, in order that you can identify the elements which will be needed to answer a particular question.

Background analysis

The starting point for any determination of strategic direction, must be a comprehensive and thorough analysis of the background situation along a number of key dimensions. These involve the company, the market, the competition, and the general business environment.

In what ways are the internal and external environments of a company likely to affect the consideration of marketing communications strategy?

The company

Since marketing communications is inextricably linked with marketing strategy, we need to develop a complete understanding of the organization and its goals. It is important to identify what business it is in; what its key products and services provided to end users are; how these are differentiated from those of its competitors; how they satisfy potential consumers; and so on.

Importantly, we need to conduct some form of audit of the organization in order to identify the particular *Strengths* it possesses, potential areas of *Weakness*; the different *Opportunities* that it might consider exploiting; and the various *Threats* which confront it. Any or all of these elements might have an impact on the development of the marketing communications plan.

If, for example, the company has only limited financial resources, then it will not be able to undertake a costly communications exercise. If there are gaps, say, in the sales force, then a communications plan which depends to a high degree on personal selling is unlikely to achieve its targets – unless the company's own personnel are augmented from an external force, or new recruits are employed and trained before the plan is implemented.

There are two important points to establish. It is probably worthwhile to establish some form of grid on which the strengths, weaknesses, opportunities and threats can be plotted. Although some elements will be immediately apparent, others will not emerge until other aspects of the analysis are completed. Secondly, although the diagram in Figure 5.1 suggests a series of *sequential* activities, in fact there is a high degree of interdependence between the variables. The information gained from one area of this situational analysis may have an impact on and relevance to other areas.

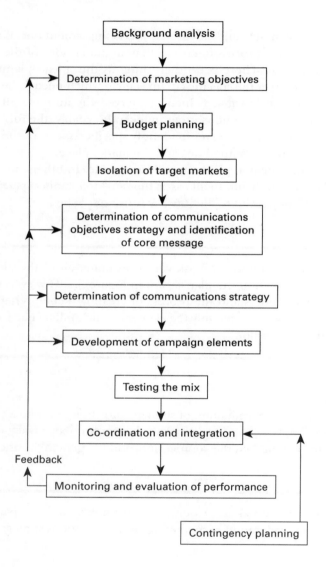

Figure 5.1

Having completed the internal company analysis, we can begin to examine the other dimensions. It is not necessary to carry out these activities in any particular sequence, as long as by the end of the exercise all of the key dimensions have been covered fully.

ACTIVITY 5.1

If you are working within an organization, carry out a SWOT analysis for its leading product or service. If you are not, 'adopt' a product or service and carry out the exercise.

The competitor

We might turn next to an examination of the competitive environment. Similar questions to those explored within the company might equally well be addressed to the competitors. Certainly it will be useful to conduct a SWOT analysis for each of the companies with whom we compete. This might identify, for example, areas where our strengths correspond with their weaknesses – in turn suggesting a direction for subsequent activity. The converse may equally well be true. If the competitors have particularly strong areas of activity, it would probably be advisable to avoid attempting to tackle them head on. Assuming that there are other areas to which we might turn our attention, attacking the competition in their own 'heartland' is unlikely to be the best use of our resources.

The market

The third area to examine is that of the marketplace. In simple terms, the issues can be summarized as follows. Who are the consumers? Where are they? To what extent do we meet their needs? Are there any untapped opportunities which we might exploit? And so on. Few companies will possess sufficient information to be able to conduct these important areas of analysis without seeking external input. Certainly some valuable information may be derived from desk analysis (see Unit 6). It is more than likely, however, that it will be necessary to conduct some form of market research, either to dimensionalize the segments of the market (for example, to see how big any gaps we have identified are) or to explore the attitudinal dimensions of the consumer.

When answering an examination question, although some information will be provided it is unlikely that you will have access to everything you need. You must identify for the examiner the areas in which you feel that specific research would be required to supplement your knowledge, and the nature of the information you would be seeking.

For any market with which you are familiar, identify the information that you would need to consider before beginning the process of marketing communications planning.

The business environment

It is equally important to establish an understanding of the broader environment in which the company operates – either domestic or international. Here, there are a number of important factors which are, substantially, outside the control of the organization, although to varying degrees it may be possible to exert some form of influence.

A useful acronym as an aid to remembering these dimensions is PEST + C. Each of these initials represents an important dimension of the external environment which will need to be considered (see Figure 5.2).

Political factors

Political influences are likely to be significant in the future development of a company's business. Inevitably, a change of government brings with it a new political agenda which may favour some aspects of business, whilst diminishing the prospects of others.

The government of the day may introduce specific pieces of legislation which curb or control particular business functions. High on most political lists is the desire to control certain perceived antisocial activities. These include smoking and the consumption of alcoholic beverages. Government action, for example, may limit access to the media either in part (as in the UK) or entirely (as in other parts of the EC). A change of government may manifest itself in the form of higher levels of taxation, which are specifically applied, and which make particular goods and services more expensive to the consumer. Equally, it may take the form of specific controls on the importation of certain product areas in order to protect domestic markets for domestic producers.

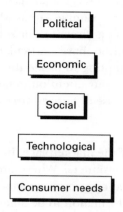

Figure 5.2

The converse may equally be true. Governments may provide direct incentives to encourage certain forms of consumer behaviour which, in turn, encourage them to buy particular goods and services. In the UK and elsewhere, government action has specifically benefitted the growth of private health-care provision and personal pensions, for example.

Some of the actions of government may be anticipated to occur in the short term – the annual budget statement, for example, will have a sizeable impact on the performance of the economy by the tightening or relaxation of personal taxation levels and interest rates. Both these factors affect the potential for growth of a company's sales.

Although the longer term is less easy to predict, a company must nevertheless attempt to anticipate likely changes which may impact on the way that its business is likely to perform.

Economic factors

By the same token, the economic elements will inevitably affect sales potential. Recent years have seen a worldwide recession which has significantly dampened down economic performance. Whilst governments have made various attempts to stimulate their economies, with varying degrees of effectiveness, the underlying factors have resulted in a reduction in levels of employment and the preparedness of individuals to embark on specific patterns of expenditure. Both of these influences have considerably reduced the sales volumes of specific goods and services.

Although currently experiencing a slight recovery, car sales have sustained a considerable downturn over recent years. Similarly, house sales have been depressed compared to previous years. However, although these factors have impacted on direct sales, there have been positive benefits in other areas. Because some people have deferred the purchase of a new car, many of them have spent more on car maintenance and the purchase of accessories – to the direct benefit of the companies operating in these areas. Similarly, there has been a growth in some areas of house and garden improvements, either because home owners have sought to improve their own personal environments, or because they have tried to make their houses more attractive to potential purchasers. Again, the suppliers of goods and services in these areas have been the direct beneficiaries. These examples serve to illustrate the fact that it is important to examine not only the broad-scale impact of economic changes, but also the effects on related areas which may experience growth.

Social changes

We have already seen that there is a series of fundamental changes in both consumer attitudes and behaviour patterns within the social environment. Here again, it is important to be aware of these factors in order to anticipate their likely impact on business performance. Since most of these will be the direct result of observable changes, it is somewhat easier to foresee their effect. A few examples will illustrate this point.

Life expectancies have increased dramatically throughout this century in most developed countries. In the UK, for example, in 1901 the average life expectancy for men at birth was only 45 years, but today it is close to 73 years. For women, the comparable figures are 48 and 78 years, respectively. Indeed life expectancy will continue to increase as a direct consequence of the underlying improvements in eating habits, living conditions and medical knowledge. This has been accompanied, for many, by a considerably enhanced standard of living. Many of these individuals have long since paid off their mortgages and, now that their children have left home, can 'trade down' their properties in order to gain access to their capital. The result has been a dramatic growth in the sales of specific products and services which are targeted to appeal to these more affluent older individuals.

A similar trend can be seen as a result of the progressive reduction in the number of births – resulting in a smaller youth market and a dampening down of demand for many products aimed at this segment.

The increased number of working women has brought about changes in the retail environment. Since they can no longer access their preferred stores during the 'normal' hours of 09.00 to 17.00, retailers have been forced to adopt longer trading hours, even opening during weekends to ensure that their customer needs are satisfied.

Smaller family units, single-parent families and similar factors have resulted in a growth in the demand for small product sizes, and so on.

An increased concern with the impact of particular goods and services on the environment has, similarly, resulted in both manufacturers and retailers being forced to become more aware of their responsibilities in these areas. Sometimes the direct result of governmental action and in other instances the result of consumer pressures, manufacturers have been forced to respond by changing the nature of their products (to eliminate chlorofluorocarbons (CFCs) and chlorates) or their packaging in order to minimize the wastage of scarce resources.

Inevitably, this brief overview can only consider a few of the important dimensions of social change. A comprehensive plan must consider them all!

What are the key social changes which might affect the marketing communications planning process for:

- A fast-moving consumer goods product.
- A service.
- A charity seeking donations.

ACTIVITY 5.3

Technological factors

It is important to recognize that a company's ability to deliver products that perform in the manner which consumers expect will often be related to the technological dimensions of production. Most organizations maintain a research and development function, part of whose purpose is to ensure that products are continuously up-dated to take advantage of new technologies. Sometimes, these reflect 'in-house' development of new ingredients and formulations; in others, they are a response to competitive improvements as the company seeks to identify the basis on which competitors' products achieve their results.

Carry out a PEST + C analysis for a product or service of which you are aware.

ACTIVITY 5.4

International dimensions

The acronym described above is sometimes written as PESTI + C, the I standing for 'International'. Increasingly, as companies expand the markets for their products and services beyond national boundaries, it becomes vitally important for them to understand the factors which impinge on their ability to perform within an international arena. Though the task is often more difficult, the same principles must be followed and the components of the PEST + C analysis repeated for each territory in which the product or service competes.

Marketing objectives

It is important to be clear as to the distinction between marketing and marketing communications objectives.

Marketing objectives are the specific goals that need to be achieved during the timescale of the plan. They will often refer to such targets as: increasing brand share by *x* per cent or to *y* per cent; increasing the return on capital investment; maintaining or increasing distribution; and penetrating an identified sector of the market.

Marketing communications objectives, as we will see later, are concerned with specific goals relating to communications. As such, they will relate to areas such as: increasing awareness; informing the market of specific features or attributes of a product; suggesting new uses for a product; explaining how a product functions; and altering perceptions of a product or service.

Try to be clear in your statements and take care not to confuse the two areas.

QUESTION 5.2

- How can you identify the differences between strategy and objectives?
- What are the key dimensions of marketing communications objectives?

Budget planning

Now we can turn to a consideration of budget planning. This is an important aspect of the marketing-communications plan and is considered in more detail in Unit 12. At the very least, the examiner will expect you to be able to justify your identification of an appropriate budget for the task set within a particular question and you must have a full understanding of the important aspects of this topic. For the purposes of this unit, it will suffice to provide a brief overview of the various methods of budget determination. It is important, however, that you carefully consider the topics covered in Unit 12 later in your study programme.

There are a variety of different methods of determining a marketing communications budget, and the approach taken will largely depend on the particular nature of the circumstances. These will include:

- *Marginal analysis* – the principles of economic theory suggest that a company should continue to increase its marketing communications expenditure until the point where the increase matches the increase in income which those expenditures generate.
- *Percentage of last year's turnover or sales* – possibly the most widely used method of budgeting is to calculate the ratio between expenditure and sales.
- *Percentage of gross profit margin* – essentially similar to the previous method, except that the gross margin is used as the basis of calculating the level of future expenditure.
- *Residue of last year's surplus* – this method is based entirely on previous performance, where any surplus of income over expenditure is determined as the budget for the next year.
- *Percentage of anticipated profit* – by calculating the expected profit to be derived from a product, a finite percentage is allocated to the budget for marketing communications.
- *Unit or case sales ratio* – this method assumes that there is a direct relationship between sales volumes and the expenditure required to create them. By calculating the anticipated level of sales, and assuming that a percentage of those sales is devoted to marketing communications, the budget is automatically established.
- *Competitive expenditure levels* – again, a frequently used method of budgeting, a manufacturer calculates the levels of expenditure of competitors, and either attempts to match this or sets budgets at some agreed percentage of their spend.

- *Desired share of voice* – rather than directly comparing absolute levels of expenditure by individual competitors, a manufacturer may start from the premise of calculating a share of total category expenditure in order to reflect a desired 'share of voice'.
- *Media inflation* – a simple approach is to calculate the take from the budget from the previous year, and allow for the inflationary pressures on those expenditures.
- *Objective-and-task approach* – arguably the most scientific approach is to determine the nature of the task to be fulfilled and to calculate the cost of achieving the specific objectives.
- *Experimentation* – on the realistic assumption that different levels of expenditure on marketing communications (or different combinations of the elements within the mix) will affect the volume of sales achieved, smaller scale tests can be run to determine the optimum levels of expenditure versus sales.
- *What we can afford* – management starts by determining the level of profit desired (or the return on investment) and then allocates the balance, after deduction of all costs, to expenditure on marketing communications.
- *New product considerations* – new products represent a special case, since no past data will be available on which to base judgements. More importantly, all instances will require significant expenditures ahead of sales. In all other respects, budgeting for new products is similar to the objective-and-task method outlined above.

Why is budget determination a critical phase of the marketing communications planning process?

QUESTION 5.3

As with other areas of marketing communications, it is important not to be prescriptive in the determination of budgets. Different companies employ different approaches, with similar levels of success. What is important is that a proper evaluation is made, and the method most appropriate to the company's situation is adopted and followed through.

The identification of target markets

We have already seen that most markets divide readily into specific segments along a series of different criteria. In order to determine the segment or segments to which a product or service should be aimed, it is vital to have a clear understanding of the consumer. Throughout this workbook, specific techniques for the identification of targets have been described in considerable detail. Indeed, the accurate identification of the appropriate target is a key task of both marketing and marketing communications.

- How do you set about defining the scale of a market and its sub-segments?
- Why is this process important?

QUESTION 5.4

In order to protect both the brand and the investment in it, much will depend on the quality of the research data available and its interpretation. Certainly, different manufacturers will place different emphasis on different aspects of the data in order to isolate the opportunities for their products and services.

The importance, in terms of planning, is to have a clear identification of the desired target market, since any degree of imprecision at this stage will have an important effect on the stages which follow. If the target market is not clearly identified, then the task of determining the appropriate communications message will be made more difficult. Similarly, if the target defined is too broad, then substantial sums of money will be wasted.

Identification of the core message

Here, again, a detailed understanding of the consumer – his or her patterns of product usage, buying motivations, and so on – will be vitally important to the accurate identification of the message to be conveyed. It is clear that the criteria for brand selection are dependent on a variety of different factors. Some relate to the individual – in terms of their desires and aspirations – whilst others relate to the product – both its physical properties and levels of emotional appeal. It is the combination of these characteristics into a single and cohesive message that is clearly understood by the target consumer which will ensure the development of effective marketing communications.

ACTIVITY 5.5

Find several examples of advertising campaigns for products in the same category. How does the core message differ for each of them?

The development of communications objectives

Related to the broader issues of marketing, we need to be specific in the development of the communications objectives. By way of a restatement, communications objectives are those communications tasks to be achieved amongst a defined audience to a defined extent and within a specific time frame and which the tools of marketing communications are uniquely designed to perform. Refer back to Unit 2 for a comprehensive examination of marketing communications objectives.

Whatever the objectives are, they need to be clearly defined in a way that all participating in the process can understand and agree on. In addition, they *must* relate to communications, not to marketing as a whole. This remains an area of considerable confusion for many students and it is important that you can demonstrate to the examiner that you can appreciate and apply a clear distinction between marketing objectives and marketing communications objectives.

The key issues to be addressed relate to the determination of specific objectives for each element of the marketing communications mix. It is clear from what has been said previously that no one element can be considered in total isolation from the others. Importantly, and given the move towards integrated marketing communications, specific communications objectives must be defined for each element of the mix, although they must contribute to a common communications message.

The determination of communications strategy

It is important to understand that, increasingly, we are in the business of communications – not of advertising, sales promotion, public relations or any of the other elements of the mix. As such we must be concerned primarily with identifying the most effective communications strategy rather than being concerned with its possible impact on the various components of the campaign which is subsequently developed. Indeed, if we are clear in the identification of the marketing communications strategy, the rest of the planning process will follow far more smoothly. As such, it will set the tone for all aspects of the communications plan. It will ensure the integration of all activity, and ensure that a cohesive message is delivered to the desired target audience.

The development of the campaign elements

Although it is important to develop the individual components of a campaign with great care and attention to detail, it is arguably more important that we should ensure that all communications devices offer a single and consistent message to the target audience. It follows then that we can only begin the process of identifying the campaign elements once we have determined the precise nature of the message we wish to communicate.

We will need to consider all dimensions of marketing communications – as indeed we will in the following units of this workbook – in order to examine the precise contribution that each of them can make to the delivery of the communications strategy. But we should not

66

take a fixated view as to which components we include in the campaign. Equally important-ly, we must determine at the outset which of the various areas should take the lead in our activity. In most cases this will follow logically from the work that we have done in the development of our communications plan.

If the primary task is that of creating increased levels of awareness for our brand, then we will be driven into a consideration of the relative merits of advertising, public relations and direct marketing. If we wish to offer a specific inducement to sample the product, then it is likely that we will use the variety of sales promotions techniques available to us, although the communication of the message may remain with advertising. If our audience is highly defined, then a direct marketing approach may be preferable to a broad-based advertising campaign, and so on.

It is highly likely that there will be several options open to us, and it is important to consider the relative merits of each approach. In some instances, budgetary considerations and time frames may dictate that a series of subjective decisions be taken. However, in an ideal situation, we should be prepared to test the various elements of the communications mix.

ACTIVITY 5.6

Although you will not need to have detailed knowledge of media costs, some limited understanding will be important to your being able to allocate a budget to the various elements of the communications mix. To help you in this process, identify the following:

- The cost of a 30-second television commercial.
- The cost of a full-page black & white press advertisement in a national newspaper.
- The cost of a 1-minute radio advertisement.

Testing the mix

Few companies can ever be sure that they have adjusted the various elements of the mix to achieve the most appropriate balance. Whilst it can provide no guarantees of ultimate success, market testing will offer substantial guidance to the planning process. As we will see in the appropriate units, there are a variety of market-research techniques which will ensure that we have refined the individual campaign components to ensure the effectiveness of their communication to the target audience.

Just because we think that our campaign says something is no guarantee that it will be interpreted by the audience in the way that we intend. It is important that we identify such discrepancies in our messages at an early stage. Equally, other aspects of the campaign can be subjected to market research to identify, for example, the acceptability of a sales promotion offer, its potential for raising motivation to purchase amongst the target audience; the validity of a direct mailing list to target the desired consumers; and so on.

For the most part, such market research activity considers the components of a campaign on a one-by-one basis. Inevitably, there are some dimensions of a communications campaign that are best tested in a holistic manner, that is as part of the whole. Often the effectiveness of an integrated campaign will be the direct result of the interaction of the separate elements, and the progressive reinforcement of the message in all the media channels. In this case, the best approach is to undertake some form of 'live' testing. In some instances, it will be possible to set up a 'mini-test' in a controlled area, although it must be recognized that such market testing will only be able to test some of the components. In order to scale down the operation, it may be necessary, for example, to substitute some of the intended media for some other form of communication. In a small test area it may be necessary to place advertising in print media rather than on television. The fundamental differences between these two media will need to be considered when assessing the results of the test campaign. On a somewhat larger scale, however, not only can the 'real' media be used but, equally importantly, different weights of advertising can be tested to determine their impact on the target audience. The same may also be true of other campaign elements which can be tested in different combinations in order to determine the most cost-effective deployment of the available funds.

To what extent will issues relating to distribution affect marketing communications planning?

Co-ordination and integration

It is vitally important that, in order to maximize campaign effectiveness, the implementation programme is carefully co-ordinated. In simple terms, this may mean the adoption of a critical timing plan to ensure that each aspect of the campaign breaks at the right time. There are a number of elements which need to be considered in this respect.

The first priority will be to ensure that the sales force is fully briefed both as to the nature and the objectives of the campaign. Their enthusiasm will need to be stimulated to ensure that all other elements can, reasonably, be put in place at the right time. At the same time, it is important to ensure that they are equipped with the appropriate sales aids to communicate the message to their immediate audience of wholesalers and retailers.

Equally important is the fact that sufficient time must be built in not only to allow them to communicate the proposition but also, in turn, to enable the distribution channels to take up appropriate volumes before the campaign breaks. If, for example, the campaign depends on a sales promotion incentive, then adequate stock of the specially prepared packaging needs to be in store to meet anticipated consumer demand. Even if the campaign is designed to build awareness of the brand, or to stimulate trial of existing product, it is important to ensure that, as far as possible, the trade is made aware of the campaign *before* it breaks to the public. Not only will this enable the selling in of stocks against demand but, more importantly, it will serve to develop the relationship between the retailer and the company.

The functional aspects of campaign implementation are important. Sufficient time needs to be planned for promotional labels to be printed, television commercials and press advertising to be delivered to the media, direct marketing lists to be profiled and de-duplicated, public relations activities to be prepared and placed in the media channels, and so on. Care also needs to be taken to ensure that all aspects of the campaign integrate well with each other. To repeat what has been said previously, the more closely integrated the various elements of the campaign are, the more effectively will the message be communicated to the target audience. Not only will we avoid confusion between different elements of the campaign, but we will also ensure that the single message is continuously reinforced.

Monitoring of performance

It is important that all aspects of the campaign are carefully monitored during their implementation. Even the best laid plans go wrong, and if a proper monitoring process is followed minor errors can be identified and corrected.

Even with careful pre-testing, there is no substitute for the real thing. The performance of the campaign in a live situation is what matters and it is vitally important that some continuous assessment of campaign achievement is implemented – possibly in the form of a tracking study, or some other form of periodic research – to identify the impact of the campaign on the target audience.

Most importantly, the information gathered will ensure that subsequent campaign planning is enhanced by the additional knowledge. Some form of feedback mechanism must be built in to enable the proper evaluation of the campaign activities against the established objectives to determine the extent to which those objectives have been met.

What is the role of 'feedback' in the marketing communications planning process?

Contingency planning

A wise general once said: 'There is no such thing as success, only limiting the damage of failure'. In marketing communications this statement is particularly apposite. However great the efforts taken to eliminate the possibility of errors creeping into the campaign, and in testing the effectiveness of the variables, one key dimension cannot be assessed in advance – the nature of competitive response. Only once the campaign is fully implemented will it be possible to identify the specific nature of competitive activities. Although these may take some time to implement, the planner can be reasonably certain that the competition will not sit idly by and watch as the campaign erodes their strengths. What form this might take can certainly be considered in advance, although its true nature will not be known until it, too, is implemented. Sufficient funds must be kept aside to make necessary adjustments to the planned campaign to ensure that the objectives can be met.

What are the stages of the marketing communications planning process? (Only list the key headings.)

ACTIVITY 5.7

Organizing for marketing communications

It is clear that, in order to ensure the maximum effectiveness of its marketing communications campaigns, a company must adopt an appropriate approach to the management of activities. This manifests itself in two forms. Firstly, an organization must consider how it needs to organize itself *internally* to deal with marketing communications issues. Secondly, it must identify the appropriate *external* organizations which can contribute to specific aspects of marketing communications planning and implementation.

Internal structures

If one took the opportunity to examine the internal structure of several organizations involved with marketing communications, the one thing which would become immediately apparent is that there is no single framework which is universally adopted.

In many organizations the responsibility for the direct control of marketing communications is vested in the marketing director; in others, control is in the hands of the sales director; for a few the whole area of communications remains with the managing director or chief executive. At a lower level (often reflecting the size of the organization) there will be a pyramidal structure of marketing management, with marketing group managers, product group managers, product managers, and so on. Elsewhere, individuals will be specifically charged with responsibilities in identified areas, possessing titles such as advertising manager, sales promotion manager, etc. To confuse the situation further, some companies retain a corporate communications director or manager whose responsibilities may embrace the totality of the organization's communications with its various publics.

Clearly, there can be no definitive prescription for the successful management of marketing communications tasks. Each company has identified its own approach, and employs the method which best suits its operational culture. Whatever the titles and reporting structure, certain key elements remain important. Indeed, given much of what has been said earlier, they will become increasingly important as the need to fuse the elements of marketing communications becomes more widely recognized.

- It is vitally important that there are nominated individuals in place to consider *all* aspects of the marketing communications plan to ensure their smooth integration. It remains true in many organizations that specific individuals will have control over the determination of the individual communications elements, often without regard to the longer-term issues involved. In many companies, for example, the brand manager is charged with the responsibility of achieving sales targets. These may be readily facilitated by means of, for example, price cutting or other sales-promotion devices. The fact that these may, potentially, undermine the longer-term impact of, say, image advertising is outside his or her remit and will be given scant consideration.

- As such, companies must increasingly accept that the responsibility for the adoption of a long-term competitive positioning strategy must be more important than the short-term achievement of sales targets. Indeed, if the internal approach is fully adopted, such conflicts will be eliminated, with the long-term strategic goals providing the framework for the short-term determination of tactics.
- One or more individuals must be responsible for the smooth implementation of the marketing communications campaign. As we have already seen – and the point will be developed further throughout this workbook – implementing a campaign is, potentially, a logistical nightmare. Even a simple communications campaign will involve the co-ordination of the efforts of a large number of people and external organizations – planners, copywriters, art directors, typesetters, printers, media buyers, etc. The more complex the campaign, the greater the need for control.
- Few organizations possess the appropriate management and creative skills to be able to develop and manage campaign activities in isolation of external expertise. However, this expertise may itself complicate the issue as a result of its inherently fragmented nature. Recent years have seen an explosion in the number of specialist companies which offer individual input in areas such as advertising, sales promotion, public relations, direct marketing, and so on. The onus for fusing and integrating the inputs provided more often than not remains within the company. Not only must this responsibility be recognized, but specific policies must be established to ensure that it happens.

QUESTION 5.7

What are the conflicts present in brand management with regard to achieving short-term marketing goals versus the longer-term development of the brand's positioning and image?

The use of agencies

Most organizations employ some number of external agencies on a semi-permanent or *ad hoc* basis to supplement their own communications skills. What particular skills they will require will depend largely on the nature of their businesses and the markets within which they operate.

Procter and Gamble, in the UK, employs at least four international advertising agencies to handle its brands, a media specialist together with other agencies in the areas of public relations and sales promotion. Similarly, H. J. Heinz uses separate mainstream advertising agencies, direct marketing agencies, sales promotions companies, public relations specialists, and so on. Even far smaller organizations call on the services of several different communications companies to supply their needs.

The task of appointing and co-ordinating these activities is a considerable one, to say the least. For the purposes of the CIM Diploma, you must be able to identify the key issues in relation to the selection and remuneration of the appropriate agencies, and this is covered below.

The selection of agencies

QUESTION 5.8

List the considerations to be applied when appointing an advertising agency or a sales promotion consultancy.

The starting point in any agency selection process must be the definition of the services which you require them to provide. Different agencies fulfil different specialist roles, and it is important to isolate which services you will require. The range is certainly broad enough to provide the flexibility to meet any circumstances.

- *Full service agencies* offer, directly or indirectly (often through subsidiary companies), a comprehensive range of marketing communications inputs.
- *Broad-based specialist consultancies* offering services in the fields of media planning and buying, sales promotion, public relations and direct marketing.
- *Narrow-based consultancies* offering, for example, creative services (copywriting and art direction), planning, or new product development.

The starting point is to identify the particular *services* that will be required in order to isolate the nature of the organization or organizations to be employed. If the needs of the organization are predominantly in the area of sales promotion or public relations, for example, there is little point attempting to secure the services of an international advertising agency. Not only are the main skills likely to be underutilized, the senior management are extremely unlikely to become involved with the management of your business.

Having identified the services required, the next step is to identify the qualitative and quantitative criteria that will be used to evaluate performance. For example, do you require the agency to be skilled in areas such as market research? Is planning a key requirement? What type of creative skills do you require? And so on. Should the agency have prior experience of your market sector? What size should the agency be – do you wish to be a major player, or are you content to be a 'small fish in a big pond'? Should the agency be part of an international network, or are you content with a domestic agency?

You can then begin the process of identifying a shortlist of agencies that can fulfil your brief. In this respect, it is important to consider a wide variety of inputs to help you in the selection process. Certainly, it is important to examine recent issues of the trade press which will help you identify which agencies are 'hot' and which are not. It may provide you with examples of work that they have produced for other clients – so that you can consider aspects such as creative performance. There are a number of specific publications which will also help you identify the current clients and other aspects of the agencies you might be considering. Among these are: the *Campaign* publication *Portfolio*; the BRAD *Advertiser and Agency List*; and the *Blue Book*. You might consider consulting the Advertising Agency Register (AAR) or the Sales Promotion Register, both of which maintain current portfolios of agencies in their respective fields and can help guide you towards a shortlist by offering advice based on their experience of agency structures and 'personalities'.

There is little doubt that rumours of an 'account change' are particularly unsettling to the working relationship with the incumbent agency. As far as possible you should avoid publicizing any impending review until as late as possible. It is important that you visit a number of agencies to get to know the personalities involved – relationships with agencies depend on people factors. These meetings will provide the agency with the opportunity to set out their credentials and, hopefully, to identify the personnel who would be working on your business, should they be appointed. At this stage, try to discriminate between the 'A' team of senior management who will be responsible for new business presentations and who (unless your account is of major significance) will be unlikely to work on your business, and the day-to-day team. It is the latter with whom your will have to develop a working relationship.

Some companies issue a preliminary questionnaire to agencies they are considering, which contains a number of specific questions to assist in the process of shortlisting. This may be used to ensure that the criteria you have established are met by the possible contenders and that other important areas, including agency remuneration, are covered before the shortlist is finalized. Similarly, there are a number of specialist selection companies who will undertake the preliminary stages on your behalf. The benefit of using such consultants rests in their experience gained from an involvement in the process over many years – unlike your own which is likely to be somewhat limited – and the fact that the identity of the company you are seeking to appoint may be protected for somewhat longer.

Whatever approach you adopt, the next stage is the creation of a shortlist and the issuing of a specific brief. The brief to the agency is used to enable them to demonstrate a specific response to your requirements. As such it needs to provide the contenders with as much information as can be provided – bearing in mind that the more vague you are at this stage, the less able they will be to provide a full response to your requirements. As far as possible, you must be prepared to allow the agencies access to the same information as you would require for the development of your marketing communications plan. Security can be maintained by including a confidentiality clause in the briefing document.

Allow sufficient time for the agencies to absorb and analyse the information provided, and to carry out their own research, if necessary, when considering the date for the 'pitch'. If there is insufficient time between the briefing and the presentation, the response will inevitably be somewhat shallow. Finally, establish some form of objective assessment against which to measure the agency presentations. Define the formal criteria so that all persons involved in the process can participate in the decision on the same basis. Whether the presentations will be assessed on the basis of strategic recommendations, or on the basis of preliminary creative work is a somewhat subjective decision. Equally it is important that, as far as possible, the key people at the company end should be involved in the selection process. It is they, rather than the senior management, who will need to establish good working relationships on an on-going basis. The importance of these interpersonal relationships cannot be emphasized enough. Once the agency selection has been made, it is important to ensure that there is a smooth and efficient hand-over between them and the previous incumbent, so that there is no interruption to the flow of work on your business. Contacts need to be formalized and the winning agency announced.

Agency remuneration

An important dimension of the relationship will, inevitably, be a reflection of what you are charged for the work that the agency produces and an agreement as to the ownership of this material. There are a variety of different bases for agency remuneration, and it is important that whichever method is used agreement should be reached at the outset.

Commission

Still the most common basis for calculating agency income is the traditional commission system. For many decades, the principle has been established that agencies receive the bulk of their income *not* from their clients, but from media proprietors. Indeed, this gives rise to the use of the word 'agency' – originally they were the agents of the media companies.

Agencies receive 15 per cent of the monies spent in the media as a direct discount from the television contractors, radio stations, media titles, and other sectors. You may sometimes see the figure of 17.65 per cent used. This is the amount required to uplift the net media expenditure to yield 15 per cent commission.

The important thing to remember is that this commission is already built in to the media rates. If, for example, a poster campaign is quoted as costing £100 000, it will contain an agency commission of £15 000. When you are preparing budgets, say for an examination answer, remember not to double cost this element. Some students show the gross cost of media plus an agency charge of 15 per cent. This is wrong!

It is also important to remember that this commission payment covers only the cost of the internal charges – staff salaries, predominantly – and that charges incurred by the agency for the production of items or the commissioning of any work on behalf of the client will be passed on, usually uplifted by a similar rate of 15 per cent. We will deal with the costs of production more fully later in this unit.

Negotiated commission

For several years pressure has been applied to agencies to adjust the commission rate to reflect more accurately the volumes of work involved in handling a clients' business. Today, several agencies are prepared to negotiate a level of commission lower than 15 per cent. Sometimes this will be a straight reduction on the entirety of the business, say to 12 or 10 per cent. In other instances, it will be based on a sliding scale.

In these cases, the first million-pounds worth of billings might be charged at the full rate of 15 per cent, the second at, say, 12 per cent, and so on down to an agreed level. In part this is a reflection of the fact that agencies, like other businesses, achieve economies of scale and that as income rises the associated costs rise at a slower rate.

It is also important to recognize that the calculation of commission can go the other way. In the case of a highly labour-intensive account, with a relatively low level of expenditure, the agency may require a higher level of commission to compensate it for the level of work involved.

However, whatever method of commission calculation is agreed, it is vitally important that it is formally agreed, in writing, at the outset of the relationship. Seldom is there more ill feeling than when either party feels aggrieved, either that it is being overcharged, or that it is being underpaid, for the level of work required.

Fee

Some agency–client relationships are based on a level of fee being calculated and agreed at the outset. Here, some assessment of the level of work involved in handling the business is agreed and a fee reflecting this determined.

It is argued that, by removing the commission element, agencies are no longer predisposed to recommending increased levels of media expenditure on the basis of their own increased income needs. By the same token, since the agency receives no more (or less) for its large recommendations than its smaller ones, the client can feel more comfortable that these are based on a proper consideration of the strategic issues. However, for the fee method to work smoothly, periodic reviews must be included within the contractual arrangements to ensure that both parties remain comfortable with the level of fee charged.

Time-based remuneration

In a few instances, the remuneration of agencies is based on similar principles to that of other professional bodies. Since, often, a great deal of time is involved in, say, the development of creative concepts, or media campaigns which for some reason do not run, an agreement is based on the time required to develop the work.

The system is based on the maintenance of accurate timesheets by all the personnel involved with the client's business, and the salary and associated costs raised by an agreed factor to deliver an appropriate level of profit.

Cost-based remuneration

An alternative approach is to apply the same principles as above to the costs of developing the associated work for a client. Again, an agreed percentage uplift is applied to all costs to ensure that the agency receives a profit for its efforts.

Production costs

The issue of production costs remains a thorny problem, and is often the source of unsettling established relationships. As noted above, whether the agency receives commission, a fee, or income based on time or costs, clients must expect to pay the costs of production for the materials required to implement a campaign. Whether this is in the form of a television commercial, or a direct mail piece is, in itself, immaterial. The principle is that agencies rarely maintain in-house production facilities.

At the time when an agency has agreed finished concepts for implementation, these will be passed on to some outside company for final production. This may involve, for example, the production of film and video, the casting of artists for a commercial or press advertisement, photographers' charges, and the typesetting of any print items.

A proper process is to agree cost estimates at an early stage in the process, so that the client company has a complete understanding of the likely costs involved in producing communications materials. Some costs, like those for a television commercial, may be extremely high. Inevitably, the more complicated the materials, the higher the relative costs. A complicated mail piece will cost considerably more than a simple letter. If both parties know the 'ball-park' costs of production early in the process of creative development, subsequent difficulties can be substantially avoided. There is no point continuing with the development of a complicated brochure involving expensive location photography, if the need is for a simple communications item!

Some latitude must be built in to cost estimates. Almost inevitably, some changes will take place during the production phase and these must be paid for. But, at a minimum, the likely cost parameters will be clearly understood by both parties, and the shock of receiving a production bill of £400 000 when the client was expecting to pay, say, £250 000 will be largely overcome.

What are the benefits and disadvantages of the different methods of agency remuneration to:

- The agency?
- The client?

Above- and below-the-line expenditure

The final area is an important one to clarify, and one that causes difficulty for some students attempting the Diploma – that is, the distinction between the terms 'above the line' and 'below the line'.

In simple terms, *above-the-line* expenditure relates to media expenditure – that is the cost of advertising on television, in the press, on radio, posters and outdoor sites, and cinema. It is these areas from which the agency receives its commission payments.

Below-the-line expenditure covers all other areas of marketing communications, whether on sales promotion, public relations or elsewhere.

In this unit we have seen that:

- The key to the development of an effective and fully integrated marketing communications plan is the adoption of a systematic process of analysis.
- In order to identify the appropriate brand positioning and creative proposition, it is vitally important to have a comprehensive understanding of the meaningful consumer dynamics.
- At the same time, it is equally essential to develop an understanding of the broader environment in which the product or service is sold, and of the factors which are likely to affect its development.
- The planning process is an important stage in the development of marketing communications, and candidates for the CIM Diploma must be able to demonstrate both a clear understanding of the process and an ability to apply the principles to an examination question.
- It is equally important to understand the management of the process, both within the organization and externally via the use of a variety of professional agencies which will provide considerable and important input.
- We have seen how these organizations are selected and how they are paid for their services.

Examination hints and specimen questions

It is important to recognize that exam questions relating to this unit may take a number of different forms. On the one hand, there will be specific questions which will relate to the various dimensions of this unit – as with the examples provided below. On the other, you may be required to use your understanding of the marketing communications process to answer some of the mini case questions which are set. These may cover such aspects as the appointment of external agencies, remuneration, and the broader aspects of the development of a marketing communications plan. It is important, therefore, that you develop a familiarity with the topics, and are able to interpret them successfully to the exam question that is posed.

The examples below are, again, 30 minute exercises, within which time frame you should allow sufficient time to read the question *carefully*, perhaps underlining the key words which the examiner asks you to address, together with time to *plan out* your answer properly.

You should always bear in mind that a slightly shorter answer which is both properly focused and addresses the issues comprehensively, will always attract a better mark than one which is broader than the examiner requires, or which lacks direction.

You work for a leading national high street grocery retailer which has an impressive record based on its commitment to marketing, product quality and the highest level of customer satisfaction. You have the responsibility for local marketing; that is marketing for one region with a population of five million. You are familiar with marketing models, have excellent interpersonal skills and budget management experience. Set out what might be your marketing communications objectives and activities for the next year, including their relative priorities.

(June 1994)

Growing competition for staff, for students and for both government and private funding is forcing academic managers to take a crash course in marketing communications. You are asked, in a brief report to the head of your local college, to recommend a marketing communications campaign for your local college. Included in your recommendations should be target audiences, communications objectives and promotional methods.

(June 1992)

Many of you will also be studying for the CIM Diploma Planning and Control paper. The issues developed within this learning will also be applicable to the issues raised in the management and control of the marketing communications process. The topic is covered in:

P.R. Smith *Marketing Communications. An Integrated Approach*, Kogan Page, 1994.

Important dimensions are also well covered in:

D. Schultz, S. Tannenbaum and R. Lauterborn, *Integrated Marketing Communications*, NTC Business Books, 1992.

The new text by Ian Linton also helps identify important dimensions of the planning process:

I. Linton, *Integrated Marketing Communications*, Butterworth-Heinemann, 1995.

Students should also consult texts on brand and marketing management, such as:

D. Arnold, *Handbook of Brand Management*, Century, 1992.
P. Doyle, *Marketing Management and Strategy*, Prentice-Hall, Englewood Cliffs, NJ, 1994.

Articles on aspects of agency selection are often included in issues of *Campaign*, *Marketing* and *Marketing Week*. The issue of the latter title published on 2 December 1994, for example, contains a major article on clients' perceptions of advertising agencies.

The strategic use of market research

OBJECTIVES

The main objective of this unit is to provide an understanding of the role that market research plays in the context of marketing and marketing communications strategies.

We have already seen that the understanding of the consumer is key to the determination of effective marketing communications. The interface between the consumer and the company is the various techniques of market research.

In this unit you will:

- Explore the stages of the market research process.
- Examine the sources of information and the roles of various research techniques.
- Explore the importance of issues such as market segmentation and product positioning, and the contribution that market research makes in identifying strategic direction.
- Examine the use of the above techniques in the various areas of marketing communications and their importance to integrated communications activities.

By the end of this unit you will:

- Have an understanding of the role that market research plays in the context of marketing and marketing communications strategies.

STUDY GUIDE

Market research represents a valuable tool in the armoury of marketing communications. As such it can make a major contribution in several important areas. However, market research does not provide all of the answers.

Some of you will already have some understanding of the techniques of market research, and this unit will help you reinforce that knowledge. However, as with the other units in this workbook, our primary concern is with strategic issues, and this unit will concentrate primarily on those aspects.

The examiner will not be asking for a detailed response in terms of the methodologies of market research, but will require clear evidence that you understand the importance and relevance of the techniques, and can identify the appropriate approach to take in a variety of situations.

Don't rush this unit. It will help underpin the rest of your studies. Allow about 4 hours to work through the unit, and at least the same amount of time to complete the various questions and activities.

Some candidates find it easier to revise from their own notes than from printed texts such as this. In any case, it will be important that you integrate any other material that you have located, such as articles from magazines, information gained from the various activities, and so on, into some logical order for this purpose.

If you haven't done so yet, divide up your material into its component parts, so that when the time comes to revise, everything you need will be in the right place.

Central to the role of planning an effective marketing communications strategy is the function of market research. In a dynamic marketplace, the gathering and assessment of information is a vital precursor to the determination of strategy. Clearly, much information will already have been gathered to form the basis of marketing planning, and this will have equal relevance to the marketing communications process. Importantly, however, there are a number of specific aspects of market research which will have a more direct bearing on the planning of marketing communications. For completeness, reference will be made to both areas, although this unit will concentrate primarily on those areas of research which are most likely to impinge on marketing communications.

QUESTION 6.1

Why is market research fundamental to the development of effective marketing communications campaigns?

The market research process

The process of market research is relatively straightforward and consists of a series of separate stages of data collection, organization and interpretation. The fundamental objectives of the process are two-fold.

Firstly, there is the need to reduce or eliminate uncertainty in the various steps of the planning process. Although there will be a number of factors that are outside the direct control of the company, it is vitally important that the company is aware of those factors which may impact on the development and implementation of the strategic and marketing communications plan. By the same token, the company will need to be aware of fundamental movements in such areas as competitive activity, consumer purchasing patterns, attitudes, and so on.

Secondly, there is the need to monitor the performance of the developed plan. We have already seen that marketing is not an exact science. The more rapid the feedback of response to the plan, the more likely it is that the company can make the necessary changes to ensure its effectiveness. And, of course, the information gained will make a substantial contribution to the long-term strategic planning process.

The stages of market research

The market research process consists of a series of interlinked stages (Figure 6.1). It is important to remember that, although the stages are linked, work can be conducted in several areas concurrently, and in many instances not all of the stages will be required.

Market planning

It is to be assumed that considerable amounts of information will already have been gathered in the development of the marketing strategy. Using internal sources and published data (secondary research) and from the commissioning of specific research programmes (primary research), a picture will have been built up of the general environment in which the brand competes, the nature of the competition, growth rates and potential, as well as information regarding the consumer.

Figure 6.1

It is this latter area which has most bearing on marketing communications. The value of desk research should not be underestimated. Much valuable information can be derived from available and published data, with the advantage that it will be significantly cheaper than commissioning dedicated research studies. Moreover, as in many cases much of the important work of interpretation will have been carried out by others, the information will be easier to assimilate.

There are many important sources of information which should be examined at this stage.

Internal information

This includes the frequent and currently available information sourced from inside the organization, such as production information, sales statistics, field sales reports, together with any previous research which has been conducted. The latter will provide an important base of benchmarking, which will be referred back to at several stages in the subsequent work.

External sources

The company will be able to access considerable amounts of information from published sources. Important amongst these are the wide range of publications available from the Central Statistical Office (CSO). Although the list of publications is extensive, certain titles should be referred to on a regular basis. These include the *Annual Abstract of Statistics*, the *Monthly Digest of Statistics* and the *Quarterly Digest of Statistics*, *Social Trends* (which is an invaluable source of information for uncovering the underlying trends amongst the population), and special surveys, such as the *National Food Survey*, the *Family Expenditure Survey* and the *General Household Survey*. A comprehensive guide to government data is the *Guide to Official Statistics* which is published by HMSO.

A second, but equally important source of market information is provided by a number of titles including The Economist Intelligence Unit's *Retail Business*, *Mintel* and *Euromonitor*. All these and similar publications provide frequent 'overviews' of specific markets which aggregate much of the information available and present it in a comprehensive form.

Thirdly, there are a number of published surveys available which will provide valuable information on different aspects of brand and consumer behaviour. These include: the AGB *Home Audits* and *Consumer Panels*, *Nielsen*, *BARB* (which provides television viewing data), the *JICNARS* readership survey, and the *Target Group Index* (TGI) which relates the purchasing of products to media habits.

The fourth important source is the plethora of trade and specialist publications which, similarly, provide important information on issues relating to their own market areas.

It should be noted that the examples given above relate to the UK market. Comparable sources from government and other agencies are available in most countries, and represent an important contribution to the planning process in the international context.

Look at any market with which you are familiar. What internal and external sources of information might you consult in the preparation of a marketing communications plan?

Understanding the market

A key area of understanding will be derived from *usage and attitude* (*U&A*) *studies*, since these provide a consumer perspective of the brand and the market in which it exists. Whilst, as with other forms of market research, it is difficult to be prescriptive in this area, there will generally be a number of specific areas which will need to be covered.

How will an understanding of the consumers' attitudes towards a brand and their patterns of usage assist the process of marketing communications development?

- *Awareness* U&A studies can indicate levels of awareness for one's own and competitors' products, as well as providing an indication of advertising awareness.
- *Usage* There are a number of dimensions of usage which will be important to understand. On a general level, information will be required on the levels of loyalty and the propensity to trial other products on the part of the consumer. Since few consumers remain exclusively loyal to any one product – rather, they tend to build up a portfolio or repertoire of brands which they are prepared to consider as viable alternatives – it is important to understand the make-up of the portfolio. On a more specific level, information will be needed on patterns of usage, in terms of frequency of purchase, source of purchase, how the product is used, on what occasions the product is used, and so on.
- *Attitudes* As the name suggests, a U&A study is the primary source of attitudinal information. And since marketing communications is concerned, in part, with the creation or reinforcement of attitudes, the study will provide important clues as to what potential consumers think about the brands available, their relative positionings and offerings.
- *Needs* Although the products purchased may be identical, the consumer needs which they fulfil may be very different. The U&A study will provide guidance as to the extent to which existing brands fulfil consumer needs and expectations and will also help in the identification of potential gaps in the market.

It goes without saying that it will be necessary to collect the information across a wide sample in order to enable a statistical analysis in terms of the demographic breakdown of the existing or potential market which it is desired to penetrate.

certain. defi
definition *n*.
precise mea
distinct, clea
definitive *a*. f
something;

DEFINITION 6.1

Qualitative research is that form of research conducted amongst relatively small groups in order to identify subjective opinions and value statements. It uses a variety of techniques to identify underlying thoughts and beliefs and is not subject to statistical analysis.

certain, **defi**
lefinition *n.* s
precise mear
distinct, clea
lefinitive *a.* fi
something; 1

Quantitative research uses specific techniques to enable the collection of data which can be quantified and analysed. This form of research requires large sample sizes in order to represent statistical validity in the subsequent analyses.

U&A studies will often be supplemented with other forms of *qualitative research*. For the most part, qualitative research is conducted either with small groups of individuals, or on a one-to-one basis. The specific purpose of such research is of an exploratory or investigative nature, although no attempt is made to draw definitive conclusions from the information gained. Its most important contribution is the ability to provide depth and texture to consumer information which would not be available from quantitative studies. In some cases, the two forms of study are used in tandem.

Qualitative studies are capable of making a valuable contribution to the strategic planning process because they are more flexible than the standardized form of research based on interviewing against a predetermined questionnaire. There are a number of specific areas where a qualitative approach will be favoured over a quantified one:

- To identify potential problem areas more fully, and in greater depth.
- To enable the formulation of hypotheses which can be the subject of further research study.
- To explore patterns of consumer behaviour, beliefs, attitudes and opinions.
- As a precursor to a quantitative study, where it is important to pilot questionnaires for comprehension.
- Especially within the field of marketing communications, where it is possible to explore concepts prior to the further development.
- To establish the comprehension of communications campaigns both prior to and after they have been exposed to a mass audience. This is especially important in the identification of deficiencies in the communications process.

Qualitative research is a methodology which uniquely allows for the exploration of 'sensitive' or 'embarrassing' issues, since questions can be set in an oblique form for subsequent interpretation. Often, a one-to-one approach will enable access to consumer information which would not be available in a group context.

Although not an ideal situation, there are instances, resulting from the constraints of time or cost, where qualitative data provide the only basis on which subsequent decisions are taken. This is particularly true, for example, in the development of communications concepts. It is clear that, on these occasions, there is a greater need for caution and care in interpretation than where a quantified study is used. Often decisions will be based on the comments of a relatively small number of respondents.

The importance, however, is not the *number* of respondents but the commonality of the *directions* of their responses. If a series of group discussions, say, are similarly negative in their views of an advertising proposition then, in most cases, it is reasonable to consider dropping the particular approach in favour of some alternatives which are more positively received.

The main contribution of such studies is in terms of the group dynamics which the techniques allow for. Unlike conventional questionnaires, where the respondent is interviewed against a preset format and where the aggregation of 'open-ended' comments may be difficult to interpret, group discussions enable the skilled interviewer to facilitate the interaction between respondents, and to explore their responses in far greater depth. This is of vital importance in the identification of appropriate communications dimensions.

A communications proposition may be rejected for a number of reasons. It may, for example, have the wrong tone of voice; there may be an inconsistency between the visual and verbal dimensions of the message; it may depict the wrong sort of people or environment. All of these, and other, facets of the message can be amended with relative ease in order to overcome the objections and enable the proper communication of the message which is desired. By the same token, such feedback can be instrumental in the determination of the most effective communications strategy and of defining the most appropriate positioning for the product or service in the marketplace.

QUESTION 6.3

- In what situations will a qualitative approach be preferable to a quantitative one?
- When would quantitative methods be required?

We will explore each of these dimensions in the following sections.

Market segmentation

We have already seen (Unit 2) that the potential consumers for a product or service can be subdivided in a variety of different ways in order to target a proposition more effectively. The socio-economic groupings, together with the important social, environmental and attitudinal factors which we have already considered, may be the basis for ensuring the differentiation of a product's positioning from that of its competitors.

A great number of the initial directional indicators will be derived from quantified studies, since these will enable us to dimensionalize the numbers of consumers who make up certain categories. We can, for example, separate out the number of young versus old, male versus female, high income versus middle income, and similar dimensions. However, the point has already been made that these are relatively crude measures.

It is far more important to consider the attitudinal and other dimensions which are likely to have a far greater bearing on the potential consumers' propensity to buy a particular product or service. It is clear that relatively few products are capable of satisfying all of the consumers' needs simultaneously. If we take a market such as that for instant coffee, we can see that some consumers prefer their beverage strong, whist others like it weak. Indeed, given the state of development of this market in most countries, it is immediately apparent that, on this one dimension alone, there are several distinct groups of consumers whose needs will require a somewhat different product delivery. The process of identifying these differing needs and requirements is of vital importance in the process of product positioning and the determination of the appropriate marketing communications strategy.

ACTIVITY 6.2

Assume that you are planning to launch a new carbonated soft drink. What questions would you need to ask potential consumers to isolate a positioning for your new brand?

By using the appropriate market-research techniques we can develop market 'maps' which enable us to see the relative positions of the various brands available in the market. We can approach this process from two different perspectives. On the one hand, we can identify factors which relate to product differentiation, such as those just described. Here we are concerned with identifying the various product attributes which are considered desirable by different groups of consumers. Alternatively, we can examine the market from the standpoint of the consumers' attitudes and behavioural patterns.

We have already seen that, in many markets, product differentiation alone between competing brands is insufficient to achieve the differentiation of competing brands in the eyes of the consumer. The inevitable consequence of converging technology is the fact that competing products rapidly become almost indistinguishable from each other. Yet, it remains true that consumers adopt very different attitudes towards those same brands based on key dimensions of image. Market research will enable us to identify the image dimensions and to scale them according to the importance which is attached to them by the consumer.

In what ways might a manufacturer segment a market using attitudinal characteristics?

Identify examples where this has been done to illustrate your answer.

The starting point is to identify the segments of a particular market. Although this may in some instances be based on specific product attributes, in most cases it will reflect a number of important consumer perceptions relating to the product category. We have already seen some aspects of perceptual mapping on brands (Unit 4), and an example was included there for you to consider. In that case, using the car market, attributes such as luxury, family use, performance and economy were used, but the consumer may consider other dimensions to be more important. The availability of servicing facilities might be an important consideration, seating capacity is another product dimension which might be important to large families, and price is an obvious consideration.

Having identified the key dimensions of image, it will be important to rank them in order to isolate the most important. Obviously, the more mentions that an individual dimension receives, the more important it is to the respondents. The next stage is to relate consumer perceptions of the various competing brands on the map to indicate their relative positions. It should be noted that the four axes do not need to contain opposite dimensions. Family and performance, for example, are not the opposites of each other, nor are luxury and economy. It is merely a device to allow the plotting of four separate dimensions of a product area.

We can then plot the various competing products against each of these dimensions, based on consumers' perceptions of their performance against each of the criteria. Even at this stage, we may well discover that one map will be insufficient for the purpose of the exercise. Often we will find that the market subdivides into several distinct categories, each of which have a series of different evaluative criteria. Clearly, small family cars do not compete with luxury saloons, both representing individual segments of the market.

The final stage is to determine the relationship between the position occupied by 'our' brand and determine the appropriate communications strategy. By understanding 'our' positioning relative to our competitors', we can identify the extent to which consumers recognize our strengths and weaknesses against the key dimensions. By the same token, it will also help to identify the strengths and weaknesses of our competitors.

It is at this point that we can begin the process of identifying the most desirable positioning for our product or service, and designing an appropriate communications strategy to provide the consumer with relevant information. There are two strategic options at this stage:

- The first is to seek to reinforce consumer perceptions if the brand's position is similar to that desired by consumers.
- The alternative is to seek to alter brand perceptions if it is found that the brand position differs.

An excellent example of perceptual mapping is demonstrated in a recent paper outlining the contribution of advertising to the Levi Strauss jeans brand in Europe (C. Baker (ed.), 'Jeans Sans Frontieres', *Advertising Works* 7, Institute of Practitioners in Advertising/NTC, 1993). In 1990, the agency Bogle, Bartle, Hegarty and its client undertook a major qualitative research study amongst young European males to identify the attitudes and behaviour with regard to the Levi brand. Some 50 group discussions were held throughout seven separate countries. The primary purpose of the study was to identify the role played by the advertising in the creation of a consistent brand image across the variety of local markets. What emerges presents a fascinating picture both of the particular market and, more importantly, the relevance of the technique.

Taking any recent advertising campaign of which you are aware, identify the areas in which market research might have made a contribution. Think particularly about the development of the message, and the placement of the advertising in the media.

Marketing communications research

Any product or service is an amalgam of values which are presented to the consumer and reinterpreted by them into some form of whole. Inevitably, therefore, there are many factors beyond those of the product ingredients which influence the consumer to purchase or to refrain from purchasing a particular item.

We have considered the important dimensions of a brand in Unit 4, and have seen that the brand and its image are made up of a number of important constituent parts:

- At the centre is the product itself made up of a series of ingredients which have been brought together to respond to some identified consumer need. This is often referred to as the *core product.*
- However, what the consumer buys – the *actual product* – is a series of features and benefits contained within some form of packaging and offered at a price.
- These, in turn, are influenced by a variety of further dimensions, such as pre- and post-sales service, guarantees, availability, and so on. In some instances, particularly with the purchase of comparatively expensive items, such factors as the warranty, finance, and instructions for use may also play an important part in the decision to purchase.
- However, the *brand* comprises a series of further dimensions which are mostly perceptual and intangible. These include the brand name, the reputation of the parent company, quality and value perceptions, and the influences of external forces, such as the recommendations of others.

Marketing communications plays a vital role in establishing these dimensions and reinforcing them in the minds of the potential consumer. Here, again, market research can make an important contribution, both to the understanding of the important dimensions and in minimizing the potential problems resulting from poorly constructed communications messages.

How do we 'position' a brand?

The contribution to strategic direction

Market research has an important role to play in this context. Before we can determine the nature of the communications message itself, we must first identify the appropriate direction for the communications strategy. This, in turn, depends on the corporate direction and marketing strategy identified for the company.

How can market research contribute to the identification of the most appropriate marketing communications strategy to be adopted?

Several distinct communications strategies can be identified, and their appropriateness needs to be considered in the context of any marketing communications campaign:

- *Pioneer strategy* When a company creates a completely new product and, in the process establishes a new market category, the purpose of the communications message is to ensure that potential consumers are told of the product's existence, its functions, its usage and the location of purchase. When, for example, Sony first introduced the Walkman, the support activity designed for the brand took on these characteristics. Similarly, when Swatch was introduced, it was important that it was not simply seen as just another watch. The marketing communications programme sought to position the product in the vein of a fashion accessory which offered other dimensions than simply telling the time. Inevitably, the thrust of pioneer activity is to develop a market category, rather than simply emphasizing the benefits of the brand.
- *Competitive marketing communications* Once a category has been established, it is likely that new entrants will begin to compete with the original brand. Accordingly, the owners of that brand must enter a phase of competitive communications. The imperative is to differentiate the brand from its competitors, and to isolate those features and benefits – real or perceived – which will induce potential purchasers to select that brand rather than another.
- *Defensive marketing communications* This is designed to offset the impact of competitive pressures. A good example of this can be seen in the current UK newspaper market where each move taken by one title is immediately matched by a comparable move by one or more of its competitors.

In their book, *Integrated Marketing Communications,* Shultz, Tannenbaum and Lauterborn identify eight key facets of the marketing communications strategy:

- The need to pinpoint customer segments.
- To identify a competitive benefit.
- To understand how the consumer positions the brand.
- To establish a unique, unified brand personality which differentiates the brand from its competitors.
- To establish real and perceived reasons why the consumer should believe the promise of the brand.
- To identify the means by which consumers can be reached effectively.
- To establish the criteria for monitoring success or failure.
- To determine the need for additional research which would help refine the strategy further.

In each of these areas of strategy determination, research techniques are available to assist the process.

ACTIVITY 6.4

Shultz, Tannenbaum and Lauterborn identify eight key facets of marketing communications strategy. How can market research assist in the first six stages?

Identification of customer segments

We have already seen how market research can provide both quantitative and qualitative information on the nature of potential consumer segments. Qualitative research, such as depth interviews and group discussions, can identify similarities in consumer attitudes and beliefs which will serve to identify potential market segments; field research can dimensionalize whether those segments are viable in terms of the numbers of potential consumers they represent.

Identification of competitive benefits

Qualitative research can assist in the identification of the key benefits – again both real and perceived – which the consumer expects from the product category and the brand.

Brand positioning and personality

Segmentation analysis and perceptual mapping techniques enable the creation of a detailed picture in which the brand exists, embracing both consumer typology and product differentiation. By identifying where the brand sits in relation to its competitors, marketing communications can then seek to reinforce the position or to change it. Similarly, we can identify the factors which serve to differentiate the brand from its competitors and provide it with a unique personality in the marketplace.

In most instances, as we have already seen, this will relate mostly to the perceptual values which consumers attach to brands, particularly in those instances where there are no tangible reasons to set one product apart from its competitors. The factors which induce the consumer to favour a particular brand of petrol, or to purchase a branded bottled water are, predominantly, perceptual rather than tangible.

Brand promise

Marketing communications needs to provide 'evidence' for the consumer to accept the promise of the brand. This may involve the depiction of a tangible benefit resulting from some emotional value. For example, testimonial advertising showing 'people like me' who are satisfied with the performance of a brand.

Effective reach of target consumers

Specific research into patterns of television viewing, newspaper readership and so on, is used to assist in the determination of both media strategy and execution. However, there is an increasingly important dimension of research to identify the appropriateness of the media environment. If we accept Marshall McCluhan's statement that 'the media is the message', then it follows that the environment in which the advertising is seen will have an important bearing on image dimensions.

Haagen Daz determined that, in order to achieve a high-quality positioning in the minds of its consumers – and to differentiate itself from other 'run of the mill' ice creams, they would only place their advertising in quality titles. The synergy between the medium and the message was apparent. In this instance, the surrounding 'noise' has a 'halo effect' on the advertising, and the same principle applies equally to the placement of an advertising message within specific television programmes.

Monitoring criteria

In determining a marketing communications strategy, it is vitally important that the criteria for performance are agreed and established at the outset. Whether this consists of some form of pre- and post-exercise measurement, or more sophisticated tracking studies to monitor performance progressively over time will depend largely on the scale of the exercise and the budget availability.

In all cases, however, it is important to understand the precise manner in which the chosen message communicates to its target audience, in order that the marketing communications strategy can be refined further to enhance its effectiveness in the future.

Market research and advertising

In the same way that advertising has a variety of different roles to play – creating awareness; communicating information, changing the brand's image or personality, developing feelings and emotions, stimulating purchase, and so on – so too there are a number of techniques designed to assist the process of ensuring that the desired message is communicating effectively. The essence of effective advertising development is the existence of a good feedback mechanism between all the parties involved in the process.

We have seen that the development of a campaign depends on the development of a clear and concise statement of the objectives – usually in the form of a creative brief. Certainly, most creative briefs will be based on the learning derived from market research. However, it can also assist at other stages in the development of a campaign.

The starting point for the development of creative work is, as we have seen, the preparation of a series of roughs. On the basis that there may well be several alternative approaches which meet the overall requirements, objective rather than subjective measures should be used to identify the appropriate route. Qualitative research will often provide valuable guidance to this task. By exposing the concepts in this preliminary form, the agency and client can secure feedback from the target audience. By explaining the nature of the research exercise, and involving consumers in the process, a far better understanding of the specific advertising message can be achieved. Indeed, on some occasions the playback from consumers serves to identify necessary revisions to the overall communications programme.

It is worth repeating the exercise with the finished versions of the advertising, since there may well be quite fundamental differences in perception when final photography or other materials are used. The same principle applies equally to other forms of advertising, such as television, where a storyboard or an 'animatic' may be used at the preliminary stage, and the finished commercial shown as the last stage before airing to validate comprehension dimensions. Fortunately, the cost of radio production is such that the practice is generally only to test the final execution. Even if it fails to communicate, the costs of scrapping it are comparatively low.

We have already discussed the need to monitor the effectiveness of advertising on an ongoing basis and, here, certainly with major advertising campaigns, the use of tracking studies operated by the major research agencies would commonly be used. The benefit of using an existing procedure is that the companies maintain a bank of normative data – on such dimensions as awareness, recall, etc. – for a wide variety of market categories, against which the performance of the new advertising can be measured.

ACTIVITY 6.5

- Identify a charitable organization.
- What contribution could market research make towards improving its message to its target audience?
- What research techniques would you employ?

Media research

Media is one area where the impact of information technology has been truly felt and, importantly, one where the research contribution has been significant. Until relatively recently, although there were considerable banks of data available to the media researcher, they dealt predominantly with consumer breakdowns into the conventional socio-economic groupings.

Information contained in the TGI (Target Group Index) relates the readership of newspapers and magazines to purchases of a wide variety of product categories, JICNARS (*National Readership Survey*) provides analyses of readership by socio-economic breakdowns, e.g. age, sex, class, etc. and similar publications provide a great deal of information which, at the very least, ensures that the media planner can determine the effective coverage of the desired target audience that an identified media channel can provide. The importance of this information should not be underestimated. The provision of such information enables the application of more scientific principles to the patterns of expenditure.

However, whilst it is certainly interesting, and useful, to know just how many ABC$_1$ viewers a particular television programme has, or ABC$_1$ readers a particular newspaper has, this is of somewhat less significance than understanding their attitudes towards specific consumer propositions. Increasingly, therefore, attempts are being made to marry the two sources of data in order to provide the media planner with a greater access to the necessary information. The media, themselves, have made important contributions in this respect by profiling their outlets in terms of important behavioural characteristics.

The result has been an increased opportunity to identify not only the nature of the viewer or reader in terms of age, sex, class and so on, but also in terms of some key behavioural characteristics which can be allied to brand purchasing behaviour. This process is inherently assisted by the progressive development of narrow casting within the media. The advent of an increased number of television channels (both land based and satellite), radio stations and newspaper and magazine titles, has meant that they too have begun the process of targeting their output to meet the needs of more 'dedicated' audiences.

Sales promotion research

Given the dramatic growth of sales promotion activity over recent years, it is not surprising that there is increasingly greater importance being attached to research in this field. As with other forms of marketing communications research, the starting point is the evaluation of objectives. Since promotions can be specifically designed to, for example, build levels of trial, increase penetration and encourage repeat purchase, as well as to secure distribution and develop trade support, it is vitally important that the objectives are clearly defined at the outset.

In some instances, there are a variety of pretesting devices using consumer panels, or simulated purchasing environments, in which dummy promotional offers can be assessed for their likelihood of take-up. Complete 'printed' mock-ups of the finished version are offered to potential consumers, amidst alternative brands and promotional propositions. In this way, it is possible to gauge the level of potential consumer participation, with the resultant benefit of being able to determine the likely budgetary impact and, where appropriate, ensure that adequate stocks of merchandise offers are available to meet consumer demand. Similarly, studies into areas such as likely levels of coupon redemption, amongst both consumers and the trade, will enable an assessment of the impact and response of both parties before the event.

As with advertising, it is important to track the impact of sales promotions to monitor the brand's performance in the competitive context, as well as the impact on consumer attitudes towards the brand. Since some consumer promotions may, especially if used too frequently, have a negative impact on the imagery of the brand, it is important that attitude movements are monitored to avoid this effect.

QUESTION 6.7

- To what extent can market research help avoid potential disasters in the field of sales promotion?
- What areas of difficulty can it help avoid?

Direct marketing research

Similar techniques to those used to test advertising concepts can be applied to the areas of direct marketing and direct mail. As with advertising, such research can assist in the determination of the best creative approach (headlines, text, visuals, incentives) as well as ensuring their effective integration with other aspects of the marketing communications programme. In some instances small-scale dummy mailings can be conducted to assist in determining the likely levels of participation. Since much direct marketing activity takes the form of mail pieces, it is important to simulate the process as far as possible in the pretesting stage in order to generate reliable information. For this reason, techniques such as telephone interviews (following the receipt of the mail piece) are sometimes used.

Arguably, this area is far more receptive to detailed analysis in terms of identifying the target consumer than any other form of marketing communications. It is important that care is taken to ensure that the appropriate market segmentation techniques are employed to ensure a cost-effective mailing programme.

Public relations research

It has to be said that the application of the principles of market research in the field of public relations lags considerably behind that of the other marketing communications disciplines. Why this remains so is a matter for conjecture, although in principle the same techniques as employed elsewhere could be equally well applied to public relations. Certainly, some progress has been made in recent years in the area of post-campaign evaluation. Tracking studies have been employed, particularly in the area of corporate imagery to identify any shifts in attitudes towards the company following campaigns.

Whilst there is little doubt that more work is needed in this area, it is certainly true that the use of market research techniques can only assist in the process of understanding both the construction of public relations programmes, and their evaluation after the event.

Researching integrated marketing communications

Given that the current drive is towards the integration of marketing communications, it is not surprising that an increased level of attention is being paid to the comprehensive evaluation of the totality of activities. As we have seen, at the moment most market research is conducted in a linear fashion. That is, specific research programmes are established to assist in the identification and development of advertising, sales promotion, direct marketing and other communications activities. There have, however, been several attempts to establish creative guidelines which embrace multiple marketing communications disciplines from the outset. The imperative has been to determine what message communicates best, irrespective of the method of conveying that message to the consumer. By the same token, manufacturers cannot avoid building an improved understanding of consumers' reactions to the communications process from a detailed examination of tracking studies.

We have already seen that, from the consumer perspective, it is irrelevant *how* the message is conveyed, only *what* that message is. Consumer attitudes towards products and services, from all communications sources, are monitored by tracking studies and the important discipline for the future will be the *interpretation* of those data.

QUESTION 6.8

What help can techniques such as tracking studies provide in the area of integrated marketing communications?

We have to recognize that, if communications programmes convey conflicting messages in different executional areas, the result will be confusion on the part of the consumer. And that must be to the detriment of the product or service that is being promoted. As companies come increasingly to recognize that every aspect of the marketing communications programme must serve to reinforce and underpin every other aspect, so too will we see more precise monitoring of the impact of the totality of those programmes.

International research

As you continue through this workbook, you will appreciate the increasing importance of international marketing communications. With an increasing number of brands being sold in the same packaging and with the same communications support across many markets, so too there is the recognition that a more detailed understanding of the 'international' consumer must be gained.

Undeniably, there are particular problems associated with conducting market research across a number of different markets. Underlying these are the problems of communications and lack of familiarity. There is, of course, the problem of conducting research in a multiplicity of languages and of ensuring (as with the marketing communications process itself) that the words used, say in a questionnaire, have the same meaning in countries which differ in terms of cultural and other values.

Even in multi-national organizations there is often a degree of unfamiliarity with the variety of markets in which the study is to be carried out. It is extremely unlikely that any one person will have a detailed understanding of all the characteristics of the markets (behavioural characteristics, customs, market structures and so on) where research is to be implemented. This may give rise to problems of implementation as well as interpretation. If the starting points are different, it may well be difficult to establish norms against which to evaluate the findings.

It is important that these and similar problems are identified and addressed. A failure to establish adequate comparability at the outset could result in considerable wasted investment when the results are received. An interesting article on this aspect of market research appeared in *Marketing* (8 September 1994) under the heading 'Europe's Uncommon Markets'.

ACTIVITY 6.6

For an international brand, such as Coca Cola or Mars, identify the role of market research in the determination of a consistent approach to its various national markets.

The limitations of market research

It would be naive to assume that market research is capable of providing all the answers. There remain too many examples of manufacturers who have 'got it wrong' to deny that the techniques can eliminate all the risks in marketing communications. The recent, and unsuccessful, launch of Tab Clear provides evidence of the fact that even the giants of marketing can get it wrong.

In a constantly changing marketing environment, there will always be situations in which the results obtained from research will no long apply – there is an inevitable time lag been the conducting of market research and the implementation of the programme. Market research must be regarded as a instrument of marketing communications. It will never provide all the answers to all the questions.

QUESTION 6.9

Market research can provide guidance, but cannot guarantee success.

What are the limitations of market research?

The interpretation of the research findings is key. However good the techniques, it is the way in which the results are interpreted and applied which ultimately makes the difference. There is no doubt, however, that the proper use of market research at various stages in the construction and development of a marketing communications programme will certainly help to eliminate some of the risks. And, with the very considerable sums involved in the implementation of marketing communications programmes, this alone is ample justification for its continued use.

SUMMARY

In the course of this unit we have:

- Examined the application of the techniques of market research to important areas of marketing communications.
- Seen that there are several stages of market research which can be used to assist in the development of marketing strategy, marketing communications strategy and the various stages of implementation.
- Seen that not all information is costly to locate. A great deal of information can be derived from internal and published sources. Indeed, these sources should become almost the 'staple diet' of the marketing communications practitioner.
- Seen that in important areas, such as the identification of market segments, the determination of a positioning for the brand, the identification of attitudes towards communications concepts, and the evaluation of the performance of communications activities, it will be necessary to commission or conduct specific research studies to provide the required information.
- Seen that in all areas of marketing communications, specific research techniques and methodologies are available, and new approaches are being developed to

assist in the process. However, certainly thus far, that process is an inexact one and the research techniques available cannot provide all the answers. It can provide important directional indications, but one has to accept that if the data are incorrectly interpreted, the destination will be the wrong one!

Examination hints and specimen question

It is unlikely that you would be asked to identify or define specific research *techniques* to be applied in particular situations. However, you are expected to understand the *principles* which apply in this area, and may well be called upon to identify the *types* of research that would be applicable to the different stages of the marketing communications process. It is therefore important that you gain a grasp of the topic and are able to relate the processes of market research to those of communications.

The following question is taken from Part 2 of the paper, and you should allow no more than 30 minutes for your answer.

Prepare a brief report on the methods that can be used to measure the effectiveness of marketing communications campaigns. In particular, you are required to show how the methods may change to match the differing objectives of two campaigns: firstly a campaign to launch a new instant coffee product; and, secondly, a campaign to promote equal opportunities in the workplace.

(December 1992)

EXTENDING KNOWLEDGE

A chapter on the subject of market research which also provides some indications of the likely costs of the various techniques can be found in:

P. R. Smith, *Marketing Communications – An Integrated Approach*, Kogan Page, 1993.

There are several alternative titles which will provide you with a more detailed insight into the topic:

P. Chisnall, *Marketing Research*, 4th edn, McGraw Hill, New York, 1992.
M. Crimp, *The Marketing Research Process*, 3rd edn, Prentice Hall, 1990.
P. N. Hague and P. Jackson, *Market Research in Practice*, Kogan Page, 1990.
L. Moutinho and M. Evans, *Applied Market Research*, Addison-Wesley, 1992.

The strategic development of advertising

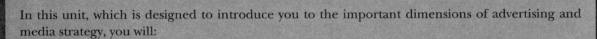

In this unit, which is designed to introduce you to the important dimensions of advertising and media strategy, you will:

- Consider the role of briefing in the fulfilment of creative strategy.
- Identify advertising objectives.
- Consider the need to relate advertising propositions to a deep understanding of consumer behaviour; the relationship between the consumer and strategy development.
- Look at the advertising process which guides the development of effective advertising campaigns.
- Consider the development of media strategy and develop an outline understanding of the roles of the various media types.

By the end of this unit you will:

- Understand the strategic dimensions of advertising and media development.
- Be able to apply this learning to Diploma questions.

STUDY GUIDE

This unit is important to your overall understanding of marketing communications, since advertising will often take the lead role in communications campaigns. You must ensure that you build up a 'bank' of examples with which to illustrate your answers, and ensure that you have a thorough grasp of contemporary advertising activity.

As you will see from the example question contained at the end of this unit, the examiner may require you to describe one or more current advertising campaigns and to examine the strategic aspects of this activity.

Allow 3–4 hours to complete this unit and attempt to carry out all of the activities. They have been specifically designed to ensure that you have understood the material in this unit.

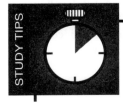

STUDY TIPS

Keep your eyes open for all suitable examples, and make sure that you read the relevant trade papers on a regular basis. They will be full of examples which you can use. Keep a file in which to store the examples you find.

> Spend some time looking at advertising, both on television and in print media, to try and work out what the advertiser is trying to achieve. The more you practise this activity, the more instinctive it will become, and the better equipped you will be to deal with exam questions.

Advertising is just one of the elements of marketing communications. Although it is capable of fulfilling a number of different roles, the specific function must reflect the objectives contained within the marketing plan. In the development of any advertising campaign, the starting point for the planner must be to determine the specific objectives. A key determinant of the nature of the advertising campaign will be the available budget. Casting the objectives too wide, or attempting to achieve too much within a limited budget, will undermine the effectiveness of the advertising message.

Since the advertising plan is an integral part of the marketing plan, it is imperative that the marketing forms the basis of all advertising planning. In many instances both the marketing plan and the advertising plan will be developed together. However, in some cases, the advertising plan will be developed separately. As such, it must contain a number of specific elements. Although there is no formal prescription, it is likely that the advertising plan will contain the following items:

- A review of the background situation.
- A competitive analysis.
- An overview of the brand.
- An analysis of the consumer.
- A statement of the marketing goals.
- A summary of advertising recommendations.
- A summary of media recommendations.
- A budget determination.
- A summary of evaluative procedures.

It is important to remember, however, that advertising does not and cannot exist in isolation from the other elements of marketing communications. For any marketing communications plan to work to its maximum demands the total integration of all communications activities. Obviously, not every marketing communications plan embraces all of the elements. However, it is highly likely that the marketing plan will demand the use of, say, sales promotion, sales-force incentives, and point-of-sale material. Care must be taken to ensure that all of these, and any other elements, are fully integrated to achieve the maximum impact on the target audiences. This is especially important in the context of the nature of the organization which may contribute to the fulfilment of marketing communications activities.

Since the early 1970s there has been a progressive fragmentation of the consultancy sector. Prior to that time, a client could reasonably expect that all the elements of a marketing communications campaign would be developed in conjunction with the advertising agency. There followed the emergence of specialist companies within the fields of sales promotion, direct marketing, media planning and others, each of which provide a high level of both input and expertise to the planning of the specific element of the campaign. Inevitably, with this fragmentation of activities, and the more narrow focus adopted by the specialist agencies, the responsibility for determining the most efficient use of resources became a primary responsibility of the brand management team.

As we have seen (Unit 6) the underpinning of any successful advertising campaign will be the use of market research. As markets become increasingly complex, it is beyond the scope of advertising planners, or even the most highly paid creative personnel, to base their work entirely on some form of intuition. Moreover, with the costs of making a mistake increasing alarmingly, few advertising professionals would fail to seek guidance from the marketplace.

In the development of an effective advertising campaign, research input is likely to be sought from a number of key areas.

- *Consumer research* The are a number of important areas of information that will be required on which the advertising campaign will be based. The planner will require detailed information as to the nature and behavioural patterns of the consumer to whom the message is to be addressed. Who are they? Where are they? How, when and where do they buy the product? How do they use the product? What specific attitudes do they hold? And so on. It is important to build up a finite picture of the target consumer in order that the message can be properly constructed and focused.

- *Competitor information* It will be vital for the development of advertising to understand the nature of the competitive environment. Who are the competitors and what are their offerings? How are their products or services positioned to the consumer, and what images – either positive or negative – do they possess? What advertising approaches do they use, and so on.

- *Strategy development* Depending on the amount of information which the planner already possesses, it may be necessary to conduct specific research to aid the process of strategic development. This will be specifically concerned with the nature of the message and is designed to identify the strongest possible positioning and consumer proposition which can be made. It is quite likely that the planner will explore a number of different alternatives at this stage, in order to identify the single proposition which is likely to achieve the highest level of impact on the target consumer. Part of this process will involve an exploration of competitor positionings in an attempt to determine whether there is a gap in marketplace which can be adopted by the brand.

Why do companies involved with industrial marketing rely somewhat less on advertising than companies involved in fast-moving consumer goods?

QUESTION 7.1

- *Monitoring research* In most instances, the planner does not start from scratch. Since most products and services already exist in the marketplace, it is reasonable to assume that they will have benefitted from previous advertising support. It will be important to understand the workings of previous advertising campaigns and to explore the image which that advertising will have created in the minds of the consumer. Indeed, such research, often conducted on a regular periodic basis, will not only yield considerable information about the company's own brands, but will also provide a valuable insight into competitor brands. Additional research is likely to be used at various stages in the development of the advertising campaign, and this will be explored in more detail later in this unit.

Most companies and, in this context, most advertising agencies, use a very specific format for the development of advertising. Although the content will differ between agencies, the aim is the same, i.e. to produce a simple summary of the advertising requirements in order that the creative department can be given the appropriate guidance.

The *creative brief* is the basis of all advertising development and should encompass, in summary form, the major findings of research and other inputs upon which the advertising will eventually be based. Two examples of contemporary creative briefs are shown in Figures 7.1 and 7.2. It will be worth making photocopies of these in order to carry out some of the exercises in this unit.

Before proceeding, it is worth making a distinction between some of the terms which will be used in this unit.

SAATCHI & SAATCHI
ADVERTISING

CREATIVE BRIEF

CLIENT	BRAND	JOB NUMBER	DATE
ACCOUNT GROUP	CREATIVE GROUP	PLANNER	MEDIA PLANNER
JOB TITLE		DEVELOPMENT BUDGET £	PRODUCTION BUDGET £

BACKGROUND REQUIREMENT

CAMPAIGN REQUIREMENT

TARGET AUDIENCE

WHAT IS THE ADVERTISING INTENDED TO ACHIEVE ?

THE SINGLE MINDED PROPOSITION

SUBSTANTIATION FOR THE PROPOSITION

MANDATORY INCLUSIONS

DESIRED BRAND IMAGE

PROGRESS CONTROLLER	BRIEFING DATE	INTERIM REVIEW DATE	FINAL REVIEW DATE
SIGNATURES GROUP DIRECTOR	PLANNER	HEAD OF PROGRESS	CREATIVE GROUP HEAD

Document3

Figure 7.1 The Saatchi & Saatchi creative brief. (Reproduced by kind permission of Saatchi & Saatchi)

Creative Brief

DMB&B

Key Dates

Date originated
....

Date allocated
....

1st cr. rev.
....

2nd cr. rev.
....

BTR
....

Ex. Cr. Dir.
....

CP
....

Copy/air date
....

Nett Budgets

Media
£
....

Prod. to Master
£
....

Illus./Photog.
£
....

Artwork
£
....

Radio/TV Prod. Budget
£
....

B form attached ☐

Brand Team Approval

Sn. Board.Acc. Dir.
....

Planning
....

Creative Group Head (1st)
....

Creative Group
Head (Final)
....

Media
....

SRB
....

Cr. S. Dir.
....

Client
....

Responsibilities

A. Manager
....

Traffic
....

Prod.
....

Art Buying
....

TV Prod.
....

Art Director
....

Copywriter
....

Planner
....

Media
....

Client: ....   Job No: ....

Brand: ....   Media: ....

Date: ....

What is required?

Why advertise?

Who to?

Critical consumer insight

What should the advertisement say?

Why should the consumer believe/accept this?

What should the consumer feel, believe or do as a result of the advertising?

Guidelines/tone of voice

Mandatories

Figure 7.2 The D'Arcy Masius Benton and Bowles creative brief. (Reproduced by kind permission of D'Arcy Masius Benton & Bowles)

DEFINITION 7.1

Advertising objective: a specific statement of what the advertising is designed to achieve.

This will define, in *measurable terms*, the role of the advertising, for example, in the context of awareness, brand choice, image change, loyalty or some other aspect of advertising communication.

DEFINITION 7.2

Advertising strategy: this is a statement of the means by which the advertising objective will be achieved.

DEFINITION 7.3

Communications objective: this is a statement of the principal thought or idea that the consumer should remember from the advertising.

DEFINITION 7.4

Advertising execution: this describes the form that the advertising will take (television, radio, press, colour or black and white, etc.).

In the following section, we will examine the various components of the creative brief, and assess the contribution each of them makes to the creative process.

The creative brief

Most advertising agencies use a very precise format for the purpose of briefing creative work. Although the topic headings may differ from agency to agency, the fundamental need is the same in all cases – that is to provide the creative department with the appropriate guidance regarding the development of creative materials, in a succinct and easily comprehensible form.

The starting point is to identify the *background requirement* in order to isolate the specific task which the creative department is expected to fulfil. This may, for example, take the form of a campaign which builds on the previous advertising heritage of the brand, and which will be used to refresh and update particular aspects of the communication.

The PG Tips television commercials are amongst the longest running British advertising campaigns. Periodically, new advertising executions will be developed to communicate a desired attribute of the product, or some other emotional value. The context of the commercials, however, remains the same with all the major characters being represented by chimpanzees.

Alternatively, the background requirement may be the development of a completely new campaign, sometimes for a new product, or be a change in the strategic direction of the brand. Recently, for example, after many years of running advertising which was based on puns on the word *eau*, Perrier adopted a totally different stance in the marketplace.

The background requirement may be to develop a single advertisement for some specific purpose, such as a tie-in with some retailer activity, for example a store opening, or a particular announcement to the target audience, as was the case with the recent advertising for Johnson's Wax recalling a specific product line.

In some instances, the advertising component will reflect some other form of marketing communications activity which has already been, or is in the process of being, developed. Here the other activity will take the lead, and advertising will provide the means by which the proposition is communicated to a wider audience. This might be a sales promotion offer, such as a competition or on-pack lottery which, otherwise, would only present its message at the point of purchase and then, predominantly, to existing purchasers of the brand.

Once the background requirement has been established, a short *justification* for the proposed advertising activity is given. If the creative department understand the purpose of the advertising, they can better fulfil the brief.

The next important stage in the process is the identification of the *target audience*. This is important in a number of respects. If the creative department understand the dimensions of the audience (young, old, attitudinal values, lifestyle factors, and so on), they will be able to reflect these in terms of the tone and style of the message. For example, advertising aimed at a youth market will probably employ different language and tonal values from a campaign designed to support the introduction of a product to an older target audience. In addition, information about the target audience will provide the media department with the key information with which to isolate the appropriate media to provide the most cost-effective coverage of the defined target.

Elsewhere on the brief, there will be an identification of the *budget* and a suggestion as to the *media* category to be used. Budgetary factors may preclude the use of certain media, such as television, on the simple grounds of cost (either of the media itself or the production of the associated commercials). Sometimes, the brand will reflect its image in particular media – often to the exclusion of others. It is important that both the creative and media departments are made aware of these issues to avoid wasting time in developing creative or media proposals which are inappropriate. It is important to recognize, however, that the creative brief should not be unnecessarily restrictive. It is not the job of the planner to predetermine media selection which, itself, may be an important facet of the creative message.

The selection of the appropriate media environment for the advertising is often as important as the message itself. A good example of this was the launch advertising campaign for Haagen Daz ice cream, which exclusively used up-market, quality colour magazines which were chosen to position the brand in the minds of potential consumers. For a full discussion of the Haagen Daz case history, which develops this and other issues, students might like to refer to *Advertising Works*, 7 edited by Chris Baker (Institute of Practitioners in Advertising/ NTC Publications, 1993).

The next area in which information is required is the 'critical consumer insight' or the 'single-minded proposition'. Effective advertising must be based on a careful study of the important consumer dimensions. What can the brand say about itself which will create a clear separation in the minds of consumers between it and its competitors? Although summarized in a very short form (there is only space on the brief for, at most, two short sentences) this a critical aspect of the creative briefing process. It will almost certainly be the culmination of a great deal of research activity and analysis, which has provided the agency with an understanding of the important consumer perceptions of the brand's characteristics.

This will be accompanied by some, again short, substantiation of the reasons why the consumer should believe the proposition. This may relate to some physical characteristic of the brand. In many instances, it is a direct consequence of the emotional values which the brand represents.

- Why is it dangerous to overclaim product benefits in advertising?
- What are the possible consequences?

QUESTION 7.2

The DMB&B version (Figure 7.2) includes two further dimensions. The first is: 'What should the consumer feel, believe or do as a result of the advertising?'. This is specifically designed to identify whether the advertising is designed, for example, to reinforce or alter consumer attitudes, or to achieve a specific response, for example, sampling the product. The second is designed to indicate 'Guidelines and tone of voice'. Here again, it is important to indicate whether the advertising proposition is to be authoritative and serious or amusing and light hearted, fashionable and stylish or down-to-earth and approachable, and so on.

Similarly, there may be specific elements of the advertising which need to be carried over from previous campaigns. Perhaps a particular personality spokesperson is used to represent the brand; on other occasions, an underlying theme needs to be reinforced (as in the 'eau' example given above). Certainly, there may be specific requirements to identify the brand with a logo, and perhaps the identity of the parent company.

The Saatchi & Saatchi version includes a section on the 'Desired brand image' which, similarly, provides the important guidelines for the tone of the advertising.

The creative brief fulfils a vital role in the strategic development of advertising. Although much of the work will have been done separately, this brief forms the framework for determining the strategic approach which the advertising will take. As such it fulfils many of the key requirements of the DAGMAR approach described in Unit 3.

ACTIVITY 7.1

Using either the Saatchi & Saatchi or the DMB&B briefing form, develop a creative brief for a product or service of your choice.

However, it is also important to recognize that the briefing document fulfils other functions. From the management perspective, it is the distillation of the major part of the preliminary strategic development which will guide the entirety of the creative process which follows. For the creative department, it provides an indication of the important directions and the thrust of the communications message, which they will be required to develop. For the media planners, it will provide the key dimensions of the target audience which they will seek to reach in the most cost-effective way possible. It will avoid unnecessary waste of time, energy and cost of developing creative messages which are inappropriate to the brand or the target audience. And it serves as the benchmark against which the creative work can be assessed.

Understanding consumer behaviour

We have already seen (in the section on consumer behaviour in Unit 1) that there are a number of different types of buyer behaviour. Understanding the process of buying behaviour will have important implications for the determination of advertising strategy.

Product categories exhibit differing levels of involvement for the consumer. Clearly, a frequently bought impulse item, such as ice cream or confectionery, requires little thought on the part of the consumer. In response to the felt need, the consumer will simply purchase a product which satisfies that need. Sufficient information will already be stored in the consumer's memory to facilitate the choice between different brands and to enable the purchase to be made with only a low-level consideration of the alternatives.

QUESTION 7.3

Why is it important for low-involvement products to seek a unique advertising proposition?

At the other end of the spectrum, major purchasing decisions which involve significant sums of money, or items which are only infrequently purchased, such as a new car or a holiday, will create a high level of involvement in the purchasing decision.

The involvement level of different product categories can be regarded as a continuum – from low level to high level – and understanding where a product is located on the scale will be important in deciding the nature of the advertising message. Advertising which is designed to support frequently purchased fast-moving consumer goods or services will, often, serve only to reinforce and underpin existing values. Advertising for expensive consumer durables will, in many instances, provide a great deal of information to provide a framework for an understanding of the product's features and benefits.

A further consideration will be the extent to which the decision is based on rational or subjective factors. *Rational* decisions are those which are based on a careful consideration of the functional values of a product or service, and in which the perceived performance will be the primary criterion for choice. *Subjective* decisions are those which are based on such factors as taste or image.

An important consideration, in both areas, is the role of the brand. Some brand names project an image of quality and performance – which will impact on the consumer's purchasing decision process. By the same token, other brand names are synonymous with style and fashion.

It is possible to create a simple matrix to depict these factors, and on which any product or service can be plotted (see Figure 7.3). Identifying the position on this scale (using objective measures such as market research) will be important to the development of an effective advertising strategy.

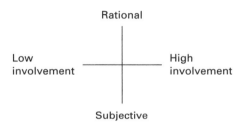

Figure 7.3

Consider any two products and any two services. Position each of them against the matrix and consider the information which the consumer will require in order to make a purchase decision.

ACTIVITY 7.2

Implications for strategy development
Routine problem solving
For products and services which are bought routinely, the fundamental role of advertising is to reinforce the values associated with the brand, and to ensure a high level of pack recognition at the point of purchase. The consumer will not spend a long time evaluating the available alternatives. They will possess adequate information on which to make the purchase decision, and advertising must ensure that the brand values are sufficiently well known and 'front of mind' to ensure that the brand, at the very least, is included on the shortlist of products to be considered.

Limited problem solving
For products and services which are purchased on a less regular basis, the primary task of advertising is to provide the necessary levels of reassurance to the consumer that the purchase is an appropriate one. Since the purchase itself is undertaken less frequently, the advertising will need to remind the consumer of the benefits associated with using the brand, and to establish clear advantages relative to the competition. Sometimes, these will

be tangible benefits relating to particular attributes of the brand, such as taste, quality, economy and so on. In other instances, these will be emotional benefits such as good motherhood (caring for the needs of the family), or social values (the type of people who use the product or service).

Extensive problem solving

In the context of products which require more extensive problem solving – as we have seen previously, these are normally expensive and very infrequently purchased items – the role of advertising will be both to establish the specific values of the brand, and to provide much of the necessary information upon which the purchase decision will be made. Sometimes, advertising in such instances will attempt to establish the evaluative criteria which the consumer will use in the making of brand comparisons. It will indicate suggested criteria for choice and, not unreasonably, demonstrate how it performs better than the competition against these given criteria.

QUESTION 7.4

How will the role of advertising differ when the product is a fast-moving consumer good as opposed to a durable?

It is important to make a distinction between the dimensions of purchasing behaviour. Not all products are purchased for rational reasons, although these may be important in the context of justifying the particular purchase to others.

Rational decisions

Some purchasing behaviour is conditioned by the need to take rational decisions as to the nature of purchase. In those instances, it is important to provide the consumer with hard factual evidence which will occasion their purchase. This may take the form of a promotional device, such as a lower price or extra product free. In other instances, it may be some statement of the functional performance of the brand, such as lasting longer than its competitors. In the case of more expensive purchases this may take the form of long copy advertising, factual comparisons, etc.

Image decisions

Many products and services are purchased more because of the image that is associated with them, than the purely functional benefits. In such instances it is important to consider the style and the image which is conveyed by the advertising, or the possibility of developing an association with famous names or personalities.

ACTIVITY 7.3

- Identify two or three examples of lifestyle advertising.
- What is the advertising trying to achieve?

Establishing advertising objectives

Advertising can, inevitably, fulfil a number of roles. As such, the objectives which advertising may be required to fulfil are somewhat diverse. Some advertising objectives are described below.

Awareness

At various times in the life of a brand, it is important to raise the level of awareness amongst target consumers. Inevitably, this is most often associated with the introduction of a new product. However, either because of competition or other pressures (perhaps a reduction in the levels of advertising support), the levels of awareness of a particular brand may fall, and advertising will seek to improve these levels. In some instances, although the consumer may be aware of the product itself, they will need information as to where to purchase it (particularly if it is in limited distribution). Advertising will seek to identify stockists of the product.

Reminder

Reminder advertising can take a number of forms. In some instances it serves (as with awareness advertising) simply to ensure that the brand is brought towards the front of the consumer's mind. In others, it will seek to communicate specific benefits or uses of the brand which may have been forgotten. Or, perhaps it will suggest new uses which will make the brand more relevant to the consumer's needs.

Changing attitudes, perceptions and beliefs

From time to time, market research will reveal a dissonance between the stance of the brand and the desired positioning. Perhaps, the image of the brand has become 'old fashioned' or more recently introduced competitor products are seen to have greater relevance to current needs. It should be recognized that the task of changing attitudes and perceptions is far more difficult to achieve, but one in which advertising can make a valid contribution (see the examples of Lucozade and Hellmanns Mayonnaise given in Unit 4).

- Identify examples of where advertising has sought to change the product benefit.
- How have the images of the brands changed as a result?

ACTIVITY 7.4

Reinforcing attitudes

Often the role of advertising is to remind consumers (particularly in the case of routine purchases) of the original reasons why they chose the product. In some instances, such advertising will reassert the original values of the brand either to offset competitive pressures or simply to reassure consumers that those brand values have not been changed. Kellogg's, for example, ran a campaign with the broad theme 'If it doesn't say Kellogg's on the box, it isn't Kellogg's in the packet' to reduce the encroachment of retailer products which might otherwise be confused with the leading brand.

Product line building

In some instances, the volumes for individual product lines, although profitable, will be insufficient to sustain advertising. Here, the manufacturer may seek to communicate values which are common to all product lines which bear the brand name (even though they may well have different functional benefits). Sometimes, although not always, this will take the form of corporate advertising to associate a series of positive values with the parent name in order that it serves to endorse the products with which it is associated.

Image

Advertising may seek to convey particular image dimensions in order that the product will be better perceived by the target audience. Much perfume advertising is of this nature.

Identify examples of advertising which attempt to fulfil the individual objectives of:

- Awareness.
- Reminder.
- Attitude change.

ACTIVITY 7.5

- Attitude reinforcement.
- Product line building.
- Image.

How does each advertisement differ from the others?

The advertising process

The development of advertising is a sequential process which, as we have seen, must relate to the marketing strategy. Only when the marketing strategy has been determined can the development of advertising strategy begin. In broad terms, the process of advertising development follows a series of individual steps, as depicted in Figure 7.4.

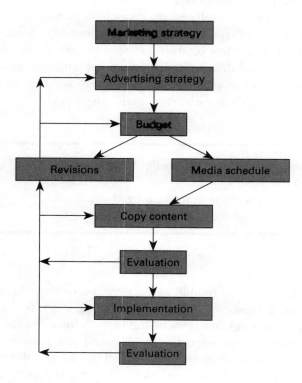

Figure 7.4

QUESTION 7.5

Justify the use of a tracking study when you have already used market research to test the copy and other critical elements of the campaign.

Advertising strategy determination

It is clear that advertising can fulfil fundamentally different strategic roles in the communications process. The following are *some* indications of possible strategies that might be considered:

Generic strategy

Sometimes, where a brand is in a dominant position in the market, advertising will simply make a straight claim of product benefit. Heinz Baked Beans or the same manufacturer's Tomato Ketchup both use advertising which has, over a number of years, established them as being synonymous with the category.

Competitive strategy

In the majority of instances, an advertiser will seek to establish a point of difference between their own and competitive products. In some cases, this will be based on a specific dimension of the product (e.g. Persil washes whiter; or Nescafé, 'Best beans, best blend, best taste'). In others, it will derive from a positioning of the brand which sets it apart, such as Avis, 'We try harder'. In all instances, the objective is to establish some point of advantage which distinguishes the product or service. It is important to remember, however, that such competitive strategies should not be taken to imply that only that particular brand possesses the attribute – rather that they have used the advertising medium to make it their own.

How does advertising contribute to the creation of brand personality?

QUESTION 7.6

Brand image dimensions

Here the advertiser will use other associations to ensure that the product or service is separated from its competitors. Haagen Daz does not use basic claims in its advertising to reinforce its quality positioning, but rather it associates the brand with desired lifestyle imagery. The current Perrier advertising communicates the values of a 'free spirit' rather than asserting that it tastes better.

Such advertising is a reflection of the desires and aspirations of its consumers, rather than a reflection of specific aspects of the product itself. The advertising will thus seek to convey such dimensions as sensory and pleasurable benefits (as with Haagen Daz), intellectual stimulation (as, for example, with *The Economist* or the *Sunday Times*), or social approval (Burberry's advertising).

Which is more important, creative strategy or media strategy?

QUESTION 7.7

Media strategy and planning

The identification of the appropriate media to communicate the message to the target audience is an important dimension of the advertising process. Each of the available media not only has a series of unique characteristics that make it more or less appropriate for the task in hand, they also represent an environment for the message which will serve to enhance or diminish aspects of that message.

Media can, therefore, be considered against three separate dimensions.

- Does it enable the communication of the advertising message?
- Does it provide cost-effective coverage of the target audience?
- Is it the appropriate environment in which to place the message?

You have a media budget of £150 000. Identify the types of media you might use to communicate a charity message to raise funds for famine relief; and a business-to-business campaign for a company involved in mining.

ACTIVITY 7.6

Communicating the message

If the nature of the communications message, for example, demands some form of 'live' demonstration of the product or service, then is likely that the media planner will be driven towards the use of television. If the nature of the conversation with the consumer requires a long explanation of product attributes and benefits, then print media uniquely offer that facility. If the purpose of the campaign is simple product or brand recognition, then posters may fulfil that requirement.

Cost-effective coverage

Inevitably, companies are concerned to achieve the effective communication of their propositions to the target audience at the lowest possible cost.

EXAM HINT

The examiner will not expect you to have a detailed knowledge of the specific costs of advertising media. However, it will be important for you to demonstrate that you understand the relative costs. If, for example, you are asked to deploy a budget across a variety of media, you will need to know (in broad terms only) the allocation of costs to your media recommendations.

Each of the available media can be ranked on this dimension alone.

Television

Traditionally, television has provided a major means of communicating to a mass market and, as such, is frequently used for the promotion of fast-moving consumer goods. However, as might be expected, the associated costs are extremely high. Not only is air-time expensive, but so too are the costs of producing a commercial for airing.

As an indication, a 30-second peak time commercial (between 07.30 and 10.30 p.m. on Carlton Television – covering the London area alone – would cost around £55 000. An off-peak spot of the same length of time in the same region would cost some £7500. The comparable rates for Channel 4 in London – which attracts significantly smaller audiences – would range from £26 000 for a peak-time spot down to £1000 for an off-peak spot. By comparison, a peak spot in the Grampian region – covering Scotland – would cost around £14 000, with an off-peak spot for as little as £250. The advent of satellite-based television stations has introduced a new dimension to television buying. A peak spot on Eurosport, for example, costs around £12 000.

Production costs are also high. It is realistic to expect to spend anything from £250 000 upwards for a 'simple' commercial, and commercials of a slightly more spectacular nature, such as those for British Airways or The Halifax, could cost £1 million or even more. Similarly, using a personality to endorse a brand does not come cheap. A famous name might add a further £100 000–200 000, and a music track (especially if it is in the charts) could cost the same again!

The key factor is not just the *size* of the audience but its *composition*. Inevitably, almost any advertiser using television as a medium will have to accept a degree of wastage – that is, viewers who are not interested in his particular message. The task, therefore, is to identify the programmes which are most closely targeted to the desired viewing audience. The consequence is that an advertiser may accept a smaller audience on, say, Channel 4 or one of the satellite stations, because the viewership is more in line with the profile of the brand. The use of viewing data from such sources as the British Audience Research Bureau (BARB) will enable refinement of the television schedule to ensure that as far as possible the viewing audience corresponds with the brand's target group.

Try to identify examples of television programmes which might appeal to:

- Young affluent viewers.
- Families.
- Well-off older viewers.

Press

The print media can be subdivided into a number of separate areas for the purposes of media planning.

There are a series of national daily and Sunday newspapers which appeal to different social groups, enabling the advertiser to reach significant segments of the population who, at least, can be segmented on socio-economic grounds.

To these can be added a variety of regional titles, which offer coverage on a geographical basis (although their stature is somewhat less). Furthermore, there is a wide range of over 3000 media titles which enable the targeting of 'special interest' groups. Whether the special interest is fishing, car maintenance or antiques collecting, there will be a number of titles specifically targeted towards the group.

As noted earlier, print media offer the ability to develop a long copy message to the target audience. Sophisticated research tools such as the National Readership Survey (NRS) and Target Group Index (TGI) will enable a profiling exercise to be undertaken.

A few indications are given below to dimensionalize the costs of using print media:

Title	Circulation	Readership (millions)	Cost per page (black and white)(£)
The Sun	3.6 million	11.5	29 500
The Times	0.6 million	1.4	16 000
Mail on Sunday	2 million	6.5	28 500
Car Magazine	132 318		2642
Antique Collector	13 878		2190
Computer Shopper	123 318		2635
Woman's Own	731 348		1550

Radio

Commercial radio, often regarded as a support medium only, is gaining credibility in its own right. As we have seen, for the most part, consumers cannot recall the source of the advertising message. Indeed, there is considerable evidence that some radio advertising will be recalled as having been seen on television! Radio may provide a means of achieving comparatively low-cost coverage of an identified target audience since, not only are the rates for using the medium relatively low, so too are the associated production costs.

With three national radio stations and over 100 local radio stations in the UK, the possibility of targeting specific audiences is improving rapidly. Due to the diversity of programming (from jazz through classical, from rock to pop, and a variety of speech-only programmes), listeners can be targeted on a variety of interest dimensions, both nationally and regionally. The recent allocation of frequencies to new radio stations will extend the opportunities for listener segmentation even further once they are all on air.

As with television, radio is purchased on the basis of time. A 3-second commercial on Capital Radio (London) would cost around £1800, whilst a similar spot on Isle of Wight radio would cost only £22.

A new dimension in radio advertising is the sponsorship of programmes. Crosse and Blackwell recently signed the biggest ever UK radio sponsorship deal with Classic FM, with a combination of sponsorship and airtime valued at around £2.2 million. Nescafé, a division of Nestlé, sponsors the 'Big Red Mug Show' on Virgin, with Cadbury's now sponsoring the album chart on the same station.

Cinema

Cinema is normally purchased on a screen-by-screen basis. This enables very tightly focused advertising campaigns down to the smallest geographical region. An average campaign, providing national coverage, would cost around £30 000 per week.

However, it is important to remember that production costs will make the investment in cinema considerably higher. Not only are the costs involved in producing a cinema commercial as high as those for television, but each screen on which the commercial is to be shown requires its own copy.

Posters

Outdoor media are available in a variety of different forms and sizes. Poster sites are available in 96-, 48-, 32- and 16-sheet sizes. The medium encompasses a range of options from taxi-cab sides to supermarket trollies. A national campaign of around 1000 48-sheet sites would cost around £150 000 for 1 month.

Predominantly posters and other outdoor media provide the opportunity of reminder advertising, reinforcing either an aspect of a campaign which is developed elsewhere (on television or radio, or in the press), but enable a tight focus on the brand identity with the featuring of the pack, the logo, and similar devices. A great advantage of the medium is the fact that sites can be purchased close to the point of purchase, underpinning the brand message close to the moment of purchase.

QUESTION 7.8

What are the advantages and disadvantages of using a specialist media consultancy alongside the advertising agency developing the creative materials?

The strategic dimension of media planning

Media planning essentially revolves around two key issues. The balancing of coverage and frequency.

DEFINITION 7.5

Coverage is the percentage of people within the defined audience who will be exposed to the advertising message.

DEFINITION 7.6

Frequency is the number of times people within the defined audience will be exposed to the message.

However large the advertising budget, there will never be enough money to maximize both elements, and the planner must determine the balance between the two. Inevitably, some form of trade-off will have to be made between a campaign which achieves the maximum level of coverage, but provides few opportunities for the target audience to see or hear the advertising message, and one which narrows the coverage to enable a greater frequency of exposure.

Although a great deal of work has been done to research the balancing of coverage and frequency, there are no definitive answers. Even today, much depends on the skills and experience of the media planner in assembling a media schedule which will achieve the objectives that have been set. This will often be seen in the way in which the media campaign is laid down. In some instances, in order to achieve the maximum level of impact, media expenditure will be concentrated into a relatively short period.

Often associated with awareness objectives, the *burst* campaign (sometimes referred to as *flighting*) compacts media activity into a series of relatively short time frames, with relatively long periods of absence from media activity in between.

An alternative approach, mostly associated with reminder campaigns, is to extend the timescale of the advertising message over a long period. The *drip* campaign provides continuity of the message, although at the cost of impact.

A compromise between the two is the development of a *pulsing* campaign. Here a comparatively low level of media activity is maintained over a long period of time, with periodic increases in the expenditure pattern, often associated with seasonal or other influences on buyer activity.

Under what circumstances would it be more desirable to use pulse advertising rather than spreading the available funds evenly over a longer time period?

A third consideration is that of the impact of the message within a given medium. The media environment will be a critical factor in terms of the way the message is received and interpreted by the target audience. In some instances, as noted earlier, the nature of the advertising campaign will, itself, determine the broader issues of media selection – television versus press or radio, and so on. However, it is in the area of the specific selection of the timing of the appearance of the commercial, the press titles or radio stations selected that will have the greatest level of influence on the advertising message.

No media schedule is ever perfect. The aim must be to maximize the effectiveness of the campaign elements by the careful determination of the format in which the schedule is planned and the specific content of the media in which the advertising will appear.

To ensure that the media campaign continues to deliver against its targets, a proper evaluative process must be implemented. Whether this takes the form of periodic *ad hoc research* activity to investigate specific dimensions of the advertising effectiveness, or continuous market research in the form of a *tracking study* is somewhat less important than the fact that appropriate objective measurements are taken.

SUMMARY

In this unit we have seen that:

- Advertising is an important dimension of branded marketing communications. Indeed, it is the primary means of establishing and maintaining a brand and creating the dimension known as 'brand equity'.
- For advertising to continue to expand markets, there must be some degree of unsatisfied demand which the brand can seek to satisfy. In most instances, markets approach a state of equilibrium. The role of advertising becomes one of maintaining the balance between competitors. As the opportunities to create a distinction between brands on the basis of product differences, price differences or availability diminishes, the role of advertising becomes even more important.
- The nature of the advertising proposition, as with other aspects of marketing communications, is totally dependent on a thorough understanding of the consumer dynamics. In this respect, market research is a critical part of the advertising planning process.
- The contribution of media selection is important and the identification of a solid media campaign plan is fundamental to the achievement of advertising effectiveness.

- Market research will be the source of the objective criteria by which the advertising campaign is monitored and evaluated.

Examination hints and specimen questions

The following specimen questions have been taken from the second section of recent CIM Diploma papers. As with the previous sample questions, you should allow no more than 30 minutes for your answers. Bear in mind, especially with the first example, that you will not have any materials to refer to whilst in the examination room. You must be confident that you have a sufficient understanding of the examples you choose to use to be able to write them up and analyse them fully for the examiner.

Choose any two current national consumer advertising campaigns which use media in significantly different ways. Describe the objectives of the two campaigns. Explain why, in your judgement, the two campaigns have used media differently. Comment on the effectiveness or otherwise of the two campaigns.

(December 1993)

You are the recently appointed marketing manager for a large car dealership with ten branches located throughout a promotional region. This region is served by a commercial television company, and by a separate independent radio company. There is one evening newspaper, and several weekly free newspapers. Your advertising spend is likely to be less than £1 million. Write a memorandum to the managing director comparing the strengths and weaknesses of the different media available, with specific reference to advertising new and used cars.

(December 1992)

EXTENDING KNOWLEDGE

The following text will provide you with a good understanding of the material required for extending knowledge within this unit:

P. Smith, *Marketing Communications – An Integrated Approach*, Kogan Page, 1993.

In addition, the two texts listed below will give you an insight into the detailed working of advertising, and the development of advertising and media strategy:

D. A. Aaker, R. Batra and J. G. Myers, *Advertising Management*, 4th edn, Prentice Hall, Englewood Cliffs, NJ, 1992.
T. Russell and W. R. Lane, *Kleppner's Advertising Procedure*, 12th edn, Prentice Hall, 1993.

A further useful text is:

J. R. Rossiter and L. Percy, *Advertising and Promotion Management*, McGraw Hill, 1987.

The strategic development of direct marketing

In this unit, which is designed to introduce you to the important area of direct marketing, and is particularly concerned with the strategic aspects of the discipline, you will:

- Examine the reasons for the dramatic growth of direct marketing.
- Consider the uses of direct marketing techniques.
- Explore the importance of the database.
- Identify the criteria for list selection.
- Consider database application.
- Identify the specific objectives of direct marketing and adopt a strategic approach to the area.
- Consider the various roles of database strategies and the contribution of market research.
- Consider the role of media and the management of direct marketing activity.
- Explore the applications of direct marketing to business-to-business, non-profit and international marketing.

By the end of this unit you will:

- Appreciate the fundamentals of direct marketing strategy.
- Be able to apply the principles to key areas of business and marketing communications.

STUDY GUIDE

Direct marketing is an area of marketing communications which is growing both in stature and importance. Increasingly, companies are concerned with increasing the cost-effectiveness of their marketing communications activities. With the ability to target prospective consumers more effectively, and to monitor the costs of activities more directly, the area is attracting considerable attention.

You should already have some understanding of the techniques of direct marketing from your earlier studies, and should be able to apply those principles to your answers. However, here we are more concerned with the strategic aspects of the subject.

You should allow about 3–4 hours to complete the unit, and spend about the same amount of time on the various exercises and activities.

Example questions taken from recent CIM papers are included at the end of the unit so that you can practise the application of this knowledge.

You should be thinking clearly in terms of how you will approach the questions in the CIM examination.

Make sure that you present your answer in a clear and legible form. Don't try to use every inch of the answer paper, leave space so that your answer is easy to read.

Make sure that you have tackled the question in the way in which the examiner requires. In some instances, for example, you will be asked to write a short report, in others perhaps a memo. Other questions will demand a more analytical approach.

Help yourself by underlining the key parts of the question so that you are sure which style to adopt.

There is little doubt that direct marketing has enjoyed rapid growth in recent years. The problem, in terms of quantifying this growth, is defining precisely what is to included within the sector, and of identifying the exact scale of the various components.

DEFINITION 8.1

The British Direct Marketing Association defines *direct marketing* as: 'an interactive system of marketing which uses one or more advertising media to effect a measurable response and/or transaction at any location'.

An alternative definition is: 'any advertising activity which creates and exploits a direct relationship between you and your prospect or customer as an individual'. (D. Bird, *Commonsense Direct Marketing*, 3rd edn, Kogan Page, 1993)

Taking either of the above definitions, the difficulties of isolating the components can be readily seen.

Certainly, we must include the entirety of the area of direct mail which, according to the Advertising Association estimates (see Unit 1) was worth some £904 million in 1993. To that we might add all, or at least the majority, of the expenditure on classified advertising, valued by the same source at £2105 million. After all, most classified advertising is placed with the aim of eliciting some form of response from the reader.

It is at this point that the going gets tougher. Most other areas – whether in the press, on television or radio, or even posters – include some form of response mechanism (an address, a telephone number, etc.) in order that the viewer or reader can obtain further information. However, it is debatable whether this device is included to establish a *relationship* with the customer which, as we will see, is the key strategic reason for using the techniques of direct marketing.

Whatever the true value, the importance of the process of this sector to marketing communications cannot be denied.

The growth of direct marketing
Several factors can be cited as contributing to the rapid growth of direct marketing techniques.

Cost
With the increasing costs of media, and the inevitability of a high wastage factor, marketers have been encouraged to seek communications mechanics which are more precisely targeted and less wasteful. For example, even for a high-volume fast-moving consumer goods product, many of the viewers of a particular television programme in which the product is advertised, will not be interested in the product proposition. For slower moving products and business-to-business propositions, the resultant wastage is likely to be considerably higher.

The importance of narrow casting

As marketing and, in particular, market research techniques have improved, it has become increasingly possible to segment markets along different lines. Because consumers are different, it is reasonable to assume that in many ways their needs, desires and aspirations will also be different. Direct marketing offers the opportunity to develop a line of communication with these identified market segments and to 'tailor' the message in ways that would not be possible using a conventional media approach.

The importance of 'plastic'

Increasing numbers of consumers have become holders of bank accounts, credit cards and similar 'charging platforms'. These have become important in two respects.

Firstly, cash is no longer the primary means of making a purchase. As more consumers become familiar with the principles of 'charging', so their patterns of purchase are likely to change. For example, as most cards offer the facility of spreading repayments for an expensive purchase over time, the consumer can consider making the purchase now, rather than waiting. And, as they become more familiar, they become equally more confident of the processes involved.

Secondly, the possession of such charging facilities itself provides the basis for the creation of databases and the more precise targeting of prospective purchasers, since it is possible to identify previous purchases which indicate areas of interest.

The growth of the service economy

An important trend in recent decades has been the progressive growth of the service sector. As material standards have improved, individuals have turned to other areas to improve their lives. Services, such as insurance, security, etc., have directly benefitted and, more importantly, have been able to utilize direct marketing approaches to achieve the most cost-effective coverage of their target consumers.

The growth of information technology

The dramatic improvement in both computers and other areas of information technology have realized the potential of direct marketing.

The creation of databases, the processing of information, the possibility of conducting cross-analyses with other sources of information, the profiling of prospective consumers and similar techniques are, potentially, made much easier with the widespread use of the new technology.

Most importantly, analyses can be conducted speedily – while the information is still fresh – and the prospective consumer can be contacted before their own situation has changed.

The desire for shopping convenience

Changing lifestyles have dictated a need for new patterns of shopping to which, for a variety of reasons, traditional retailers have been slow to respond. With the increasing numbers of working women, for example, shopping can no longer be restricted to the normal 'daylight hours'. In the absence of conventional retailers responding to their needs, consumers have turned to mail-order catalogues, telephone marketing, and other forms of non-retail outlets to satisfy their needs.

The same principle applies equally to the services sector. If the consumer wants to renew an insurance policy or pay a bill at 9 o'clock in the evening, they need to access those services even if the retailers providing them are closed. Telephone response mechanisms provide the consumer with the potential of 24-hour shopping and, from the standpoint of the operator, avoids the need to invest in costly high street retail premises.

Outline the reasons why direct marketing has become one of the fastest growing areas of marketing communications.

QUESTION 8.1

The advantages of direct marketing techniques
Targeting
Some forms of direct marketing, especially those relating to direct mail, can be very precisely targeted. By accessing lists of named individuals who can be identified as having an existing interest in the market category, the advertiser can be reasonably sure that the recipients of the message will be more likely to be motivated by its offering. Business travellers, for example, can be offered, via direct marketing techniques, information on hotels, airlines, etc., which is directly relevant to their needs.

Relationships
A key aspect of direct marketing is the creation of relationships between the company and the prospect. Once a contact has been established, the ensuing messages can be directed and personalized to a *named individual*. The likelihood of securing a positive response is greater if the recipient of a message believes that it is geared to his or her specific needs.

Interactivity
Unlike conventional advertising, which communicates with all prospective consumers in a somewhat indiscriminate manner, direct marketing has built-in response mechanisms which encourage a flow of information from the prospective consumer back to the manufacturer. The *feedback* of communication between the prospect and the company may be especially useful in avoiding, for example, post-purchase dissatisfaction, or identifying potential new product opportunities.

Motivating action
Most direct marketing activity is designed to encourage a specific response, often using in-built incentive programmes. Whilst many other forms of marketing communications have a similar objective, it is the speed of monitoring the levels of response which provides direct marketing with its unique appeal to marketers.

Databases
By encouraging response, the company can build up a database of named individuals. Recognizing that many individuals will not make a purchase on their first exposure to a proposition, such individuals can be recontacted at intervals with similar or varied messages in order to achieve the sales objective. Moreover, once a sale has been secured, those individuals can be recontacted, either to encourage them to repurchase, or to secure the purchase of another product or service from the same company.

Transactional information
Over time, it will be possible to build up specific profiles of customers. These might include, for example, the frequency of purchasing, the nature of purchases, differential responses to incentive programmes, characteristics of purchasers, and so on. Such information, which would not be available in the context of conventional marketing techniques, provides a basis for developing cost-effective sales amongst defined audiences.

Measurement
Because direct marketing produces a measurable response, it is possible to calculate the effectiveness of a specific campaign with a considerable degree of accuracy. Moreover, as enhancements are made to the database, it will be possible to predict levels of response to subsequent activities.

Testing
With the high degree of control associated with direct marketing, it is far easier to mount small-scale test exercises. The impact, for example, of different advertising messages, or of different mail pieces, can be assessed in advance of full-scale activity.

The importance of the database
At the heart of successful direct marketing activity is the database and, for this reason, the area is often referred to as *database marketing*.

Databases may be *internal*, that is created from the names and addresses of previous customers, or *external*, that is purchased from a third party or organization.

Internal databases

Most companies have a great deal of information about previous customers. The primary issues are whether they bother to access this information and, if they do, do they make the best use of the information available to them.

Almost without exception, the manufacturers of durable goods (fridges, freezers, toasters, cars, etc.) demand the return of some form of card following purchase. From the consumer perspective, the return of the registration or warranty card is the means of ensuring that they are logged on for the purpose of securing repair or replacement if the purchased product fails to perform properly during the warranty period.

From the manufacturer's perspective, it is a primary means of compiling the names and addresses of purchasers of their products and services. And, sadly, for many that it as far as it goes. Despite the fact that these consumers have already evidenced their preparedness to purchase products bearing the particular brand name, comparatively few companies recognize the importance of the marketing opportunity which this represents. Not only does the list represent the means whereby a *relationship* can be established with existing customers, it also represents the means of selling them additional products from their range. Both these dimensions may be of crucial importance in the longer term.

By establishing a relationship with existing customers, potential difficulties which may be experienced with the product may be overcome. If, for example, some consumers find that the product does not perform as expected, they may experience dissatisfaction with the product, and make their views known to other potential purchasers. (We have already seen the importance of post purchase evaluation in Unit 1.) The company may eliminate the source of these concerns by, for example, establishing a contact line where they can provide additional usage advice to purchasers. This, in fact, is a process which has been successfully adopted by many computer software companies. Even at this level, customer dissatisfactions can be minimized and those individuals converted into 'positive promoters' of the brand.

Furthermore, as most companies manufacture a range of products and services, establishing a positive relationship with existing customers may be the key to achieving additional cost-effective sales to those same individuals. Moreover, by using market research to identify the elapsed period after which the consumer seeks to replace the purchase, the company can then recontact them at the appropriate time to incentivize them to buy from their range rather than from one of their competitors.

ACTIVITY 8.1

Keep all the direct mail pieces you receive over a short period of time. Identify the approaches which have been used by the companies, and compare the extent to which they have targeted your specific personality and interests.

External databases

From time to time, companies need to supplement their own lists with those acquired from external sources. These range from general *compilations* (such as the Electoral Roll, or the Census) to those which are developed as the direct result of a relationship of the membership or subscription to an organization. The latter are more targeted to the extent that the list represents participation in some form of activity which can be assessed for its relevance to the potential user. For example, a company offering some form of financial service may purchase lists of people who have previously responded to similar, but non-competitive, offers.

Although lists are widely available – a current advertisement in *Marketing Week* offers no less than 1500 separate lists which allow access to, for example, 551 716 people who are interested in fine art and antiques, 174 392 people who have a television satellite dish, 27 979 people who have a 4 × 4 vehicle, and 108 549 who drink Heineken beer – it is vitally important to adopt a strategic approach in terms of their selection. In most instances, companies will need to use a list broker who can provide access to a wide range of category lists, although it may be possible to deal directly with a third-party organization whose database corresponds to the particular needs in hand.

Obtaining the appropriate list or lists is fundamental to the ultimate success of the campaign, and it is important to define a series of criteria to be met.

Source of list

As far as possible, it is desirable to identify the original source of the listings. This is important to avoid conflicts between the original owner's use of the list and the purpose for which it is intended. At the same time, the way in which the list was originated will provide some guidance to its likely validity. For example, names and addresses of people who have *purchased* a product or service will tend to be more valuable than those collected, for example, as a result of entries to a competition.

Restrictions on use

It is important to identify any restrictions which may be applied to the subsequent use of the list by the original owners. These may cover such things as the categories of product or service for which the lists may or may not be used – to avoid offers of a directly competitive nature – or the use in certain areas which the owner deems 'inappropriate'.

When collected

The original collection date will be a guide to the accuracy of the lists. The longer the time since its original compilation, the higher the incidence of 'gone aways'.

Frequency of use

If the list has been used often, this may affect the likelihood of achieving a positive response, especially if the list has been used for a parallel market.

Size

It is important to dimensionalize the scale of the list. Often small numbers may be sufficient to conduct a market test, but the overall numbers will be required to scale up the exercise to a partial or complete roll-out.

Profiling information

Many lists will contain only the titles, names and addresses of potential respondents. More sophisticated lists will be accompanied by profiling data, for example ownership of particular goods and services, age and lifestyle data, and so on.

Other information

Apart from the obvious question of the cost of acquisition, it will be important to determine whether you will have direct or indirect access to the database, and the form in which the list will be supplied. You may wish to profile the information against your own database, or to de-duplicate lists to eliminate the possibility of more than one mailing being sent to the same individual, and so on.

Finally, you will need to identify when the list will be available to you, and on what terms. Some list suppliers, for example, discount the price to cover the cost of returns and 'gone aways', others don't. This may have a sizeable impact on the overall cost effectiveness of the exercise.

QUESTION 8.2

What are the benefits of direct marketing techniques to companies which currently sell their products through conventional retail outlets?

The use of the database

Once the database has been compiled, it represents a major opportunity to augment conventional marketing communications techniques. But, unlike conventional communications, the successful implementation of a direct marketing strategy is the repeated use and reinforcement of the database itself. In practical terms, it provides the ability to achieve some of the benefits of the one-to-one relationship normally associated with personal selling, but without the attendant costs.

The objectives of direct marketing

Database marketing can fulfil a variety of objectives which build upon the market penetration achieved by other marketing communications tools.

- **Generating repeat purchase** Once the name and address of a purchaser has been captured, he or she can be recontacted in order to achieve further sales of the same product. Some products will be restricted to direct marketing channels, and hence the only opportunity to achieve additional sales will be by these means. Recently, a number of compact disc and tape offers have been heavily advertised on commercial radio. Having logged a purchase, the prospective customer receives a series of follow-up mailings accompanied by an incentive to purchase additional 'exclusive' compact discs.

- **Introduction of new product** Having established a database, it may provide the platform for the introduction of a new product or service which is likely to appeal to the same target audience. Importantly, a test campaign can be conducted with a high degree of security, and at significantly lower cost than would be associated with other testing formats.

- **A platform for cross selling** As noted earlier, once a manufacturer has sold a single product or service (and assuming that the purchaser is satisfied with that purchase) the consumer can then be motivated to buy additional products from that company. The same principle applies to a supplier whose reputation rests in the selection and pricing of relevant merchandise. This may often encourage a previous purchaser to buy again. This applies particularly to catalogue operations, such as Kaleidoscope who have built up a major business operation through direct marketing techniques.

- **Provision of a new distribution channel** In some instances, a manufacturer will have the opportunity to create a direct distribution channel in parallel with conventional outlets. Products will continue to be available to 'all' consumers in the normal way, but the direct marketing channel will remain the exclusive preserve of the manufacturer – who can restrict competitive encroachment with the use of incentive devices.

- **Targeting minority markets** Conventional marketing communications may make the process of niche marketing unaffordable. We have already considered the high wastage factors associated with conventional media, for example. By precisely identifying niche opportunities, the manufacturer can continue to derive a profit even from comparatively small sales volumes, since the costs of achieving those sales will be far lower.

- **Establishing loyalty** Through establishing a positive relationship with the consumer, the company can create a high degree of loyalty by providing additional benefits to the consumer which are often not available through conventional channels. Sometimes this may involve the provision of a tangible incentive, such as a free gift or discount. In some instances, it may simply rely on periodic contact between the company and the consumer to provide additional new and relevant information. Many manufacturers create some form of 'club' for this purpose, for example, owners of particular makes of car, or users of particular computers or software.

- **Identification of prime prospects** By isolating the best prospects within a database – people who spend most, or who purchase most frequently, for example – the company can direct its activities towards the achievement of the greatest return on its marketing investments.

What marketing communications objectives are better served by the use of direct marketing techniques?

Building relationships

The establishment of positive relationships is the primary aim of direct marketing. The process can be described as having five distinct stages, as shown in Figure 8.1.

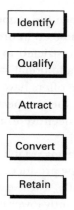

Identify

Qualify

Attract

Convert

Retain

Figure 8.1

The identification of prospects

The initial stage is to ensure the identification of prospects or, more effectively, to motivate potential purchasers to identify themselves. In many instances, a mass media approach will be used, with some built-in response mechanism. Often, although not always, an incentive to respond is also included. Most mail-order catalogue companies, for example, use mainstream media to communicate their proposition and invite respondents to supply their name and address in return for some free gift together with the catalogue. A similar approach is adopted by many book clubs.

To qualify consumers

It is inevitable that not all respondents will want or be prepared to move to the second stage. Sometimes, repeat activity, mailings or incentives will be required to motivate them to purchase. Where, however, the consumer makes an 'off-the-page' purchase, they are automatically qualified as future prospects. In all cases, some form of proof of initial purchase identifies the consumer for inclusion in subsequent direct marketing activity.

To attract consumers

The third stage is that of increasing consumers' knowledge of the products and services offered by the company. The Automobile Association (AA) periodically mails its members with details of merchandise and services which distinguish them from their competitors, and enhance the consumers' awareness of the benefits of membership. Other companies, such as computer software companies, mail owners with additional information to improve their image of the product. This may, for example, detail new or unusual usage which increases the reliance on the product. Or it may be based on providing information about third-party products which, similarly, augment the value of the base product.

To convert prospects

Here the company targets existing users to try additional products. These may take the form of 'upgrades' on the existing product, which are offered to the existing user base at preferential prices. Recently, for example, Lotus – the makers of a wide range of software products – offered the users of any *one* of their products the opportunity to trade up to a suite of five programmes at a massive saving against their individual retail prices.

Why is retention regarded as a key facet of direct marketing?

Retention

The retention of existing customers is of vital importance to overall success and profitability. In all instances, customers are expensive to identify. Having found them, direct marketing affords the opportunity of developing programmes which will ensure their loyalty to the company's products or services.

A variety of mechanisms can be used for this purpose. Some provide for the direct incentivization of loyalty through the offering of some form of collector device, for example a display unit to house the items purchased. Others may offer a sequential discount so that each subsequent purchase becomes progressively cheaper. In the same way, 'club' magazines may provide both a vehicle for on-going communication and incentivization. Exclusive free gifts, invitations to special events, and other forms of discount may be offered to customers to secure their loyalty in the longer term.

The strategic approach to direct marketing

As with other forms of strategic management, direct marketing needs to be considered in the context of the longer term goals and objectives of the organization. The development of a cohesive and integrated direct marketing strategy follows a similar format to that of other aspects of marketing communications and requires the sequential analysis of the organization and its environment. The process is described in detail in Unit 5.

We need to identify the specific *objectives* for direct marketing and, as we have seen in earlier units (see, in particular, Unit 2), these must be succinct, finite and measurable, agreed by all those involved in the process, and have built-in mechanisms for the monitoring and control of the activities.

It is only at this point that we will be in possession of sufficient information to begin the process of *identifying potential strategies*. Direct marketing, as we have already seen, provides the means whereby a relationship can be established between the company and its prospects to motivate a transaction. Thus, whilst direct marketing strategies may be similar to those of other forms of marketing communications, they are likely to be subtly different. Most importantly, the strategic goals of direct marketing will be designed to ensure the *creation of the most effective database* for subsequent communications activities.

Identify a small local retailer. Consider how you might develop a direct marketing campaign to promote their business. Remember – the budget will be small!

The contribution to database strategies

Effective database management can make a major contribution to many key strategic areas.

Campaign planning

The database is a unique source of information to enable the identification of potential customers with particular needs. The analysis, for example, of previous purchasing information will enable far more precise targeting of potential consumers with a high propensity to respond to a particular type of product or service, or a particular type of offer.

Monitoring of activities

By its very nature, database marketing provides rapid feedback on the effectiveness (or otherwise) of campaign activities. By extrapolating the data it is possible to predict the ultimate achievements of the campaign, even at a very early stage. Importantly, if things aren't going well, it is possible to take early remedial action to correct the situation. Moreover, it is possible to conduct regular analyses as to the individual performance of the various elements within the campaign mix. If individual components fail to deliver against targets and expectations, they can be modified without interrupting the overall campaign.

Campaign evaluation

It follows from the above that, at the end of the campaign, specific and quantified data will be available to enable a comprehensive evaluation of all aspects of the campaign. If comparable data are available for previous campaigns, the differences in performance between these and current activities can be compared and evaluated. In this way, a long-term information source is created which will assist in subsequent campaign planning activities.

QUESTION 8.5

What contribution can market research make to the improvement of direct marketing?

The use of market research

As we have seen (Unit 6), market research is at the centre of all effective marketing communications. Uniquely, however, in the field of database and direct marketing, direct access to existing and potential customers is already available on the database itself.

Until comparatively recently, little use was made of market research within the area of direct marketing. Perhaps because of the short-term nature of some activities, or because of the lack of a recognition of the value of a database, limited efforts were made to take advantage of the potential integration with market research techniques.

Some commentators have suggested that, because testing is part of the process of direct marketing, direct marketing is synonymous with market research and obviates the need for market research. Indeed, many practitioners still maintain this position. They argue that, because databases themselves are increasingly subjected to sophisticated examination and analysis, market research and the techniques it employs can offer little in the way of new information. Certainly it is true that direct access to a database does make the conducting of certain *quantitative* forms of market research somewhat easier. The identification and location of target segments is simplified, as indeed is the access to groups that are difficult in conventional research terms.

However, it is in the area of *qualitative* research that usual market research procedures can provide considerable assistance. Where, for example, there is a need to explore creative strategy or creative concepts, or to gain a deeper understanding of consumers' needs, the various qualitative approaches (described in Unit 6) come into their own. The ability to judge consumer reactions to the various individual components of an overall proposition can be achieved far more readily, for example, in the context of a group discussion. Similarly, the use of the various projective techniques can only be conducted with the direct participation of the respondent on a one-to-one or group basis. Where the database can simplify the process is by providing speedy access to qualified respondents. Ordinarily, pre-interview procedures must be followed to identify, for example, people who have recently purchased a particular product, or who are contemplating such a purchase in the near future. Identifying such individuals may be achieved by interrogating the database.

The other area in which market research procedures are normally employed, however, is that of market testing. There is little doubt that this may sometimes be carried out far more cost-effectively by conducting the test against the database directly. By extracting matched samples from the database, alternative propositions can be exposed to them and their response levels compared against each other.

QUESTION 8.6

Given the level of consumer antagonism towards direct mail and telephone marketing, how would you justify their continued use?

The use of media

It is fair to say that there are few *rules* that govern the selection of the most appropriate medium for use in a direct marketing campaign. Much will depend on a consideration of:

- The nature of the proposition.
- The nature of the target audience.
- Access to targeting information.

In general terms, **television** is a very expensive medium. The ability to target selected audiences is somewhat limited and, whilst it is capable of generating leads, the cost per contact is often quite high. However, with the advent of direct response television channels – already well established in the USA, and beginning to take off elsewhere – the situation is likely to improve.

ACTIVITY 8.3

An increasing number of advertisers use direct response mechanisms in their campaigns. Examine three television commercials and three press advertisements and determine how they seek to motivate a response from their target audiences.

Radio involves lower capital outlay and the facility to target is similar, if slightly better, to that of television. Nevertheless, in general terms, the cost per contact remains at a high level.

Print media, in its variety of forms, enables far better targeting. The existence of titles which are geared to the needs of specific interest categories ensures that the readers of such publications are, at the very least, predisposed to the product category. Providing that the appropriate titles are selected, the cost per contact can be extremely low.

ACTIVITY 8.4

Identify several media titles which provide the platform for targeted messaging. What benefits do they provide compared with broad-scale media?

Posters are of somewhat limited value. The ability to target, other than on a geographical basis, is extremely limited, and whilst the capital cost is not too great the cost per contact is likely to be high.

Public relations activities have an important role to play in this context. The placing of relevant releases with appropriate media – particularly in the press – and the building in of a response mechanism such as a telephone number or address, is capable of generating significant numbers of enquiries. Unfortunately, the outcome is rarely predictable and the costs are, therefore, highly variable.

The two areas which are particularly responsive to direct marketing are of course **direct mail** and the **telephone**. Both offer extremely good potential to target precisely and, if used correctly, are very cost-effective forms of marketing communications activity.

A comparatively new medium to be considered for direct marketing is that of **door-to-door** activity. The advent of increasingly sophisticated systems based on the analysis of geo-demographic data – such as ACORN and PiN – have enabled more precise message targeting. This is an area which is proving to be of considerable value to fast-moving consumer goods products, where the opportunity to provide physical product samples and purchasing incentives to identified households is generating positive response levels.

QUESTION 8.7

What procedures would you recommend a company to adopt to ensure the smooth development and implementation of a direct marketing campaign?

The management of direct marketing activity

The great benefit of direct marketing activity is the far greater ability to identify the outcome than in almost all other forms of marketing communications. Since all direct marketing campaigns have a response mechanism built in, the performance of the campaign can be speedily determined. However, that benefit has a price attached.

There is a far greater need for comprehensive management programmes to deal with the complexities of direct marketing. The very nature of direct marketing activity requires, in many instances, a large number of different suppliers and agencies. To give just one example. An individual campaign might necessitate using: a list broker to identify available listings; a computer bureau to conduct a profiling exercise to analyse the data against other criteria; the use of an agency to de-duplicate the lists, which may be compiled from a variety of different sources; an agency to develop the creative proposition; perhaps a market research company to assess alternative treatments; a printer to produce the items; a handling house to effect the mailings; and a fulfilment agency to ensure that consumer requests are met. And this represents a much foreshortened version of the list of areas which must be covered. Thus project management itself is a vital ingredient of direct marketing activities.

ACTIVITY 8.5

For a company of which you are aware, identify their use of direct marketing techniques within their overall marketing communications activity. Are there ways in which they could make better use of direct marketing?

Business-to-business activity

Although direct marketing techniques are increasingly being applied to consumer goods and services, they are especially relevant to the business-to-business area. Indeed, to a far greater degree, business-to-business marketing relies on the underlying mechanics of direct marketing as a key platform for marketing communications. There are a number of reasons which serve to explain this situation.

- **Identification of contacts**   In many instances, the sales universe for business products is comparatively small. Often, we are talking about thousands of potential customers (or even hundreds) against multiple millions for most consumer goods. It is thus relatively easy to identify – by name and title, in many cases – the individual targets for a business-to-business proposition.
- **Sales-force size**   Few business-to-business organizations maintain large sales forces. In some cases, the number of representatives is in low single figures. Accordingly, some mechanism is required to maximize their effective strike rate. Maintaining conventional contact with potential purchasers would otherwise be extremely hit and miss, or over a very extended time frame.

- **The need to create/reinforce awareness** The interval between purchases may be extremely long and relationships with alternative suppliers may be quite strong. In this context, organizations need to ensure cost-effective contact with potential purchasers over an extended time period in order to maintain an awareness of their company and its products at a reasonable level.
- **The decision-making unit** In many company purchasing decisions, it is unusual that a single person will have the necessary authority to arrange the purchase. Often there will be several people, fulfilling different functions within the organization, who will all contribute to the decision-making unit. Each of them will need to be exposed to the product or service proposition, and it is quite likely that they will require different aspects of the offering to be detailed. Some, for example, will be interested in the performance of the product itself; others in the financial aspects of the proposition; yet others in the technical aspects of integration with existing machinery or materials; and so on.

For many organizations, direct marketing represents the most cost-effective solution to their marketing communications requirements. In this context, direct marketing can ensure:

- Cost-effective lead generation by maintaining regular contact with potential purchasers and prospects.
- Corporate and product awareness, by targeting specific messages which are 'tailored' to the needs of named individuals or job functions.
- A more effective sales visit, by ensuring that prospects have pre-awareness of the proposition – and may be motivated to request a sales call.

QUESTION 8.8

- How would you explain the techniques of direct marketing to a not-for-profit organization?
- What are the advantages and disadvantages compared to other forms of marketing communications?

Non-profit organizations

Direct marketing can offer similar benefits to non-profit organizations, where the cost per response may be the key to their long-term financial survival. With the exception of the very largest charitable bodies, non-profit organizations have extremely limited budgets to support their communications activities.

The nature of the message to be conveyed may have a highly specific appeal to comparatively small numbers who comprise their target audience. Here again, the ability to reach small sectors of the population, or individuals who possess certain characteristics, may be the critical factor in effective communications campaigns. Existing databases may be interrogated to ensure consistency against the defined criteria in order to maximize the response rate. Often, the message itself requires detailed communication, which would otherwise not be possible within the bounds of conventional media.

Finally, direct marketing and, particularly, direct mail can be more readily controlled within limited financial constraints. Even where a large list of potential contacts exists, a non-profit organization may not have the funds to finance the mailing to them all. A small proportion can thus be mailed in the first instance, and part of the revenue generated by this first mailing can be used to fund subsequent activity.

Integrating direct marketing

The fundamental need, as we have already seen in Unit 2, is to ensure the total and complete integration of all marketing communications activities. The potential consumer cares little about the source of the message, only its content. Even then, they will give only scant attention to what the company has to say about its products or services. The imperative must be to achieve the most cost-effective communication of the message to the target audience using the appropriate vehicles for its communication. In this sense, therefore, the selection of the techniques of marketing communications must be based entirely on their appropriateness for the task, and their ability to deliver against the defined objectives.

QUESTION 8.9

What are the factors which inhibit the growth of international direct marketing?

International direct marketing

Direct marketing has a unique ability to achieve cross-border communications, especially through the use of targeted direct mail and the use of the telephone.

Large variations exist between countries in terms of their response levels to direct marketing and, for the most part, direct marketing activity continues to operate on a national rather than on an international level. Nonetheless, it is clear that a major opportunity exists for the expansion of direct marketing techniques as the processes themselves achieve better understanding and as knowledge is gained regarding the response to these techniques within different markets.

Already, the availability of satellite channels, which are beamed consistently throughout Europe or, separately, throughout Asia, have brought with them the opportunity to achieve direct response messaging throughout several countries simultaneously. As elsewhere, however, the vital need is to ensure an adequate understanding of the consumer in these diverse markets. Only in this way can we isolate those areas which are held in common in order to ensure the effective communication of a constant message which will be received in different countries and by different cultures.

SUMMARY

During the course of this unit we have seen:

- Some of the reasons why direct marketing techniques are attracting a considerable level of attention.
- The progressive fragmentation of markets – both consumer and business-to-business – demands more sophisticated techniques to enable the precise targeting of prospects in a cost-effective manner.
- The establishment of sophisticated databases – itself dependent on the improvements which have taken place in the area of information technology – enables the profiling of prospects against a range of dimensions.
- In an environment which is justifiably concerned with the costs and measurement of marketing communications activities, direct marketing techniques enable a speedy response in both areas.
- The techniques have been adopted across the range of markets, but are particularly appropriate in the areas of business-to-business and non-profit organization marketing, where the prospect base is narrowly defined and is often more difficult to reach using other communications techniques.
- Direct marketing will, increasingly, come to the fore in the context of international marketing communications, as the relevance of the techniques is appreciated, and as greater convergence between diverse national markets and cultures enables the delivery of a constant message.

Examination hints and specimen questions

The examiner will be far more concerned that you can demonstrate an understanding of the *strategic issues* relating to the area of direct marketing than the various *techniques* which are employed within the discipline. Nevertheless, it will be useful to have a solid grasp of the principal techniques in order that you can underpin your response to the questions with contemporary examples of direct marketing practice.

Two questions from recent CIM papers are reproduced below, which specifically relate to this important area of direct marketing. You should attempt them both, although it is probably a good idea to write your answers on separate occasions rather than one immediately after the other. Again, you should try to restrict the time you allow for each question to no more than 30 minutes.

The experience of many leading companies shows that database marketing, when used strategically, can transform the way a company does business and therefore achieve competitive advantage. Understanding the strategic role of information technology has also been increased by the work of Michael Porter, which has shown how to strengthen customer relations and overcome supplier problems. For an organization of your choice, illustrate how information technology and database marketing can make a significant contribution to marketing strategy.

(December 1993)

Direct marketing is an interactive system of marketing that uses one or more promotional media to effect a measurable response at any location. You have just been appointed the first ever marketing manager of a company selling a range of outdoor leisure clothing and equipment. These are at present only distributed through exclusive retail outlets. Your priority is to increase sales by direct marketing techniques. Write a short report setting out how you would do this in the next year

(June 1993)

Most general marketing texts will provide a good introduction to the principles and techniques of direct marketing, and it is strongly recommended that you read the appropriate chapter in the text of your choice. For a more detailed insight, the following titles are recommended:

D. Bird, *Commonsense Direct Marketing*, 3rd edn, Kogan Page, 1993.
Various Authors, *The Practitioner's Guide to Direct Marketing*, The Direct Marketing Centre, 1992.
G. McCorkell, *Advertising That Pulls Response*, McGraw Hill, New York, 1992.
A. Baines, *Handbook of International Direct Marketing*, Kogan Page, 1992.
R. Fairlie, *Database Marketing and Direct Mail*, Exley, 1990.

EXTENDING KNOWLEDGE

The strategic development of sales promotion

In this unit you will:

- Consider the background and environmental factors to sales promotion.
- Identify the factors relating to the determination of sales promotion objectives.
- Examine the various sales promotion techniques and consider their advantages and disadvantages.
- Examine the application of sales promotion techniques.
- Look at such considerations as brand loyalty and brand franchise.
- Recognize the importance of the determination of sales promotion strategy and the integration of activity with other marketing communications tools.
- Consider the use of market research techniques.

By the end of this unit you will:

- Appreciate the importance of sales promotion in the overall marketing communications context.
- Be able to identify appropriate sales promotion techniques to respond to specific marketing communications needs.
- Recognize the important strategic issues relating to sales promotions.
- Be able to plan and control the applications of the various techniques.

Sales promotion is an important part of marketing communications, and you should ensure that you have developed a thorough understanding of the principles underlying the techniques and the techniques themselves.

It is unlikely that you will be asked to answer specific questions on the techniques, but without an understanding of these it will be far more difficult to appreciate the strategic issues which are considered in this unit.

You should allow 3–4 hours to work through the main content of this unit, although the questions and the activities described will take a further 3 hours.

As with the other areas of marketing communications, it is vitally important that you are aware of contemporary issues relating to the topic and that you are able to introduce examples of the application of sales promotion techniques from current marketing practice to your answers.

Make a special effort to read as many articles on the subject as possible, and to examine examples of activity on products, in stores, in service outlets and elsewhere. Make notes for yourself of the promotions you have seen and try to list the reasons why the particular techniques have been selected.

In recent years sales promotion has become a particularly dynamic area within the overall context of marketing communications. Although accurate figures are difficult to come by, most industry pundits agree that more money is now spent 'below the line' than 'above the line'.

Since the impact of sales promotion is primarily geared to the short term, it is inevitable that the area should enjoy considerable growth in times of economic recession. However, it is also true that this growth has been influenced by changing attitudes amongst marketers. In an increasingly competitive retail environment, and with the concentration of buying power into relatively few hands, manufacturers have turned to sales promotion to achieve on-shelf differentiation between their own products and those of their competitors.

Moreover, since the appeal of retailer products is often based on price, sales promotion has provided manufacturers with the ability to adjust the retail price to the consumer – in the short term – and minimize the differential. Undoubtedly, a major influence has been the desire for short-term sales achievement in its own right. In many instances the performance of product management may be monitored by its ability to deliver volume sales. Since sales promotion potentially has an immediate impact on consumer sales, there has been a tendency for product managers to turn to these techniques in order to achieve their sales objectives.

At the same time, pressure on margins has made for a closer attention to the detail of the achievement of cost-effective sales volume. Since the results of the applications of many promotional devices can be predicted with a high degree of accuracy, product management can be confident in their volume forecasts. Similarly, with the increasing costs of other forms of marketing communications, especially that of advertising, management has turned to areas which are perceived to be more cost-effective – especially for the achievement of short-term sales.

A further factor is the growing belief of product and sales management in their ability to handle the techniques of sales promotion. Unlike other areas of marketing communications, sales promotion is rarely subjected to the same level of internal debate as would be the case with, say, advertising. This enables product managers to be more 'independent' and self-motivated in the determination and implementation of sales promotional activities.

The growth of specialist sales promotions agencies has also contributed to the increased recognition of the importance of the area, and the growth in credibility which the application of sales promotion techniques has enjoyed. Historically, sales promotion has been viewed as an adjunct to other marketing communications techniques, but today it is recognized that the use of sales promotion has an important impact on marketing strategy.

The tactical and strategic implications of sales promotion will be explored in this unit. Varied though the array of sales promotions is, together they represent a variety of methods to achieve an aspect of the total strategy for the brand.

Get hold of two or three editions of current practitioner magazines, for example, *Marketing* or *Marketing Week.* Identify all the sales promotions campaigns described.

In contrast to some of the other marketing communications tools, however, sales promotion predominantly works on a short-term basis. Unlike advertising or public relations, for example, it may have no lasting impact on the brand. Research by Ehrenberg et al. in 1991 indicated that: 'Consumer promotions have large immediate sales effects, but do not appear to be brand building' (Ehrenberg, Hammond and Goodhart, *The After Effects of Large Consumer Promotions*, London Business School, 1991).

QUESTION 9.1

What justification is there for the increased percentage of marketing communications budgets which have been devoted to sales promotion in recent years?

The audiences for sales promotion

In the vast majority of instances, sales promotions are designed to impact on both the trade and consumers. In some instances, however, specific promotions can be developed to achieve defined objectives within the trade alone (Figure 9.1).

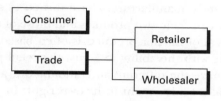

Figure 9.1

Sales promotions objectives

Although sales promotion has an important role in the context of ensuring the speedy achievement of sales objectives, to consider sales promotion in this way is somewhat limiting. It is clear that the techniques available are capable of fulfilling a wide range of specific objectives. Before exploring the nature of those objectives, it is important to establish the key principles.

- *Sales promotion objectives must be defined clearly and succinctly.* It is vital to define precisely what is expected of the campaign and over what duration it will be run. Few promotions are open ended and a timescale must be established for the fulfilment of commitments. Promotions which, for example, are designed to establish consumer loyalty, will cause consumer alienation – and will almost certainly fail – if the timescale is too far beyond normal consumer purchase patterns.

- *Sales promotion objectives must be amenable to measurement.* Some numerical value must be attached to the objective. Is the campaign, for example, designed to achieve a 40 per cent level of trial, or repurchase amongst 25 per cent of existing users? Not only will this establish the parameters for the campaign, it will also enable a proper evaluation once the campaign has been completed. By monitoring the results, it will be possible to determine whether the objectives have been met or exceeded, over what timescale the results have been achieved, and the cost-effectiveness of the expenditure. Apart from the immediate benefit of evaluation, the process will add to the sum of knowledge to ensure the efficient use of resources and the selection of the most appropriate techniques in the future.

- *Sales promotion objectives must be achievable.* There is an inevitable temptation to set grand objectives for any form of marketing communications activity. Whilst it obviously makes sense to establish real targets, it is also important that they are felt to be realistic within the constraints of the budget available and the organization's structure. A promotion which, for example, sets unrealistic targets for the number of salesforce contacts will, inevitably, fail.

- *Sales promotion objectives must be budgeted realistically.* Few companies have limitless financial resources. Almost all activity will be constrained by budgetary limitations. It is imperative that the objectives are related to the financial resources and not set at an unrealistic level. By the same token it is important that the organization is aware of the likely cost impact of the achievement of the objectives. All promotions cost money, and if the level of consumer demand for the promotional offer exceeds the level of affordability the consequence will be disappointed consumers and a failure to meet the commitments of the campaign.

We will now consider some of the objectives which specific sales promotion campaigns can be addressed to achieve.

Enquiries/list building

An increasing concern amongst manufacturers is the desire to build accurate lists of actual and potential consumers. Promotions can be designed specifically to ensure that consumers provide this information. As the costs of conventional media increase, companies are seeking more cost-effective ways of reaching their target audiences. Access to lists of names and addresses enables the subsequent communication to these named individuals with a minimum of wastage. We will explore this issue in greater depth in Unit 8.

Product trial and sampling

A key area of sales promotion rests in its ability to generate product trial and sampling, of either an existing or a new product. A properly constructed promotional offer will have an immediacy of impact which will attract the potential consumer.

Product repurchase/loyalty

The generation of repeat purchase and, in the longer term, the establishment of consumer loyalty to a product, is a major facet of sales promotion activity. Such promotions can be targeted specifically to recent trialists, for example, to encourage them to purchase on another occasion. Long-term promotions are frequently used to provide an overlay to the purchase which provides the consumer with a valid reason – over and above the specific product benefits and performance – to purchase the brand on a number of separate occasions.

Increasing rate/frequency of purchase

A similar requirement will be that of increasing the rate and frequency of purchase. This may be achieved by the presentation of new usages for the product, or the suggestion of new-use occasions.

Trading up

Often, and particularly at the time of the introduction of a new product, the manufacturer will make available a smaller size of the product for trial purchases. Subsequently, however, they will wish to encourage the consumer to purchase larger quantities. This will be encouraged through the use of a variety of promotional techniques.

At the very least, the manufacturer will ensure that purchases of the product are brought forward. In many cases, however, this will also be accompanied by a greater frequency of use simply because the product is immediately available to the consumer.

By ensuring that the consumer holds a greater 'stock' of the product in home, the manufacturer removes the consumer from competitive attack for a period of time.

Introducing a new product

Sales promotional techniques, because of the immediacy of their impact, are conventionally used at the time of a new product introduction. Often, either through the use of successive promotional executions, or the specific nature of the execution, the manufacturer will incentivize the consumer to pass through the various initial stages of the product life cycle.

As sales promotion manager for a new convenience food, you have been asked to develop a plan for activity to stimulate trial and repurchase. What issues do you need to consider in relation to the sales promotional techniques which might fulfil this requirement?

In the same way that sales promotion can be targeted specifically towards the consumer – although there is an inevitable trade impact – techniques are available to target the trade.

Traffic building

Some techniques, particularly those which involve, for example, in-store sampling, may also serve to increase the volume of traffic for the retailer. Although the consumer will be motivated to visit the outlet because of the specific incentive, it is highly likely that he or she will make other purchases whilst in store – to the benefit of the retailer who participates in the promotion.

Inventory building

In precisely the same way that the manufacturer might seek to encourage the consumer to purchase larger packages of the product, so they might also wish to ensure a deeper inventory on the part of the retailer. There are a variety of stock-loading techniques which will be discussed later and which may be employed for this purpose.

Stock reduction

At certain times, the manufacturer may wish to ensure that there is effective pull through of their products and thereby reduce the level of inventory held by the retailer.

Offsetting impact of competitive activity

One great benefit of sales promotion over other forms of marketing communications is its speed of implementation. Certain forms of promotional activity can be introduced literally within days of determining the need. For this reason, sales promotion will often be employed to minimize the impact of competitive activity.

Promotional support to trade

In certain instances, promotions will be designed to provide either general or specific support to the trade. Some of the objectives which can be fulfilled by such activities are: feature pricing; the provision of displays and display incentives; in-store demonstrations, which will provide for trial of a product and will often be accompanied by some additional incentive to the consumer (e.g. discounted price) to purchase the product.

Other in-store support may provide the opportunity to build on special events; for example, a new store opening, some themed activity in which the brand can participate (Italian week, cookery week, etc.); seasonal activity to promote sales (spring cleaning event, midsummer sale, etc.); cross-promotion, where two products are sold together. Safeway have recently mounted a large campaign in which pairs of one branded product together with an appropriate Safeway own-label product were sold together at a discount.

As noted above the motivation of the sales force, dealers, etc., by the use of incentives – often linked to sales targets – is an important area of sales promotion activity.

Identify the areas in which sales promotion can make a special contribution to the achievement of marketing communications objectives

Sales promotion techniques

We have seen that there are many different objectives which can be established for sales promotion activity. Similarly, there is a wide variety of executional techniques which can be employed to meet these objectives. The following section details some of the major techniques and describes both the advantages and disadvantages in use.

Reduced-price offers

Money off

Money-off promotions, in their variety of implementation, remain the most commonly employed promotional device. Often referred to as 'price packs' or 'RPOs', these promotions offer the consumer the most powerful incentive to purchase – money!

In essence, the promotion consists of a price reduction which is communicated either on or off the pack. The size of the price reduction will be determined by an assessment of the brand requirements and the competitive environment. Most often, the offering consists of an on-pack flash detailing the size of the price reduction, either as an absolute price or as a reduction on the normal price. However, it may be communicated to the consumer with a notice at the point of purchase. By providing an *immediate* price reduction, a manufacturer makes the most impactful offer. All consumers will be made aware of the offer and will receive the benefit at the time of purchase.

An obvious disadvantage to be considered is the fact that all consumers receive the incentive, despite the fact that some – the loyal users – would probably have purchased at the normal price. Equally, such promotional offers are easily, and potentially speedily, matched by the competition. Moreover, they lack distinctivity, as all products and services can offer money off. A further, and possibly the most important disadvantage, is the fact that frequent use of money-off techniques may result in a reduced price expectation on the part of the consumer (the reduced price becomes the norm), and may denigrate the image of the brand.

Since much sales promotion is involved with actual or effective price reduction to the consumer, why don't manufacturers simply cut the price permanently, and have done with it?

QUESTION 9.2

Against these disadvantages must be set the obvious advantages. Money-off promotions can be speedily implemented. If the offer is a simple price reduction on-shelf, the promotion can be implemented within a few days. Moreover, since most companies have built up considerable experience of the technique, there is little need for testing and the results can be predicted with a reasonable level of accuracy.

The impact of the technique is considerable. It has a universal appeal and both the trade and the consumer like the promotion.

Importantly, the promotional device is available to all manufacturers and service providers. Not only are there no specific economies of scale (which would otherwise restrict the use of the device to larger companies), a means of transmitting the offering to the end consumer is similarly available to all – the pack is not the only vehicle.

Coupons

There are a number of different ways of transmitting a money-off offer to the consumer. Although the manufacturer's product is an ideal vehicle for carrying the coupon, there are many alternative carriers and means of communicating with the end consumer.

On some occasions, a manufacturer will use another product within the range to carry the coupon. This has the dual advantage of providing an incentive to purchase product A, whilst encouraging trial of product B. This is sometimes referred to as *cross couponing*. On other occasions, a manufacturer will negotiate with another to carry his coupon on their product. This has a similar benefit to the carrier since the value of the purchase is enhanced. However, it may also ensure that the two products are related in the consumer's mind. For example, money off toothpaste when you buy a toothbrush, or money off butter or jam when you buy bread.

Although far more costly, money-off coupons can be distributed within the media or even on a door-to-door basis. These may be used to target new users (who might not be aware of the offering in store) or to employ a more cost-effective carrier to reach the target audience.

ACTIVITY 9.4

Describe a sales promotional offer which specifically induced you to buy a product or service. Why did it have this effect?

Obviously, on-pack coupons will take longer to implement, since the revised pack design containing the flash will need to be fed into the production pipeline. If another carrier is to be used, negotiations will be required before the offer can be implemented. Coupon offers are significantly more expensive and time consuming in terms of implementation. But they sometimes offer a particular benefit.

Where the coupon is designed to be redeemed at the time of a *subsequent* purchase, such offerings have a similar appearance of immediacy and impact, although in practice many consumers forget to redeem the coupon! Hence money-off coupons may have a similar visual impact to that of an immediate money-off offer, but will represent a lower real cost, since the level of redemption will be lower. They thus represent an effective way of inducing sampling and, because they can be transmitted via alternative carriers to designated groups of consumers, they are particularly effective in encouraging new users.

The pack

A third form of promotion which has the same effect as reducing the price is that of bonus or multi-packs. These offers represent an alternative expression of the money-off proposition, by providing the consumer with additional product at no extra charge. As noted, there are two forms of the offer.

The **bonus pack** consists of an enlarged pack size although the price charged is that of the 'normal' pack which it replaces. In some instances, such packs are specially produced and provide the consumer with 10, 20 or more per cent extra product free. In other instances, partly to offset the additional manufacturing costs and difficulties, the manufacturer simply offers a larger size for the price of the smaller size.

An alternative execution, especially important to manufacturers whose product format precludes the bonus pack offer, is that of the **banded pack**. Here, two or more packs are banded together at a reduced price: 'save x per cent when you buy two'; 'three for the price of two'; and so on.

Both promotional formats reflect the fact that there is a differential between the cost of the product and the consumer's perception of value. Indeed, such is the relationship that these promotions can sometimes offer greater consumer value at a considerably lower cost to the manufacturer. Both devices can encourage the consumer to increase the frequency of purchase or, in the case of the bonus pack, to trade up to a larger size. They obviously have a high perceived value and can offer considerable on-shelf impact.

The choice between the two devices will depend on manufacturing circumstances. Bonus packs require a flexibility of packaging and manufacturing which is not available to all manufacturers. The latter requires minimal production changes, although it must be recognized that the process of banding may be both labour intensive and time consuming to implement.

Free gifts

Many manufacturers seek to incentivize the purchase by the offering of a free gift item at the time of purchase. Once again, there is the advantage of immediacy in that if the consumer is attracted by the gift they are more likely to purchase the product. There are four distinct forms of free gift offer.

The **on-pack free gift** is any item of merchandise which is presented to the consumer by affixing it to the external surface of the product. The application of the technique is commonly seen in a wide variety of areas. A free spoon attached to a jar of coffee, for example, or a computer program affixed to a magazine. Indeed, it is in the latter area where the promotional device is most frequently available. The obvious disadvantage is that of pilferage.

The **in-pack free gift** is used by a number of packaged goods manufacturers, with a description of the gift on the pack surface, and the item only available once the packaging has been opened. Cereal products are regular users of this promotional tool.

The **with-pack free gift** is an execution which relies on the co-operation of the retailer, since the free item of merchandise is detached from the purchase item. However, it offers the advantage of not requiring any changes to the manufacturing process and is, therefore, available both to manufacturers of products and providers of services alike. The application of this technique is particularly popular within the cosmetics trade, and free gifts of substantial value are offered by the makers of perfumes and aftershaves.

The fourth important area of free gift is **the pack itself**. Once it is recognized that the packaging, or some alternative presentation, may represent added value to the consumer, it can be appreciated that this is an area of considerable potential. This format has been used by a variety of packaged goods manufacturers, either with reproductions of previous packaging (history has value), or to present the consumer with some reusable container that will be retained after the product has been consumed. Most mustards in France, for example, come to the consumer in small glass containers which can be used as drinking glasses once the mustard has been used.

All four varieties of gift incentives have the attraction of immediacy and, if well selected, can add considerable value to the brand. Often their use serves to extend the brand values by a close association of the free gift with the primary product, for example, offering a tumbler with a bottle of spirits. A variation is to offer sequential free gifts which serve to deliver loyalty over an extended period of time. Above all, they represent a distinctive form of promotional activity which will serve to differentiate the brand from its competitors.

The key problem associated with free gifts is that of identifying items of sufficient perceived value at an appropriate cost to the brand. Low-cost items may be of poor quality and value, and thus serve to detract from the brand rather than add value to it. A good decision basis is to ensure that the quality of the free gift is perceived to be at least the same as that of the brand itself. The costs of a free gift promotion may be quite high if the quality requirement is to be met.

Other disadvantages of the technique are associated with the different executions. As already noted, on-pack free gifts are subject to pilferage, and this may annoy the real purchaser. Overcoming the problem by seeking to insert the free gift inside the packaging may require significant alterations to the packaging machinery and, particularly with food products, the gifts themselves require additional packaging to avoid contamination of the contents. With-pack free gifts require a substantial level of trade co-operation which may make their implementation more difficult to achieve.

Free mail-ins

An alternative to the free gift item offered at the point of purchase is to invite the consumer to send in an appropriate number of proofs of purchase for a gift item. Although somewhat more complex in its implementation, the technique has a number of direct advantages.

As the free gift may be occasioned by multiple purchases of the product, the gift item may be more expensive and, hence, more attractive to the consumer. As such, it may add to the differentiation of the brand from its competitors. There is an obvious loyalty aspect to the execution since the consumer will have to make several purchases in order to obtain the necessary proofs of purchase. And, as with some couponing techniques, although motivated to buy the brand with the intention of redeeming the free gift, many consumers forget to do so.

Similar problems arise with free mail-ins as with other free gifts in terms of the difficulty of obtaining suitable merchandise to offer. Additionally, however, it must be remembered that the extra costs of postage, packaging and handling may make the promotion too expensive to run. The promotion lacks immediacy and consumers will be far less motivated to buy the brand if they are expected to collect wrappers and wait to receive the free gift – to a large extent this will depend on the free gift being offered. Finally, the technique has relatively low appeal to the trade.

As with all forms of free-gift merchandise, it is important to test the items, both to ensure the level of acceptance of the gifts and to anticipate the likely levels of redemption.

QUESTION 9.3

How do the application of sales promotion techniques differ according to the life-cycle stages of a product or service?

Self-liquidating offers

As the name suggests, these incentives are 'paid for' by the consumer. In effect, the manufacturer uses his bulk-buying power to purchase gift merchandise which is then offered to the consumer at cost. Obviously, depending on the item to be offered, and the skills of negotiation, it is possible to offer such items at considerably less than their perceived retail value. The resultant offer, for example, 'free cutlery set with a retail value of x, yours for only half x and proofs of purchase', is thus attractive to manufacturers.

The promotional costs of self-liquidating offers are low – the consumer bearing the costs of the item itself, whilst the brand bears the cost of distribution and display. They offer the opportunity to create an offer of apparent value without having to bear the associated costs.

As such, they represent useful vehicles for the creation of a presence at the point of purchase and, as with other gift-based promotions, represent the opportunity to provide 'dealer loaders', where the manufacturer gives examples of the merchandise to retail staff in exchange for display space or some other consideration.

However, as a general rule, they are unlikely to generate major trade enthusiasm. Retailers are aware that self-liquidating promotions generate relatively low levels of consumer redemption, and hence are not likely to create significant increases in sales volume.

ACTIVITY 9.5

Identify examples of current sales promotion executions from local retailers. Define the objectives which you believe they were designed to meet. Consider the alternatives available to the organizing company

Contests and competitions

This is an area which has enjoyed considerable growth in recent years, especially with the development of pseudo-lotteries in which the consumer is, apparently, offered the opportunity to win a prize of sizeable value.

Contests and competitions are good point-of-sale vehicles, as they represent an opportunity to add to the brand aura. The offer of a substantial prize fund in cash or merchandise is likely to attract the attention of the potential consumer. The chance to win, say, one of ten cars, or a luxury holiday, will be likely to motivate considerable numbers of consumers to fulfil the competition entry requirements. However, set against the sales volume, the costs of such activities are relatively low.

The disadvantage of this promotional format is that it lacks the immediacy of other forms of incentive. Once again, the retail trade is aware that they will often generate only low levels of consumer participation. In many respects, the success of the format will depend on both the creative treatment and the scale and nature of the prizes offered.

One word of caution, however. Most countries require that participation in competition formats depends on the exercise of some form of skill. The absence of inherent skill in a competition may render the promotion illegal. An alternative option is to remove the purchase requirement on the part of the consumer! Although this sounds less than sensible, the reality is that most consumers intending to enter the competition will continue to buy the brand as if it were a requirement of entry.

A recent 'World Cup' promotion mounted by Coca Cola on a worldwide basis to reinforce their sponsorship activities of the event are a perfect example of the implementation of this form of pseudo-lottery. The 'instant win' prizes were obtained by revealing the identity of the prize by removing the ring pull from the can. The rules of the competition provide, however, that anyone can enter the competition simply by sending in their name and address to the handling house who will open a can on their behalf.

In-store sampling

Although relatively expensive, in-store sampling may provide the opportunity to provide a direct interface between the product and the consumer. Particularly in instances where the product is complicated to understand, or new, the opportunity for a sales person to explain the functions of the product and for the consumer to sample it may be very desirable. The trade likes such promotions as they generate in-store activity which tends to encourage a higher level of all product purchases – not just the product which is being sampled.

The application of sales promotion techniques

Table 9.1 can be used as a simple checklist to establish the specific nature of a promotional technique to meet a defined objective. It must be remembered, however, that the list is not exhaustive and that, in some instances, several objectives may be combined.

Table 9.1 Promotional techniques and the objectives they meet

Objective	Technique								
	Money-off packs	Money-off coupons	Banded packs	Bonus packs	Free gifts	Free mail-ins	Self-liquidators	Contests & comps	Sampling
New product launch	**	*	*	*	*				**
Induce trial	**	**	*	*	*				**
Encourage new usage	*	*	*	*	*				**
Gain new users	**	**	*	*	*				*
Retain existing users	*	*	**	**		*	*	*	
Increase frequency of purchase		*			**	**			
Increase purchase size				**	*				
Increase distribution	*	*	*	*	*				*
Increase inventory	*	*	*	*					*
Reduce inventory	*	*							
Activate slow-moving lines	*	*	*	*				*	
Gain special featuring in-store							*	*	*
Increase shelf facings	**			*	*				

- What sales promotion techniques are relevant to service companies?
- Does the application of these techniques differ from those applied to consumer goods products?

QUESTION 9.4

A consideration of brand loyalty factors

An important dimension of sales promotion, which is sometimes overlooked, is the fact that certain forms of activity reward all users with the incentive, irrespective of whether or not they would have purchased the product anyway. It has to be remembered that the consumers of any product or service make up a continuum ranging from *loyal users* to *promiscu-*

ous buyers. Loyal users are those consumers who purchase regularly or on all occasions, whilst promiscuous buyers will be those who usually purchase only in response to some form of incentive.

Most promotional techniques are indiscriminate in this context, and tend to reward all purchasers. Thus, whilst a promotional device may be attractive in terms of attracting new users, it will also be received by those users who would have purchased the brand without the incentive. When costing out the benefits of promotional activity, this factor must be taken into account.

There is also a number of other factors which need to be considered in the determination of promotional strategy.

Level of involvement with purchase

There is some evidence that, where consumer involvement with the product category is low, promotions which have an immediacy of impact will work better than those which impact over time. Thus, clearly identified money-off promotions, or the offering of bonus free product, will have a high level of impact compared with money-off next purchase and similar offers. In this regard, it is important that the discount or offer is clearly 'flagged' to the consumer. As many consumers are not aware of absolute prices, an on-shelf offer which effectively reduces the price, but which is not clearly identified to the consumer as such, will have far less impact.

Purchase frequency

It is important to understand the nature and frequency of purchase for the target consumer. Ideally, incentives should be timed to coincide with the patterns of purchase of the heavy user, so that they are encouraged to buy within their normal rate. If a phased incentive (with, say, on-pack vouchers that need to be saved) has too short an interval, even heavy users will not be able to buy sufficiently often to achieve their goal. Petrol promotions, which in the past have offered vouchers for items, or collectable free gifts (World Cup coins, car badges and so on), can result in considerable irritation of consumers if insufficient time is allowed for them to complete their set.

By the same token, a differential impact can be achieved by addressing the issue of pack size. It is reasonable to assume that regular users will, in the main, tend to buy a larger pack size. If an incentive is offered on a smaller size, it will tend to attract more new users than existing ones.

Coupon distribution

We have already seen that all recipients of a promotional incentive will be rewarded, irrespective of whether or not they would have purchased the product at the 'regular' price. By targeting discount offers by, for example, including the coupon in a newspaper or magazine advertisement, or by the use of direct mail, it can be more effective in attracting new users than those who are loyal to the brand.

Brand franchise

Much has already been said about the potential risks of short-term promotional incentives undermining the desired image of a brand. In addition to assessing the ability of a promotion to achieve short-term volume goals, careful consideration needs to be given to the likely impact which it will have on overall consumer perceptions. Too great a reliance on price-based offers will tend to encourage consumers to focus on the price, not only of the preferred brand, but also of potential competitors, and sometimes to the detriment of the brand.

The determination of sales promotion strategy

As with any other form of strategy determination, the starting point must be the correct *assessment of the situation* or need. What is the promotion designed to achieve and what is the problem that needs to be rectified? In this respect, it is important to analyse the situation of the brand relative to its competition in order to identify the true cause of the problem. For example, is the low sales volume caused by some deficiency in the product or, perhaps, the result of competitive activities? Sales promotion may help in the latter situation but is unlikely to remedy the former. Indeed, it may accentuate the problems as more trialists will become aware of the imperfections in the brand!

Given that many companies use several marketing communications tools simultaneously, how can the effects of sales promotion be differentiated from the others?

As with other forms of marketing communications, it is important to set *precise objectives* for the activity. Is the promotion expected to increase trial and sampling, or reward loyal users? Not only must the objectives be specific they should also be measurable. What level of trial is to be generated – 10, 20 or 30 per cent or higher? If no value if given to the objective, it will be extremely difficult to determine whether the goal has been achieved on completion of the promotion.

Having determined the objectives, the next stage is to *identify the potential solution*. We have already seen that a number of promotional techniques can achieve similar objectives. Selecting the appropriate promotional technique is a vital part of the process; Table 9.1 will provide some guidance in this respect.

Pre-costing of the promotion must be an important element of the process. Perhaps, with the use of market research techniques, it will be possible to identify the likely take-up of a consumer free-gift offer or coupon promotion. At the very least it will be important, for budgetary reasons, to be able to anticipate the likely costs of the exercise. In the instance of merchandise offers, it will be important to ensure that adequate quantities of the items are available to meet expected levels of consumer demand (avoiding consumer disappointment). Similarly, at the other end of the spectrum, it is important not to overorder and thereby be left with unused stocks of the free gifts.

List the various skills you would expect from a newly appointed sales promotion agency.

Control mechanisms must be established at the outset to ensure the smooth implementation of the promotion. How will the company respond to changes in the levels of consumer demand? Is there sufficient manufacturing capacity, for example, to cope? What happens in the event that the promotion goes wrong? Are there adequate monitoring procedures to identify what is going on in the marketplace? And so on.

Finally, once the promotion has been implemented, the results must be carefully *measured*.

The integration of sales promotion activities

QUESTION 9.7

How should sales promotion activities be integrated with other aspects of the marketing communications plan?

It is important in the planning of sales promotion plans, to ensure the continuity of communication with other elements of the marketing communications plan. There is little point running sales promotion activities which only serve to confuse consumers' expectations of the brand. In this sense, it is vital to ensure that there is a consistency of image and functional values before a sales promotion technique is employed and that it is fully integrated with other aspects of the marketing communications plan. It is important to understand that adopting a strategic approach to sales promotion does not preclude the tactical use of sales promotion techniques. The purpose of the strategy is to provide a framework in which tactical planning can exist and be improved.

Research into sales promotion

QUESTION 9.8

Outline the techniques you might use to pre-evaluate a sales promotion campaign.

Some mention is needed of the research techniques which are available to assist in the process of sales promotion planning. These fall into two broad areas:

- Testing.
- Monitoring.

Sales promotion, like other forms of marketing communications, is responsive to market research techniques which can help to avoid the many pitfalls that might otherwise occur.

Qualitative research methods can be used to assess such factors as the likely impact on the image of the brand of a particular range of promotional techniques. Identifying how consumers will react to an offer is important both in the tangible sense (such as, how will it affect their propensity to purchase the brand) as well as the intangible aspects, such as how the promotion affects their overall perceptions of the brand. Is a particular offer more likely to cheapen than improve the image, for example?

Techniques such as 'town hall tests' in which the purchase environment is simulated and the results of exposure to different consumer offers are monitored, can make a considerable contribution to the determination of the most effective incentive.

Similarly, quantitative techniques can be used in which consumers scale their preference for different forms of promotional offer. If possible, it is desirable to include some previous promotion – for which results are known – as a benchmark against which the performance of alternatives can be assessed.

In some instances, especially where the scale of the promotion is likely to be large, it may be advisable to stage a 'mini-test market'. By running the promotion in a small region of the country, it will be possible to gauge the impact of the offering in a live environment, where the brand has to compete with real competitors.

The close monitoring of consumer response once the promotion is implemented is, similarly, an important part of the process. Constant feedback from the market will serve to alert the company to any potential difficulties, which may be avoided with a speedy response.

It has to be said that these techniques are often ignored or overlooked in the context of sales promotion activity. Market research will provide some assurance that the particular chosen technique is the appropriate one to fulfil the task set and, most importantly, to provide some indication of the likely outcome of the activity.

International sales promotion activity

The rules, regulations and codes of practice which govern sales promotion are far from being universal. Indeed, the application of the principles of sales promotion in the international context are fraught with difficulties. Free mails-ins, for example, are not permitted in Germany; promotions designed to encourage consumer loyalty with the offering of collector schemes are prohibited in Austria, Germany and some parts of Scandinavia; self-liquidating offers may not be run in Norway or Switzerland and special permission must first be obtained in Holland. The same problems exist with other forms of promotion and, whilst there is some movement towards common practice, at least within the EC, the situation for the moment remains somewhat confused.

It is imperative that any sales promotion planned for international implementation is checked for legal and other compliance on a country-by-country basis. It certainly cannot be assumed, as the examples above demonstrate, that simply because a promotion is 'legal' in one country it will be equally so elsewhere.

SUMMARY

In this unit we have seen that:

- Sales promotion can make an important *tactical* contribution to marketing communications, and offers a variety of techniques to motivate the consumer and the trade which are not paralleled elsewhere in the field.
- The techniques of sales promotion are many and varied and can make a significant contribution to the communications process, providing that the proper disciplines (defining objectives, ensuring budgetary and other controls are in place, monitoring and evaluation) are observed.
- It is important to view the contribution of sales promotion in the *strategic* context, both to ensure that it makes its proper contribution to the overall programme and, perhaps more importantly, does not contradict other activities that are being planned.
- With legal and other convergence towards common practice, it is to be anticipated that the growth in the area of sales promotion which has been experienced over recent years will continue. However, in the international context, such convergence remains a long way off. Perhaps more than in any other area of marketing communications, the legal framework precludes the true international implementation of activity.

Examination hints and specimen questions

Below are two further 'short' questions taken from recent CIM papers. As with the others that you have tried, you should allow yourself no more than 30 minutes to tackle each of them. By now, you should be more aware of this time frame and have gained more experience in ensuring that the key issues raised in the question are answered to the satisfaction of the examiner.

When answering any question, you should take a few minutes to *map out your answer*. Few of us have the ability simply to pick up a pen and start writing. The analysis of a question –

to see what the key points to be covered are – and the preparation of the answer are important stages in getting good marks.

There are a variety of techniques available to help focus your mind and it is worth practising one or two of them to see which is best for you. Several examples are contained in a text by Simon Majaro, *The Creative Gap – Managing Ideas for Profit* (Longman, 1988); this book covers such techniques as 'mind mapping', the 'fishbone approach' and many others. Apart from their value in the context of organizing your approach to exam questions, the many techniques described will also assist in other problem-solving areas, such as those experienced in the working environment.

Petrol can be regarded as a commodity, with the major oil companies such as Shell, BP and Esso, battling to attract car owners to their particular forecourts. These company owned sites have become smarter and many of them offer convenience stores. The 1990s has also signalled a sea change in the way oil companies carry out forecourt promotions. Describe two such promotions with which you are familiar. Compare their relative effectiveness and suggest how they might be improved.

(June 1994)

In 1992, Hoover, the manufacturers of electrical appliances, offered two free return flights to America from Britain to customers who purchased Hoover goods with a value in excess of £100. This apparent bargain immediately attracted thousands of customers. Stocks were soon exhausted and Hoover factories had to work overtime. Some consumers, however, complained about difficulties in booking their holiday accommodation through the travel agent recommended by Hoover. Evaluate the advantages and disadvantages of this type of sales promotion campaign from the points of view of the manufacturer, the retailer and the customer.

(June 1993)

EXTENDING KNOWLEDGE

There are few specialist texts which cover the area of sales promotion. However, the following are titles that you might like to consider reading:

W. P. Dommermuth, *Promotion – Analysis, Creativity and Strategy*, 2nd edn, PWS-Kent, 1989.
J. F. Engel, M. Warshaw and T. Kinnear, *Promotional Strategy*, 8th edn, Irwin, 1994.
J. Rossiter and L. Percy, *Advertising and Promotion Management*, McGraw Hill, New York, 1987.
D. Shultz, and W. Robinson, *Sales Promotion Management*, NTC Publishing, 1992.

You should also be referring to the weekly issues of *Marketing, Marketing Week* and *Campaign*. Apart from carrying regular reports on sales promotion issues, they conduct surveys into such aspects as consumer reactions to the techniques, considerations relating to the selection of specialist sales promotions consultancies, etc.

The strategic development of public relations

In this unit, which is designed to assist your understanding of the important dimensions of public relations, we will:

- Consider the broad role of public relations and the various publics to whom activity may be directed.
- Examine the functions of public relations, and the nature of the public relations process.
- Consider the nature of public relations programme planning, and the management of public relations activities.
- Look at the important aspects of public relations in the context of financial and charitable activities.
- Study the important aspects of event management and sponsorship.

By the end of this unit you will:

- Have a comprehensive understanding of the key strategic issues which must be addressed in the planning of public relations.
- Be able to apply this learning of CIM examination questions.

STUDY GUIDE

Public relations is an important aspect of the marketing communications mix. Unfortunately, because of its 'intangible' nature, in tends to receive less consideration from a strategic standpoint. However, it is important both from a practitioner standpoint, and from a need to fulfil the requriements of the CIM diploma, that you consider all the strategic issues which relate to this important communications area.

The unit, in common with those which have preceded it, contains a number of questions and activities specifically designed to assist your learning. Try to spend enough time on the questions to reinforce the points which are made in the workbook. Allow about 2 hours to read through the topics, and about 3–4 hours to complete the tasks which have been set.

Unlike other areas of marketing communications, it is somewhat more difficult to identify tangible examples of public relations activities in the media. Despite this, it is important that you develop a number of specific illustrations which you can use to clarify your answers. Some of these will be found in this unit, others in textbooks. However, it will be of considerable benefit for you to develop your own examples.

Take care to read through newspapers and examine other media for instances where public relations may have been the source of the story. Try to imagine how the information was conveyed, and the intention of the source in providing the material. In some instances it may be possible to track a story over time, especially in the case of a major news event relating to an organization. Where possible, maintain a file so that you can explore how the story develops and identify the final outcome.

In the course of this unit, we will consider some of the important dimensions of public relations. Two specific areas, those of corporate communications and crisis management, although considered by some as public relations functions, are here separated out from the main body of public relations because, although they may depend in large measure on the techniques of public relations, they also call upon other marketing communications techniques. Both these topics will be considered in more detail in Unit 11.

DEFINITION 10.1

certain. **defi**
lefinition *n.* s
precise mea
distinct, clea
lefinitive *a.* fi
something; r

The Institute of Public Relations defines public relations as: 'The deliberate, planned and sustained effort to establish and maintain mutual understanding between an organization and its publics.'

Although this is the definition of the main professional body, we might take issue with it. The Public Relations Society of America adopts a broader based definition and, more importantly, identifies a series of specific functions relating to public relations.

- Anticipating, analysing and interpreting public opinion, attitudes and issues which might impact, for good or ill, the operations and plans of the organization.
- Counselling management at all levels with regard to policy decisions, courses of action and communication.
- Researching, conducting and evaluating, on a continuing basis, programmes of action and communication to achieve informed public understanding necessary for the success of the organization's aims.
- Planning and implementing the organization's efforts to influence or change public policy.
- Managing the resources needed to perform the functions of public relations.

It is important to make a distinction between public relations and publicity. In simple terms, *publicity* may be any form of information from an outside source used by the news media. It is largely uncontrollable, since the source of the news item will have little control over how and when the story will be used and, most importantly, on how it will be interpreted. Although much public relations is concerned with the gaining of publicity, not all publicity derives from public relations. The responsibility of public relations is to create and influence publicity in such a way that it has a positive impact on the company for which the activity is undertaken.

QUESTION 10.1

- What are the differences between public relations and publicity?
- How does an organization generate publicity for its activities?

The 'publics' of public relations

It is clear that public relations programmes relate to a variety of different audiences, each of which may represent a different role in terms of the effectiveness of the overall campaign. It is important to remember that not all publics will be important at the same time, and part of the public relations process must be to identify and prioritize the specific audiences for a particular campaign message.

In the planning of a public relations campaign, any or all of the following may be targeted as recipients of the desired message:

- Employees and potential employees.
- Shareholders and investors.
- Suppliers to the company.
- Distributors of the company's products and services.
- Buyers and consumers.
- The local community.
- The national community.
- Opinion formers.
- The media – local, national and international.

QUESTION 10.2

- How are the 'publics' of public relations identified?
- What are their roles in relation to each other?

The nature of the audiences will, similarly, depend on the nature of the organization's activities. A large commercial company will, at different times, seek to communicate with some or all of those listed above. A smaller company may have a narrower base against which to target its message. A charity, similarly, will generally seek to influence a somewhat more limited group of publics. As with a commercial organization, these will include those who work for the body, the general public – although focused on those who are currently (or in the future) likely to be interested in the aims of the charity – opinion formers who might impact on the latter group and the media in general.

A key issue will the identification of the primary audience for a particular public relations campaign. Although in may instances these will be those people likely to be affected by the activities (or lack of action) undertaken by an organization, often they may be a different group which, by virtue of its standing or reputation, may be able to influence the opinions and attitudes of others. For example, a company wishing to secure a land site to extend its business operations will recognize that its audience will embrace all those likely to be affected. However, the primary audience is likely to be those decision makers (possibly in local or national government) who will determine whether the expansion can be permitted or not.

The functions of public relations

Public relations may, at different times, fulfil a variety of different functions. The following list identifies some of the most important aspects of public relations but, undoubtedly, there will be a number of other activities which might be added:

- Opinion forming.
- Counselling senior management.
- Liaison with public officials.
- Communications policies.
- Community relations.
- In-house activities.
- Product or service publicity.
- Financial activity.
- Media relations.
- Event management.
- Business sponsorship.

QUESTION 10.3

Identify the key roles of public relations.

Opinion forming

An increasing thrust of contemporary society is the development of opinions concerning governmental policies, the activities of companies and organizations and other aspects beyond the nature of the products and services which those companies produce. To the extent that companies operate within the bounds of public attitudes, it is likely that the products they manufacture will be well received (or at least favourably considered). The converse, however, is equally true. Organizations must, increasingly, recognize that they cannot sit idly by ignoring the underlying attitudinal changes which are taking place within society. In fact, it is increasingly important that they take a proactive approach to shape and form those opinions.

Whilst few would doubt that positive moves to protect various aspects of the environment will improve society in general, the desire for rapid change (beyond, say, the state of technological knowledge) may impact unfavourably on an organization's performance. To counter the possible dangers, companies must continuously seek to demonstrate, for example, how they are responding to these environmental pressures but, at the same time, ensure that the various publics are made aware of the possible consequences of the abandonment of current technology.

Counselling senior management

More and more companies are recognizing that all aspects of their internal and external actions are likely to have an impact on the public's perceptions of their organizations. Senior management must be continuously aware that they must frame their activities in a way which makes them, as far as possible, both socially and politically acceptable. Public relations counselling can make an important contribution not only to the way in which companies behave, but also to the way in which they communicate their activities.

The recent adverse publicity which has surrounded the departure of a number of senior managers with multi-million pound pay-offs has, for example, resulted in a number of organizations giving careful consideration to the management's remuneration packages.

Liaison with public officials

Many decisions which affect the company require either the positive decision of local and national officials or, at least, their tacit acceptance. Maintaining close and realistic relationships with local and central government officials and other regulatory bodies is a key dimension of positive public relations.

Communications policies

As we will see in Unit 11, which deals with corporate communications, it is not just the specifics of communication which must be addressed, but the framework in which such communications activity takes place. Public relations, therefore, is a key management function which, potentially, can influence all aspects of the organization's internal and external communications. The image and identity of an organization is, increasingly, recognized as a vital dimension of its commercial well-being.

Your company is involved in the business-to-business sector. Recently it has dveloped a new process for recycling glass products which is both more economical and efficient than other methods. How would you set about developing a public relations campaign to explain the process, and who are your key target audiences?

Community relations

No organization exists in isolation of the various communities within which it exists. Like other aspects of its operations, these are multi-dimensional.

On one level, the company operates within a localized environment. It is simultaneously an employer and a source of local income and wealth; and it is the user of a variety of resources which may affect community life. The siting of a manufacturing plant may, for example, result in heavy lorries having to travel down narrow country lanes, possibly to the detriment of local residents. It may be the source of a variety of community benefits, which enhance its reputation in its immediate area – the traditional provision of clubs and other facilities enhanced the early reputation of companies such as Cadbury's and others,

A company will often possess membership of trade and similar organizations which will respond, variously, to the activities of the company in relation to its other members.

In an international context, the company may serve as the 'representative' of the national identity in the countries in which it operates.

Identify stories currently being reported in the media where public relations is the likely source. Consider both general stories and those in the financial press.

In-house activities

Most companies recognize the need to maintain positive relationships with all the members of its staff. Rather than distancing management, the role of public relations will be to explain and secure support for the variety of management decisions which will be taken. Often the organ for such communications will be some form of in-house journal designed to create a bond between the people who work within the organization.

Product or service publicity

The external perception of public relations is its involvement with the creation of publicity for the products and services which the company provides. Whilst this is undeniably an important aspect of public relations, it is only one dimension of public relations activity.

Financial activity

To varying degrees, companies are dependent on the interpretation of their activities – positive or negative – by financial analysts, in order to secure additional funding or to maintain the value of their shares. Public relations can seek to maintain and improve these relationships and ensure that the financial sector is provided with relevant and appropriate information upon which to base their judgements.

Media relations

The appearance of positive publicity for a company or organization does not happen by chance. Invariably, it is the result of carefully nurtured relationships between the various media and the company over a long period of time. Journalists, like others, are people with opinions. How they interpret, for example, a press release will be affected by the underlying views of the organization responsible for creating the release. Even positive news may be interpreted negatively, if the opinions held towards the company are unfavourable.

Event management

An increasingly important aspect of public relations activity is the management of events, either on a local or national basis. Most often, such events are used to create positive relationships between the company and one or more of its target audiences, often of an 'informal' nature. The company may, for example, invite staff, key suppliers, retailers or others to some 'entertainment' event during which social relationships can be established to reinforce the day-to-day business relationships which exist.

Business sponsorship

A similarly important area of activity is that of creating business sponsorships which serve to associate the company with some specific activity designed to enhance the image associations of the organization. Inevitably there is some degree of overlap between this and the previously mentioned area, although they may well be separate and distinct.

The public relations process

The development of effective public relations campaigns, like that of all other aspects of marketing communications, is dependent on the adoption of a systematic approach towards the public relations process.

As such, it consists of four sequential stages – as shown in Figure 10.1.

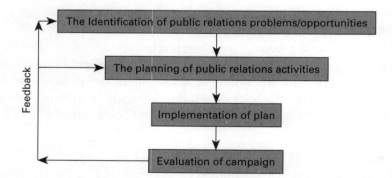

Figure 10.1

The identification of public relations problems and opportunities

Effective public relations is a continuous process, relying on a continuous examination of the relationships which an organization maintains between itself and its various publics. As with other areas, it is important to ensure that feedback mechanisms are used so that the company is aware – at the earliest possible opportunity – of any concerns which might exist in relation to the organization, or of opportunities which may exist for it to enhance its reputation. It has to be said that, to a somewhat lesser degree than in other areas of marketing communications, the techniques of market research are used to provide this feedback.

To quote Cutlip, Centre and Broom in *Effective Public Relations* (Prentice Hall, 1985): 'Historically, few practitioners have studied research methods. Moreover, many employers and clients view research as unnecessary. . . . For years, executives and practitioners alike bought the popular myth that public relations deals with intangibles that cannot be measured'. In all practical terms, the application of market research to identify problems and opportunities, and to evaluate programmes of activity is as important here as in other aspects of marketing communications.

The starting point for any public relations campaign activity must be the appropriate use of research to identify possible causes of concern with the organization or its operations amongst the various publics with which it deals. Until the organization is aware of the nature of the concerns, and can identify the specific identity of the publics who are affected, then appropriate campaign activity cannot be planned. By the same token, the use of similar research approaches will identify particular areas of opportunity which might present the company with the means of enhancing or changing its reputation.

- What is the role of market research in public relations?
- Why are the techniques often not used?

QUESTION 10.5

Programme planning

The development of a cohesive and effective public relations plan is dependent, as we have seen, on a thorough understanding of the audiences for the campaign message. Here, as elsewhere, the adoption of an orderly approach will greatly assist both in determining the specific campaign objectives and in monitoring the extent to which they are achieved (Figure 10.2).

The situational analysis, both of the internal and external aspects of the operations, will identify any areas of shortfall between the desired image and the actual image. Only then will it be possible to begin the process of identifying campaign objectives and, with them, the target audiences for campaign activity. The latter may be, as we have already seen, those people who are directly affected by the activities of the organization, although in some instances it may be preferable to target some group of opinion formers who, in turn, will impact upon that group.

The selection of the strategy will depend on a series of key dimensions:

- The specific nature of the objectives. Secondly, the skills required.
- Will the company implement the programme using only its internal resources, or will it employ an external public relations consultancy?
- The scale of the budget.

Once these factors have been considered and resolved, the identification of specific campaign components can commence. It will be important to remember that the campaign elements, although desirably cohesive in terms of the message, may well need to be varied to reflect the different values of the groups to whom the messages are targeted.

Using the example of a company wishing to expand its local operational base, the message to the local community (and local government decision makers) may revolve around the benefits of increasing local employment opportunities; to the financial community (from whom the funding may be sourced) the nature of the message may be the profitability which will result from expansion; and so on.

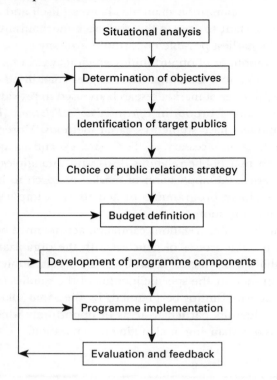

Figure 10.2

ACTIVITY 10.4

Identify two examples of instances where public relations have been important. These may be negative public relations, such as that affecting the Reed Group or the British Airways 'dirty tricks' campaign, or positive public relations.

Once the selected programme has been determined and implemented, it will be important to monitor the effectiveness of the campaign activity. In the short term, it may be necessary to refine specific elements to ensure the achievement of the campaign objectives. In the longer term, it is important to assess whether the overall objectives were met, how each of the campaign elements performed, and the cost-effectiveness of the campaign.

The management of public relations

To a much greater degree than in other areas of the marketing communications process, the management of public relations remains, for many, the preserve of the senior management team. As we will see below, in the area of financial public relations this is not surprising. There is little doubt that, to achieve the benefits of integration, public relations activities must command the full attention and support of the management of the company. However, other than in the smallest companies, the task of public relations demands a higher volume of input than can be provided by senior management. To meet these demands, varying structures have been established within organizations, although in the majority of instances the senior management remains involved – at least in the strategic direction of activities.

Many large companies maintain a *public relations department* which is responsible for all aspects of communications with its internal and external publics. In effect, they act as the interface between senior management and the various publics, although for the most part, this can be taken to mean the media. They are often responsible for co-ordinating the in-house publications; developing appropriate press releases to draw attention to company news stories; preparing the annual financial report; and, sometimes, having the responsibility for the implementation of the company identity programme.

An alternative approach is the appointment of a specialist *public relations consultancy*. These will be appointed either to fulfil a specific programme of activity which has been developed against a company brief, or to assume the day-to-day responsibilities which would otherwise be carried out by the internal public relations department. It should be recognized that such input is not without cost. The fees charged by the larger consultancies will often run into several hundreds of thousands of pounds, to which must be added the physical costs of the materials produced (press releases, photography, travel, etc.).

A compromise approach is most commonly adopted, in which the in-house operation deals with the day-to-day public relations requirements, and a consultancy is appointed to take responsibility for the more strategic issues that require to be addressed.

What approaches can management take towards the handling of its public relations activites?

What are the advantages and disadvantages of each approach?

QUESTION 10.5

Financial public relations

In recent years financial public relations has emerged as a specialist function within the broader field of public relations. This is a direct consequence of the greater importance of the financial institutions and the financial press in the well-being of companies. Associated with this has been the recent spate of flotations by large public institutions (e.g. the Water Authorities and British Telecom) the scale of which has demanded specialized attention to achieve the desired objectives.

The responsibility for this aspect of public relations is largely assumed by the key members of the management team (chairman, managing director, financial director, corporate affairs director). Since these people are regarded as the primary determiners of company policy, they are often assumed to personify the strategic direction of the organization. Mostly, however, the primary focus rests with the chief executive. Sir Colin Southgate at Thorn EMI, Lord Young at Cable and Wireless, Sir Alan Sheppard at Grand Metropolitan and Lord Hanson of the Hanson Trust, are all examples of this.

Financial public relations deals specifically with four identified publics – the City, the shareholders, the staff and employees and, of course, the financial journalists. The *City* remains the focal point for all activity, since it represents the means whereby the company can communicate effectively with its main audiences. Amongst these are the financial analysts and stock-broking houses whose advice is key to the desired outcome. Ensuring that they are provided with important financial information on a frequent basis is the key to the maintenance of a company's financial reputation. Their advice and action will, in turn, impact on two further areas: the volume of *institutional investors* who maintain the majority shareholdings in most publicly quoted companies; and, the *private investors* whose actions, for the most part, rely on the advice of city specialists. Equally important are the *financial journalists*. In many cases these are non-specialist writers who rely for much of their information on the reports and comments of the city analysts whose advice is considered as independent and credible.

Financial public relations remains a key strategic issue for many organizations. Its purpose is to promote the reputation and financial stability of the company and, inherently, needs to take on long-term dimensions.

What are the roles of public relations in the context of an organization's financial activities?

QUESTION 10.6

Charity public relations

Charitable organizations and other non-profit organizations are prime users of public relations activities. Although, with the recent relaxation of advertising regulations, these bodies are now able to access the media through conventional advertising routes, the costs are often prohibitive. Public relations (together with direct marketing activities) represent a more cost-effective route to their communications needs.

A primary requirement of charitable bodies is the need to raise funds to finance their main activities. At the same time, however, it is important for such organizations to ensure the continued participation of their supporters to enable their aims to be fulfilled. Since the majority of charities depend both on voluntary contributions and voluntary participation, activity is needed which will maintain interest in the areas of concern.

Clearly in this context publicity must be generated which will expose the work of the charity to a wider audience to enable a fuller understanding of the operation. Not only will this be designed to secure wider approval of the charity's actions, it will also aim to secure continued funding and participation. In some instances, special events will be staged to provide exposure for these activities. Sometimes, these will take the form of 'static' displays featuring some of their achievements. For example, the Council for the Protection of Rural England (CPRE) has mounted a series of photographic exhibitions, both to highlight its work and to focus attention on areas of the country which are under threat. Other charitable bodies have staged more participatory activities – such as 'fun runs', charity walks and similar events – to achieve fund-raising objectives. In all cases, the use of public relations must relate to the strategic aims of the organization. It is important that any such events are designed to fulfil specific objectives which relate to the overall goals.

QUESTION 10.7

Define the functions of public relations in contributing to the communication of the aims of a charitable organization.

Event management and business sponsorship

As noted above, event management and sponsorship are areas which are attracting increased attention in the field of public relations.

At the lowest level, *event management* is the creation, implementation and administration of short-term activities designed to promote the organization. In some instances, these will be specially created to provide a vehicle for 'hospitality' which can be extended to clients and customers of the organization. In others, they will take the form of participation in conferences and exhibitions the themes of which are relevant to the functions of the company. Such activities may have different aims and objectives, and it is important that the company should understand, in advance, the reasons for its participation.

Hospitality events provide the opportunity for the organization to express its gratitude to those people who have assisted it in achieving its aims in the past or those who it is hoped will provide assistance in the future. Often, these events will take the form of sporting or other 'entertainments' in which the company can participate by purchasing admission tickets and inviting its own guests (several companies, for example, purchase block tickets for events such as Wimbledon or the British Grand Prix). In some instances, they will be specially organized events which are only available to invited guests of the company.

QUESTION 10.8

Conferences and exhibitions are an important vehicle for communication. Discuss the public relations context.

Many commercial organizations mount periodic events at major venues which have a special appeal to a specific audience. *Exhibitions* and *conferences* staged at such venues as Earls Court, Olympia or the NEC in Birmingham may be used either simply to gain exposure for the products and services of the company, or to mount activities similar to those described above.

Sponsorship is a more embracing activity, and often involves the organization in substantial levels of expenditure. It is the association of the company or organization with some third-party activity, designed to achieve a series of separate but mutually agreed objectives.

QUESTION 10.9

What are the benefits and drawbacks of sponsorship activites?

Inevitably, sponsorship may take a wide variety of forms. For example, it may be the re-naming of an established event to feature the name of the company or organization which, in return for an annual or other payment, takes 'ownership' of the event. Recent examples are the Carling sponsorship of the Premier Football League, TSB's involvement in athletics, Budweiser's sponsorship of American football, and the Skoda snooker grand prix. The sponsor seeks to achieve either name recognition or image association by their involvement with some particular sporting or other event. Such sponsorship may take on global proportions, as with the recent involvement of McDonald's and Coca Cola in the football world cup.

Company involvement with charitable bodies is another important form of sponsorship activity. In these instances, the organization promotes the aims of the charity with the objective of raising funds, for example. The objective is similar to other forms of sponsorship activity in which the sponsor seeks to achieve image benefits as a result of its association with the aims and objectives of the charity with which it participates. Examples are the involvement of Tesco with Save The Children, and Texaco's association with the Royal Society for the Prevention of Accidents and so on. Sometimes, sponsorship involvement is specifically designed to gain media exposure which might not otherwise be possible.

Sporting and cultural events gain considerable levels of coverage in the media. The featuring of the sponsor's name alongside the event may generate a level of mentions worth hundreds of thousands of pounds. In some cases, such activity will be undertaken by products whose media activities are otherwise circumscribed – cigarette brands, for example, gain exposure on television from which they are banned in terms of advertising.

A new form of sponsorship activity has emerged recently with the decision to allow companies to sponsor television and radio programmes. Here the objective is to derive benefit from the association of the company name and a programme which has relevance to a desired target audience.

ACTIVITY 10.5

You are the marketing manager of a car manufacturer and responsible for the launch of a new small vehicle. Identify your approach to the selection of an activity to sponsor on behalf of the new car.

Other forms of sponsorship may include professional awards, educational awards, books and publications (for example, the Shell Egon Ronay Guide and the Guinness Book of Records), and a wide variety of local events. As with other forms of public relations activity, such involvement must be planned against a series of clearly identified objectives and monitored to ensure that these objectives are fulfilled cost-effectively.

Integration of public relations activities

It is extremely unusual for companies to use the tools of public relations in isolation from other forms of marketing communications. To achieve the maximum benefit from the activities, it is important that they are carefully planned to ensure thorough integration. This inevitably demands that all parties to the communications process work together to ensure that the objectives are mutually understood and realized.

Undeniably, public relations activities can make a major contribution to the overall effectiveness of communications campaigns. Often, they can achieve a level of credibility for the activity which does not derive from other forms of marketing communications. However, to achieve this effect, common strategic goals must be determined and the same principles of research and evaluation applied to the tool of public relations as to other areas of the communications mix.

International public relations

As marketing activity increasingly takes on global dimensions, so too public relations must be considered as a vital ingredient in the global marketing communications mix. Public relations activities can be used to target important areas of influence and decision making in a cost-effective manner, often in advance of a product's launch into a foreign market. As such, it can provide a foundation against which other marketing and marketing communications activities can function effectively.

Public relations may provide the vehicle for adapting a global message to achieve local impact, thus assisting the process of ensuring the acceptance of a global brand in markets in which cultural and other factors may inhibit the potential for growth.

SUMMARY

In this unit we have seen that:

- Public relations must be seen as an important dimension of marketing communications and, as with other aspects of market communications, must operate against a sound basis of planning and evaluation.
- Public relations provides the opportunity to communicate with a wide variety of different publics with whom the company or organization must deal on a consistent and regular basis.
- Identifying the nature of the audiences, and the nature of the message to be communicated, is an important aspect of the public relations process.
- Compared with other forms of marketing communications, control of the outcome of public relations is far more restricted. The issuing of a press release itself can never guarantee either the appearance of the story or, if it does appear, that the interpretation will be one which favours the organization.
- Good public relations is dependent on establishing good relationships with the various audiences with which the organization must communicate. Inevitably, this takes both time and money.
- Increasingly, practitioners recognize that to fulfil the necessary requirements they must draw upon the benefits of the tools of market research, both to assist in the process of planning activity, and to ensure the evaluation of campaigns during and after their completion.

Examination hints and specimen questions

Two example questions relating to public relations activities are included below. Remember, that the priority in answering these questions, as with others in the Diploma paper, is to deal with the *strategic issues*. Certainly, you may wish to illustrate your answer with the techniques which would be employed to achieve the identified objectives, but the description of the planning process and the identification of the appropriate strategy will ensure that you gain the highest possible marks.

As with previous questions, allow no more than 30 minutes for each, and remember to prepare a structure before you begin to write your answer.

Livewire is a scheme supported by Shell that is designed to encourage young people to consider self-employment. There are two elements to the scheme. Firstly, each young person is allocated an individual voluntary adviser. Secondly, Livewire participants are encouraged to join a competition which awards grants to the best business plans. Acting as a consultant, submit the outline of a public relations programme to generate and sustain interest and support for the Livewire scheme on a national basis.

(December 1993)

An international children's charity, Dr Barnado's, which has been in existence for over 100 years, has decided that it needs to update its identity. The goal is to replace the former orphan image with an accurate perception of the charity's innovative childcare work. Acting in the role of a consultant, suggest ideas for a public relations plan which uses the change of identity as a public relations platform to relaunch the charity.

(June 1993)

Many of the general texts recommended in previous units contain sections on public relations. For a more in-depth text, you might wish to consider:

R. Haywood, *All About Public Relations*, 2nd end, McGraw Hill, 1990.
Institute of Public Relations, *Institute of Public Relations Handbook*, Kogan Page, 1992.
M. Nally, *International Public Relations in Practice*, Kogan Page, 1991.

The development of corporate image and identity

Increasing importance is being attached to the areas of corporate image and crisis management. In this unit, which is designed to improve your understanding of both these topics, you will:

- Identify the importance of corporate communications.
- Examine the means by which organizations communicate with their various publics, and the various media which need to be considered.
- Review the relationships between an organization and its brands.
- Determine the process of creating a corporate identity and the objectives of corporate communications.
- Consider the contribution of market research.
- Examine the role of crisis management and its key dimensions, and consider the process of handling a crisis.

By the end of this unit you will:

- Have a comprehensive understanding of the areas of corporate image and crisis management.
- Be able to apply this learning to real situations.

The topics covered by this unit represent an important aspect of marketing communications, and the Chief Examiner frequently sets questions either explicitly on these areas or within the framework of a broader question to test your understanding. It is important that you attempt to answer the various questions and activities set within the unit before you tackle the example questions which have been extracted from recent examination papers.

As with the other units, do not try to rush this work. Spread it out over a few days and try to read around the subject in newspapers and magazines. There are frequent articles on aspects of corporate communications. Allow about 3 hours to read through the unit, and the same again to carry out the various activities.

The task of learning a new topic is a difficult one, especially if you are not familiar with the area. For this reason, the workload in this unit has been divided up into separate sections, and the various questions and activities have been designed to reinforce your learning.

Make sure that you develop your own examples to use in the examination, rather than simply repeating those covered here. The examiner wants to see that you can apply your knowledge to the types of situation described in the questions, rather than simply writing out long lists of points – only some of which are relevant!

Recent years have seen an increasing role for corporate advertising, and an increasing recognition of the importance of developing a corporate identity. When these tasks are carried out effectively and efficiently, they are the epitome of good integrated marketing communications. The process is an important one, and has significant strategic implications. Above all, it is the means by which an organization communicates the very nature of itself to its various publics. Importantly, it is more than just a change of logo, the typeface used on the company letterheads, or the external colour of the corporate headquarters. The task is, primarily, to ensure the consistency of communication across all media of a common message to a variety of audiences.

Corporate identity is the programme of communication and change that a company undertakes, sometimes in conjunction with an external consultancy. An organization's identity is its sense of self formed by its history, its beliefs, its philosophy, the nature of its technology, its ownership, its ethical and cultural values, its people, the personality of the leaders, and its strategies (adapted from Nicholas Ind, *The Corporate Image: Strategies for Effective Identity Programmes*, Kogan Page, 1992).

There are sound commercial and communications reasons for this increased level of interest. There has been an increasing recognition that consumers choose between the various products and services available to them for a wide variety of reasons. Not all of these are derived exclusively from the product or service itself. In many purchase situations, company recognition and image are important factors in the decision-making process. Moreover, as the costs of marketing communications increases, the ability of a company to provide support for all the products in its portfolio becomes more remote.

The market segment, whilst profitable, may be too limited to justify media expenditure. Or the share of market might be too small to fund a marketing communications campaign. Those brands which are embraced by an identifiable and positive corporate identity will tend to be chosen by consumers in a purchasing environment over those which have no identity or which stand alone. This may be exemplified in the purchase of a medicinal product. Whether it is taken to alleviate the symptoms of the common cold or to relieve a headache, the nature of consumption attaches considerable importance to the purchase decision. Familiarity with the corporate name of Smith Kline Beecham or Fisons will help overcome the relative unfamiliarity of names such as Venos Cough Mixture, Ralgex or Opticrom.

Look out for some brands which are owned by large companies. Identify how the company image affects your perceptions of their brands.

ACTIVITY 11.1

A further impetus to the process has come from the expanding rate of globalization. Mergers and acquisitions, together with organic growth, have resulted in many corporate operations opening up in different parts of the world. As operations expand and become more dispersed, there is an inherent danger that each operating unit, by retaining responsibility for its own communications programme, produces materials which are inconsistent with other parts of the operation. The development of a cohesive corporate identity programme has the twin benefits of avoiding inconsistencies and of binding the diverse parts of the operation together. The alternative is the lack of a shared identity, with the risk that the operations move apart and the benefits of globalization are lost.

Inherent in this statement, however, is the recognition of the need for corporate identity programmes to work across national divides, and with different languages and cultures. Not only words, but symbols and colours may communicate a different impression from the one intended and desired. There is a need to ensure that companies in competing industries identify a means of differentiating themselves from each other. But it must be remembered that image and identity change are no panacea for other ills. A simple audit of the present identity will establish whether images perceived by the target audiences are positive or negative. In the latter instance work needs to be done to enhance the image. However, if the reality falls short of the image – actual or desired – then it is clear that there is a fundamental problem within the organization which needs to be addressed. The corporate identity can provide the focus for the organization and provide a unique position in the marketplace. In many respects the corporate identity reflects the personalities and values which are associated with a company.

ACTIVITY 11.2

Think of some global companies. What image do you have of their organizations?

Anita Roddick and the emotional values she projects have become synonymous with the corporate identity of Bodyshop – the company she founded. In the same way, Virgin and Richard Branson are inextricably linked together, as are Alan Sugar and Amstrad. It is obvious that companies communicate, whether they do so deliberately, or by default. The issue to be addressed is how companies go about the process of communicating to their various publics.

QUESTION 11.1

Why do charities need to be concerned about their image?

Comparatively few companies have a corporate communications strategy, although the number that do is growing along with the recognition of the importance of the area. The result is that the image and identity which many companies portray is one that 'happens' rather than one which is deliberately fostered for the overall benefit of the company.

Several years ago, the then Chief Executive of GrandMet saw a refuse disposal lorry bearing the corporate name. As part of its diversification at that time, the company had entered a number of service areas which delivered to the overall income. However, it was recognized that the lorry would be seen by, amongst others, people in the city or in the media, and that the image conveyed would be contrary to the one desired. It didn't take long before a directive was issued, not only to remove the GrandMet name from the rubbish van, but from all other operating companies that did not have permission to use it. Although this is a long way short of developing a proper corporate identity programme, it was the first step in the appreciation of the fact that all means of communication impact on the various publics who are exposed to them.

Companies which don't communicate – internally or externally – do a great disservice to themselves. A lack of communications may often be interpreted as negative communications, implying that the organization has something to hide. If a company says nothing about an issue, its publics will infer a response. Increasingly, the public is becoming more concerned with how a company relates to it, and the beliefs that it holds or the actions that it takes, than simply with the nature and quality of the products or services it provides.

David Ogilvy, in his excellent book *Ogilvy on Advertising* says:

> Big corporations are increasingly under attack – from consumer groups, from environmentalists, from government, from antitrust legislators – who try their cases in the media. If a big corporation does not take the initiative in cultivating its reputation, its case goes by default.

Bob Worcester of Market and Opinion Research International (MORI) who, for many years have conducted specific studies into aspects of corporate image and identity, suggests three elements of corporate advertising:

- This is who we are.
- This is what we can do for you.
- This is what we think.

Corporate advertising is only one of the means by which a company communicates with its various publics.

What are the key dimensions of company image?

QUESTION 11.2

David Bernstein (*Corporate Image and Reality*, Cassell, 1989) identifies nine distinct media which serve to communicate and convey a company image:

- **The products the company produces**   Every company offers a range of products or services to its customers. The perceived quality of the products and the way in which they are presented underpin or diminish the identity of the parent company. If a consumer has a poor experience or image of a product or service which is closely identified with its provider, their perceptions of that company will be diminished.
- **Its correspondence**   The materials used for correspondence – the letterheads, envelopes, etc. – as well as the style and content, will impact on the image of the company.
- **Public relations**   The image of an organization will be substantially influenced by the relationships which it has with its various publics. A company which has a good, open and honest reputation is likely to be regarded as producing good products; the opposite is equally true.
- **Personal presentation**   Many companies are, quite rightly, concerned with the way that people who represent the company present themselves. Shoddy dress, poor use of language – written and verbal – poor manners, and so on will reflect adversely on the company they personify.
- **Impersonal presentation**   The same principles apply equally to the intangible aspects of a company's presentation. The style of its buildings, company vehicles, offices, etc., will all depict the stature of the organization to others.
- **Literature**   All companies produce large quantities of printed material, from brochures and annual reports to leaflets and handouts. The care and attention which goes into those items will reflect favourably or unfavourably on the way in which the company is perceived. Quality materials tend to evoke a positive response. Items produced 'on the cheap' are likely to undermine the image.

- **Point-of-sale material** Point-of-sale material designed to support a product or service at the point of purchase will have the same impact as other items of literature. Shoddily produced items - even though cheap to create – can do a great deal of harm to both the brand and the company's identity in the minds of those who see it.
- **Permanent media** Permanent media comprise signage, showcases and other items which are on continuous display. Sometimes, although not always, old-fashioned typefaces and logo styles will present the company as possessing a similar identity. Care must be taken not to confuse heritage and history with an old-fashioned image although, even in the former case, attention to detail is important and a 'quality heritage' may need to be modernized from time to time.
- **Advertising** Advertising is the focal point of communication for many organizations. The style and tone will say as much about the nature of the company as will the content of the message.

QUESTION 11.3

All companies must communicate – but to whom? List the various audiences for a corporate communications message.

In the same book, Bernstein identifies nine different audiences for corporate communications:

- **Internal** Many companies tend to forget that their staff and workforce all represent potential ambassadors for the organization. If employees have a positive relationship with their employer, they will tend to communicate a favourable impression. To engender such feelings, it is vitally important that employees feel involved with the company and, wherever possible, are exposed to the company's thinking at regular intervals.
- **Local** Companies need to develop positive relationships with the community in which they exist. If, for example, the company is seen to be a contributor to the local economy, they will tend to receive more support for things such as planning applications.
- **Influential groups** Whether on a local or a national basis, there will be a variety of external bodies which will have an impact on the company's activities. These may consist, amongst others, of pressure groups and public officials. Their relationships to and perceptions of the organization will have an impact on the way that they respond to the company's activities. Shell, for example, have cultivated a positive relationship over many years with environmental groups who, in turn, have been more supportive than might otherwise have been the case.
- **The 'trade'** Most companies are dependent on wholesalers, retailers and others who act as the intermediaries between them and their ultimate customers. The cultivation of good relationships and a positive image will be an important factor in gaining their support.
- **Government** The actions of central government will have a marked impact on company performance. The introduction of unfavourable legislation may well diminish a company's profitability. The support of government agencies who represent companies in overseas markets, for example, may be pivotal in gaining major foreign contracts.
- **The media** The media, in general, are the recipients of a variety of messages concerning a company. Some messages derive from positive public relations activities, others from impressions received from other sources. The interpretation the media place on stories about the company will have a substantial impact on the way in which those messages are communicated.
- **Financial** The financial community will require a great deal of information about a company, both regarding its past performance and its prospects for the future. In

order to secure a continued flow of investment, these relationships will need to be developed to ensure a positive response to company actions.

- **Customers** We have already seen that, to an increasing degree, customers are concerned as much about the nature of the company, the actions it takes on important issues, and its general beliefs, as with the quality of the products and services it produces. Because of the recent focus on environmental issues, companies have been able to secure positive images (and negative ones) from the actions they have taken in this area. In turn, this is likely to impact on the sales volume they achieve. Remember, there are always alternatives available, and a company which is received poorly may well find that its customers turn to others to obtain products and services.
- **The general public** The image of the company to the general public is of similar importance. Ultimately, for many companies, the general public are their consumers. How a company is thought of will often determine whether people purchase from that company or another. Periodic research, such as that carried out by the MORI, repeatedly demonstrates that companies with a positive image are expected to produce 'better quality' products.

How does a corporate campaign (such as that run recently by the Hanson Trust or ICI) affect perceptions of the company?

Many organizations simply assume that they need only communicate when they want to. However, it is inevitable that deliberate and unintended messages get through to audiences all the time. Failure to control all aspects of the communications process may result in the offsetting of those aspects of communications which are more within the company's control, such as advertising and public relations, and result in a confused image.

The recent adverse publicity associated with Group 4 following its appointment to transport remand prisoners to their court appearances and the subsequent escape of some of their charges had a negative impact on the way people perceived the company and the services it provided.

What are the dangers inherent in an organization's failure to adopt a positive approach to corporate communications?

Shell has been consistent, both in its advertising and in its other activities, in identifying itself with environmental issues and concerns. The result has been the creation of a very favourable and positive image of an environmentally friendly and caring organization. The change of image and identity of British Petroleum to BP has moved the company into somewhat similar territory.

Corporate image is the feeling and representation that the various publics may hold about a company, and is the result of the aggregation of all the messages they receive about that company.

157

It is important to remember that corporate identity and corporate strategy will be closely related to each other. The strategic direction of an organization will be influenced by its identity, whilst its identity will be affected by the nature of the strategy.

A core strategic decision which an organization must take is its approach to the market. Wally Olins (*Corporate Identity*, Thames & Hudson, 1989) divides corporate identities into three distinct categories (Figure 11.1):

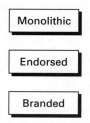

Figure 11.1

- **Monolithic**   The organization uses a single name and visual style throughout all its operations, where each item of communication that the company uses serves to reinforce the identity of the parent company. Examples would be those of IBM, BMW, Shell and Prudential.

- **Endorsed**   The organization maintains a separation between its subsidiary companies and the activities it pursues, but endorses those activities by the addition of the group name and identity alongside that of the operation company. Here, examples would be BAT and P&O. The former has diverse interests in the fields of tobacco, insurance, etc., and uses its corporate name to add stature and credibility. The latter, similarly, owns companies in areas such as housebuilding (Bovis), exhibition halls (Earls Court and Olympia) and others, alongside its more familiar cruise liners and cross-channel ferries. It is only in the last two operations that the P&O name is used directly. Elsewhere, the P&O logo and identity is used alongside the operating name.

- **Branded**   The company operates through a series of brands which may be unrelated to each other. Procter & Gamble owns operating companies in diverse markets such as soap powders, toiletries, perfumes, etc., with brands such as Oil of Ulay, Vidal Sassoon and Pantene. In some cases, the identities are deliberately kept distinct in order to enable products to compete in the same market. Unilever has adopted a similar posture.

The process of establishing a corporate identity

Having decided upon the corporate identity, the company must determine the best means of communicating that identity and its corporate strategy to its various audiences. The starting point is to consider all aspects of printed or visual communications in order to assess the consistency of the approach. It is inevitable that the larger the company, the more dispersed will be the responsibility for commissioning and producing these materials – with the consequent loss of consistency and the danger of delivering a confused message.

The organizational structure and the naming policies for the subsidiary operations needs to be examined in the light of the corporate strategy. Here again, it is important to ensure consistency. Many organizations have responded to this need by creating a corporate identity manual which embodies the look and style of the parent company and its subsidiaries.

ACTIVITY 11.3

Think of a recent example of a campaign to change opinions. This may have been conducted by a government body, company or a charity.

What opinions did it set out to change, and how did it seek to change them?

This approach provides both the focus for internal examination and ensures the consistent application of the principles in all forms of communication. At the same time, it will be possible to ensure that there is a logic and consistency in the visual representation of the organization in all printed materials such as letterheads, advertisements, mailers, etc. The question to be asked is whether all parts of the company look similar, or can they be seen as independent operations. In addition to ensuring that typography, colours and other aspects of printed communication are consistent in their representation of the corporate image, it is also important to question the tone of voice which is used in these materials. Does it convey a sympathetic feeling or does it stand in sharp contrast to other aspects of the image?

The objectives of corporate communications

What would a company seek to achieve by running a corporate communications campaign?

QUESTION 11.6

The process of developing a consistent corporate identity delivers many opportunities and advantages to the organization. The following is a list of the key objectives which may be met:

- *The creation of a strong internal identity.* Many organizations suffer from being dispersed, both nationally and internationally. The provision of a strong and consistent identity for all parts of the operation will serve to unify the attitudes, goals and motivations of the employees, and ensure that they feel part of an overall structure.
- *The enhancement of external awareness of the organization and an understanding of its businesses.* As has already been seen, the diffuse and diverse nature of communications may be inconsistent with the desire to present the company as a cohesive whole. A single organization will appear to be stronger if its component parts are unified in their representation to external audiences. Recently, a television campaign for Hanson has used a series of commercials featuring pastiches of famous films such as Orson Welles' *Citizen Kane* and *The Graduate* to communicate the diversity of Hanson's interests and activities.
- *Provision of flexibility for expansion.* This is especially important in a global context. The limitations imposed by, for example, a national name may inhibit the opportunities for expansion in overseas markets. The perceptions of British Petroleum are more narrow than those of BP, and BT has become a global player. Would the same opportunities be open to British Telecom or the Royal Mail? However, it is equally applicable to companies which may discover that their sphere of activities is restricted by their operating name. The change of the parent identity from Woolworth's to Kingfisher served to embrace a variety of acquisitions including Comet, Superdrug and B&Q alongside the original Woolworth's company, whilst removing the focus of attention from the latter – whose fortunes were less positive.
- *Integration of operations following merger or acquisition.* A singular corporate identity presents the opportunity to fuse acquisitions with existing operations and ensure a single consistent identity for the new company.
- *Enhancement of the share price or other financial aspects of the company in order to secure investment.* This issue is one which enjoys sharp focus at times of takeover bids or defences. In order to maximize the perceptions of corporate strength, the corporate identity will be a vehicle for raising awareness of different aspects of the operation.
- *To withstand or launch a takeover or merger.* Although the specific target audience, that is those with the power to influence the final outcome, may be small, the sphere of influence is much wider. Increasingly, takeovers are being fought out in public, with each of the participants seeking to communicate its virtues and strengths.

- *Communicating new strategies.* The recent demerger of ICI and the establishment of a separate operation – Zeneca – is a demonstration of the new corporate direction which the company proposes to take.
- *Advocating change.* Organizations may use corporate communication to encourage change – social, political, attitudinal – which may be useful to the organization or its publics. This area is particularly, although not exclusively, associated with charitable bodies. The recent campaigns conducted by the RSPCA designed to bring about the introduction of dog registration or the ending of live animal transportation are both examples. It also applies to advertising conducted at times of industrial unrest, to explain an organization's position in a dispute.
- *Resolving organizational structures.* The acquisition by Philip Morris of a number of companies within the food industry has been addressed by the change of identity in order to present a consistent approach to the various audiences. After operating as separate companies, Kraft was merged with General Foods to become KGF; the subsequent restructuring following the acquisition of Jacobs and Suchard has been resolved by naming the new company Kraft Jacobs Suchard.
- *Defining the positioning of the organization.* Corporate identity programmes enable the company to address what is, arguably, the single most important issue, i.e. their overall positioning, in order to present a unique identity.
- *To aid the process of recruitment and staff retention.* An organization which is seen to be well established or one which has a reputation for graduate recruitment and training will enhance its prospects of securing the best of each year's crop of potential applicants. Employees will be more likely to remain with a company which has a positive reputation in terms of its dealings with them.
- *Demonstration of the company's achievements or contributions to the economy.* Companies will use corporate communications to bring industry or national awards, e.g. the Queen's Award to Industry, to the attention of a wider public. By the same token, a particular policy to, for example, export more, or recycle waste, may be used as the basis for image enhancement.
- *To overcome poor attitudes towards a company.* This may be the result of previous poor performance in a particular area, of some form of crisis, or simply its failure to communicate effectively in the past.

Corporate communications is the process that translates corporate identity into corporate image.

In order to communicate with all of an organization's audiences, both internal and external, the process of communication must be addressed systematically. Although the process of design may be the initial focus of activity, corporate communications embraces far more than simply the change of name or logo. However, it is important to recognize that this process will result in a visual statement which identifies what the company stands for, and presents a consistent message to diverse audiences, including external audiences such as consumers, customers, suppliers and the financial sector, together with management and employees within the company.

Measuring corporate communications

How can market research help a company identify weaknesses in the perceptions held by external audiences?

As with other aspects of marketing communications, the application of scientific rigour is an important part of the process. Without proper measurement, few organizations can hold a true picture of the ways in which they are perceived by others. Indeed, research will assist in the identification of the key dimensions that are important to the various audiences, and that will provide the subsequent basis for defining the corporate communications programme.

Research will need to be undertaken amongst all possible audiences for the corporate message (see list above). The key dimensions of image can then be plotted against a multi-attribute scale, as shown in Figure 11.2.

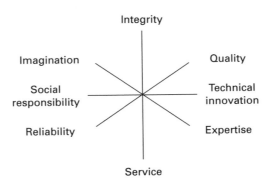

Figure 11.2

The next stage will be that of plotting the company's results on these image dimensions against the established scale (see Figure 11.3). Only then will it be possible to undertake the process of improving the perception of the organization in those areas which are seen to be weak. The process should be on-going. Not only do image values change as a result of both internal and external factors, but the scales themselves may differ over time.

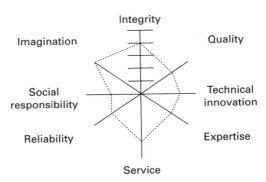

Figure 11.3

Not that long ago, few companies would have been concerned about the environmental issues relating to their operations. Today the increased importance which is attached to this area has forced companies to address this issue as a matter of urgency. Remember also that the strong and positive image attributes need to be maintained. The publics will have short memories and past strengths can soon be forgotten.

Corporate identity programmes should not be considered as the unique province of major manufacturers, or those involved within the field of fast-moving consumer goods. The process is equally applicable to both profit and non-profit organizations. One only has to look at work carried out by government departments (such as the Department of Trade and Industry), charitable bodies (Barnado's, World Wide Fund for Nature), trade unions (National Union of Teachers) and other organizations (British Rail, British Telecom) to recognize that their respective identities have all been re-examined and redesigned in order to convey the appropriate desired images to their target audiences.

Key aspects of corporate communications

- **The need for a long-term perspective** In a dynamic and changing environment, corporate communications activities must focus on the longer term aspirations of the organization. They must not inhibit change or potential movement into other operational areas.

- **Clear statement of objectives**   Effective corporate communications, like all other aspects of marketing communications, must be based on a series of clearly stated and quantifiable objectives.
- **Commitment of management**   Corporate communications is the embodiment of the corporate philosophy. The involvement of senior management in the process is imperative if the activities are to achieve the desired objectives.
- **Involvement of employees**   Steps must be taken to ensure the active and positive involvement of staff at all levels. People within the organization must feel a pride of ownership if the activity is to secure their support.
- **Consistency is paramount**   All aspects of the organization and its operations must be examined to ensure that the communications process provides a single unified view. In addition, all aspects of the communications process must be integrated to provide the consistency desired.
- **People and systems must be in place**   Corporate communications demand constant attention. They do not happen on their own. It is important that a process is established to ensure the consistency of approach and application in all areas of the company's operations.
- **Evaluation**   No marketing communications campaign is perfect, and this is no less true of corporate activities. A proper programme of research and assessment must be an integral part of the corporate communications plan. Feedback and revision will be essential components of successful implementation.
- **Only make changes for good reasons**   The oft quoted adage 'if it ain't broke, don't try to fix it' applies here. Changes to the strategy should only be made for solid reasons. Change for its own sake will often result in more problems being caused than resolved.

QUESTION 11.8

How can a company ensure that it presents a consistent message in its corporate communications campaign?

Crisis management

Crisis management is a further area of corporate communications which is increasingly becoming recognized as a major aspect of the management of corporate identity and image. Perrier in the UK, Tylenol in the USA, and Group 4 in the UK have all faced varying degrees of 'crisis' with which they have had to deal. The nature of their respective responses to their individual problems illustrates the importance of having a positive approach to crisis management. The company that is seen to fail in its response to a disaster, or whose response is deemed to be inadequate, has only itself to blame for the subsequent decline in its perceived persona.

QUESTION 11.9

Why do companies need to have a crisis management policy in place even when their business is functioning smoothly and their external relationships are good?

Companies need to be prepared in advance to deal with a crisis – even though it is unlikely that they will know its nature – and have an established system and process to deal with and respond to the issues as they are raised. The process of anticipation is key.

It is important that there are clearly established and identifiable pathways of responsibility within the organization. Ideally, nominated individuals will be in place to deal with enquiries and become the focus for company statements – both internally and externally. Too many people acting on behalf of the company can result in confused or contradictory responses, or responses based on poor information or knowledge of the situation.

Ideally, a company should have some form of plan in place which will be used to identify all areas of potential risk and, importantly, how to deal with them. This will enable a rapid response. As we have seen earlier, the lack of a direct response may itself be inferred by some members of the audience as being intentional.

In any organization, it is possible to ensure that some 'crises' are identified in advance – although they cannot be prevented or eliminated. It may be inherent in the nature of the business that some problems will occur, e.g. deaths in hospitals, or the lay-off of staff during a downturn in the economy. Other crises cannot be so readily foreseen, but the need for a speedy and informed response is the same.

Identify an example of a 'crisis' which has befallen a company recently. How did they respond to the problem they faced, and what was the outcome in terms of the organization's image?

Key dimensions of crisis management

- Develop a specific programme to deal with a 'crisis'.
- Identify specific personnel, at a senior level, whose responsibility it will be to deal with events as they occur.
- Identify potential 'crisis' areas in advance, and devise programmes to avoid their occurrence.
- Formulate specific strategies to deal with crisis events.
- Devise effective communications channels.
- Formalize the plan and ensure that it is communicated throughout the organization.

Handling a crisis

Several dimensions can be readily identified which will assist in the process of handling and dealing with a crisis:

- Take the initiative by maintaining close contact with the media.
- Provide accessibility by designating named individuals who should be contacted.
- Do not offer speculation or guesses – only established facts should be released.
- Defer answering questions until facts are available.
- Ensure that internal communications are good.
- Anticipate the questions and keep the responses simple.
- Think in terms of 'people' implications.
- Monitor all media coverage.
- Follow up.

In this unit, which is concerned with the important and intimately related issues of corporate communications and crisis management, we have seen that:

- All aspects of a company's communications to its various publics will serve to create the image of that company. Indeed, the very lack of a communication may well be interpreted negatively by those publics.
- Although an identity must be communicated to have any validity, the various

163

ways in which this is achieved must be clearly defined and managed from the outset.

- It is vitally important that all the communications techniques that are employed must be integrated and work together to deliver a cohesive and consistent image of the organization.
- To achieve integration of communications, a succinct plan must be developed by the company to ensure not only that the various communications channels receive the same message, but also that all important audiences for the message are covered adequately.
- As elsewhere, market research is a vital means of understanding existing perceptions and of monitoring the effectiveness of campaigns intended either to reinforce or to alter the company image.
- No company or organization can act in isolation of the various publics with which it must deal. As, increasingly, those publics are concerned with the reputations of the companies they deal with or buy from, so too companies must adopt a positive approach to dealing with their public identity.
- Because of the underlying changes which continue to occur in the environment, which are often rapid, companies must continuously re-examine and re-evaluate their perceived identities in order that they can continue to communicate an image which is consistent with their corporate strategy.

Examination hints and specimen questions

The issues covered in this unit are frequently addressed, in different forms, by the Chief Examiner. It is important that you understand the principles covered, and are able to apply them to the contemporary marketing environment.

In order to give you practice in dealing with the various topics, three 'short-form' questions have been extracted from recent papers. These will enable you to determine whether you have understood the main themes and, importantly, whether you can apply them appropriately.

By now, you will have developed a familiarity with these questions, and will be much better at organizing your time profitably. Allow no more than 30 minutes to answer each of the questions, and think carefully about how to approach each of them. Try to develop a simple plan or outline which you will follow in your answer. This will give you a proper framework to work with and enable you to get the important points organized before you begin to write out your answer. This is an important aspect of dealing with all questions, but remember that the time for doing this must be included in the overall 30 minutes allocated.

In recent years, crisis management programmes have been put in place by an increasing number of organizations in an attempt to mitigate the potential damage that would result if a crisis strikes the organization. The off-shore oil industry is the type of organization that needs to be prepared in this way. Accidents do happen in what is a hazardous industry. You are the public relations manager for the operator of an oil platform producing off-shore. You are asked to set out your crisis management objectives and what you would do in the case of an oil spillage.

(June 1994)

The retail group the Bodyshop does not advertise but uses other methods to communicate its products, services and ideas. With reference to the Bodyshop or another retailer of your choice show how:

(i)   The power of the attributes of the retailer's product communicates.
(ii) The price and packaging can communicate loudly.
(iii) The nature of the retail outlet sends a distinct message.

(December 1992)

In recent years British Nuclear Fuels Limited (BFNL) has adopted an 'open-door' communications strategy. It believes in its dealings with the public it must be open, honest and credible. This has led them to set up a Visitor Centre at its Sellafield nuclear operation in Cumbria, which is open 364 days a year. The international group at BFNL have asked you for an independent report giving your evaluation of:

(i)   The objectives behind such a strategy.
(ii)   Who are the target audiences.
(iii) The degree to which you expect the strategy to achieve the objectives.

(December 1992)

There are several books that you might consider reading which will assist you in gaining a deeper understanding of the principles covered by this unit. Remember that reading around the subject will undoubtedly assist you in the process of learning. However, don't try and read everything available. The following are alternatives for you to consider:

D. Bernstein, *Corporate Image and Reality*, Cassell Educational, 1989.
N. Ind, *The Corporate Image: Strategies for Effective Identity Programmes*, Kogan Page, 1992.
W. Olins, *Corporate Identity*, Thames & Hudson, 1989.
E. Selame and J. Selame, *The Company Image*, Wiley, 1988.

Determining the budget

OBJECTIVES

This is a somewhat unusual unit in the sense that the topic is not normally directly examined within the CIM Diploma paper. Nonetheless, the issues that it addresses and the topics which are covered will, frequently, be encountered during specific examination questions – especially the case study exercise.

Therefore, in this unit, which covers a number of topics which are important to understand, you will:

- Examine the various methods which are used to determine marketing communications budgets.
- Consider aspects of budgetary allocation.

By the end of this unit you will:

- Have examined the major approaches to budgeting and will appreciate their respective benefits and drawbacks.
- Be able to apply the principles to practical situations.

STUDY GUIDE

There are many important and, at first sight, potentially complicated issues covered in this unit. With careful study, the task will be far less daunting and you will rapidly grasp the principles established.

Take care to study the various elements of the unit and to consider each of the issues carefully. Where possible, carry out the various exercises at different times in order to reinforce your learning of the key aspects of the budgeting process.

Allow about 2 hours to read through the topics, and a further 3 hours to answer the questions and do the activities that are included.

STUDY TIPS

This unit is much more about application than the simple ability to state information. Often you will be given some of the financial dimensions of a brand scenario and asked to develop a marketing communications budget.

Practice with the tasks provided in this unit will ensure that you are far more able to cope with the requirements of the examination on the day.

A key task within the framework of marketing communications is the appropriate determination of the levels of expenditure required to fulfil the task established. The amount of money spent on marketing communications differs widely amongst companies, even within the same industry.

The annual brand survey published by *Marketing Magazine* in conjunction with Nielsen (the worldwide market research organization), which is the source of the following figures, provides a comprehensive analysis of many consumer goods markets. For example:

- Dolmio pasta sauces, estimated to be worth some £34 million in 1993, spent £1 million on advertising. Ragu, a direct competitor, worth an estimated £15–20 million spent almost as much at £0.7 million.
- Carling Black Label, worth more than £58 million, spent some £4.4 million on advertising; Heineken, with a value estimated at around £55 million, spent £6.5 million; whilst Tennent's Super, with a similar brand value as Heineken, spent only £0.2 million in 1993.
- Flash cleaning liquid, estimated to be worth around £40–45 million, spent some £9.1 million. Fairy Excel, also owned by Procter and Gamble, spent some £7 million to defend its estimated value of over £72 million.

The primary issue is that of identifying the reasons for this wide variation in expenditure patterns, and of determining an effective approach to the setting of a budgetary level. It should be clear that the determination of the correct level of expenditure must depend on a proper analysis of the situation, rather than the use of 'norms', rule of thumb, or 'gut-feel'. According to Simon Broadbent, author of *The Advertising Budget*, the amount to spend is determined by a process, not a formula. Hence, there is no simple solution. Various methods of budget determination have been suggested and the issue is one of deciding which approach is right for the situation.

In the course of this unit, we will examine some of the most important approaches that have been suggested and consider their application to the real environment. The following list gives most of the ways used to determine the budget:

- Marginal analysis.
- Percentage of previous year's turnover (sales).
- Percentage of product gross margin.
- Residue of last year's surplus.
- Percentage of anticipated turnover.
- Unit or case/sales ratio method.
- Competitive expenditure.
- Desired share of voice.
- Media inflation.
- Objective-and-task method.
- Experimentation.
- What we can afford.
- New products.

Marginal analysis

Several attempts have been made to transfer the learning from the principles of economic theory to that of budget determination. In essence, the principles of marginal analysis suggest that a company should continue to increase its marketing communications expenditure until the point where the increase in expenditure matches, but does not exceed, the increase in income which those expenditures generate. This can be shown graphically, as illustrated in Figure 12.1.

Unfortunately, the application of the theory of marginal analysis does not transfer readily into the real-world situation. The first problem to deal with is the fact that the theory assumes sales are a direct function of marketing communications expenditures. Whilst it is possible to postulate situations in which this might be the case – for example, in the area of direct marketing – this may be somewhat wide of the mark.

The level of expenditure is only one of the variables which needs to be considered. The theory makes no attempt to consider, for example, the location of the activity in terms, say, of media placement, or of the copy content of the advertisement or sales promotion tool. It simply assumes that every pound spent is likely to achieve the same impact on the market. Clearly, other marketing activities will have an impact on the level of achievement which will render the formula almost incalculable. Importantly, most marketing communications activities rely on a built-in time lag. Even in the area of direct marketing, where a more precise correlation can be established between patterns of expenditure and achievement, it will be necessary to make an allowance for other indirect variables.

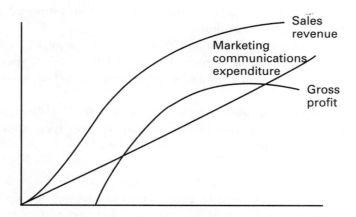

Figure 12.1

The nature of the message, its placement, the competitive environment and other factors will all have to be allowed for if the theory is to stand up in practice. Certainly, until the advent of rapid response computer programmes, the amount of detail which would need to be built into such a calculation proved unwieldy at best. Several attempts have been made to build econometric models against which to 'test' different levels of expenditure. Suffice it to say that, at best, they provide some guidance as to the likely impact of the proposals in the real world.

Percentage of sales

Probably the most widely used method of budget determination is the calculation of a ratio between past expenditure and sales. The calculation itself is quite straightforward. The previous year's expenditures are calculated as a percentage of total sales, and the resultant figure is used to calculate the budget for the coming year. Thus, if £12 million worth of sales was achieved against a communications budget of £300 000, the percentage would be 2.5%. Assuming that the sales forecast for the coming year was £15 million, this would yield a budget of £375 000.

Whilst the process is a quick and easy one, there are flaws in the argument. In the first place, the data used will be considerably out of date by the time that it is implemented. As we do not have a full picture of the current year's sales, we must rely on, at best, the latest 12 months for which we have information on which to base our calculations for next year's activity. Secondly, the model creates a situation in which the budget only increases against an expectation of higher sales. If sales are expected to decline, then the future communications budget must be reduced to bring it into line with the defined ratio. The inherent danger is that a brand that is under threat – and losing volume – actually has a reduced budget rather than an increased one. Thirdly, the model fails to recognize that marketing communications activity can create sales volume for a brand. The application of the principle in fact operates in reverse – with sales being the determinant of expenditure levels.

Percentage of product gross margin

This approach is, essentially, similar to the previous one, except that the gross margin rather than the level of sales is used as the basis for calculating the future level of expenditure. Here, a percentage of either the past or expected gross margin – net sales less the cost of goods – is used.

Given that your objective is to increase your share of the £550 million pet food market from 10 per cent to 15 per cent, and the leading brands spend approximately £7–9 million on advertising, what marketing communications budget would you recommend, and how would you support your argument?

Residue of previous year's surplus

This method is entirely based on prior performance, whereby the excess of income over costs in the previous year is designated as the budget for the following year. Although simple in principle, it clearly demands that a surplus is achieved in order for monies to be spent in any future period. It fails to recognize the need for investment in growth brands or, for that matter, the impact of competitive activities.

Percentage of anticipated turnover

This approach is based on the allocation of a fixed percentage of future turnover to the marketing communications budget.

Unit or case/sales ratio method

This method, sometimes referred to as the *case rate*, requires that brand volumes for the next year are estimated and a fixed sum per unit is allocated towards marketing communications expenditure. It is then a simple process of multiplying the expected sales volume (in units or cases) by the fixed allocation to arrive at a total communications budget.

After several years of growth, your market has begun to decline at a rate of approximately 5 per cent per annum. Although your share has held up, the volume has begun to decline.

What recommendations would you make, as brand leader, for the setting of next year's marketing communications budget?

In some instances comparisons are made between the company's own case rate and those of its competitors in order to explore the relationships between them. Obviously the approach is a simple one, but it begs the question as to how the case rate itself is calculated. In some instances it may be based on past experience. Usually it is a company or industry norm.

Here again, as with other ratio-based approaches, expenditure patterns reflect past achievement or anticipated sales. As such, the method tends to benefit growth brands and disadvantage those which are declining. It ignores the fact that a brand which is suffering in the marketplace may need increased levels of expenditure in order to arrest the decline, rather than a reduced budget which would be the automatic result of applying the method.

Competitive expenditure

Another frequently used approach is to base a brand's expenditure levels on an assessment of competitors' expenditures. Often a calculation is made of the level of category expenditure and a percentage – usually related to a brand's share of market – is chosen as the basis of calculating the expenditure levels for the brand. In other instances, an attempt is made to achieve parity with a nominated competitor by setting a similar level of expenditure to theirs.

At the very least, this approach has the benefit of ensuring that brand expenditure levels are maintained in line with those of the competition. However, it suffers from the obvious difficulty of being able to make an accurate assessment of the level of competitors' spends. Whilst it is obviously possible to obtain a reasonable fix on advertising spend from published information (from *Register MEAL*), the same is not true of sales promotional spend and other categories of marketing communications. Figures for the latter are rarely published. Moreover, the model fails to recognize that the expenditure patterns of a competitor may well be dictated by a totally different set of problems and objectives.

QUESTION 12.1

You are attempting to introduce a new product to the £670 million hot beverage market and are targeting a share of 5 per cent in year 1. What factors would you consider to help you determine the budget for marketing communications?

Desired share of voice

This approach is an extension of the previous one, where management relates the volume share of the product category to expenditure within the category as a whole, and is primarily related to advertising expenditure. Thus, if a brand has a 15 per cent share of the market in which it competes, and total advertising expenditure for the category is £8 million, in order to retain a proportional share of voice a budget of £1.2 million would need to be set. By the same token, the company would have a benchmark against which to establish the levels of expenditure required to drive a brand forward. Hence, it might decide to increase its share of voice to, say, 20 or even 25 per cent in an attempt to gain a greater level of visibility for its brand and a greater share of the overall category.

QUESTION 12.2

Set out your arguments in favour of adopting a share-of-voice approach to budget determination.

Media inflation

This approach makes the simple assumption that a budget – usually the previous year's – should be increased in line with the growth in media costs to ensure a similar delivery of the message to the target audience. At the lowest level, this approach ensures that the real level of advertising expenditure is maintained. However, it fails to acknowledge any of the other variables which will have an impact on the achievement of marketing objectives.

Objective-and-task method

This method is based on a more realistic examination of the specific objectives which the marketing plan needs to meet, and was established as an attempt to apply a more scientific approach to budget determination. The basis of the approach was a paper commissioned by the American Association of National Advertisers and published in 1961. In the paper 'Defining advertising goals for measuring advertising results' (DAGMAR) the author, Russell Coley, proposed that advertising should be specifically budgeted to accomplish defined goals or objectives.

The DAGMAR approach – also known as the objective-and-task method – requires that specific objectives for the campaign are defined at the outset. These may be expressed in terms of, for example, increasing brand awareness, encouraging sampling and trial, promoting repeat purchase and so on. In each case a finite numerical target is given, and the costs of achieving this target are calculated. The resultant budget is thus based on a series of goals rather than on past or future results, and is thus the most realistic in marketing terms.

The method offers the benefit of being able to monitor the campaign achievement against the targets set, and provides a more accurate guide to budgetary determination for the future. The limitation on the accuracy of the method is the ability to access sufficient information to ensure that all relevant variables can be considered.

Although the original paper dealt specifically with the task of establishing advertising budgets, the method is equally applicable to other areas of marketing communications.

QUESTION 12.3

Why is the objective-and-task method of budget determination increasingly preferred over other approaches?

Experimentation

A guiding principle for budget determination, as with other aspects of marketing, is the need to, on the one hand, protect the company investment, whilst, on the other, ensuring that sufficient new and innovatory approaches are taken to drive the brand forward. It is for this reason that most major marketing companies use an experimental approach at various times.

Having established the overall marketing communications budget by the normal or most appropriate means, it is possible to create a 'mini-test market' for the purposes of experimenting with a variation. By isolating, say, one region of the country, it is possible to experiment with alternative budget constructions. In many cases, and in the absence of definitive data, it is useful to determine the impact of, for example, an increased level of media expenditure or of a particular sales promotion technique.

The benefit of this approach is that the main sources of business are 'protected', in the sense that they receive the 'normal' support levels. Hence, the position of the brand is not unduly prejudiced. By 'hot housing' a different approach, real experience can be gained and the budgetary process enhanced with the additional knowledge.

The method thus represents an attempt to apply an empirical approach and, therefore, a more scientific method to the process of budget determination. However, it is important to restrict the number of 'experiments' in order to ensure that the data are readable against the norm, and that the individual variables can be properly assessed within a real market environment.

QUESTION 12.4

Write a short note to your managing director justifying the adoption of a more scientific approach towards budgeting as opposed to its arbitrary determination.

What we can afford

This approach is based on a management assessment of either the brand itself or the overall company position. In effect, management determines the level of profit desired, or the return on investment, and the marketing communications budget is the amount that remains after calculating that level. Of course, the approach fails to recognize the contribution of marketing communications itself, and ignores other environmental factors, such as competitive pressure, which might mitigate against the profit level being achieved.

Although this is a somewhat arbitrary approach to the budgetary process, it should be recognized that the issue of affordability plays an important part in any financial procedure. There will always be competing demands for funds within a company – to support the activities of other brands within the portfolio, to fund areas such as production capability, to finance research and development, and so on. It is a fundamental role of management to determine company priorities and to allocate funds accordingly.

Budgets for new products

QUESTION 12.5

- Why do marketing communications budgets for new product launches have to be given special consideration?
- What criteria would you consider using as the basis of budget determination?

One area that demands a separate mention is that of developing a marketing-communications budget for a new product. Clearly, past data will be unavailable and hence many of the usual budgeting approaches cannot be applied.

At the simplest level, the approach to new products is similar to the objective-and-task method described above. Calculations must be made of the amount of money required to achieve the objectives established for the brand.

It must be recognized that, in most instances, new products require investment in advance of sales performance. Indeed, without the appropriate levels of investment in marketing communications, most new products are unlikely to succeed. A realistic time frame for achieving the goals set must be established at the outset. It is unrealistic to expect a new product to make a major contribution in the short term.

ACTIVITY 12.3

List the methods of budgetary determination described in this unit, and write a few lines explaining each of them.

It is important to re-state that there is no hard and fast formula for defining a marketing communications budget. It is important to experiment with a number of the methods described above, and to ensure that appropriate use is made of previous company experience, industry data and experimentation. The imperative for all companies is to ensure that a database of information (both within-company information and information on competitors) is built up, which can be used to enhance the process.

The process of budget determination

Whichever method, or methods, of budget determination is adopted, however, the task must be to consider the process of budget determination itself. Broadbent suggests that the process is made up of six separate stages (Figure 12.2).

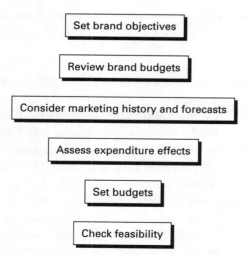

Set brand objectives

Review brand budgets

Consider marketing history and forecasts

Assess expenditure effects

Set budgets

Check feasibility

Figure 12.2

Stage 1 – brand objectives

Here we must consider the role of the brand within the company and the importance of the brand to the achievement of the overall objectives. The consideration should encompass both the short-term time frame of the plan, e.g. the year ahead, as well as longer term considerations, e.g. over the next 3–5 years. It is also important to examine the relationship between volume and profit contribution. At this stage also the source of the brand's sales should be identified. The larger the audience, the greater the likely budget requirement. By the same token, by adopting a more concentrated approach, the media budget may be lowered.

Why are long-term brand objectives important in budgetary determination?

Stage 2 – review the brand budgets

It is important to consider how the brand has performed in the past, as this will have significant implications on its ability to perform in the future. If a brand has been in decline, then the previous budget will need to be increased if the decline is to be arrested or reversed.

Stage 3 – marketing history and forecasts

As well as a consideration of the brand itself, it is important to consider the market category which will help place the brand in context. This will reveal a number of important factors which will assist in the brand planning process. Although volume sales may be increasing, it is important to determine whether they are keeping pace with the category as a whole. In fact, the brand may be losing share of market which, in the longer term, could endanger its position.

What information is required to assist in the process of budgetary determination?

Stage 4 – assess expenditure effects

It is important to examine the effects of previous advertising and promotional expenditure in order to determine the level of brand responsiveness to marketing communications activity. Previous experience is a valuable guide to likely future performance. And remember that, in this respect, it is possible to learn as much from competitor performance as from that of your own brand.

Stage 5 – set budgets

When setting budgets consider the application of a number of the standard approaches to budget determination (these are set out in detail above). This is very much a preliminary exercise in budget determination, as it will suggest a range of possible amounts to be spent, with affordability and feasibility being checked in the final stage.

You have 20 per cent of the UK spread market (which includes butter and butter substitutes) worth £550 million. Currently you spend around £3 million on advertising, primarily on television and in the colour press. You are planning to enter the European market, and have targeted

France and Belgium to spearhead your activity. What financial recommendations would you make for your launch campaign and what assumptions would you make?

Stage 6 – check feasibility

The final stage of this proposed process is to ensure that the budget determined is feasible and practical within the context of the established objectives.

Allocating the promotional budget

QUESTION 12.8

What are the important considerations in the allocation of funds between marketing communications tools?

Having established how the overall budget is to be calculated, the allocation of funds within the budget must be addressed. Again, the emphasis must rest with integrated marketing communications and the identification of the most appropriate and cost-effective communications channels for achieving the specific task. That having been said, however, it must be recognized that there are no set formulae for allocating budgets between competing communications approaches.

In many instances, the appropriate channels will be easily identified by carefully examining the objectives and the techniques which can best meet them. Since all marketing communications tools have identified roles in the communications process, it will be apparent that a careful consideration of the needs will, similarly, identify the areas likely to be most appropriate. If the task is defined as generating high levels of awareness amongst a wide target audience, then it is probable that advertising will absorb a substantial proportion of the communications budget. If the task is to generate trial and sampling, the budget will need to be apportioned primarily between sales promotion and advertising. If the need is to promote the corporate identity, the budget is likely to be spent on corporate advertising and public relations. If the task is to reach a narrowly defined and readily identified group of consumers, direct marketing techniques will come to the fore. The imperative in all cases is the need for integrated marketing communications.

We have seen, from the beginning of this workbook, that the consumer does not discriminate as to the source of the message. Our fundamental objective is to deliver the brand proposition in the most cost-effective manner to the defined target audience. As such, we need to identify and integrate those marketing communications techniques that best achieve this goal.

QUESTION 12.9

During the recent economic recession, many major manufacturers cut back on the expenditure on marketing communications. How would you suggest that adopting the opposite approach, i.e. increasing spend, might have benefitted the company?

SUMMARY

Although this is not a directly examinable area, candidates for the CIM Diploma will often be asked to identify the approach they would adopt to budget determination, and to justify the apportionment of funds. This is often a component of the case exercise, which is the compulsory part of the examination – it was an element of the recent Jaguar Case Study (June 1994) as well as previous case studies – Nescafé (June 1993), Swatch (December 1993).

Make sure, therefore, that you have a thorough grasp of the various approaches, especially the task-and-objective method and, equally importantly, that you can apply this learning to the material provided by the examiner.

EXTENDING KNOWLEDGE

Although its focus is primarily on advertising the following text provides a truly comprehensive examination of the issues relating to budget determination and the principles are equally applicable to other areas of marketing communications:

S. Broadbent, *The Advertising Budget*, Institute of Practitioners in Advertising/NTC, 1989.

Useful sections on budget determination are contained in:

D. A. Aaker, R. Batra and J. G. Myers, *Advertising Management*, 4th edn, Prentice Hall, 1992.
D. Arnold, *The Handbook of Brand Management*, Century, 1992.
D. E. Shultz and W. A. Robinson, *Sales Promotion Management*, NTC Business Books, 1992.

International considerations

In this unit, which is designed to consolidate your knowledge of marketing communications, and assist you in applying this knowledge in the international context, you will:

- See that, with the increasing tendency towards globalization, operators within the field of marketing communications must be able to consider the wider implications of the international markets for the products and services for which they are responsible.
- Examine the pressures that are resulting in this trend towards globalization.
- Consider the implications of international versus national marketing communications.
- Look at the benefits of standardizing international communications and the needs of the 'international' consumer.
- Consider the role of the international marketing communications agency.

By the end of this unit you will:

- Have a thorough understanding of the international dimensions of marketing communications.
- Be able to apply your learning to the type of examination questions that the examiner is likely to set.

The field of international marketing communications is an important one and, in recent years, many of the questions set by the examiner have had an international dimension. This particularly applies to the compulsory question which takes the form of a case study.

This unit provides you with the opportunity to reinforce the learning that has taken place since you started on this workbook. By now you will have developed a detailed understanding of the major topics of marketing communications strategy. If necessary, refer back to the individual units which cover aspects of the marketing communications process in more detail, in order to remind yourself of the topics covered at that time.

This unit will probably take about 3 hours to complete, although it is worth spending at least as much time again on the exercises and mini questions as these will help you in the learning process.

We are almost at the end of the programme, and you have done much of the work to cover the ground in readiness for the CIM Marketing Communications paper. This unit will help you begin the process of revision, which is vital to ensure that you have a good enough command of the subject to approach the examination with confidence.

It is a good idea to re-read all the work units to identify any gaps or weaknesses in your knowledge. If you can identify and rectify any problems now, you will have no problem when it comes to the examination.

The trend towards globalization

Recent years have seen an increasing tendency towards the globalization of brands. As domestic markets have reached positions of virtual saturation, manufacturers have turned to new and often distant markets to ensure a continuation of their growth potential. It is argued by some (see, for example, P. R. Caetora, *International Marketing*, 8th edn, Irwin, 1993) that global marketing is the final phase in a progressive process of this desire for market extension (see Figure 13.1).

Figure 13.1　From: P. R. Caetora, *International Marketing*, 8th edn (Irwin, 1993)

- **Domestic markets**　These comprise the first stage of the process, in which companies design products and services to satisfy the identified needs and wants of domestic consumers.
- **Infrequent foreign marketing**　This is often dictated by a short-term need to eliminate production surpluses which cannot be absorbed by the domestic market. However, there is no real desire on the part of the company to exploit these opportunities on a longer term basis, and once the domestic 'problem' of oversupply or low demand has been eliminated overseas sales are curtailed.
- **Regular foreign marketing**　The manufacturer devotes some resources to the exploitation of overseas opportunities on an on-going basis, but the primary focus remains the need to respond to domestic demand. In these instances, the company often uses middlemen, but may create its own selling operations in important markets.
- **International marketing**　As companies perceive the major opportunity to derive profits from foreign markets, they progressively commit more resources to the development of this potential and, in the process, become more committed to the tasks of international marketing. In general, they perceive their markets as possessing unique characteristics for which individual marketing and marketing communications strategies must be developed.
- **Global marketing**　At this level, companies view the world as a single market. This is accompanied by a tendency towards the standardization of business activities and the adoption of marketing and marketing communications strategies which reflect those elements of commonality throughout the many markets they serve.

What are the key factors motivating the shift towards globalization?

QUESTION 13.1

Multinational versus global marketing

We can make an important distinction between these two approaches to foreign markets, and these have significant implications for the determination of marketing communications strategies.

The *multinational company* readily perceives the fundamental differences between the various markets it serves. In general, it believes that its success is dependent on the development of individual marketing and marketing communications programmes for each of its territories. As a result, it tends to operate through a number of subsidiaries which, for the most part, act independently of each other. Products are adapted, or developed independently, to meet the needs of the individual markets and the consumers within. By the same token, the other elements of the marketing mix are developed on a local basis. Although there may be some cross-fertilization of ideas through some form of central function, the primary aim is to satisfy the needs of individual country markets, rather than the specific identification of common elements which might allow for the standardization of activities.

The *global organization* strives towards the provision of commonality, both in terms of its products and services, and the propositions which support them. As far as possible, it attempts to standardize its activities on a worldwide basis, although even within this concept there is some recognition of the need for local adaptation to respond to local pressures. The fundamental objective is the identification of groups of buyers within the global market with similar needs, and the development of marketing and marketing communications plans that are as standardized as much as possible within cultural and operational constraints.

ACTIVITY 13.1

- Find examples of three or four similar magazines from different countries.
- Examine how the advertising presentation differs in each of them.
- Are there any advertisements for the same product in the different magazines? Are they the same or different?

The impetus for a more detailed examination of the implications of international marketing was provided by a seminal article by Theodore Levitt (*Harvard Business Review*, 1993, **61**, 92–102). The thrust of his argument in 'The globalization of markets' is that a variety of common forces, the most important of which is shared technology, is driving the world towards a 'converging commonality'. The result, he argues, is 'the emergence of global markets for standardized consumer products on a previously unimagined scale.'

From a personal standpoint, I would argue that it is the convergence of communications which has, and will continue to have, the far greater impact. We have already seen (Unit 1) that consumer motivations towards the purchasing of products and services are the result of the influence of a wide range of factors. One central factor which impacts upon many, if not all, of them is the mass media. As the peoples of the world are exposed to the same messages via television, film and other media, it is inevitable that their attitudes towards the products and services depicted will move towards a common central point.

ACTIVITY 13.2

Find examples of products or services featured in the media (foreign films, imported TV programmes, etc.). How does their usage and positioning differ from that of the domestic market?

Irrespective of our geographical location, it is likely that most of us will listen to the same music (the bands that top the charts in one country enjoy similar levels of success in others), the same films (which country has not yet been exposed to *Jurassic Park*, *The Flintstones* or *Star Trek*, to name but a few?), the same television programmes, the same computer programs, and even the same articles in the media. Whilst it is undeniable that cultural differences will continue to prevail, at least for some considerable time into the foreseeable future, so too are we witnessing the coming together of many attitudes and beliefs, which enhance the potential for products and services that respond to those common and shared values.

The forces of internationalization

There are many factors that can be cited as contributing to this growth of an international rather than a purely domestic outlook. We have already seen that, from an attitudinal perspective, there are growing similarities between countries. With improved communications, the physical distances between markets matter far less. There is, as mentioned by Levitt, the integrating role of technology. The capacity to produce similar or even identical products in dispersed markets is enhanced as the technological base of manufacturers becomes similar. At the same time, we are witnessing the progressive removal of the former barriers to international trade – tariffs. Most regions of the world are joining together in supra-national groupings for their mutual economic benefit. Amongst others, these include the EC (European Community), USA/Canadian trade agreements, ASEAN (the Association of South East Asian Nations), CARICOM (the Caribbean Community and Common Market), and CACM (the Central American Common Market).

With slowing domestic economic growth in many areas, manufacturers are being forced to seek potential markets away from their home base. Indeed, specific government actions are being taken to incentivize foreign trade. A similar impetus comes from the recognition that, as products reach the maturity or decline phase of the product life cycle, they will need to identify new markets which are in a different stage of development.

The intensity of domestic competition may also force companies to look elsewhere, where perhaps the costs of market entry are lower or their offerings appear to be more innovatory and exciting. And, of course, there is the opportunity for manufacturers to secure the benefits of differential pricing. A product sold for a premium price in one market can be sold in another for a lower price and still make a profit contribution, so long as the marginal costs are covered. The changing base of competitive advantage and the emergence of global competitors is forcing other manufacturers to seek joint ventures and coalitions, often with foreign partners. Apart from the benefits of shared technologies, the participants in such deals obtain 'ready-made' set-ups which enable them to access other markets in return for a comparatively low investment.

The forces restraining standardization

As much as there are many forces driving the move towards internationalization, so too there are a number of factors which preclude, or at least slow down, the rate at which manufacturers from one country can introduce their products directly into another.

National and cultural characteristics remain a fundamental point of difference. Although, as many have argued, there is a progressive convergence of attitudes and behaviours, many such patterns are sufficiently ingrained to be unchangeable in the mid-term. We will discuss these factors in more detail later in this unit, as they have important implications for the determination of marketing communications strategies.

The different levels of economic growth and national living standards will, similarly, act as restraints in some areas. However attractive a particular offering may be, if the individual is on a low income or unemployed, he or she will not be able to make the desired purchase.

There will be fundamental differences between markets which cannot be altered in the short term. Whilst some will relate to the ingrained behavioural patterns mentioned above, others will be a direct consequence of environmental factors – the comparative penetration of such items as fridges and freezers, the availability of domestic storage space, distribution factors, and so on.

There may be a more basic resistance to change which will inhibit the acceptance of products and services which are commonly accepted in other markets. Also, there remain a number of legal and regulatory factors which may preclude the penetration of particular markets where the sale of individual products may be limited or even banned. And, finally, there is the political environment which may discourage foreign trade in general, or that from individual companies in particular. At the same time, manufacturers may be wary of making substantial investments in markets with unstable economic or political environments where they do not have sufficient confidence of being able to secure an adequate level of return because of underlying changes.

QUESTION 13.2

How does the information required for the development of an international communications campaign differ from that required for domestic planning?

QUESTION 13.3

Can a brand develop global appeal? Find three examples of brands which have adopted a global communications strategy and three which have adopted a multinational communications strategy. In what ways are their communications strategies different from each other?

The development of global brands

It is inevitable that the progressive standardization of products results in significant economies of manufacture which, potentially, lead to lower prices and a more competitive positioning for the brand. The high investment in product development will be rapidly amortized if the market for the resulting product is global and enormous rather than domestic and limited. Such developments, however, will not obviate the need in many instances to adapt the product to meet 'special' local needs, however these are occasioned.

Some manufacturers perceive the world of the future to be one in which global brands dominate. The perceived benefits of a single worldwide brand identification outweigh those of country-specific products with separate brand identities. However, it is important to remember that, even here, it is not essential that the product delivered in each market is identical – only that the branding and the imagery associated with it are the same. Nestlé, for example, have adopted the same packaging and style for their leading brand of instant coffee across most international markets. However, the specific product may well be different in many of those markets to reflect local taste characteristics.

ACTIVITY 13.3

Locate examples of some products sold in your market but originated elsewhere. How have they been adapted to suit local needs? Consider product, packaging, advertising, etc.

Even where it is necessary to subjugate the current brand identity in favour of a single consistent worldwide brand mark, major manufacturers have determined that the long-term benefits are likely to outweigh the short-term losses. Despite enjoying considerable consumer acceptance in the UK with their Marathon brand, Mars opted for a standardization of the brand under the name of Snickers across all markets.

QUESTION 13.4

In what ways does the construction of a marketing communications campaign differ in an international context?

The move to global marketing communications

In the same way that we have seen a progressive move towards the standardization of brands, so too has there been a movement towards the development of standardized marketing communications programmes. The rapidly accelerating costs of producing separate campaigns for individual markets, the difficulties of co-ordinating separate campaigns in physically close markets, together with the desire for the establishment of a single worldwide identity for its brands, have induced many companies to explore the potential of single campaign development across many, if not all, markets. Inevitably, there are polarized views on the merits of such moves.

At one extreme, as a response to the pressures indicated above, some companies have developed central campaigns which provide the core of all of their marketing communications activity in all markets. For a number of years, Coca Cola have run essentially similar campaigns in many markets, with all or most of the elements being constantly applied in all of the territories in which they operate. Their recent sponsorship of the 1994 World Cup, for example, was featured prominently on cans sold as far apart as Thailand and Malaysia and the UK. Similarly, identical advertising, save only for the language of the voice-over, has been run by the brand across all territories.

At the other end of the spectrum are a wide range of international brands for which 'local' advertising propositions have continued to be developed and which, in their producers' view, enable them to reflect more readily the needs and desires of the individual markets in which they operate.

Between these two positions are those brands which adopt a common communications strategy, but allow for the local development of specific executions. In these instances, there is a cohesion in the underlying message of the brand in all of its markets, but room for the development of tightly focused and tailored propositions which reflect the subtleties and nuances of the local marketplace. Some manufacturers have developed this approach to the position where they develop 'pattern book' communications campaigns. An overall stance for the brand will be taken centrally, with semi-finished examples of advertising and sales promotion approaches laid down centrally. These, however, provide the 'shell' of activity and the local operations have the flexibility to adjust the specific content to meet their local requirements. It is this latter area which has witnessed the greatest growth over recent years. Indeed, even the ubiquitous Coca Cola have recognized the need to develop specific messages for individual markets to respond to pressures on the brand's position.

QUESTION 13.5

The emergent 'new Europe' – the old Eastern European nations – represents a major market opportunity for many manufacturers' products and services. To what extent should they plan to use existing marketing communications campaigns to support the introduction of their products to these markets?

The merits and demerits of standardized communications

We have already seen that the proponents of standardized communications campaigns cite the cost savings to be accrued from the development of a single campaign, together with the comparative ease of co-ordination, as partial justifications for the move towards common global marketing communications activities.

It cannot be denied that the cost savings may be enormous. For example, the average cost of production of a television commercial is of the order of £200 000 to £300 000 and, very often, very much more than that. British Airways are rumoured to have spent around £2 million on their 'World' commercial, whilst *Campaign* reported the production costs of the recent Vauxhall Nova launch campaign as being around £3 million. Moreover, if several creative teams are working in different parts of the globe to resolve the communications needs, the time involved and the associated costs will be considerable. As we have seen, there may be an underlying commonality of requirements, and thus much of that time will be spent covering the same ground as others in the search for the communications message.

Not only does a standardized process eliminate the problems of conflict arising from dissimilar messages being communicated in adjacent territories, it also saves a considerable amount of management time involved in resolving such difficulties. Similarly, management would otherwise need to be involved – within each market – in the briefing and approval of creative work, the development of separate sales promotion campaigns, public relations activity and even packaging changes.

Ultimately, the key benefit results in the creation of a single consistent image for the brand across all markets. The management and monitoring of the campaign can be more consistent, and the implementation process simplified. Against these, however, it can be argued that there are a number of significant disadvantages.

Inevitably, if the brand is at a different stage in its development, it may be less responsive to a marketing communications campaign developed for all markets, than to one specifically designed to deal with its own particular needs. We have already seen that different objectives, such as creating awareness, stimulating repeat purchase, and so on, will require different motivations and, hence, different messages. Similarly, in order to ensure universal appeal and comprehension, the resultant execution may be bland and boring and satisfy none of the individual requirements satisfactorily. This may, in turn, inhibit the opportunity to generate sales volume and result in management frustration.

Indeed, the problem is often one of motivation for staff, both within the company and the agencies it uses. As they may not be involved with the development of the marketing communications programme, they may perceive it as being irrelevant to their needs. And they will often feel no commitment to its successful implementation. As multinational campaigns take a long time to create and produce, this may reduce the ability, on a local level, to respond rapidly to local pressures.

Understanding the international consumer

QUESTION 13.6

- What are the key issues to be addressed in the development of an international marketing communications programme?
- What approaches should be used to minimize the potential difficulties?

If marketing communications demand a thorough understanding of the consumer and the environmental factors which surround them, this is even more true of marketing communications in an international context. Where we can reasonably expect to understand important facets of consumer behaviour in a domestic context, this is far less likely to be the case in different and separate markets where culture, tradition, and other factors may result in vastly different meanings being attached to the communications message. Market research will play an important part in identifying areas of similarity in order to allow for the development of a single consistent message, if that is the objective.

It should be clear that, in order to develop an effective multinational or global communications strategy, a number of 'new' dimensions will have to be considered, beyond those which would be appropriate for a single-market communications strategy.

- Language.
- Culture and tradition.
- Legal and regulatory requirements.
- Buying habits and motivational factors.
- Standards of living.
- Media availability and usage.
- The competitive environment.

Language

Multinational communications campaigns often fail because the message is simply *translated* rather than *reinterpreted*. This is not merely a semantic difference. Not only is it true that specific words often will not have a corresponding word in another language, sometimes the true translation will have a negative impact on the target audience. Furthermore, the same principles apply equally to body language and gestures. As we move increasingly towards non-verbal communications, it is vitally important to ensure that the visual imagery we employ communicates positively rather than negatively.

Culture and tradition

Arguably, this is one of the most difficult areas of multinational communications. Perceptions which are based on tradition and culture are extremely difficult to overcome. Fundamental areas, such as pack colours or symbols, may have totally different meanings resulting from cultural interpretation. White may indicate purity in many markets, but in others it is a symbol of death. Certain numbers may be symbols of good luck in some countries, but have opposite meanings in others. More significantly, the cultural values, sometimes derived from religious views, result in markedly different attitudes towards products and services. For example, it would be an anathema to show pork or shellfish ingredients in a product intended for a predominantly Jewish market, the same would apply to beef in Hindu communities, or alcohol for Muslims.

Find examples of packaging and advertising campaigns which, in their current form, would be inappropriate for other markets. Identify the reasons for this and decide how you might change them to make them more acceptable.

ACTIVITY 13.4

Whilst the specific advertising message might avoid such obvious errors, it is important to remember that the surroundings in which the message is set (a home, a retail outlet, etc.) may, similarly, contradict existing cultural beliefs in some markets. In some markets, for example, it would be inappropriate to depict a woman wearing Western clothes; in others, a commonly used motif of a man stroking a woman's skin to connote smoothness would be regarded as taboo.

Legal and regulatory requirements

There are few common standards for marketing communications across all markets – although there are progressive moves towards harmonization is some areas, such as the EC. Yet tobacco advertising, for example, is still commonplace in many parts of Europe, whilst limited or totally prohibited in others. Most countries now see condom advertising as part of the global campaign to control AIDS. However, in certain countries, such advertising would be unthinkable due to strong religious beliefs. Sales promotion techniques which are commonly accepted and widely used in some markets are not allowed in others (see Unit 9).

Buying habits and motivational factors

The patterns of purchasing frequency differ markedly between countries, sometimes resulting from differences in income levels and on other occasions being the results of patterns of usage. In some parts of the East, for example, fresh produce is bought on a daily basis, whereas in the West shopping, even for fresh ingredients, may be carried out weekly and the purchases stored in the fridge or freezer. Motivational factors and aspirations are, similarly, different from one country to another, leading to difficulties in communicating aspirational 'norms' where such values either do not exist or have different parameters.

Standards of living

Products which are consumed on a daily basis may be considered as luxuries in others, particularly if the relative cost is high. Cigarettes, for many purchased in packets of 20, are sold singly in some African markets, with the resultant difficulties of the lack of packaging to communicate brand values. Elsewhere, the incidence of fridges may preclude the sale of some packaged convenience foods, and so on.

Consider the implications for marketing communications of the growth of multinational media such as satellite television, international newspapers, transnational radio broadcasts, etc.

Media availability and usage

A primary consideration, especially in the context of global campaigns, is the need to access constant media outlets. After all, if a major aim of standardization is to eliminate costly production, then the same media must be available in all markets. However, not only are certain media not available to the marketer in some areas – certain countries, for example, have only limited television penetration, whilst others do not allow advertising – the patterns of usage may also differ. In some countries, spot advertising throughout the day is commonplace. In others, all advertising is grouped together and broadcast at set times of the day.

Other aspects of media are equally important. In different markets, different media have a different status, such that advertising placed in them have greater or lesser credibility. This is particularly the case in those markets where media have a distinct religious or political orientation.

The competitive environment

Just as consumers differ between markets, so do the brands available to them. Identifying the aspirational values of a brand, in order to define a unique positioning, becomes more difficult as the number of markets increases and the competitors differ in their stances. Often, a desired positioning is already occupied by another brand in a particular market. As we have seen, the relative position of a brand – leader or follower – will have important implications for communications strategy determination. It is extremely unlikely that all but a very few brands will occupy the same position in all of the markets in which they are available.

It is clear from the above that the task of developing a singular marketing communications strategy, whilst not impossible, is an extremely difficult one. Many companies have accepted that, in order to achieve their communications objectives, they must adopt a somewhat different stance. Indeed, such consensus as exists suggests that the policy towards multinational marketing communications campaigns should be based on the statement: 'Think globally, act locally.' Inherent in this statement is the acceptance of the fact that common communications strategies can be developed across all markets, but that their implementation must be effected on a local basis, in order to reflect the multitude of differences which, despite convergency, continue to exist.

The development of multinational communications agencies

In the same way that companies have become international, so too have advertising agencies, public relations and sales promotion consultancies, etc. Two important and parallel trends have occurred.

There has been a progressive 'internationalization' of the service companies to the point where few do not have representation in all of the key markets. As a result of mergers, acquisitions and alignments, the major practitioners in the fields of marketing communications have subsidiaries or associates in all the major countries of the world. In addition, global clients are increasingly appointing global agencies to handle and co-ordinate their marketing communications business across all their territories.

The recent appointment of Ogilvy & Mather to handle the IBM account typifies these movements. Indeed, the key requirement to inclusion on the shortlist for many such accounts is the extent to which a company has the ability to service the business on a multinational basis.

Often, companies will maintain a roster of agencies to handle their business, particularly where they have multiple brands. In most cases, the same agency will be used across the brand in all markets. Examples of this practice may be seen with Procter & Gamble, Mars and others.

The selection of an agency for international business

The principles underlying the selection of an agency to handle business across a number of markets are essentially the same as those involved in the appointment of an agency to handle an account within a single market.

What skills would be required by an international marketing communications agency as opposed to one dealing exclusively with domestic business?

These principles were detailed in Unit 5, but are summarized here:

- Determine the overall nature of the service you require:
  - (a) Full service.
  - (b) A la carte.
- Decide which services you will require:
  - (a) Creative.
  - (b) Planning.
  - (c) Media.
  - (d) Market research.
  - (e) New product development.
  - (f) Public relations.
  - (g) Sales promotion.
    etc.
- Define the quantitative criteria:
  - (a) Should the agency be large, small or medium?
  - (b) Should the agency be independent or part of an international network?
  - (c) Is previous experience in the category relevant or essential?
  - (d) What are the desired terms of business – billings/fee/combination?
- Define the qualitative criteria:
  - (a) What sort of agency style are you looking for?
  - (b) What sort of creative work do you require?
  - (c) Should your agency have won creative awards?
  - (d) Do you require direct access to the various departments (e.g. creative, media, planning)?
  - (e) Do you want a formal or informal relationship?
    etc.

In the case of the appointment of an agency to an international account, item (3b) will take on special importance.

Obviously, the decision as to agency selection will, to a large degree, be governed by the strategic direction of the company. As such, there are a number of separate options to be considered:

- The appointment of a single, multinational agency.
- The appointment of an international agency network.
- The appointment of a series of local agencies.

Multinational agencies

As noted above, the trend has been for the large agencies either to acquire or establish branches in all those markets in which they might reasonably expect to generate international client opportunities. Indeed, some of this process has been client inspired, in the sense that the agency is encouraged to establish an office in a country in which the client is intending to operate. Over the past two decades, led originally by US agencies, but more recently by British and Japanese agencies, groupings have been assembled to respond to client needs.

WPP which owns, amongst others, J. Walter Thompson, Ogilvy and Mather, Primary Contact, Lansdowne Conquest, is the largest agency grouping in the world. In Europe, however, J. Walter Thompson ranks ninth and Ogilvy and Mather tenth. By contrast, Euro RSCG claims the top European spot, but is only fifth in the UK.

Interpublic, which comprises McCann, Lowe Howard-Spink, Lintas and a variety of other agencies specializing in public relations, direct marketing and sales promotion, has a billings total of £1267 million, which places it second in the UK.

Such has been the growth of this process that the lists of the top 10 agencies in most countries are broadly similar in content – although not in order – to each other. Table 13.1 shows the top ten advertising agencies in just four countries; it can be seen that many of the same agencies are present in all four lists.

Table 13.1   The top ten advertising agencies in Spain, the Netherlands, Germany and the UK (from *Campaign*)

No.	Spain	Netherlands	Germany	UK
1	Tapsa NW Ayer	Ogilvy & Mather	BBDO Group	Saatchi & Saatchi
2	McCann Erickson	PPGH J. Walter Thompson	Publicis FCB	Ogilvy & Mather
3	Tiempo BBDO	FHV/BBDO	Lintas Group	J. Walter Thompson
4	Bassat Ogilvy & Mather	PMSvW Young & Rubicam	Grey Group	Abbott Mead Vickers BBDO
5	Delvico Bates	Publicis FCB/Prąd	McCann Erickson Group	DMB&B
6	Tandem DDB Needham	Grey Advertising	Young & Rubicam	BMP DDB Needham
7	Young & Rubicam	ARA/BDDP Group	Ogilvy & Mather	BSB Dorland
8	Euro RSCG	DDB Needham	BSB Group	Lowe Howard Spink
9	J. Walter Thompson	Result	J. Walter Thompson	WCRS
10	Grey Advertising	DMB&B	Euro RSCG	Grey London

Independent networks

To offset the competitive threat posed by the multinational agencies, networks and confederations have been formed to provide the global coverage demanded by some client companies. CDP Europe, Alliance International and ELAN (European Local Advertising Network) are three examples of such groups. From the agency perspective, these associations meet clients' needs to operate on a global basis, whist preserving their own independence. Usually, these groupings are based on 'like-minded' philosophies, with agencies of similar views of the marketing-communications process (creative style, media prowess, the role of planning, and so on) coming together.

Local independent agencies

In many countries, newly emergent agencies remain bitterly jealous of their independence and, at least in the short term, are prepared to forego some international accounts. Indeed, many such agencies remain independent in the longer term as a means of offering their own unique positioning in a crowded market.

Criteria to be considered in selection of an agency

Before deciding on its agency, any client must consider a set of important criteria in the international context.

To what extent is it planned to implement a single communications strategy in all markets?

For those companies wishing to pursue a global communications strategy, it is sensible to consider only the first and second options i.e. a multinational agency or an independent network. The benefits of already established links will ensure the speedy transfer of knowledge and understanding which, in turn, should facilitate the process of implementation in the variety of countries in which the campaign will run.

To what extent will the intended agency be precluded from operating in other market areas?

Some companies adopt a strict policy whereby the incumbent agency is not only precluded from handling directly competitive business, but also from those other areas in which the client company has an interest. This, it has to be said, is becoming an increasingly untenable situation. As multinational companies expand their businesses, both horizontally and vertically, they embrace increasingly diverse market segments.

Acquisitions of companies and brands result in their taking an interest in markets far beyond their original businesses. For example, P&G have interests in diverse fields including hair-care preparations, sanitary protection, cough and cold remedies, soap powders and toothpaste, to name just a few. Apart from their coffee interests, Nestlé operate in the following markets: confectionery, bottled waters, cereals, tinned soups and yoghurts and mousses. Here again, the list is only a partial one.

Clearly, to function profitably, the multinational agencies have to think carefully about client conflicts, both current and in the future, before taking on a new account. Though the short-term increase in billings might be attractive, their tenure of a particular client might inhibit their growth potential in the future. In turn, therefore, some agencies with otherwise desirable credentials may be precluded from consideration.

Do the multinational or network agencies possess all the appropriate skills in all markets?

Often, a multinational agency may have relatively weak representation in one or more of the markets considered important to the company. The same is equally true of agency networks, where not all of the participants may have the same reputation and skills.

Are there specific local skills which need to be accessed?

In some instances, a local independent agency may have a far greater in-depth knowledge or understanding of the market, the consumers or the general environment which it may be important to access. Indeed, the independent local agency may have greater prowess, for example, in media planning or creativity. It should not be assumed that simply because an agency is part of a wider international grouping it will possess all the skills required.

Where co-ordination is not a requirement, some companies have taken the decision to locate the creative development with one agency – usually referred to as the 'lead' agency – and to appoint several local agencies to handle the implementation. In other instances, they have chosen to appoint the 'best' agency in each market, to ensure access to the necessary skills in all areas.

How will the company cope with co-ordinating the campaign globally?

Deploying company personnel to the co-ordinating task may be one solution to this requirement. An alternative, particularly where a multinational agency is appointed, is to devolve that responsibility to the agency. Usually, a senior member of the agency structure is appointed to the specific role of ensuring consistency, both of creative work and implementation, throughout all markets. It will be his or her role to ensure cohesion between all aspects of the campaign in all markets, although ultimately it will be the client's responsibility to determine whether the role has been fulfilled adequately.

This internal agency role is often of considerable importance to other aspects of the smooth running of the campaign. The task involves overcoming the 'not invented here' syndrome, whereby the local brand responsible for the implementation of the activity may feel detached from it, since it was created elsewhere.

Similarly, the international co-ordinator may have the responsibility for allocating funds between branches to ensure that such tasks as market research are carried out adequately. In many cases, although the work is an important aspect of the understanding of the communications task in the market, the branch office may not generate sufficient income to afford their contribution.

QUESTION 13.9

What are the benefits of using a local marketing communications agency to launch a new product rather than the branch office of an international network?

International market research

A critical area of international marketing communications is the role of market research. We have already seen (Unit 6) the various techniques that are used to plan, develop and evaluate marketing communications. Given the complexities involved in developing creative work for implementation in separate markets – especially given the cultural and environmental factors mentioned earlier – market research must be used at all stages to ensure that the intended message communicates effectively. It can never be assumed that simply because a campaign works effectively in one or two markets, it will work equally well elsewhere. Specific research testing of the concepts and executions will be required in each market in which the campaign is intended to run.

QUESTION 13.10

Recently, McDonalds was a major sponsor of the 1994 World Cup. To what extent should they, and sponsors of other global events, integrate this activity with the other aspects of their marketing communications programmes?

SUMMARY

In this unit we have seen that:

- Although there is some evidence of a progressive move towards international standardization, the bulk of marketing communications activity is developed either locally or across only a few of the total number of markets in which a company operates. There are many reasons for this situation.
- Certain cultural factors may present barriers to the effective communication of a single message across all markets.
- As individual markets may have developed in different ways, and to varying degrees, the needs of the brand may well be different. The same brand may be well established in some markets, whilst in others representing a comparatively new proposition to its prospective consumers. It may be the brand leader in some areas, whilst only a minor brand in others.
- In addition to the brand strategy being different, therefore, there will also be a need to develop marketing communications strategies which are responsive to the localized requirements.
- Market research is an essential tool in the determination of the appropriate marketing communications strategy and, even where the brand exhibits similar traits in different markets, it is important to ensure the appropriateness of the message in each of those markets.

Examination hints and specimen questions

By now, you will have completed most of the work in the previous units and will have honed your skills with the example examination questions provided. Below, you will see two very different *styles* of question. The first, like those you have tackled so far, is taken from the second part of the paper. By now you have become familiar with this type of question and have understood the need to restrict your answer to the time allowed – typically 30 minutes.

The second is a new type of question for you to attempt. All CIM Diploma papers in Marketing Communications consist of two parts. The first part of the paper is a case study which, in recent years, has often had an international slant to it. Importantly, the case study is *compulsory* and carries 50 per cent of the marks for the whole paper. You should plan to allocate half of the overall time for the paper to answering this question.

Whether you decide to answer the shorter questions first or to tackle the case study immediately is a matter of personal preference. However, whichever approach you take, ensure that you allow $1\frac{1}{2}$ hours for the case study. Do not, however, be tempted to spend more time on this section. It is equally important to gain good marks in both parts of the paper. By spending too much time on the case study, you will have insufficient time to do yourself justice in answering the questions in the second part of the paper.

You are the marketing manager of a company that is expanding its international operations. You are considering undertaking a corporate advertising campaign to establish a common identity worldwide and to reinforce campaigns in particular markets. You are asked to justify, to your colleagues, in a memorandum, the detailed reasons for such a corporate campaign. Set out the difficulties you could experience and the ways in which you may overcome them.

(June 1994)

The Big Cat's on the Prowl

Jaguar is a British based, luxury car manufacturer that markets its products on a worldwide basis. The Company is now owned by Ford which bought Jaguar in 1990 for £1.6 billion, partly reflecting the value of the brand. Worldwide sales reached 50 000 cars in 1988 but then followed a period of recession which has badly affected luxury car sales. In 1992 sales had fallen to less than 25 000. The new owners, Ford, however are now much more optimistic and are planning for worldwide sales of 100 000 by the end of the century. This represents a massive challenge for marketing and marketing communications.

Jaguar is already active in most developed countries but is planning a massive push over the next five years into new markets: South America, Asia, Eastern Europe and Russia in particular. Over this period £700 million will be invested in new product development. The marketing director of Jaguar states 'our task over the rest of this decade is to make Jaguar more like the company it was in 1960, with a wider model range'. The speed and scale of the changes ahead represent a severe challenge for Jaguar. 'It's going to be a very interesting balance between bringing in all the new technology and maintaining Jaguar's much prized reputation as a brand which holds its price well in the second-hand market' says the marketing director.

1993 proved a better year for Jaguar with bullish signs in the four key markets of Germany, the USA, Japan and the UK. The pick up is in part due to sterling's devaluation in September 1992 but radical changes in product and marketing strategy have also played their part. The new models come with an unprecedented range of technological upgrades, most visibly the driver's side air-bag and a new alarm system, both as standard. To tempt buyers there is a three year/60 000 miles warranty which has catapulted Jaguar ahead of many of its luxury rivals in Europe.

Another sign of the new marketing revolution taking hold at Jaguar is its bold new buy-back initiative. If purchasers are unhappy with their car, they have 30 days in which to return it and receive a full refund. The move has proved incredibly successful, with less than 2 per cent returned and half of these exchanged for another model. This programme has helped Jaguar increase its rating in customer satisfaction surveys in America.

Jaguar management realize that substantial investment will be necessary in their marketing communications strategy if they are to achieve their ambitious marketing objectives. They have appointed the international advertising agency J. Walter Thompson to handle their account. The campaigns being planned will once again focus on the enormous emotional appeal that the brand has. The company wants its public to say 'Jaguar is back in a big way, in a highly visible day'.

The company has asked its agency to explore every element of the marketing communications mix. In the UK, the company's bread-and-butter market, £3 million has been earmarked for an advertising campaign and, equally important, the below-the-line activity has been boosted with a budget of £750 000. The company has also revealed that it wants a better use of its 36 000 customer database. The marketing director believes, with the decline in the number of luxury car customers, that 'it is not difficult to actually communicate with every one of them, so long as you're very careful about how you select your promotions and your direct mail. Once you've got them, you make sure that you give them what they want.'

In the past, car manufacturers have been guilty of last-minute marketing, believing that a great product, supported by a lot of expensive advertising, would be greedily snapped up by an admiring and grateful public. It is now realized that this will not do in the new area of lifestyle targeting. The average age of the Jaguar customers is 50 years old and the company wants to bring that down. The company's plans include a much more accessible model, codenamed X200, scheduled for production by 1998. Currently the XJ6 model costs less than £30 000 and has been voted 'best luxury car' against competition from the more expensive Lexus, BMW740i and Mercedes 600SEL. A sports car version of the XJ6 is to be launched which will attract younger customers. At the top end of the range is the Jaguar XJ12 and the Daimler Double Six, costing over £50 000. These are more clearly differentiated than in the past, with the Jaguar being aimed at 'the driving enthusiast' and the Daimler, with a more elegant and restrained ride, for the ranks of company chairmen who remain key to the car's success.

(Source: interview given by Jaguar's Marketing Director to *Marketing* magazine.)

Compulsory question

In your capacity as the Marketing Communications Manager of Jaguar, you have been asked to prepare notes to be discussed at an important meeting with J. Walter Thompson to assist them fully in planning the effective promotion of the Jaguar brand on an international basis over the next five years. These notes should be structured to provide clear guidelines for the agency on positioning, media selection, creative rationale, budgeting and monitoring.

(June 1994)

As well as the Marketing Communications paper, many of you will be studying for the CIM International Marketing paper. Remember that the knowledge gained in this area can equally be applied in this important area of marketing communications. Make sure, for example, that you read the appropriate chapters in your international marketing texts.

The following contain good sections on international marketing communications:

W. Keegan, *Global Marketing Strategy*, Prentice Hall, NJ, 1989.
C. Phillips, I. Doole and R. Lowe, *International Marketing Strategy*, Routledge, 1994.
V. Terpstra and R. Sarathy, *International Marketing*, Holt Reinhart & Winston, 1990.

To gain a deeper insight into issues relating to international marketing communications, the following texts will be particularly useful:

T. Griffin, *International Marketing Communications*, Butterworth-Heinemann, 1993.
R. Rijkens, *European Advertising Strategies*, Cassell, 1992.
N. Vardar, *Global Advertising. Rhyme or Reason?*, Paul Chapman, 1992.

UNIT 14

Other issues in marketing communications

It this last unit we will:

- Consider the requirements of the business-to-business sector and the objectives of marketing communications in this area.
- Examine the dimensions of services marketing and the differences with the communications of products.
- Look at low-budget campaigns.
- Address some of the important ethical and legal considerations applied to marketing communications.

By the end of this unit you will:

- Have completed the tasks of the workbook.
- Be ready to sit the CIM Diploma.

STUDY GUIDE

This unit contains a number of important topics for you to study before you complete the course. They will enable you to fill in any gaps which remain in your understanding of the principles relating to marketing communications, and the strategic issues which remain. Do not assume that because the topics are shorter they are any less important than those which we have covered previously.

Allow plenty of time to carry out the various tasks and begin the process of preparing yourself for the examination itself. You will need to spend a couple of hours considering the topics contained in this unit, and a further 2–3 hours to complete the tasks. It is especially important to read the last section of the workbook which will help you prepare yourself for the examination.

STUDY TIPS

Now is the time to start thinking about the examination itself. Make sure that your notes are all in order and that you have everything to hand so that you can begin the process of revision. If you find any gaps (missing examples, articles which you would like to re-read) make sure that you get everything in place in readiness for the last stage in the process.

Revision will ensure that by the time of the examination you will have the knowledge to pass. Be sure to take note of the guidelines for answering the questions. They may make the difference.

This unit covers a series of outstanding issues of which you will need to be aware in order to complete the syllabus of the CIM Diploma paper in Marketing Communications Strategy.

The development of marketing communications activity

Much of the material contained in this workbook deals specifically with the area of consumer goods and services, although there are equally a number of specific examples taken from the important areas of business-to-business and non-profit marketing.

In many respects, the initiatives which are now broadly applied to all marketing communications had their origins in the highly competitive nature of fast-moving consumer goods. This reflected the need to develop progressively better techniques for communicating with the identified target groups. However, it must be recognized that some of the techniques, used frequently in fast-moving consumer goods marketing communications, may not be available to other areas, either for strategic reasons, budgetary reasons or both. Candidates for the CIM Diploma will need to be able to apply their thinking to all aspects of marketing communications, not just the area of fast moving consumer goods.

The sections which follow immediately deal with specific issues relating to other areas of marketing communications.

Business-to-business communications

Business-to-business communications is the promotion of goods and services to businesses rather than individuals.

Traditionally referred to as 'industrial marketing communications', this term fails to recognize the diversity of the products and buyers involved within this area. The importance of the sector is underpinned by a report contained in the *Financial Times* (2 June 1989) which stated:

> Ten years ago, the average company spent around 40 per cent of its sales revenue in buying goods and services. Today that is more like 70 per cent.

It is also a reflection of the fact that many business-to-business markets are larger than most consumer goods markets.

There are, of course, a number of similarities and differences between consumer markets and those involved in the business-to-business area, as can be seen from the following chart (reproduced from T. Yeshin (ed.), *Inside Advertising*, Institute of Advertising Practitioners, 1993).

Business-to-business markets	Consumer markets
The differences	
Use company money	Use own money
Small number of buyers	Large number of buyers
Group buying decision	Individual or family decision
Extended buying timescales	Often short timescales
The similarity	
All buying decisions are taken by people	

It is often believed that, whereas consumers often make irrational buying decisions – based on the image dimensions of a brand, for example – businesses base their decisions on a rational consideration of the variables. This, to say the least, is something of an oversimplification. Companies, as such, take no decisions at all. The decision to purchase or not to purchase a particular good or service on behalf of the company is taken by one or more individuals. These, in other circumstances, are the same people who are responsible for buying goods and services on their own behalf or for the benefit of their families. Whatever role they fulfil, they are influenced by the same demographics, personalities, aspirations, lifestyles and so on. Both consumer purchases and business-to-business purchase decisions are, therefore, influenced by a complicated array of factors, some rational and some irrational.

QUESTION 14.1

How will the approach to marketing communications differ between a company selling a conventional consumer product and one involved in business to business marketing.

However, it is important to recognize some key differences between the two types of market. Firstly, in the business context, buyers are using the *company's money* not their own, and this fact may have ramifications for the way in which they consider the purchase.

Not only is it important that they spend the company's money in a way that delivers value for money, it must be perceived as achieving that. For many years, the litany of 'Nobody ever got fired for specifying IBM' dimensionalized this factor. So long as IBM was perceived as the primary source of computing equipment, the purchase decision was unlikely to be challenged, even if it failed to deliver the best value.

A second consideration is, in many instances, the relatively *small number* of potential buyers in business-to-business markets. Often, the target audience for a company's products or services may be numbered in the hundreds, rather than the many millions of potential consumers in the vast majority of retail markets.

The most important difference, however, is that with only a few exceptions business buying decisions are taken by *groups* of people rather than individuals. A key strategic issue may, therefore, relate to the identification of the individuals who comprise the decision-making unit rather than any one person.

QUESTION 14.2

What is the role of the decision-making unit? How should the members of the unit be targeted by marketing communications?

Most business decisions are taken as a result of the interaction of a number of different individuals who fulfil different roles within the organization. These may include specifiers (responsible for identifying the specific goods or services), users, purchasers and authorizers. Any or all of these may be able to exert an influence over the ultimate purchase decision. A successful sale can only be achieved following the identification of all members of the decision-making unit, and the key factors which will affect the part they play in the decision-making process.

ACTIVITY 14.1

Identify the composition of the decision-making unit for any industrial marketing company of your choice.

Another important distinction between business-to-business and consumer goods marketing is that the product itself may be *modified* to suit the needs of the individual user, as indeed can other aspects of the specification. Despite the fact that the product is often more complex than its consumer equivalent, the nature of satisfying the consumer's needs may be dealt with by adaptation to the specific requirements of the customer. Adjustments may be made in the terms of trade, delivery, training of the user's staff, repairs and spare parts to ensure that the offer matches the individual needs of the customer.

Moreover, because the typical business-to-business market is comparatively small, *personal contact* is the most widely used method of promotion. Often the scale of the order, the length of the negotiations, and the technical nature of the purchase will demand that the supplier maintains in-depth contact on a regular basis with the potential customer. The role of other forms of marketing communications is often to provide the essential support to the personal selling effort.

QUESTION 14.3

What are the important strategic issues to be addressed in business-to-business marketing?

In the business-to-business sector, marketing communications can fulfil a variety of specific objectives which will vary according to the circumstances:

- To create awareness.
- To generate sales leads.
- To pre-sell sales calls.
- To contact minor members of the decision-making unit.
- To build corporate and product images.
- To communicate technical information.
- To support the promotional effort.

Whilst personal selling is often the most motivating form of communications, it is also the most expensive technique, and other forms of marketing communications must be used to ensure maximum cost-effectiveness. As with consumer goods marketing, business-to-business communications will depend on the successful identification of the appropriate mix of communications tools to achieve the objectives.

The *planning process* is, essentially, the same as that for other forms of marketing communications, and it is important to identify the key objectives of the activity at the outset. Inevitably, however, given both the nature of the objectives and the scale of the budgets available, the planning considerations may be somewhat different.

ACTIVITY 14.2

Prepare an outline marketing communications plan for a company involved in industrial cleaning. You have a marketing communications budget of £75 000.

Integrated marketing communications is no less important here than in other areas of business. Indeed, it might be argued that the relative sizes of budgets require an even more careful consideration of the dimensions of integration to ensure that every element of the marketing communications campaign reinforces the others.

In his book on *Integrated Marketing Communications* (Butterworth-Heinemann, 1995), Ian Linton cites the example of ICL, a major player in the computer industry. At the time of the launch of their customer services division, ICL sought to ensure that every element of their external and internal material presented the same series of core messages. Product literature, direct marketing activity, exhibitions, videos, and internal materials reinforced the proposition that customer services were strategically important, and underpinned the statement that customer services contribute to corporate efficiency. Over a 3-year campaign period, these messages were reinforced and, where appropriate, altered to reflect the changing perceptions of the organization.

Services campaigns

The promotion of services, which has been referred to throughout this workbook, is similar to that of goods, although the application of the principles may differ to take account of the intangible nature of the service offering. As a result, the *objectives* of promotional activity are substantially the same. They may be expressed as:

- The building of awareness of the service or the company that provides it.
- Communicating the benefits of the service.
- Persuading the consumer to sample the service.
- To induce re-purchase of the service.
- Differentiating the service from that of competitors.
- Building an image and reputation for the service company.
  etc.

In what ways does marketing communications support differ for service organizations?

However, it is equally important to recognize that there are also fundamental differences in terms of services marketing that must be considered when developing marketing communications programmes. In the first place, unlike consumer goods, many *service provisions* differ in both form and quality to the end consumer. Ultimately, the delivery of the service is dependent on the performance of some intermediary. Even though efforts may be taken to ensure that certain standards of consistency are applied, the reality may be that the end result differs widely. An example might be in the field of fast food. The quality of the hamburger purchased from a chain of restaurants will, despite the consistency of the ingredients, be dependent on the performance of the staff who prepare it at the point of purchase.

Personal involvement is often a key dimension of quality perceptions of service provision. Unlike products which take on a constant tangible form, the provider of the service is synonymous with the quality of provision. Often, marketing communications will be used both internally and externally to reinforce this aspect of the service.

Internally, it may be used to motivate staff to deliver to a high standard; externally, it may be used to convince potential purchasers that the service provider understands the needs of the consumer.

How should marketing communications activity respond to an inconsistent delivery of a service at the point of purchase?

Secondly, there may be *sector constraints* which limit the nature of promotion within the category. The medical professions are restricted from actively promoting the services they provide because of codes of practice imposed by their professional bodies.

Thirdly, in many instances, the *scale of service provision* may limit the type of promotional activity. In the determination of the promotional campaign designed to support a service company, the available budgets may restrict the use of all but a limited range of marketing communications tools.

ACTIVITY 14.3

- How do airlines and other travel operators promote their services?
- What techniques do they use to differentiate themselves from their competitors?

Low-budget campaigns

There may be instances where candidates are asked to consider the implications of marketing communications planning in the context of low budgets. Although the access to financial resources will, inevitably, limit the scale of the communications activity, this should not be interpreted as a reason for ignoring the basic precepts of the role of planning. The same rigour as that applied to the planning of large-scale marketing communications plans must be applied to the planning of small budget activity.

QUESTION 14.6

How does the process of marketing communications planning differ when applied to small business?

Indeed, it can be argued that the significance of following a series of set procedures assumes greater importance because of the scarcity of the financial resource. Having said that, it must be recognized that some dimensions of planning will not be available to small-scale campaigns. Market research procedures, for example, may be innately too expensive to be affordable on a small budget. Nonetheless, this is no excuse for a failure to gather as much information as possible to complete the situational analysis. Much relevant material is available from published sources and will be available at limited cost. At the minimum it will ensure that the subsequent campaign is developed against reliable data. Similarly, it will be immediately apparent that specific forms of activity will be precluded from consideration. It is important, however, to ensure that you give appropriate consideration to the relevant methods of communication which are affordable on a low budget.

ACTIVITY 14.4

What marketing communications techniques are likely to be used by a charitable organization?

Ethical considerations in marketing communications

One major issue remains to be dealt with. This relates to the ethical and legal considerations which apply to the field of marketing communications. It has to be recognized that marketing communications is often described as an immoral business activity, responsible for exerting a pernicious influence on society in general. By the promotion of products and services which are beyond the reach of many consumers, marketing communications is held responsible for many of the underlying ills of society.

Undeniably, marketing communications stimulates the desire of individuals to aspire to a superior lifestyle and, with it, to have access to a wider range of goods and services. However, whether this is a reflection of the values of marketing communications, or of society as a whole, is a more difficult question to resolve.

Defend the position of advertising against the argument that it creates unnecessary needs and wants?

QUESTION 14.7

It is a fundamental dimension of human nature to 'seek to improve one's lot'. What was an acceptable lifestyle 20 or 30 years ago would be significantly below the level of today's desires. Products which were then considered aspirational are now considered to be the very staples of existence. Inevitably, it is a facet of an open society that individuals have the right to choose the products and services which they wish to have access to. The alternative is a more rigid society in which choice is restricted – based on the value judgements of others.

On a more fundamental level, criticisms of advertising often relate to the issues of selective emphasis and exaggeration. Since advertisers choose to highlight only those areas in which their product performs well, or better than their competitors, rather than providing a comprehensive analysis – warts and all! – such advertising may be criticized as failing to communicate the true nature of the products or services it promotes. By the same token, some advertisers use exaggerated claims to promote the appeal of their products.

Ultimately, there are a series of responses common to all societies which will limit these excesses. It may be a cliché, but if the product or service fails to deliver against the expectations of consumers – largely created by marketing communications – the product will fail. We have already seen that the area of post-purchase satisfaction (or dissatisfaction) is an important dimension of marketing communications. Manufacturers who seek to use marketing communications to promote inferior products, or whose claims for performance exceed their ability to deliver will rapidly appreciate the impact of the dissonance which such activity creates.

However, it must remain true that there are a number of areas in which the consumer must be protected against the excesses which might otherwise be against their interests. To this end, the governments of most countries have created a variety of legal and other regulatory frameworks which ensure that marketing communications performs in a manner which is acceptable to the public at large. These, in turn, are augmented by self-regulatory procedures which have resulted in the creation of codes of conduct to which practitioners are required to subscribe.

What are the roles of legal and self-regulatory controls within marketing communications?

QUESTION 14.8

In the UK, for example, the codes of practice of the Institute of Practitioners in Advertising, the Institute of Public Relations and the Institute of Sales Promotion, amongst others, provide detailed guidelines for the best practice within their respective fields of activity.

Identify examples of codes of practice which apply to advertising and public relations.

- What do they seek to achieve?
- How are they enforced?

The ultimate sanction rests with the consumer. The historical development of marketing and, with it, marketing communications, has entered a new phase. As described by Philip Kotler in *Principles of Marketing*, (5th edn, Prentice Hall, 1991), we are entering a new phase in which marketers must balance their own needs with those of society in general:

> The social marketing concept holds that the organization should determine the needs, wants and interests of the target markets. It should then deliver the desired satisfactions more effectively and efficiently than competitors in a way that maintains or improves the consumer's and the society's well being.

The underlying changes in consumer attitudes will result in the exertion of a number of pressures on marketing organizations. The ultimate power of the consumer remains the freedom of choice. If manufacturers fail to recognize and respond to these changes, then they must accept that they will be forced to accept the consequences of their actions, or lack of them. If manufacturers act in ways that consumers find detrimental or harmful to their well-being, they will reject their products. By the same token, if they are seen to be taking positive steps to improve the general environment in which the consumer exists, those same consumers will reward them by buying their products.

How should marketers adapt their marketing communications programmes to reflect the requirements of societal marketing?

These concerns should not be overstated. An annual survey conducted by the Advertising Association repeatedly reports that the level of those expressing concern or disapproval with advertising is falling progressively. Only 7 per cent of the population express such mistrust. For most, the field of marketing communications makes a positive contribution to society in general. It communicates information about products and services efficiently and cheaply and provides consumers with confidence in the goods and services that they purchase. It stimulates competition to produce new products and to improve old ones, and helps to ensure choice on the part of consumers. It helps to fuel economic prosperity, with the subsequent contribution to employment, by the opening up of new growth areas. And it expands media choice, by funding diverse and independent media which, substantially, rely on the income derived from advertising.

Marketing communications is a function within all developed economies which, despite comments to the contrary, makes a valid and realistic contribution to economic well-being.

In the course of this unit we have:

- Examined the implications of marketing communications in the important area of business-to-business activity. The fundamental principles governing the application of the techniques remain, substantially, the same although specific consideration needs to be given to the identification of the target audience which, in this case, will be those individuals who comprise the decision-making unit. Moreover, constraints of budget may demand a revised balance of activity to ensure that the available funds are deployed in the most appropriate and cost-effective manner.

- Seen that similar principles apply to the area of services marketing where we are dealing with intangible rather than tangible dimensions of the proposition. Here the role of service delivery plays an important part in the overall execution of the proposition and care must be taken to ensure that those responsible for service delivery reflect the desired image dimensions.

- Seen that, in the case of developing limited budget campaigns, the same guiding principles must be applied, although you must be careful to ensure that the chosen strategy is capable of being fulfilled within the financial constraints. The integration of communications activity is important to ensure that the desired message is reinforced to the target audience.

- Considered a number of ethical factors within the context of marketing communications. Most societies have established effective controls to ensure that the interests of the consumer are adequately protected but, ultimately, it remains the responsibility of producers to ensure that their activities are consistent with the general good. Indeed, the increasing power of consumer groups makes the acceptance of the principles even more important.

The series of books published by the Institute of Practitioners in Advertising under the title *Advertising Works* provides many examples of fully developed case histories in these areas. The most recent edition contains small-budget campaigns for Whipsnade Wild Animal Park, the launch of K Shoes, the International Fund for Animal Welfare, and the launch of Limelite:

C. Baker (ed.), *Advertising Works 7*, Institute for Practitioners in Advertising/NTC Publications, 1993.

The same volume also includes several service marketing campaigns for Scottish Amicable, Alliance and Leicester Building Society and Direct Line Insurance, which will help your understanding in this area.

The following books contain excellent coverage of the societal implications of marketing communications activity, together with chapters covering the other issues raised in this unit:

D. A. Aaker, R. Batra and J. G. Myers, *Advertising Management*, 4th edn, Prentice Hall, 1992.

W. L. Dommermuth, *Promotion Analysis, Creativity and Strategy*, PWS-Kent, 1989.

J. Engel, M. R. Warshaw and T. G. Kinnear, *Promotional Strategy – Managing the Marketing Communications Process*, 8th edn, Irwin, 1994.

Preparing for the examination

This unit, which will help you prepare for the CIM Marketing Communications Strategy examination (although the principles apply equally to all of the other examination papers which you might be attempting):

- Emphasizes the importance of revision to consolidate the knowledge which you have gained from working through this text.
- Provides you with guidance on the important area of examination techniques.
- Describes the examination structure, and provides you with some guidance as to how to tackle the examination as a whole.
- Emphasizes the importance of practice.

By the end of this unit you will:

- Appreciate the importance of developing a proper approach to the examination.
- Have a sound understanding of the techniques which must be employed to satisfy the requirements of the Chief Examiner.

Think carefully about the issues raised in this unit. Examinations are daunting for everyone. Unless you have done sufficient work prior to the examination you will lack the essential ingredient of confidence. How much effort you put in is largely up to you. But there is no substitute for real effort to master the skills and to build up the base of knowledge required.

In carrying out the various tasks within this workbook you will have had plenty of opportunity to determine whether you have really understood all the key issues. If you feel that there are still areas of weakness, use the time now to reinforce your understanding of the topics.

If you have followed the recommendations made at various stages throughout this workbook, and have carried out the different exercises and activities in each unit, you will be well on your way to ensuring that you have mastered the important dimensions of marketing communications strategy. However, the real test of your knowledge will take place during the examination, and it is important that you prepare for it properly.

Revision

If you have allowed sufficient time for each unit, much of the knowledge which you have developed will now be firmly settled in your mind. By practising the example questions you will have identified your areas of strength and weakness, and you can spend some time ensuring that you have overcome any deficiencies.

Re-read all your answers to see if there are ways in which you might improve them. Are there any clear gaps in your knowledge which need to be covered before you sit the exam?

Are you clear on the processes of marketing communications, which will provide you with a framework in which to answer the questions set by the examiner?

Now is the time to make sure that you are well prepared for the examination.

Examination technique

More candidates perform poorly in the examination because of the lack of an adequate examination technique, rather than the simple lack of knowledge. Consider, first, how you will approach the exam paper.

It is advisable to *read through the paper in its entirety* before attempting to answer any questions. That way, you can identify any questions which you feel confident with from the outset. Try to *shortlist the questions* which you might answer. There may be one or more 'gift' questions which, because of special knowledge, personal experience or some other reason, will help you achieve your goal of passing the Diploma examination. Having decided which questions you are going to tackle, don't rush into writing your answer.

Re-read the question carefully to make sure you are clear as to what the examiner expects of you. Does the question ask you to take on a particular role, such as a consultant, marketing executive or similar? This will be important to the structure of the answer you provide. Does the examiner ask you to write in a particular way – write a memo, letter, report or, perhaps, use some form of checklist against which to make your points? If so, make sure that you adopt the appropriate style.

What are the points that you will need to cover? If appropriate, underline the key words in the question so that you know what to cover. Many candidates assume, wrongly, that if they write a lot on the general topic, it will gain them marks – it won't! *Your answer must be specific* to the question.

Prepare an outline answer before you write your response in full. To make sure that you present a clear and concise response to the examiner, it is worth spending some time outlining your answers. This will enable you to create a logical flow to your arguments rather than having to return to an aspect of the question which you did not cover adequately at some other point in your answer.

Be careful with *time management*. You must allocate your time in proportion to the marks available for the questions. By now, you will have had plenty of practice with the short form (30 minute) style of question to be able to pace yourself properly. Do not be tempted to spend more than 30 minutes on any of these questions – you will simply run out of time before you complete the paper. Remember, if you fail to complete the paper, you will need to achieve your pass on the basis of the questions which you have tackled! That is a hard task for anyone.

Whether you tackle the mini case or the short form questions first is entirely a matter of personal preference. Remember, the examination requirement does not stipulate *the order in which you answer the questions*. Certainly, all candidates feel under pressure when beginning the examination, and it may help you to build your confidence by attempting a shorter question where your are confident about your knowledge than one where you are less sure.

Write clearly and precisely. The examiner will want to see a careful response which is easy to understand, rather than one which is full of crossings out, asterisks to refer him back to a previous part of the question, writing in the margin, and so on. The latter are all examples of a poor approach to the examination, and should be avoided.

The examination structure

The examination consists of two parts.

- Part A contains a *compulsory mini case question* which all candidates must answer. It is worth 50 per cent of the total marks and you should allow $1\frac{1}{2}$ hours on this question.
- Part B contains *eight short questions* from which you must *choose three* to answer. This part of the paper is also worth 50 per cent of the marks.

The mini case

As noted above, the mini case is a compulsory part of the examination. The Jaguar mini case is included in Unit 13 so that you can see the style used by the examiner and the type of questions asked. (Hopefully, you have also by now practised this question so you have got a 'feel' for the mini case.) The principles of preparation, and the way in which you tackle the question (described above) apply equally to the mini case.

However, there are a series of special points to note, which apply specifically to this area.

The mini case will continue to use 'real-world' examples. The examiner will supply you with information taken from a particular market and will ask you to respond to a series of questions which relate to the text.

Make sure that you deal with the *specific issues* raised in the individual questions. The nature of the mini case should not be taken as an excuse for writing your comments on some other topic which the examiner has not asked you for!

Often the mini case will contain numerical information. Make sure that, if appropriate, you use this properly in your answer. Marketing communications is, increasingly, a quantitative subject – and you should make sure that you have practised the skills appropriate to dealing with number-based information.

Remember that, as elsewhere in the field of marketing communications, there is no single correct answer. What the examiner will require is that you demonstrate an understanding of the strategic issues contained in the case, and that you justify your position or recommended course of action.

As previously, it is important that you read the question carefully. Because of the amount of information provided, it is often the case that individual items of importance will be located in different parts of the text. If you do not read everything thoroughly there is a danger that you might miss something of importance. Plan out your approach to the questions carefully. Use the same techniques described for the short questions to prepare an outline before you begin to write your response to the question in full.

Manage your time carefully. Spend enough time to get a grasp of the key issues. A shorter answer which is more direct and covers the points required will be better received than one where the candidate rushes straight in, writes a lot, but fails to consider what is really expected.

Here, you *must deal with the questions in the order that they have been set by the examiner*. Often, one part of the question will relate to a previous one, and the examiner will expect you to deal with them in the correct sequence.

Quite often, the information will be incomplete. You might, for example, require additional information from market research, or other areas, to supplement your knowledge. In such an event, make sure that you clearly *indicate any assumptions you are making*.

You will be required to write your response in the form of a management report, a marketing communications plan, or some other format. The question will indicate the nature of your task and position. Take care to ensure that you adopt the style which is appropriate to the requirement, rather than providing an essay!

Clearly identify any recommendations you wish to make by separating them from other elements of your answer.

Remember, practice is an essential requirement for good performance. Few candidates can enter the examination room, write out their answers and expect good marks unless they have prepared carefully before the event. Use the time you have available to ensure that you have mastered the techniques of good examination performance.

A specimen examination paper, together with answer guidelines, follows.

Marketing communications strategy: specimen examination paper

The duration of this examination is 3 hours.

This examination is in two sections:

- *Part A* is compulsory, based on a mini case and worth 50 per cent of total marks.
- *Part B* has eight questions, select three.

Each answer will be given equal marks totalling 50 per cent of the whole for the paper.

DO NOT repeat the question in your answer but show clearly the number of the questions attempted on appropriate pages of the answer book.

Rough workings should be included in the answer book and ruled through after use.

The Mondex Card, Electronic Wallet

National Westminster Bank and Midland Band could save hundreds of millions of pounds by replacing cash with an electronic wallet. The two have set up a joint venture to begin offering customers a plastic 'smartcard' called Mondex, to be used as a substitute for cash.

The banks have refused to reveal the size of their investment in the service. But estimates put the figure at about £70 million between 1990 and 1995.

Recent figures show the cost to the UK's banks of shifting cash to fill dispensing machines is £4.5 billion a year. Electronic purses would dramatically reduce that figure.

The two banks are working with BT, which is adapting pay phones to accept the card and is developing a new phone for use at home so that customers will be able to transfer cash from bank accounts to the cards. Analysts estimate that if the service is successful it could add £100 million a year to BT's revenues by the year 2000 as the group expands into home services.

Yesterday's announcement surprised others in the banking industry as it came just a day after Visa and Mastercard had announced that they were working to develop a common chip standard for smartcards. John Hutchinson, managing director of Visa UK, described Mondex as 'a very interesting experiment'. He said similar initiatives were afoot in South Africa, Spain and Denmark.

However, he issued a warning: 'We need to make sure that we do not have, like the video world did for a while, three different standards.'

Bert Morris, NatWest's deputy chief executive, said NatWest had approached Midland to take part in the project because the two banks had worked well together on cash machines and Switch debit cards. Other UK banks may be invited to participate in the scheme at a late stage.

The Mondex card will be tested in 1995 in Swindon, Wiltshire, where all 40 000 of the banks' customers will be eligible. The partners hope to win customers over from other banks and have all 1000 or so retailers in Swindon taking part. If Mondex is successful, it will be rolled out to the banks' 11 million customers nationally a year later.

Mondex is a plastic card that stores a cash value electronically on a chip. This card can be updated using cash machines or specially adapted telephones. Customers will also be able to increase the values on their cards when they do their shopping, in the same way as they are able to ask for cash back when they use a debit card in a supermarket. An electronic wallet will also be available, enabling customers to store cash for transfer to cards, or to transfer cash from one card to another.

Tim Jones, the senior NatWest executive who conceived the idea in March 1990, predicted that in 10 to 15 years time, 'the telephone will be the dominant way in which electronic money is withdrawn and deposited.'

NatWest said it would begin approaching banking partners worldwide next year as part of a plan to establish Mondex as a global cash payments system.

The card is designed to be used by children as young as five years old, while the Mondex partners hope it could be used in the future for such things as paying government benefits.

(From *The Times*, 9 December 1993)

Part A

Compulsory question

1 Acting as a consultant to the National Westminster Bank Consortium you are asked to write a report recommending a marketing communications strategy for this financial service innovation. In your report you are expected to address the following aspects.

   (a) What are the problems that the marketing communications strategy must address?
   (b) What alternative marketing communication activities can be used to solve those problems?
   (c) Make recommendations on a choice of strategy for the Swindon test marketing.
   (d) Define the means of measuring the effectiveness of your recommended strategy.
   (e) Briefly discuss the implications for a roll out nationally and internationally.

Part B

Answer three questions only

2 Central to the definition of marketing communications is the concept that all marketing mix variables, and not just promotional variables alone, communicate with customers. You are asked to prepare notes for a talk to business people which is intended to described the ways in which an organization should go about developing a completely integrated marketing communications campaign.

3 Some models of how the communication process works in a marketing environment are very simple whilst other models borrowing from the behavioural sciences are complex

and more difficult to apply in practical situations. However, it is believed that a theoretical understanding of marketing communications is important. Describe and evaluate three different models which can be used in developing marketing communications strategy.

4   You are the newly appointed marketing communications manager of a company that is already well experienced in marketing planning. The managing director, to whom you report, has asked you to set out the steps necessary in developing and implementing an integrated marketing communications plan. Specifically, he has asked you to show how promotional planning is derived from marketing planning. It is likely that you will use diagrams to illustrate your answer.

5   In the last decade, the power of national manufacturers of consumer goods has declined relative to the power of the multiple retailers. The manufacturers' brands have suffered increasing competition from own-label or retailers' brands. You are the marketing manager of a manufacturer of a nationally branded food product. In a memorandum to your managing director, set out guidelines for changes in your future marketing communications strategy brought about by changes in the power of retailers

6   Many Government organizations have made their internal services either self-supporting or profit centres. The changes are intended to improve the quality of the work or to achieve high levels of efficiency. Often this means that compulsory competitive tendering occurs involving both inside and outside suppliers. For an organization of your choice show how a particular department may go about marketing itself within its own organization. Make your recommendations in the form of an outline internal marketing communications strategy and plan.

7   Choose any two current marketing communications campaigns with which you are familiar. Describe the objectives of the two campaigns. Explain why in your judgement the two campaigns use the marketing communications mix differently. Comment on the effectiveness or otherwise of the marketing communications strategy adopted in the two campaigns.

8   1993 has seen the launch of the Single European Market with the elimination of frontier controls and the consequent free movement of goods between member states. You are asked to evaluate the effect of these changes on the marketing communications strategy of a manufacturer of consumer goods, who currently manufactures and markets in one European country. The goal of the company is to enter at least two other European countries.

9   The experience of many leading companies shows that database marketing, when used strategically, can transform the way a company does business and therefore achieve competitive advantage. Understanding the role of information technology has also been increased by the work of Michael Porter in value chains, which has shown how to strengthen customer relations and overcome supplier problems. For an organization of your choice, illustrate how information technology and database marketing can make a significant contribution to marketing strategy.

Answer guidelines
This section of the workbook is reproduced from the manual prepared by the Chief Examiner and represents his recommendations and comments on answer structure and contents.

Question 1
This is a case deliberately focused on the future. The test market takes place in Swindon in 1995. Although the location is the UK the principles apply internationally. The case has been chosen to illustrate strategic aspects of marketing communications. It is hoped that students find the case interesting and challenging.

Report: Recommendations for Marketing Communications Strategy for Mondex Test Market and Roll Out.

Prepared for: National Westminster Bank

                   Midland Bank

Prepared by: A Marketing Consultant

Report date: January 1994

(a)
- Executive summary of purpose and content.
- Outline critical factors of the project. The project has a number of key points:
  - Test market followed by roll-out nationally.
  - New technology is involved.
  - There will be customer and trade resistances.
  - The project involves many organizations.
  - There will be worldwide interest in the experiment.
- Problems to which marketing communications must contribute. There are two key problems:
  - Educating pepole about the scope and benefits of the system.
  - Overcoming resistance to the new system.
- Using the simple AIDA model the chosen marketing communications used must deal with:
  - Increasing awareness of what the system will do.
  - Developing interest in the benefits.
  - Stimulating desire to register as a user.
  - Creating action to use the system.

(b) Alternative marketing communications activities:
- A greenfield situation exists. Therefore it is important to consider all the alternative methods of marketing communications, either in the context of the test market or of the national roll-out programme.
- Limiting factors will be:
  - The availability of media in Swindon.
  - The size of the promotion budget.
  - The identity of the target audiences indicated by the initial research.
- It is likely that a complex mix of methods will be used including:
  - Advertising: to reach wider audiences.
  - Public relations: because of novelty/newsworthiness.
  - Direct marketing: use banks customer database.
  - Sales promotion: at the point of usage retailers/banks.
  - Signage: 'use your Mondex here'.

(c) Recommendations on strategy:
- Develop strong brand image.
- Maximize on public relations potential.
- Develop high impact local press advertising.
- Direct mail bank customers.
- Personal selling to retailers to encourage take-up.
- Wide availability of literature.
- Freephone number for information.
- Tracking research to monitor.

(d) Means of measuring:
- Levels of take up, number per 1000 of population.
- Number of transactions.
- Freedom from difficulties/complaint.
- Measurement of attitudes and awareness.
- Public relations coverage in the media.

(e) Implications for roll-out nationally and internationally:
- Learn lessons, modify branding or message if necessary.
- Consider further test region, consider television advertising.
- Test market in another country (after one year's operation).
- De-bug the system. What about fees for users of the system?

Question 2   The marketing mix communicates

This question continues the theme of recent marketing communications papers that promotional campaigns must be integrated to be efficient and effective. This particular question also tackles the contribution of the other elements of the marketing mix; product, price, place, service towards promotion. The answer is required in the form of notes for a talk to business people. Bullet points are therefore acceptable and welcome.

- Assumptions about audience: knowledgeable, interested, but not technical specialists.
- Objectives of the talk: to convince them of the value of marketing and marketing communications.
- The marketing mix and the communications mix:
  - The 4 Ps or more: Product, Price, Promotion, Place, People, Policies, Physicals.
  - The promotion mix.
  - Advertising, sales promotion, public relations, direct marketing, POS.
- How to use the marketing mix:
  - How companies distinguish themselves, with examples.
  - Segmentation and differentiation, hopefully with diagrams.
- How to use different media:
  - Show fragmentation of the media and promotions industry.
  - Identify some major changes, i.e. direct marketing, satellite television.
- Develop model or customer behaviour/promotion: show effect of communications on customer behaviour using models to illustrate answer.
- Need for integration:
  - Refer to complex buyer behaviour.
  - Show cost savings from common purpose/design.
  - Show need for integration into timetable/budget.
  - Show integration into sales/production/finance.
  - Show integration into supply chain.
  - Importance to customer service.
  - Importance to relationship marketing.

Question 3   Marketing communications models

- *Importance of understanding.* This area will become increasingly important in future as more research is done on the effectiveness of promotion methods and as earlier work on consumer behaviour is translated into workable theories of promotion. The advent of computer modelling may also be a contributing factor. The theoretical understanding of the process of marketing communication is important because:
  - The need to make promotion more effective.
  - The need to plan in a consistent manner.
  - The need to evaluate various alternatives.
  - Alternatives are becoming more varied and complex.
  - Marketing is becoming more competitive.
  - The rapid development of information technology.
  - The power and reducing cost of computing.
  - More knowledgeable marketing persons.
  - Academic studies of marketing communication.
  - The realization that integrating marketing communications in a systematic manner is vital.
- *Description of models/evaluation.* Three models of various complexity are used here. The first is an extension of the well-known AIDA model developed in the 1920s (see Unit 3). It is very useful both in conceptual terms for understanding the processes involved and for selling objectives for each distinct stage of that process.

The second (after Joyce 1967) (illustrated in Unit 3) is an attempt to improve on the AIDA model by showing that the consumer is not a passive individual and that the process is not linear but is a more complex cyclical one. Again it helps to plan and understand how advertising may work.

The final model is an attempt to understand the consumer buying process in terms of a decision-making process together with the possible influences in the decision process. The increasing complexity of this model can be seen, which limits its practical applications.

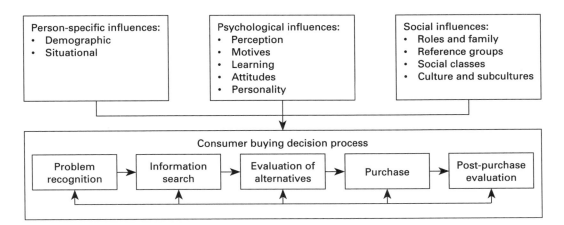

Figure 1 Consumer buying decisions process and possible influences on the process. (From: S. Didd, L. Simkin, W. Pride and O. C. Ferrell, *Marketing: Concepts and Strategies*, 2nd edn, Houghton Mifflin, 1994)

Question 4   Integrated marketing communications plan
An internal memorandum is a useful format for your answer.

MEMORANDUM
To: Managing Director
From: Marketing Communications Manager
Date: 1 January 1994
Subject: Marketing Planning and Promotional Planning

1. You have asked me to set out the steps necessary in developing and implementing an integrated marketing communications plan and specifically to show how promotional planning is derived from marketing planning. I understand that out company is already well advanced in marketing planning. This will make the early effective adoption of marketing communications planning much easier.
2. I am a firm believer that marketing communications must be integrated within itself and with the other elements of the company's marketing mix. Planning for marketing communications strategy is every bit as important as planning the other aspects such as product policy, pricing policy and distribution policy.
3. The complete marketing planning process can be described by the diagram. At each stage of this process marketing communications planning is involved as the following examples show:
    – Understanding customer needs leads to the development of appropriate communications messages.
    – Evaluating competition leads to the choice of a correct promotions strategy.
    – Marketing research measures communications effectiveness.
    – In developing segmentation the choice of media is important.
    – Targeting segment often means targeting media audiences.
    – Positioning must substantially be supported by effective branding, images and campaigns of the right weight and tone.
    – Developing the marketing mix includes the correct choice of promotional media and implementation of a marketing communications campaign programme must be integrated into the overall marketing programme.
    – Finally, control of the resources and effectiveness of the marketing communications process must be maintained.

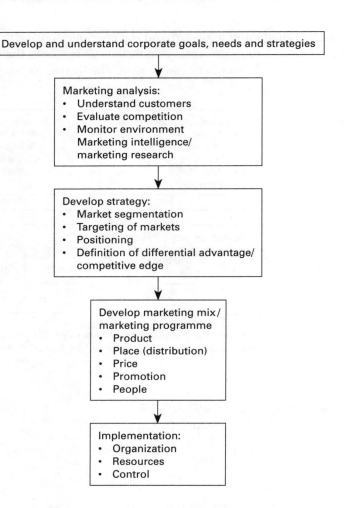

Develop and understand corporate goals, needs and strategies

Marketing analysis:
- Understand customers
- Evaluate competition
- Monitor environment
Marketing intelligence/
marketing research

Develop strategy:
- Market segmentation
- Targeting of markets
- Positioning
- Definition of differential advantage/
competitive edge

Develop marketing mix/
marketing programme
- Product
- Place (distribution)
- Price
- Promotion
- People

Implementation:
- Organization
- Resources
- Control

Figure 2

Question 5   The power of the multiple retailers
MEMORANDUM
To: Managing Director
From: Marketing Manager
Date: 14 December 1993
Subject: Changes in marketing communications strategy

1. Analysis of market changes:
    – Power of multiples.
    – Usual pull strategy of consumer advertising not enough.
    – Need for radical changes in the way we deal with multiples.
2. Gaining listing/long-term relationships.
    Most vital part, negotiation at senior level.
3. High-class service/quality control
    Ongoing high levels of service.
4. Change in advertising balance:
    – Include trade magazines, *The Grocer*.
    – Several customers have in-house magazines.
    – Co-operative advertising, i.e. KWIKSAVE.
5. Merchandising.
    Regular stocking and best position.
6. Point-of-purchase and promotions.
    Gain co-operation on regular promotions and point of purchase display.
7. Labelling to multiples requirements.
8. In-store research to monitor performance in store.
9. Marketing tracking studies to monitor against competition.
10. Annual reviews and renegotiations.
    Building long-term relationships.

Question 6   Internal marketing communications plan

The best students will first describe the organization which they have chosen. Ideally, it will be one in which they work or of which they have strong knowledge. Public sector companies are likely to feature in this question and novel ideas will be rewarded.

A sound internal plan should have the following elements:

- The reasons why marketing communications are important.
- The definition of internal marketing communications objectives. These are likely to be difficult to define. Aim for solid attempts at qualification.
- The specification of target audiences within the organization. Internal segmentation is as important as external customer segmentation. Good students may draw a diagram demonstrating relationships
- Description of media and methods. Good students will identify novel methods besides the usual meetings, company newsletters, annual reports, posters.
- Statement of financial resources required. Likely to be smaller than for external promotion but should still be qualified.
- Statement of human resources required. Likely to be related to usual organization patterns.
- Description of control and evaluation techniques proposed.

Question 7   Current marketing communications campaigns

This question offers students an open choice of any two current marketing communications campaigns. Future papers will contain similar questions. These are designed to encourage students to keep themselves up to date and to conduct thorough preparation before the examination. It is difficult, given the free choice, to be prescriptive about what students should write but answers deserving a high grade are likely to have the following elements written in an outline report style.

- The two campaigns will be described in outline with perhaps a personal view of the reasons for their choice.
- The objectives of both campaigns will be described clearly with quantification being expected.
- The target audiences will be described as this is likely to affect the marketing communications mix choice.
- Differences in the promotional mixes will be detailed and justified. These differences may be linked to a whole variety of factors including product life cycle, target audiences, availability of media and the size of the total promotion budget.
- The final stage will be the evaluation of the effectiveness of the two campaigns. Personal judgement is permissible and is to be encouraged, but reference to achieving the objectives is vital. Quantification and research results will gain extra marks.

Question 8   Entry into the Single European Market changes in marketing communications strategy

Although the problems facing any consumer goods manufacturer waiting to enter Europe are likely to be very similar, the better students may wish to particularize the product area to, say, food or drink. This will allow the students to provide more detail in their answer.

Students are not expected to have detailed knowledge of the market or media of particular European countries, but are expected to know and apply broad principles. Among the changes that should be evaluated are:

- Criteria for choosing two new countries, similarities and differences from home market affecting knowledge of customers.
- Decisions on the method and scope of market entry, whether exporting from UK or manufacturing in Europe, and the possibility of a joint venture. What effect will this have on communications strategy?
- Exploration of the effects of language, culture.
- Exploration of differences in media availability/channels.
- Possible appointments of local advertising agents.
- Cost and control elements.
- Possible proposals on test marketing.

Question 9   Strategic database marketing

The students is asked to choose an organization with which to illustrate this answer. This may be the candidate's own organization or one with which they are familiar. Students should be rewarded for choosing real practical examples. Because there will be a wide variety of organizations it is difficult to be prescriptive about the answer. Good students are expected to cover the following elements:

- The strategic use of information:
    - Long-term view of links between organizations.
    - Shifts in boundaries between co-operating bodies.
- Michael Porter's value chains (use diagram):
    - Supplier value chains.
    - Firm value chains.
    - Channel value chains.
    - Buyer value chains.
    - Links giving competitive advantages.
- Description of chosen organization, showing the organization's approach to database marketing.
- Use of databases within the organization:
    - Specific examples and the benefits accruing
    - Customer segmentation, marketing planning, new products.
- Scope for future developments.
    The scope for database marketing will increase in the future with the power of computing and the increasing capture of customer information.
- Examples:
    - Direct Line Insurance: tremendous profitable growth.
    - Marks and Spencers: charge card customer mailings.
    - Volvo customer databases.

Appendix Marketing communications strategy – syllabus overview

The new paper in Marketing Communications Strategy is designed to build on the learning undertaken by students who have completed the Advanced Certificate paper in Promotional Practice. Where the latter concentrates primarily on the application of practitioner knowledge, the former is concerned with the strategic aspects of marketing communications. It is assumed that all candidates for the Diploma will have an understanding of the Advanced Certificate material. Where appropriate, this workbook reinforces that knowledge and understanding to assist your understanding of the strategic requirements.

Aims and objectives:

- To enable students to build a sound theoretical and practical understanding of the formulation of promotional strategy and the management of the marketing communications process.
- To develop an understanding of the economic and creative justifications for marketing communications.
- To develop an understanding of the present limits of communications theory and the need to make the process of marketing communications more soundly based.
- To be sensitive to legal and ethical considerations in the formulation and the implementation of marketing communications strategy.

Learning outcomes

Students will be able to:

- Plan marketing communications strategy effectively.
- Relate communications objectives to marketing and business objectives.
- Choose the most appropriate communications elements to ensure the achievement of marketing communications strategies.
- Integrate communication elements together in a timed and targeted plan.
- Decide appropriate levels of appropriation.
- Analyse successful campaigns and learn appropriate lessons.
- Be aware of legal and ethical considerations of promotion.
- Be aware of the impact and development of information technologies on the marketing communications sphere.
- Be sensitive to marketing communications strategies in European and international contexts.

Indicative content and weighting:

The following schedule sets out the content of the syllabus and the weighting which will be applied to each section. By considering the relative importance of the different parts of the syllabus, you will be able to adjust your studies to ensure that you devote the appropriate amount of time to each of the areas covered.

1.1   Marketing communication strategy – an overview (10%):
    1.1.1   A definition of marketing communications strategy.
    1.1.2   Economic and creative justifications for marketing communications.
    1.1.3   The marketing mix communicates: product, price, distribution.
    1.1.4   Promotion strategy and the marketing concept.
    1.1.5   The importance of an integrated marketing communications strategy.
1.2   Developing a theoretical understanding of marketing communications (15%):
    1.2.1   What communications are all about?
    1.2.2   Communication in marketing.
    1.2.3   Consumer response to persuasive communications.
    1.2.4   The influence of the social and cultural environment.
1.3   Managing the marketing communications process (30%):
    1.3.1   The analysis of promotional opportunities.
    1.3.2   The concepts of segmentation and target marketing.
    1.3.3   Promotional strategy formulation and competitive positioning.
    1.3.4   Determination of promotional objectives.
    1.3.5   Deciding the promotional appropriation.
    1.3.6   Implementing the objective and task approach.
    1.3.7   Integrating the marketing communications programme.
    1.3.8   Organization and use of human resources to achieve strategies.
    1.3.9   Commissioning and contracting external resources.
    1.3.10 Managing the brand, nationally and internationally.
1.4   Successful marketing communications strategies (15%):
    1.4.1   Successful low-budget campaigns.
    1.4.2   Successful consumer campaigns.
    1.4.3   Successful service campaigns.
    1.4.4   Successful industrial campaigns.
    1.4.5   Successful charity and not-for-profit campaigns.
1.5   International marketing communications (15%):
    1.5.1   To globalize or not to globalize.
    1.5.2   Cultural and geographical differences.
    1.5.3   The role of international advertising agencies.
1.6   Wider issues of marketing communications (15%):
    1.6.1   Financial implications, long-term effectiveness, brand strategies and evaluation.
    1.6.2   Legal and ethical considerations of promotional strategy.
    1.6.3   Impact of information technologies on marketing communications strategy.

Index

your chance to bite back
Marketing Communications Strategy

Dear student

Both Butterworth-Heinemann and the CIM would like to hear your comments on this workbook. All respondents will receive a FREE copy of a CIM marketing book.

If you have some suggestions, please fill out the form below and send it to us at:

> Business Books Division
> Butterworth-Heinemann
> FREEPOST OF/1639
> Oxford OX2 8BR

Name and address: _____

_____

College/course attended:

_____

If you are not attending a college, please state how you are undertaking your study:

_____

_____

_____

How did you hear about the CIM/Butterworth-Heinemann workbook series?

Word of mouth ❑
Through my tutor ❑
CIM mailshot ❑

Advert in _____

Other _____

What do you like about this workbook (e.g. layout, subjects covered, depth of analysis):

What do you dislike about this workbook (e.g. layout, subjects covered, depth of analysis):

Are there any errors that we have missed (please state page number):

First Published October 2004
by
Total Detail Publications Ltd.

ISBN 1-904900-01-1

Printed in Hong Kong

TOTAL DETAIL
Sd Kfz 250 Alt & Neu
Volume 3 - Part 2
ARCHIVE

Martin Kögel

One

INTRODUCTION

DEVELOPMENT

Factory fresh Scheutzenpanzerwagen (SPW) Sd Kfz 251/1 Ausf Cs and Sd Kfz 250 'Alt's await allocation to combat units. These were photographed at one of the Army depots that accepted vehicles from the manufacturers rather than in a factory storage area.

As seen in 250 Archive Part 1, which deals with the earlier 'Type 1', these photographs show the change-over from the early design to what could be termed the 'classic' 250/1 or in this case 'Type 2'. There was no official separation between the first and second versions of the Alt, but for clarity it has been decided to name them Type 1 & 2 in both books.

The Type 2 was a subtle re-design, (see History in 250 Archive – Part 1), with fewer pieces to the armoured body. The driver's glacis plate was set at an improved angle and the rear panel was designed at a more vertical angle that avoided the need for the valance. The vision port in the door was deleted and the footstep bracket was no longer required because of the change to the rear armour. It also differed from the Type 1 in the mounting position of the headlamps, registration plate, the introduction of the 'one-slit' armoured visors for the driver and co-driver in the front plate and amongst other technical details a new radiator shutter design.

The 'classic' Type 2 also saw the introduction of new track and mudguards, the re-positioning of the tools and the deletion of the supplementary toolbox and lifting hooks. (However, some early versions of the Type 2 (see page 8) were built to the new design, but without the beaded edge.) The basic interior remained the same save for a few minor detail changes beyond the scope of this book. For complete details of the 250/1 Alt Type 2 with all the accompanying line drawings, the reader is kindly referred to the Total Detail Volume 3 - 250 Technical Book.

RIGHT & TOP RIGHT: Chassis numbers are chalked on the vehicle's sides. The first two digits of 310413 denote this vehicle manufacturer as Buessing-NAG, based in Berlin-Oberschoenewalde; the last four indicate the 413th vehicle or chassis. Buessing-NAG was originally involved with the production of the D7p chassis for the 252 and allocated the chassis serial numbers 310001 to 311000. It is not clear what 'E K.' translates as, but the tactical symbol identifies that these 250's are supposedly equipped with the MG34 'heavy mount'.

Photographic evidence shows that nearly all Type 1's and some of the first Type 2's destined for Reconnaissance units utilised a mount based upon the MG34 'heavy mount' instead of the shield arrangement already in use on other 250 variants. This was designed to allow the firer to remain down inside the vehicle and considered beneficial to the user.

These 250s cannot be thought of as the classic 250/1s for two heavy MGs, (see page 223) as none of these 'reconnaissance' 250s were equipped with the shield or the rack from, which to hang the Laffette. There is in fact no mention of this version of the 250 in any of the wartime manuals, yet this arrangement was obviously considered the best solution for Reconnaissance units at the planning stage.

It was also an excessive solution to mounting forward firing armament and was soon replaced by the more practical and certainly cheaper shield arrangement on subsequent vehicles. Whether a 250 equipped with the heavy mount can be considered the 'first' 250/1 is difficult to judge, but it was certainly superseded by what we know as the 'classic' 250/1.

Type 2   Type 2

Type 1   Type 2   Type 1   Type 2   Type 1

A

The Type 1 (second closest to the camera) is marked up 310314, the Type 2 nearest the camera 310390. This indicates that at some point between the 314th and 390th Buessing-NAG produced chassis, a switch has been made to the second version.

What gives away the early vehicles original identity is the U-shaped plate (A) welded onto the right rear upper panel of the third vehicle. This was the entrance point for the aerial on the 253. (In other photographs of 253-based 250's there is evidence of work done in the same area. See 250 Archive book Part 1). This particular Type 1 has all the late 253 details, with slightly more rounded (viewed from the front) mudguard edges.

On the Type 1, the curved shield under the nose armour is set back from the bottom edge and two brackets hold the registration plate just proud of the nose. See how the driver's visor is half open but the co-driver's visor is unlocked. The top of the cover is set away from the body because of a spring on each supporting arm. If it did not do this, the top edge would not clear the immediate bodywork to open. There is only provision to clamp a small axe on the right front wing. Note the different mount positions and angles of the width indicators.

BA101I-811-2231-37

Two

1942

8

Throughout 1942, Germany's armoured Divisions underwent a restructuring to accommodate the latest combat lessons, weapons and equipment then available. In part, this saw the Panzer Division merging its reconnaissance elements (armoured cars) with its motorcycle borne infantry (Kradschuetzen). This amalgamation resulted in a flexible grouping of armoured cars, mounted infantry and 'heavy' support weapons suitable for aggressive and exploitative reconnaissance. However, the term 'Kradschuetzen', along with the appropriate tactical symbol, was initially retained for these new Reconnaissance Battalions despite the allocation of armour in the form of the 250.

The clothing and vehicles seen here indicate that these men are perhaps HQ elements of an armoured car company. As such, this was the spearhead company of the Reconnaissance Battalion and the crews (rightfully) regarded themselves as their Division's 'pathfinders'. This elite status was reinforced by regulations allowing such troops to wear the black 'tank' uniform, and the use of cavalry parlance and traditions (for instance, companies could also be referred to as a Schwadron). The crewmembers wear a variety of 'fatigue' uniforms. Most appear to be wearing either a black (supposedly discontinued in 1940) or dark blue Arbeitanzug (work uniform). Intended for motorised units, these garments differed from the standard fatigue uniforms in small details, such as a 'stand up' collar and no external pockets. All wear the distinctive M34 'Schiffchen' (little ship) side cap.

The 250/1 in the middle is interesting because the headlamps are mounted through the front of the mudguards and not from underneath. The width indicators are in the correct position for the later models, however there is no beaded edge to either set of guards.

The StabsWachtmeister (Staff Master Sergeant) holds court in this unidentified French town. The unit represented here remains unidentified too, but they could be reconnaissance elements of either the 6th, 7th or 10th Panzer divisions, as all were in France refitting through the summer of 1942. The vehicles are factory finished in 'dark grey' (often referred to post-war as 'Panzer grey'), a colour deemed suitable for the built up landscapes of the European continent and confirmed as a standard in July 1940. Note the difference in tone between the grey paint and the tyres on the Sd Kfz 247 armoured car.

TOP LEFT: The crews are put through their paces. As one puts a drift in place, the other makes ready with a hammer to knock out the track pin. The vehicles wooden jack block has been wedged under the track to stop it slipping once freed. Only from this position is there sufficient clearance behind the rear idler and the chassis to remove the pin.

OPPOSITE PAGE: The track pin is almost out. Note the shape of the registration plates, the rear door lock and *Verbandkasten* (literally 'bandage box') in its cage. Inside it is possible to see that all of the radios, including the *Funk Sprecher Gerat f* (voice transmitting set, Type f) in the front of the vehicle, have their respective covers in place. Note the generator under the large rack in the rear and the beaded edge track guards. A canvas gaiter covers the aerial base.

BELOW: With the track pin out, the driver edges the 250/1 forward. By using the drift or the original pin, the track is held so as to prevent it from fouling. Note the lack of beading on the track guard and that a repair patch with a straight edge has been welded in.

BA101I-259-1399-07A

BA101I-259-1399-09A

Note the open toolbox and the wooden trays. The 250/1 is on the left and the 250/3 on the right. The track is still being held to stop it catching as the *SchuetzenPanzerWagen* moves forward. In the picture opposite top, the track pin is now being re-fitted.

BA101I–259-1399-10A

BA101I-259-1399-11A

BA101I-259-1399-14A

13

OPPOSITE TOP: The crew of the 250/3 have to do the same drill. Note the track tensioning information plate riveted to the side of the mudguard.

OPPOSITE BOTTOM: The driver has rolled as far forward as possible without running off the track, the end of which now lies on the ground below the drive sprocket.

BELOW: The 250 is now reversing and judging by the lack of track under the rear idler, this crewman has his work cut out as he has allowed the links to bunch up between the wheels and track guard. Note there is only one registration plate and no rear light on the right track guard. The unusual padlock and bar arrangement on the exterior locker indicates that it is not a factory made item.

RIGHT: And all of this under the watchful eye and stopwatch of the Master Sergeant. His shoulder boards display the Gothic 'A' for *Aufklaerungs* (Reconnaissance) and NCOs tress and three 'pips' to denote the rank. It is thought that the *Waffenfarbe* (branch of service colour) seen here is 'Golden-yellow', traditionally regarded as a cavalry colour and a common sight in pre-1943 Reconnaissance units. It is not clear what the decoration commemorates?

BA101I-259-1399-14A

BA101I-259-1399-16A

Another *StabsWachtmeister* inspects the tool kit and spares stowed both inside the vehicle and in the exterior tool locker. The cavalry trousers and boots he is wearing are indicative of NCOs and Officers serving with Reconnaissance units, and an attempt to link the (then) modern German Aufklaerungs units to the traditions and heritage of the earlier horse mounted cavalry.

This is a different 250 from the previous two. It has a standard exterior side locker (of which the front end can be seen to the left) to complement the toolbox locker behind the front wheel. It also has late pattern mud and track guards from which the beaded edge is missing.

BA101I-259-1399-21A

17

BA101I-259-1399-23A

OPPOSITE PAGE: Here we have a superb picture of all the tools carefully laid out for inspection.

1.   2 litre blowlamp for water heating.
2.   Four wick-heaters for the batteries.
3.   Brake-fluid can.
4.   Funnel.
5.   Tin of spare brake-fluid (?).
6.   2 litre blowlamp bracket.
7.   Grease gun with hose.
8.   Venting pump for brakes.
9.   Small oil can.
10. Push insert pipe for grease gun.
11. Two keys for brake adjustments.
12. Grease nipple cleaner.
13. Traffic wand.
14. Tensioning pliers for anti-skid chains.
15. Anti-skid chains. (Snow cleats)
16. Mechanics hammer.
17. Small punch.
18. Set of extended sockets.
19. Tow hook.

20. Shackle for tow hook.
21. Sparking plug wire brush.
22. Spare track pins.
23. Drift to remove track pins.
24. String.
25. Spare bulbs.
26. Set of double open-ended spanners.
27. Spark plugs.
28. Ring spanner for track bolts.
29. Double ended ring spanner.
30. Adjustable wrench.
31. Can of grease.
32. Oil can.
33. Flat chisel.
34. Water pump spanner.
35. Pincers.
36. Combination pliers
37. Screwdrivers (large and small).
38. Half-round file.

BA101I-259.1399-24A

BA101I-748-0096-02

BA101I-748-0096-03

20

OPPOSITE TOP: By the middle of June 1942, the freshly raised *Kradschuetzen Battalion 'Grossdeutschland'* had been transported from Germany to the south of Orel for further training. Here the untried unit was acclimatised to Russian conditions before being committed to battle. Judging by the relaxed atmosphere in these three photographs, the day's exercise is over. Three officers (possibly Battalion CO Horst Von Usedom with back to the camera and 2nd squadron CO Hans Klemme extreme right) look on as a 250/10 crew attach the canvas cover over a muzzle capped 37mm PAK 35/36. This vehicle was normally found in platoon command groups under direct control of the *Zug* (platoon) leader, but the low number (4) suggests this one may have been attached to the squadron command group. A brand new example of the Type 2 with the classic rib-edged mud and track-guards and driver's visors, it still retains the hubcaps on the drive sprockets. It is unusual that this vehicle should be towing a *Sonderanhanger 32* ammunition trailer, usually associated with the Sd Kfz 252.

OPPOSITE BOTTOM: Having secured the vehicle, the crew settle down for the evening. Note the belts and holsters hanging off the rear *Notek* light, use of the '88' ammunition crate to store personal belongings, and what appears to be a wash bag and bar of soap on the trailer. Lined with straw for insulation, the *Zeltbahn* 'four-man' tent has been correctly erected with taut sides.

BELOW: As the Armys premier and newest Division, it seems that for propaganda purposes a war photographer accompanied the Battalion for a short time as it advanced across the Steppes in July 1942, and in doing so captured a wide variety of vehicles originally found within the Reconnaissance Battalion. If ever there were a set of photographs that show the depth of equipment afforded to GD during the war, the following two pages justify the reality. Although others in this series have been seen before, it is still a remarkable set of pictures.

Of the four 250's seen here, only the lead vehicle is a Type 1, with split-front visors and early style stowage box (behind the semaphore indicator). It is interesting that all the 250's as well as the Sd Kfz 222 use 2 metre rod aerials, and not the 1.4 metre whip aerial. All four 250's are the heavy MG versions and have added racking for fuel cans on the right track guard. The DKW motorcycle belongs to a despatch rider from the squadron command group. Making up the rest of the column are two Sd Kfz 222s, an Sd Kfz 263, Sd Kfz 260 and a late model 261 based on the 222 chassis, all from the 1st squadron. Their crews were entitled to wear the black Panzer uniform. Note the *Zug* designation inscribed on the bucket on the first 250.

(For larger format pictures see '250 Vol. 1 Living History')

BA1011-748-0100A-16

ABOVE: It would appear that the majority of the 2nd Squadron is on the move complete with some of the supply trucks. Note the rack on the rear of the Horch Kfz 15 and the squareness of the canvas tilt frame on the Henschel truck behind. The 250's are a mixture of Type 1 and 2's, the second, third and fifth all appear to be the later vehicles.

RIGHT: The entire column featured in these pages (and other, previously published photographs) is held up by this hole in the road. For some reason the Battalion has to cross here and not go around it. Perhaps it is a gully that runs across the terrain and can only be crossed at this point? Note the dog peering over the top of the armour.

LEFT: The driver now attempts to cross over the hole, but judging by the angle of the axle and how far the right wheel is raised under the mudguard, a log has shifted. Given that there is an Sd Kfz 263 waiting in the column behind (which weighed 3 tons more than the 5.3 ton 250), they will need to find a few more logs to solve their predicament.

BA1011-748-0100A-06

BA101I-609-1906-01A

BA101I-748-0100A-07

23

BA101I-609-1906-03A

BA101I-609-1906-02A

OPPOSITE PAGE: Seen in countless other books, this photograph is still worthy of inclusion for various reasons. It comes from the same series of the GD column, but neither of these crewmen wears the distinctive GD shoulder boards. One possibility is that this crew are attached from a non-GD unit, but other photographic evidence (see 250 Vol. 1 Living History) proves that lacking the correct insignia was not unusual at this time. As the new (18,000 man) Division had just been expanded from a combat bruised Regiment, it can be imagined that the factories responsible for the appropriate insignia would have been initially slow in meeting the upsurge in demand.

Part of the 1st (armoured car) *schwadron*, this 250/3 is equipped with a *Fu 12SE 80* radio set comprising of a *Torn. E.b (Tornister Emphanger B)* in the upper rack and an *80 W.S.a (80 Watt. sender. a)* below. The rack is interesting because it is a derivation of the more usually seen three-rack set for the Fu4 and Fu8 sets, (see page 188/189). The conduit running to the left across the top of the radio rack carries the cable to the frame aerial above and the sheet metal cover protects a voltage regulator.

This is not a 250/5 with scissors periscope mounted behind the driver (as suggested in other books), as the 250/3 had the classic bench seat that the two operators are sitting on. The radio set does not appear to have a clock (to time incoming and outgoing messages). These were normally mounted to the right of the lower radio set. Something like a sock has been placed over the rear MG post, either to protect it against rust or to prevent uniforms from coming into contact with the greased surface. The rubber edging above the rear door is to protect the crew from a potential serious injury when exiting the vehicle. Compare the difference between the grey paint on the rear door and the dusty exterior.

ABOVE: With the double-slotted visors and secondary toolbox on the track guard, a Type 1 250/1 leads the way. Note the MG34 wrapped in its canvas dust cover *(Bezug fuer MG34 in Einbein 34)* and the stowed helmets. The side engine doors have been opened to help cool the engine. Laden with bedrolls, the platoon continues over the endless horizon in search of the enemy.

HQ elements of the 4th Artillery Regiment (14th Panzer Division) take up position somewhere in southern Russia, 1942. It is thought that this photograph was taken during 'Operation Blue'. Note the square metal pennant of the commander planted in the ground behind the 250 and the command post (Gefechtstand) sign. The staff are tucked into a temporary position scooped into the bank, formulating fire plans and ready to move at a moments notice to assist in exploiting any breakthroughs.

With a capitol "K" on the right rear flank of the 250/3, the 14th Panzer Division was part of von Kleist's 1st Panzer Army (Army Group South, later Army Group A) and ultimately destroyed in Stalingrad. Note the copy of 'Das Reich' on the right behind the individual manning the telephone line (see the field phone to his left). This was one of several frontline newspapers delivered via the field post. Bottom left is the cross rigged aerial for what is possibly a Tornister. Fu.f (Tornister Funkgerat f) utilised by Artillery Regiments.

BA101I-218-0516-07

Elements of an unidentified unit form up in the southern Russian summer of 1942. The Horch 830 field car (extreme left) bears an 'M', possibly denoting affiliation with Colonel General von Mackenson's III Panzer corps, in turn part of Colonel General von Kleist's 1st Panzer Army (hence the 'K'). As part of operation Blue (the offensive that would ultimately result in the disaster at Stalingrad), in July 1942, Army group south was split into Army groups A (Field Marshall List) and B (Field Marshall von Bock). Seconded to Army group A, the 1st Panzer Army participated in the advance to Rostov on Don. An order of battle for Army group A dated 4th July 1942 shows that the III Panzer Korps had both 16th Panzer (later destroyed in the Stalingrad pocket) and 22nd Panzer Divisions under its wing. By the 8th August 1942, the III Panzer Korps consisted of the 16th Motorised (later Panzer grenadier) and 19th Panzer Divisions.

Visible on the left is the front shield of a Sd Kfz 251 in front of the Horch 830. Note the coach built wooden body of the 830R Kfz 17 radio car *(Funkwagen)*, built by the coach-building firm of Glaser in Dresden. Of interest is the canvas covered roof and valance. It would also appear that they have experienced a puncture at some point because the tyre on the spare wheel is flat.

Wearing tinted goggles, the crew of a Sd Kfz 7/1 scan the skies for enemy planes. Of interest on the closest 250 is the condom protecting the *MG34* whereas the MG on the other 250 has a standard issue expendable muzzle cap.

Five 250's, three 251/1's, a single 251/10 (all Ausf C's) plus another towing a *PAK 38* aptly shows the problems of everyone going through the same place at the same time. The Divisional sign of the 11th Panzer Division (a yellow circle dissected by a vertical bar) can be seen below the tactical symbol on the nose. The 250's belong to the 4th Company of the 61st *Kradschuetzen Battalion*, later merged (in 1943) with the 231st Reconnaissance Battalion to form the 11th Panzer Reconnaissance Battalion. It is not clear how the individual vehicle numbering system worked here, but it is reasonable to postulate that '48' represents the 8th vehicle of the 4th Company. All the 250's are Type 2's.

The 251's belong to one of the two Battalions of the 110th *Schuetzen Regiment*. Each of these Battalions had one *SPW* mounted Infantry Company complete with three 50mm *PAK 38's*, 38 MG's, two 8cm mortars and three anti-tank rifles.

If the co-driver is sitting in his seat, there is a total of twelve people making a hasty exit from whatever has caused the thick black smoke.

BA1011-792-0138-18A

Whatever they have been up to of late, the 250 front wings have taken a hammering with no headlamps or *Notek* front light mounted. It is interesting that this 250 is not equipped with any visible main armament, and has an odd-looking antenna or strip of metal mounted vertically onto the top plate of the nose in front of the bonnet doors.

BA1011-792-0138-23A

A superb picture of an Sd Kfz 251/1 Ausf C (welded body) from the 110th *Scheutzen Regiment* with an accompanying 250/3 from the Signals Platoon making their way forward out of the pall of smoke. Note the MG anti-aircraft tripod has been moved from its original position behind one of the seat bins and stowed on the track guard. Of the two *Scheutzen Regiments* (110th and 111th) within the 11th *Scheutzen Brigade*, only the 110th was equipped with 251s.

Another 250/1 but this time working with tank and Motorised *FlaK* units from the 11th Panzer Division. In the dust of the main photograph it is possible to see the Pz Kpfw III Ausf H featured in the inset picture (which is the first photograph taken in this set of two) disappearing down the road to take up a forward position and cover the Reconnaissance halftrack. Note the single 'Jerry can' holder on the rear plate.

This is the only photograph of a 250/4 *Truppenluftschuetzpanzerwagen* (armoured vehicle for troop air protection) with the shield in place that I have seen. The only real reference to this vehicle* lists it as the original variant for the 250/4 that never went into production. However, it appears that at least one prototype progressed as far as field trials to evaluate the design. An expedient marriage of two existing pieces of equipment, but now offering armoured protection to the crew, this was an obvious improvement in comparison to the Stoewer based *Leichter Truppen-Luftschutz Kraftwagen Kfz 4* that preceded it.

It is not clear if the front shield rotates with the *Zwillingslafette 36* (dual mount 36), or whether the entire mount actually rotated through 360 degrees, but given that the shield is set so far back, the gun mount must support it. The fact that the same system was mounted in the back of a Stoewer (which is not that large) suggests that perhaps it is fully functioning. The roof over the drivers head appears to have been extended rearward with a radiused inner edge to match the traverse arc of the gun shield itself. There would have been no room inside for a cupboard or seat box but, like a 250/9, there could be ammunition racks built onto the armoured petrol tank cover. Perhaps an extra seat, as found in a 250/5, could be found just inside the rear door?

Like most variants of any 250, all were hampered by a lack of space. Ultimately, this version of the 250/4 did not see full production, but perhaps it served as the catalyst for the larger Sd Kfz 251 armed with the more effective *20mm KwK FlaK 38*.

Encyclopaedia of German Tanks of WW II. Chamberlain/Doyle/Jentz. Arms and Armour Press.

With its relative lack of ground clearance beneath the chassis, a 250 could quite easily become immobile as the vehicle caught its belly and lost drive. With three 250's in trouble and a waiting 251, this *Luftwaffe* 8-ton prime mover will be kept busy for a while. Receiving the tow is a classic Type 2 250/3. Note the two aerials. One is for the *Fu. Spr. f*, the other a 2-metre aerial for the *Fu 4* and *Fu 8* radio sets.

An *MG13* with a saddle drum magazine can just be seen behind the greatcoat-wearing passenger.

BA1011-453-1033-25

Elements of a Panzer Division gather on a reverse slope. Judging by the craned necks of the group in the background and the individuals to the left, something of interest is happening in the sky. The men gathered at the back of the 250 could be participating in an order group, but are just as likely having a smoke. The two factory fresh wooden '88' ammunition crates on the back of the Panzer III Ausf L's were intended to hold 1,500 rounds of 7.9mm. When emptied, such items were to be returned for repacking, but many crews found them ideal for storing extra provisions and personal items.

BA101I-218-0526-08

BA1011-218-0526-03

Finally able to wash the dust out of his hair after weeks of action, for a few roubles a crewmember from the 40th Reconnaissance Battalion takes up an offer from one of the locals. The symbol for the 14th Panzer Division is just visible on the top right of the nose plate. Along with the 60th Motorised Infantry Division, the 14th Panzer formed the XIV Panzer Corps, one of the two armoured corps found in von Kleist's 1st Panzer army in the high summer of 1942. Note however the painted out 'M'. This indicates past service in von Mackenson's corps.

Prior to the summer offensive of 1942 the Division's 64th *Kradschuetzen Battalion* was amalgamated into the 40th Reconnaissance Battalion. In many of these new 1942 'armoured' Reconnaissance Battalions, the symbol of the *Kradschuetzen* unit saw continued use until slowly phased out by the 'motorised' version from mid 1943 onwards. Subsequently, this too was replaced by the more apt 'armoured half track' symbol. The *Balkenkreuz* between the two front visors was never a common practice, as it provided the perfect aiming point for any enemy gunner.

ABOVE: Well-camouflaged elements of the 59th Kradschuetzen Battalion return from what appears to be a rainy scouting mission. Once an operation was complete, re-fuelling and the replenishment of ammunition took highest priority. The Infantry on the far side of the bank are hitching a lift across the river, as evidenced by at least four extra passengers on board the 250 in the river.

OPPOSITE PAGE: Theoretically, each Reconnaissance Battalion had its own supply train, responsible for the surplus to requirement baggage of the combat elements as well as collecting and supplying provisions.

The tailboard of this Skoda 6 ST 6-L wears the tactical markings for the 2nd Company of the Kradschuetzen Battalion and the number 56, probably an individual vehicle number. Looking at the two-tier load of jerry cans, it will probably need all of the 4- ton capacity to carry this cross-country up to the front-line units. Note the Notek rear convoy light and the wheel jack fastened on top of the rear of the chassis frame.

47

The markings have faded with a coat of dust, but the *Kradschuetzen* tactical sign with the digit '2' plus the capital 'Y' with two tick marks of the 9th Panzer Division can be seen on the rear plate. To the left of the symbol is written "311", could this be the method of this particular companies use of the three digit vehicle numbering system to identify its place within the company?

Note the amount of 300-round MG ammunition tins in the doorway and the stack of 7.9mm 15-round cartons on the rear shelf.

BA101I-216-0421-30

Crewmembers share a meal. The individual on the right wears a civilian jumper and a Red army belt while his comrade has a *M40* tunic. Both wear the *M34 Feldmuetze*. The registration plate could not be more fitting!

A veteran of a recent fire-fight inspects one of the bulletproof vision blocks. Made with two thin and one thick sheet of optically superb glass, he owes his life to it. He too wears a civilian roll-neck jumper and carries the rank of *Oberschuetze*.

ABOVE: A 250/3 belonging to either the 10th or 11th Panzergrenadier Regiment (9th Panzer Division) in southern Russia, 1942. These Regiments fielded two Infantry Battalions each but, theoretically, only the 1st Battalion of the 10th (and possibly part of the 2nd Battalion) had *SPW's*, the rest were mounted in cross-country cars or lorries. Where one would expect to see the appropriate armoured tactical symbol, this vehicle still retains the symbol for a Motorised Infantry Company. Alternatively, it is possible that a smattering of these command and control vehicles were farmed out amongst the HQ elements of the non-armoured Battalions.

The summer crops and steppe grasses often stretched to the horizon and could grow to remarkable heights. Although useful for concealment, the crops could hinder in more ways than one. Armoured vehicles in such conditions were in great danger from motivated enemy infantry and continual observation was vital. In 1943, the 250's of the Reconnaissance Battalion Grossdeutschland were participating in a counter attack through a sunflower field when the tracks got snagged on the crop. Temporarily trapped, the crews fought off repeated attempts by grenade lobbing Red army troops before successfully recovering most of their vehicles.

OPPOSITE BOTTOM: Although located in the original position for an aerial, this crew utilise the shorter 1.4 metre version. (Compare to the 250/3 above. This has the rigid 2-metre model). The 9th Panzer Reconnaissance Battalion was formed in April 1943 by the merging of the 9th Reconnaissance Battalion and the 59th *Kradschuetzen Battalion*. Even though they have traded in their motorcycles, they have yet to change the *Kradschuetzen* symbol on the rear of the 250.

BA101I-217-0488-04A

A converted Sd Kfz 250 from the 24th Panzer Division belonging either to the 21st or 26th Panzer Grenadier Regiment in the Summer of 1942 as they push on to the Don River.

TOP LEFT: Probably best known for its inclusion in the 'Panzer Colours' trilogy*, on close inspection of the original photograph, it is questionable whether the base colour is *dunkelgelb*. Receiving a paste of mud to flatten the colour (by an individual probably wondering what he has done wrong to deserve such an 'honour' on the day he received his 'Iron cross second class'), the base colour is almost certainly 'dark grey' covered in so much dust that it appears to be lighter. Because the mud paste is wet it is much darker now than it will be when it has dried. Note (top right) how the mud coat has now dried leaving the darker patches of grey showing through.

* *Panzer Colours I - III Bruce Culver Squadron/signal publications*

This 250 and the example top left are either two separate converted vehicles or the same, but at two different dates. The 250 on the right has a grenade screen hinged behind the two occupants. It carries a 2 metre aerial on the upper rear superstructure and a 1.4 metre aerial on the left track guard. Perhaps it did start life as a standard 250/3? The example on the left has a forward hinging hatch (?), which is not seen in the right hand picture. Somebody fairly important has requested these field modifications. Certainly with a raised roof like this, it is far easier to work in than the two other 24th Panzer Division vehicles on the previous page, and far more useful than an Sd Kfz 253 which surely was the originator of this idea.

The commander's pennant on the 250/3 is coloured (from top to bottom) red, white and black. The 'v. E.' denotes von Edelsheim, while the 'S' is possibly for *'Stab'* (staff/headquarters). A Regimental commander utilised a square pennant whereas the Divisional Commander was signified by a triangular pennant. It is known that Lieutenant General Reichsfreiherr (baron) Maximillian von Edelsheim commanded the 24th Panzer Division from 1943 to late 1944, but perhaps he was a Regimental commander before he was promoted to lead the Division?

205

Photographed in 1942, vehicles of the 24th Panzer Division nose into the outskirts of Stalingrad. The Pz Kpfw III Ausf J's have the tactical numbering 24/2 (of the 24th Panzer Regiment), the converted 250/1 of the *1st Ko./89th Artillerie Regiment*

LEFT: It appears that a workshop Company have built a roof with hatches for the top of this 250/1. In the picture left, the top angle of the side armour is not parallel to the track guard. The same angle can be seen in the photograph below. These are definitely not 253's. Both are modified 250 *'Alt's*, the one below a Type 1 and left a Type 2. It looks as though the roof angles up from the rear to the halfway point on the side armour, and then flattens out. It is a shame that it is not possible to see what was done at the front but, judging by the arms resting on the roof, perhaps the roof continues flat to meet a plate welded to the top of the driver's roof? (See following page). This particular adaptation does not have a front MG shield.

BELOW: Whoever painted the mud paste onto this early 250 went to the trouble of removing all the tools beforehand. Note the extra piece of plate welded to the top edge of the side armour, which could form a roof over the rear compartment. This example retains the MG shield.

BA101I-217-0488-02A

BA101I-218-0525-07A

ABOVE & LEFT: A Luftwaffe 250/3, almost certainly crewed by a *Panzerverbindungsoffizier,* (armoured liaison officer). Unlike the *'Flivo'* (*Fliegerverbindungsoffizier* or air liaison officer) who was attached to combat divisions at command level, the *Luftwaffe* 'armoured officer' was found at the front line directing ground attack aircraft against specific targets. Often known as the *'StukaLeiter',* this individual was usually an experienced *Stuka* pilot rotated into this position to advise the *Flivo* of requested air strikes. Once a squadron was overhead he would take control, advising them of enemy air defences on approach, their method of attack and ultimately confirming the intended target.

The Spanish civil war provided the first real opportunity to formulate liaison between the *Heer* and *Luftwaffe,* most notably initiated and subsequently practised to great effect by the air commander Wolfram von Richthofen, a cousin of the 'Red Baron'.

This background, combined with the successes of the Stuka squadrons in the early years of the war, resulted in the pilots developing a language of their own. Code words intended to minimise mistakes (for example friendly troops were termed *'Blaue Truppen'* [blue troops]), while a ground reference point was *'Otto')* ensured that it was advisable for someone who recognised the parlance to control their attack. Despite this, 'friendly fire' casualties could, (and did), occur.

BA101I–218-0524-31

The individual in the back of this 250 wears his summer flying helmet *(Kopfhauben LKP s100)* for liaison with the squadron. This is the commander's model with earphones and a throat microphone that allowed communications both within and outside an aircraft.

The front MG shield now resides at the rear and the MG AA boom has been discarded. In place of the shield there is now a steel box to house the base plate and ceramic isolator assembly for the aerial. There are at least four possible versions of a 250/3, two of which were used as ground liaison vehicles by the Luftwaffe and only differed in the radio equipment carried.

This version with the frame aerial carried the following:
Fu 7 (20 W.S.d1/ Ukw.E.d1)
The above two sets are used to communicate between the ground reconnaissance, air reconnaissance, spotter planes and the fighter-bombers and ground attack aircraft.

Fu 8 (Mw.E.c./30 W.S.a)
The *Fu 8* provided communication with ground units (including command vehicles like the Panzerbefehlswagen III).

ABOVE & NEXT PAGE: A group gather for a smoke round the back of a 250/3. Four sample the latest pipe tobacco on offer; a fifth has a cigarette, perhaps 'rolled' from the same source. One would expect them to be carrying a little less kit if they were *'Panzer Grenadiers'*, but they have anything other than white piping on their shoulder boards, indicating that they are not infantry. Either way, all bear the evidence of combat, and one is almost tempted to speculate that this is the remnant of a section participating in a battle group action.

This is an almost classic portrait of the 'mid-war' German soldier. All wear the M36 or M40 tunic (note the bulging lower pockets) and M35 or M40 helmet. Individual 'A' has a field made helmet cover. It appears to be camouflaged material, but it is unclear what pattern or type. It has at least two camouflage attachment loops and is secured to the helmet by what could be modified SS helmet cover clips. He has scratched his initial onto his mess tin. Note that 'B' has placed a rubber muzzle cap over the end of his rifle, whilst 'C' is without doubt a squad leader *(Unteroffizier)*.

'D' is the 'odd one out'. It is not clear whether he is an NCO/officer or a despatch rider, but his nonchalant stance probably indicates the latter. *Obergefreiter* 'E' also has his entrenching tool tucked through his belt, a common practice at the front. *Gefreiter* 'F' is clearly responsible for a machine gun. However, it is not clear why he has a 7.9mm ammunition pouch attached to his belt. He carries his 'bread bag' slung over his shoulder on its strap.

The Pz Kpfw III Ausf L's of the 7th Panzer Regiment armed with the *5cm. Kw.K39 L/60* cannon and the latest 20mm spaced armour on the superstructure (but with only the frame over the gun mantlet).

The anti-aircraft mount on the lead Pz Kpfw III appears to be a crew devised use of the *MG34* from the tank (note the armoured barrel) with supporting pipe-work and bracket welded to the commander's cupola. All of the Pz Kpfw III's are equipped with searchlights.

Units of the 10th Panzer Division are seen here on exercise in France sometime towards the end of 1942. The Division returned to France to re-equip in April and would have spent the intervening period with daily training exercises to familiarise themselves with their new equipment.

The headquarters vehicles are from the 2nd Company (both 250's) and the 1ton Zugmachine (Sd Kfz 10) belongs to the 3rd Company of the 10th Kradscheutzen Battalion. There are two umpires standing to the side of the1 ton and what appears to be a senior Officer from both the Panzertruppen and Aufklaerungs in the rear of the Sd Kfz 10. Various other individuals (including an officer on the 3rd Pz Kpfw III) in this photograph wear the white umpire's armband (and at least one of the bystanders has a white cap band). The crew of the closest 250 have placed the anti-aircraft boom on the front pintle and because there is no travel lock, the MG34 hangs down into the crew compartment.

Whilst the Aufklaerungs still retain the original grey, the tanks have already been re-sprayed with their new camouflage scheme of dark tan with secondary stripes of grey in preperation for their transfer to Tunisia. They are subsequently seen driving through Marseilles for the entire world to see and letting anyone know they were bound for an overseas destination. It has been previously suggested that the Division was rushed to Tunisia. However they obviously had time to re-paint the vehicles in good time before they arrived in Marseilles, and only afterwards did they then transfer on to Naples for embarkation to Tunisia. Perhaps the 10th were earmarked for Tunisia sometime in the summer of 1942 but were only rushed there once the German high command realised the magnitude of Operation Torch?

BELOW: This brand new 250/5 belongs to the 10th Panzer Division and wears both the original diagonal stripe from Russia and the new symbol by the left of the rear door. The *Kradschuetzen Battalion* received their new 250's in Amiens in their re-fit after the Russian campaign and other units within the 10th Panzer Division, including the Artillery Regiments, also received equipment and vehicles during the course of the summer.

It is marked with the tactical sign for the *6th battery / II Abteilung of the 90th (Mot.) Artillerie Regiment.* This classic Type 2 bodied 250 is equipped with a 2-metre *Sternantenne D* (star) aerial to replace the earlier frame aerial which was used in conjunction with *Fu4* and *Fu8* sets. Note the individual shape of both the rear number plates, which are unusually symmetrical, perhaps attached to the track guards, and not painted on like later versions.

Because the front and rear posts are identical, it is possible to mount the front shield on the rear post normally used for the anti-aircraft boom. The problem with the shield is that it overhangs the cabin roof and with a MG in place, it takes up a surprising amount of space above the driver and co-driver's heads and both were in real danger of hitting the shield as they climb out. With the radio rack taking up so much space within the 250, it has been fitted with an exterior stowage box on the right hand track guard.

OPPOSTIE TOP: Judging by the amount of civilians watching, the sight of German troops on the streets is a new experience. This is another 250/3 from the 10th Panzer Division passing through the centre of Chalon Sur Saone. The signpost in the background indicates the towns of Louhans and Dole. Unlike the 250/5 top right, this radio half-track does not have the armoured aerial box for the star antennae on the upper rear right panel. Of interest are the four prongs on the roof (two on the front and one either side), angled up to retain a stowed tarpaulin cover if no space was available inside. Both the front visor openings have the windscreen inserts in place.

OPPOSITE BOTTOM: A 250/3 from the 10th Panzer Division crossing the Saone River Bridge in the City of Chalon sur Saone. Approaching the border post with Vichy France on the 11th November 1942, this vehicle belongs to the commander of the 7th Company (II Battalion) of either the 69th or 86th Motorised Infantry Regiment. The Division only received the classic Type 2 version with the single slot front visors, 'late' mudguards, and brackets under the front wings to mount the headlamps. The individual standing in the back is holding a signal baton with which to indicate his intentions to both oncoming and following traffic. The manual states that this baton was to be omitted in wartime, but there are countless pictures to show that this was not the case.

BA1011-362-2214-16

WH-1261691

BA1011-256-1250-17A

OPPOSITE & BELOW: One of a series of pictures of the 7th Panzer Division in occupied Vichy France. This pristine condition Type 2 250/5 bears the tactical insignia of a battery from 78th Panzer Artillery Regiment (above the yellow 'Y'). Like other vehicles seen in the same set, a national flag is draped over the bonnet for air recognition purposes. Note the lack of a MG and the windscreen insert in place in front of the driver.

The 250/5 *Beobachtungs PanzerWagen* became the primary forward observation vehicle for German artillery units. The crew would observe the fall of shot, track the position of opposing batteries, call in counter strikes and plan general fire patterns for their particular battery. Half hidden by the boys head is the new armoured shroud for the aerial. This is now placed on the rear left, unlike the 250/3 on page 20/21 & 22/23. The original position was a throwback from the Sd Kfz 253.

The *Stabsgefreiter* hanging off the side of the 250 wears a Field-grey 'assault gun' tunic. Note the *Totenkopf* insignia, a sure sign either way that this unit regarded itself as a 'Panzer' force. Of interest is the shoulder strap on the *Obergefreiter*. Mounted on a standard *M40* tunic, the shoulder board could be the *M36* 'bottle green' type, but perhaps is dark enough to be black?

The posture the boys have adopted, the bent arms and turned heads are an emulation of *"Stillgestanden! Augen rechts!"* (Attention! Eyes right!), an every day sight to impressionable young minds in occupied Europe?

74

Elements of the 58th Pioneer Battalion (7th Panzer Division) rumble down the quayside of a harbour in the South of France. It is possible that this photograph was taken in Marseille. The ship is the 'Marechel Lyautey', one of a number that ran the Marseille –Casablanca route and probably confined to port because of the occupation.

Note that in this and other photographs of 7th Panzer Division vehicles (pages 26, 27 and 31), the tactical symbol has a rectangular box outline. Also in common is the habit of draping a national flag over the front of the vehicles for air recognition purposes. Given where the crew are standing and the double radio rack resting on the front right mudguard, this is in fact a 250/3. The aerial position on the left side of the vehicle is unusual as is the lack of an MG shield or the post that it mounts onto.

BA1011-620-2840-16A

ABOVE: In response to the Allied invasion of North Africa on the 8th November 1942, Hitler secured his southern flank by moving German forces into Vichy France. Despite the assurances of the French, he was convinced that he was being hoodwinked and ordered that 'operation Lila' be put into action, an attempt to seize the French fleet moored at Toulon. This represented a huge prize for whoever controlled it and, not prepared to take any chances, the Germans began massing tanks on the outskirts of the port.

In response to a tip off, the French Navy scuttled its fleet on the 27th of November. Amongst a host of other vessels, the 'casualties' included the battleship Provence and the battle cruisers Strasbourg and Dunkerque. This photograph is one of a set taken just hours after the deed was complete. Having initially got lost in the back streets contending with sporadic pockets of resistance, the German units finally arrived to find thousands of apprehensive sailors and dockyard workers milling around their luggage considering what to do next and wondering what the reaction of the Germans would be.

Between the two closest 250's it is just possible to see a pile of suitcases and rucksacks, probably belonging to the sailors. In the background there are four immaculate 250/3 half tracks complete with double rear registration plates. The 250 on the left is numbered 762 (2nd vehicle/6th platoon 7th Company). These vehicles are either from the 7th or 10th Panzer Divisions. Both, along with elements of the *SS 'Das Reich' Kradschuetzen Battalion*, had been drawn up on the outskirts of Toulon ready to seize the fleet intact.

OPPOSITE & FOLLOWING 2 PAGES: With the news that the Vichy forces in North Africa had capitulated, it was necessary to provide immediate defensive measures along the south coast against a possible invasion. The 7th Panzer Division remained in position until the end of 1942.

It is just possible to see the 'Y' of the 7th Panzer Division below the tactical sign for the 2nd Company of a motorcycle *(Kradschuetzen)* unit. In 1942 the Division had both the 7th Kradschuetzen Battalion and 37th Panzer Reconnaissance Battalion on its books, the two being merged into the 7th Panzer Reconnaissance Battalion in 1943. However, the best available source on such matters* does not indicate which of the two Battalions were equipped with 250's in 1942. One would have thought that the 37th Panzer Reconnaissance Battalion would have received the armour, but this photograph suggests otherwise.

However, it is also possible that just the HQ elements of the 7th *Kradschuetzen Battalion* received some 250's. Note how the '1' has been daubed to lessen its visibility and the *PanzerAbwehrKanone 38* being readied in the distance. If the 250/3's in the opposite picture are also from the 7th Panzer Division, compare the difference in condition from one picture to the next. All have what appears to be telephone cable hung off the back.

---

* *The German order of battle: Panzers and Artillery. G.F. Nafziger. Greenhill books*

78

Three

1943

Having spent a large part of 1942 rebuilding in France, in November the 6th Panzer Division was transferred from the comparatively balmy climes of Brittany to the bitterly cold, endless plains of southern Russia. Having survived numerous partisans attacks en route, the Division assembled southwest of Stalingrad as the most powerful unit in von Manstein's Army Group Don. Participating in the attempt to relieve the besieged 6th Army (including beating off an attack by a Red Army camel Regiment!), the 6th Panzer Division slowly ground to a halt some 48 km short of its objective.

Here, 2 motorcycle combinations and a 250/1 from the recently formed 6th Panzer Reconnaissance Battalion scan the horizon for the enemy. This 250 has the *Kradschuetzen* symbol with the digit '2' for 2nd Company (a half-tracked 'armoured car' Company), plus the 'XX' of the Division. Note the positioning of the *Balkenkreuz*. Hanging over the rear is the fold up chair usually sited in front of the locker in the rear right of the vehicle. The snowshoes are made of reeds for insulation; all the helmets appear to have been camouflaged with paint under which is a section of spare track. The track pin section is just visible.

Another 6th Panzer Division vehicle photographed in the winter of 1942/43, except that this is a 250/5 from the 76th Panzer Artillery Regiment from within the Division. Note the wide variety of winter uniforms, from two-piece reversible suits, greatcoats and what appears to be a soldier wearing the longer-length SS winter parka.

A 250/1 of an unidentified unit heads up a mixed bag of vehicles on convoy duty. Immediately behind the *SPW* is an Opel staff car, followed by a Gaz truck and then a 3-ton Opel Blitz truck. Note the rectangular heated screen element in the Ford car and Renault cargo truck parked up on the left.

A classic Type 2 250/3, but note the position of the headlamps. Normally found closer to the front of the mudguards, they are not back far enough to be mounted in the nose (like an early production 250). It seems as though in order to better protect them, the crew or workshop unit have fabricated new headlamp mount brackets to the top of the track guards.

BA101I-216-0422-13A

See how much darker the inside of the roof tarpaulin is compared to the grey paint and the contrast with the tan leather edging to both colours. The helmet covers seen here look field made. The one on the left is almost certainly *'splinter'* pattern material. It is hard to identify the cover on the right, but the smock is the *'splinter'* version.

BA101I-216-0422-17A

BA101I-216-0421-06

The sleeping *Unteroffizier* is wearing a herringbone fatigue tunic with wool field-grey shoulder straps. He has an issue pullover underneath, just discernable by the edge of the green 'ring' on the cuff, and also has the cotton *Kragenbinde* (collar liner) attached to the inside of the collar. This protects the neck from chafing against the coarse material of the tunic. The helmet cover is unusual. It almost looks like a cut up fatigue tunic. It is not hessian (more usual in lieu of issue camouflage covers), as the weave appears too fine. The other two crewmembers wear woollen tunics.

A   B   C   D

BA101I-216-0421-27

Field made helmet covers using camouflage material (possibly a cut up *Zeltbahn*) apparently secured with a pull string seem to be de rigueur in this unit. Issue helmet covers were a lot better fit and tended to have foliage loops attached. The despatch rider handing out the rations wears the standard motorcycle coat, and has apparently brought the (cold) rations up to the front wrapped in a blanket; a common practice. Soldiers 'A' & 'B' both wear M40 tunics, whilst 'C' appears to wear a fatigue tunic over his woollen tunic. Soldier 'D' is wearing some sort of two-piece overall set.

ABOVE & LEFT: Note how the headlamp cable runs down and under the chassis front, and the red paint lined chassis number plate on the shock absorber plate. The headlight covers (to restrict the beam at night) are a simple sheet metal fitting that sits directly on the glass. Interestingly this 250 is armed with a *MG42*.

OPPOSITE: Here is an almost perfect example of a 250/10, complete with headlamps and metal covers, width indicators, rear view mirror and all but one of its tools. The wire cutters are missing from the left front mudguard. The crew are wearing the field grey 'assault gun' uniform with a full complement of *Totenkopf* insignia. All appear be officers or NCOs.

The *37mm. Pak 35/36* could fire both armour piercing and high explosive rounds to a maximum range of 7.000 metres, and carried approximately 216 rounds of mixed ammunition. As the platoon leaders vehicle, it would provide covering fire for the MG armed 250's against ground troops and enemy positions. It proved effective against soft skinned vehicles, armoured cars and light tanks, and despite being christened as no better than a 'door knocker', it was continuously employed until the end of the war.

Looking through the archives, it becomes obvious that because of their role, the enemy especially targeted the 250/10's. By the end of 1943 they became rare items, and were never officially superseded with a *'Neu'* version.

WH - 1387052

BA101I–259-1389-16A

BA101I-259-1389-15A

With seven people on board, the lead 250 is now somewhat crowded. An officer perches on top of the armour with his feet on the seat-box. Traffic wands are held aloft in the first, second and fourth 250's as a child looks on in possible amazement at the sight before him. Note the lack of MG shield on the lead 250 and that the second in line is the 250/10 seen earlier.

Heavily camouflaged 250's from the *9th Panzer Aufklaerungs Abteilung* return to their billeting area outside a small village. Because of the summer crop colour, the panzer grey now makes their vehicles highly visible against the yellow of the fields. The photographer has obviously caught their attention as they pass by. Note the ubiquitous bucket hanging from the tow hook.

BA101I-216-0425-11A

With *Zeltbahn* neatly rolled up at the rear and 'Jerry can' and bowl roped to the left front mudguard, note the difference in colour between the dried mud under the rear chassis and front wheel hubs compared to the muddied tracks.

BA101I-216-0425-13A

Both a Type 1 (in the foreground) and Type 2 are visible here, *laagered* next to the camouflaged truck. The bright line angled up at 45 degrees on the Type 1 is the front hoop for the tarpaulin cover. The buildings have taken a fair amount of damage, and parked up in front of the houses to the left are other vehicles, perhaps also belonging to the Reconnaissance Battalion?

Vehicles of an unidentified Armoured Reconnaissance Battalion somewhere in the Ukraine, mid-1943. This factory-finished *dunkelgelb* 250/1 has been 'dug in' and camouflaged, standard practice when in reserve just behind the front line and no other cover is available. Note the track tensioning instruction plate riveted to the rear of the track guard. In the background, crews gather to collect their rations.

A fine shot of a late version Sd Kfz 260 equipped with a short range *Fu7* and *Fu. Spr. a*. Unlike the 250's seen in this set of photographs, this 260 crew have added a light green over-spray on top of the dark yellow. The 250 in the background is the same one from the previous page, seen delivering food to the troops.

Most German soldiers took their civilian 'wash kits' into service with them and, judging by the evidence, used a wide range of every day products (here 'Nivea' toothpaste, priced at 39 *Reich Pfennig*) to keep themselves clean.

Nominees gather with their mates mess tins for the ration handout, brought along in a 250 Type 1. Built some 18 months to two years previously, its original 'Panzer grey' finish now exhibits a worn dark yellow over spray. This specimen is in poor condition compared to the 250 Type 2 on page 106/107.

It is hard to find any other fighting force in the Second World War that had such a diverse range of uniforms, insignia and awards as the Wehrmacht. Rather than sticking to one good idea and then mass producing it, the Germans continued to refine, update and attempt to replace old items on an almost yearly basis. This resulted in a bewildering array of types, models, and rules and regulations so baffling that they can cause military researchers sleepless nights sixty odd years on. Add to this the tendency of frontline troops to ignore the regulations, wear something their mother sent them, or personalise themselves with unofficial insignia, and you have a very interesting set of photographs!

Several variations of the same idea can be seen here, all worn in an attempt to keep cool on an obviously hot day. It is tempting to assume with both armoured car and 250 crews are present that there are definitely two distinct styles of dress. Armoured car crews were allowed to wear the black 'tank' clothing, 250 crews (with rare exceptions) tended to look like Infantry/Panzer Grenadiers. Prominent is the individual with the pre-war *Drillich* fatigue tunic. He appears to be receiving the contents of a tin (jam?) and has another in his left hand.

BA101I-705-0272-23

BA101I-705-0272-22

BA1011-705-0272-24

There are a real mix of veterans and youngsters here. The *Stabsgefreiter* 'B' displays the Panzer assault badge and has the ribbon for the 'war merit cross 2nd class' in the buttonhole. The bar of medal ribbon miniatures is hard to identify. The 'Iron cross second-class' hanging from the buttonholes of the two lads have only recently been bestowed. Regulations stated that the recipient could wear the award like this for one day. After this, the cross was removed and the ribbon sewn in place. (See 'A' for final result). The smaller of the two seems to have mislaid his cross already!

It is not clear what the unofficial insignia denotes. On enlargement, it appears to be an arrow crossed at the lower shaft by two lines. It also appears extremely similar to the insignia of the 22nd Panzer Division, an almost unremarkable unit that was disbanded in February 1943. However, its dissolved subunits were absorbed into the 23rd Panzer Division which, strangely enough, had a divisional emblem of an arrow crossed at the lower shaft by one line. Whatever it is, it was only important enough to be worn on two of the half dozen black caps visible.

The food containers *(Essenbehalten)* have an inner lining to provide insulation. Theoretically each scoop of an issue ladle corresponded to one of the two indentations seen on the side of the mess tins. Three scoops (and a bit) should fill the mess tin. Note the difference in colour of shirts, (F) still wearing his woollen trousers despite the heat, and the civilian jumper on (E).

BA1011-705-0272-26

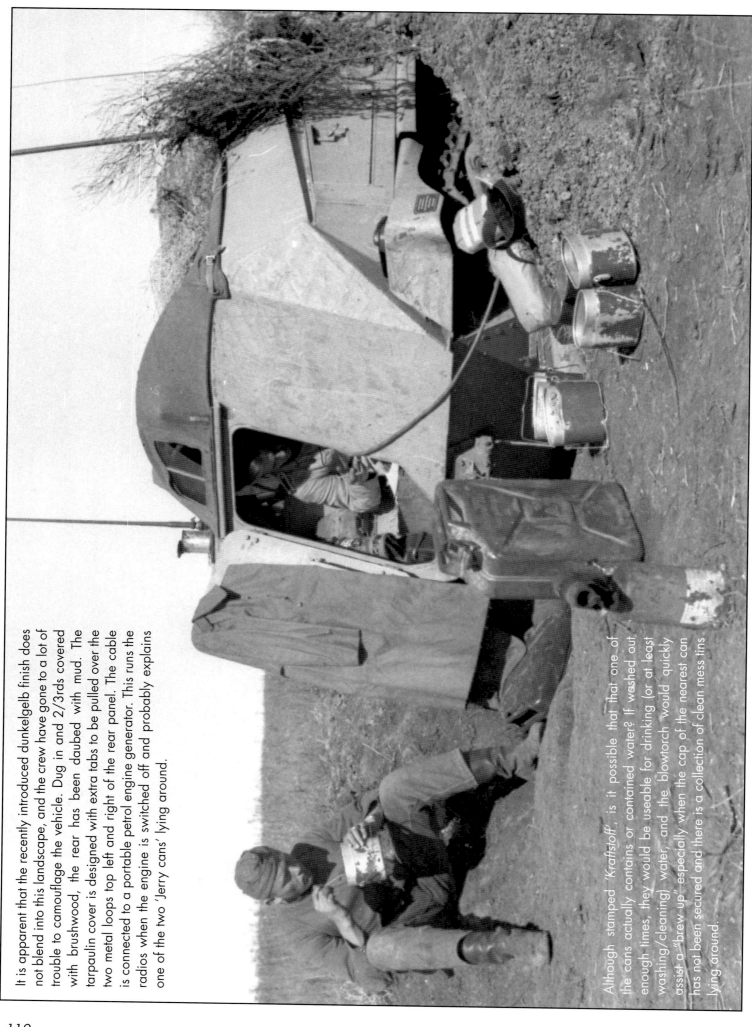

It is apparent that the recently introduced dunkelgelb finish does not blend into this landscape, and the crew have gone to a lot of trouble to camouflage the vehicle. Dug in and 2/3rds covered with brushwood, the rear has been daubed with mud. The tarpaulin cover is designed with extra tabs to be pulled over the two metal loops top left and right of the rear panel. The cable is connected to a portable petrol engine generator. This runs the radios when the engine is switched off and probably explains one of the two 'Jerry cans' lying around.

Although stamped 'Kraftstoff', is it possible that that one of the cans actually contains or contained water? If washed out enough times, they would be useable for drinking (or at least washing/cleaning) water, and the blowtorch would quickly assist a "brew up" especially when the cap of the nearest can has not been secured and there is a collection of clean mess tins lying around.

ABOVE: The tarpaulin is pressed hard against the rear MG AA boom, seen through the plastic window above the door. Directly at the base of the post, a leather strap and sheet metal 'slot' secures the canvas cover by passing through a metal eyelet attached to the bodywork. The window element can be unfastened at the bottom, rolled up and held with straps inside to keep it open.

LEFT: Apart from the track adjustment information plate, notice the different style of locker catch, more in keeping with the later *'Neu'* version. The piece pointing 45 degrees down to the right is in fact the padlock. Even though this is a Type 2 250, there is no beaded edge to the track guard.

OPPOSITE PAGE: The crewman tucking into his rations wears the two-piece herringbone fatigue uniform, favoured for hot weather, and a *M42* cap. The *Unteroffizier* making notes in the shade of the 250 wears what appears to be the pre-war *'Drillich'* tunic. To this he has attached shoulder boards and, on the right breast, the national emblem.

BA101I-705-0278-33A

ABOVE: This particular 250/5 could belong to the same unit as the previous page. It has the same exterior door locks and the same textured finish over the original grey paint, which is still showing on the chassis. Just visible on the side locker is the tactical sign for an artillery unit and semi hidden by the trees is the armoured housing for the *Sternantenne D*. Note the lack of a number plate on the right and the missing tow hitch.

OPPOSITE TOP: A 250/3 of an unidentified SS unit parked up with a *5cm PaK (Sf) auf Zugkraftwagen 1 ton* (5cm anti-tank gun, self propelled, on a 1 ton half tracked vehicle). The stowage box normally found immediately behind the driver and co-driver has been discarded and a new, heavier mount to accept the carriage has been welded in place. Now minus the wheels, the trail legs of the gun carriage have been retained along with the tarpaulin roof of the original Sd Kfz 10. Both vehicles appear to have green patches sprayed over the base grey colour.

RIGHT: This classic shot is always worthy of inclusion in any book about 250's. Developed to replace the Sd Kfz 222, the 250/9 made a fine reconnaissance vehicle with its good mobility and relatively powerful armament. However, if it came in contact with a similarly armed opponent, the armour (even the 14mm thick nose plate) would not prevent the loss of the vehicle. Note the spare track blocks strung out on the vehicles sides and the links fastened to the front tow hooks of the closest vehicle.

BA101I-711-0447-27

BA101I-711-0447-31

117

Classic Type 2s of an unknown SS unit moving out of town. Note the purpose-built short stowage box on the track guard and the unusual headlight covers.

206

BA1011-704-0128-06

Two Sd Kfz 250's from the *2. Kompanie/Panzer Aufklaerungs Abteilung 11* pass by a village well. The 'Zitadelle' alternative marking is clearly visible here, as is the tactical sign for a (Motorised) *Aufklaerung* unit (note the 'A' in the top left corner and the diagonal 'cavalry' stripe).

Parked up beyond the well is further proof that the Germans were not shy about utilising any vehicle they could lay their hands on. The 'Studebaker' is a US 'lend lease' now liberated from the Red Army and eagerly drafted into one of the Division's supply units. German veterans recall being impressed by the sturdy American trucks. One was captured by the Panzer Regiment Grossdeutschland (11th Panzer's left hand neighbour during the Kursk offensive) and served with its supply train until the end of the war. Beyond this is either a Stoewer of Mercedes-Benz *le.gl.Pkw* and parked beside it a Mercedes-Benz Typ L 1500 A *Mannschaftswagen*.

BA101I-219-0584-39

An Sd Kfz 250/1 belonging to the *3. Batterie/ Panzer Artillerie Regiment 76* is followed by a brand new *Munitionstraeger auf Fahrgestell III/IV.* This rare vehicle is theoretically one of two ammunition carriers serving the battery's six *15cm Schwere Panzerhaubitze auf Geschutzwagen III/IV (Sf) (Hummel).* Some 100 *"Hummel's"* were built in time for the Kursk offensive and records show that the 11th Panzer had a battery on their books by August 1943. This example is one of the original versions with the narrow driver's superstructure. Later versions incorporated a radio operator's position. It is presumed that the *StuG III* belongs to *Sturmgeschuetz Abteilung 911.* Raised in March 1943, this independent assault gun Battalion was attached to the 11th Panzer Division for the duration of the Citadel operation until April 1944.

Note that the divisional sign is formed from four separate rectangles. Hastily re-sprayed with dunkelgelb, the tactical sign has been re-painted in white and overlaps the registration plate. The 250 is now in a sorry state with bent mud and track guards and a missing crank access cap. The shield under the nose has gone and, at some point, the entire nose has been removed for servicing as the headlamp cables have not been re-attached correctly and now hang loose from the armour. It also appears to have a set of truck tyres instead of the usual bulletproof cross-country *(gelande)* examples. When re-sprayed the headlamp glass lenses have been simply painted over, leaving a clear illumination slot.

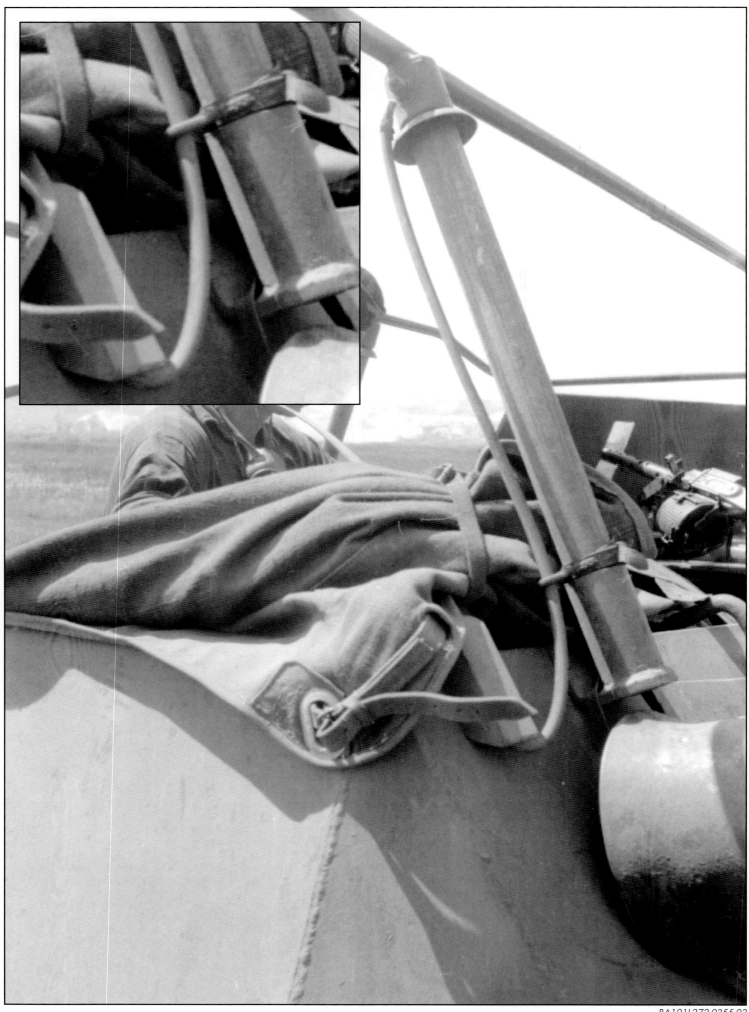

BA101I-272-0355-03

RIGHT: Frame aerial posts were either made of wood or the same compressed wood pulp used for wire cutter handles, to isolate the aerial from the vehicle itself. In this picture the original pole would appear to have been lost and a replacement has been found but is made of steel tubing (note the holes that have left an indent when drilled). Because the metal post cannot isolate the aerial it is deliberately not placed in the support mount and is perhaps jammed in this position with a piece of wood unseen from this angle? The leather buckle is there to attach the aerial cable to the post and not a vain attempt at securing the post.

Note the armoured cable cover that angles over the side that feeds the cable from the radio sets out to the aerial. Note also the aerial base cover, which is made of canvas with a spring steel retaining band and clip. This is the first version of the aerial base that is slightly less deep in its base and has a shorter drop over the side from the top edge. Half hidden by the shadow the rear post has a protective cover.

BELOW RIGHT: The Knights Cross winning Major and his *Leutnant* pose for pictures with their crew. Note the different texture of the aerial support poles compared to the metal cups that they sit in and the aerial frame itself together with the positioning of the extra bracket with block to clear the side armour. Interestingly this 250/3 is equipped with the armoured barrelled version of the MG34 normally used in tanks.

OPPOSITE: The metal ring to hold the aerial cable is riveted onto the leather strap and fastened to the post with a buckle. In this larger picture it is possible to see the texture of the wood or compressed pulpwood used to make the posts. The canvas has been reinforced with a second layer where the eyelet passes through the material as it takes a lot of strain at the corners.

NEXT PAGE: Whilst the track guard retains the beaded edge, the mudguard (like so many others) has seen better days and appears to have lost most of the tool brackets as well. Note the mounting holes along the edge to screw the wooden bead onto the metal. The toolbox has also received its fair share of mistreatment and a new door has been cobbled together to replace the original.

BA101I-240-2137-31A

BA1011-680-8282-29A

ABOVE: Even though the registration plate says differently, two *Luftwaffe* soldiers share a chat and cigarette in this classic but tired 250 Type 2. Using individual stencils, the numbers have been applied by someone not particularly fussy as to whether they were straight or not. The circle between the 'H' and '1' is in fact the original (faded) plate colour and *Feldpost* stamp, carefully avoided when re-painted. Note how the over-spray of the camouflage colour has caught the left edge of the number plate.

The front wings show a different method (also seen in other pictures) of attaching the headlamps in front of the mudguards. The bracket passes through a slot in the wings rather than appearing from underneath the leading edge. Note how bent and buckled the front wings have become and the misshapen

right hand width indicator. On the extreme left of the picture (the right side of the 250), there seems to be a smoke canister discharger (normally found on tanks) mounted onto the top of the exterior stowage box.

It would be easy to assume that the colours seen here are grey and green, but with the front visors open it is possible to see the original *dunkelgelb* finish. This has remained here because the visors were obviously shut when the camouflage colours were applied. So this could be Tunisia, with a *dunkelgelb* 250 re-sprayed with the darker tan with grey camouflage on top of that, or units who were originally destined for Tunisia but re-routed when the Tunisian campaign ended. The crews dark blue issue tunics were not often seen in North Africa lending weight to the idea that this is the Eastern front.

This is the same *Luftwaffe* crewed 250 as left, note the difference in vehicle colour between these two pictures one taken in overcast conditions and this one in bright sunshine has changed the look completely.

BA101I-680-8282-24A

BA101I-524-2258-16

BA101I-524-2258-21

At the end of 1942 the 1st Panzer Division was withdrawn from the frontline at Rzhev and travelled back to France to rest and re-equip the Division. In April 1943 the Division was transferred to Greece to continue re-equipping and provide coastal defence and were fully operational by June. This parade took place in August 1943 in Athens in front of General Kruger commander of the 1st Panzer Grenadier Regiment (standing in the Opel Admiral convertible) and Major von Zitzewitze.

In the top left picture a 250 'Alt' heads a Company of the 37th Panzer Pioneer Company in their Sd Kfz 251/7s,

whereas in the picture above the 250/3 bears the tactical sign for Motorised Infantry and could be either a Company or Battalion headquarters vehicle. Note that behind the four 250's are a selection of radio cars and the difference in locker design between the first and second 250's.

The two pictures opposite both appear to be marked up or rather were marked up in the same way except that the tactical and Divisional signs that were saved during the over-painting of the original panzer-grey have now been painted out. Either for the censor or that these 250's belonged to another unit within the Division and now require new tactical symbols.

A pair of Sd Kfz 250's from an unidentified artillery Regiment parked up back to back. The crew have used branches and several Zeltbahn buttoned together to form a roof between the vehicles. With the tarpaulins in place it is impossible to know if they are both 250/5's. The tarpaulins were a grey-brown colour while the leather edging and buckle straps were light tan. Note the individual to the left. The shorts and tropical (leather and canvas) ankle boots he wears suggests that this is somewhere in Italy, 1943.

Both of these 250's were originally finished in the 1940 'dark grey'. On the right-hand vehicle, evidence of this can be seen on the interior door and lower rear chassis. On the left, further clues can be found in the worn paintwork along the edge of the body armour and the hand painted loading plate (see inset picture). The body colour on both appears to be slightly darker than the 20 litre 'Jerry cans' (compare previous photograph). These examples were specifically intended for carrying water and therefore are almost certainly factory finished (during the manufacturing process, fuel cans were stamped *Kraftstoff*, water cans *Wasser*. They also bore the obvious white cross). Note the two different styles of exterior side lockers and the rear mud flaps that have been painted over. The tactical symbol for an artillery unit can just be seen on the rear of the vehicle on the right.

BA101I-175-1271-39

ABOVE & TOP: A standard 250/1 Type 2 receiving a lot of attention from the local Italian population in 1943. I do not know exactly what the *813* stands for and the number 6 cannot be for the 6th Panzer Division, as they never served in Italy during the war. It is interesting that this vehicle has never received a proper coat of *dunkelgelb* and the unit were obviously content to make-do with the fast wearing second coat over the original panzer grey.

OPPOSITE PAGE: A 250/5 'Alt' in France on field exercises in the summer of 1943. The greenery is attached to rope netting and they appear to have collected quite a few specimen trees, including oak, horse chestnut and various ferns to camouflage the vehicle from passing planes. Note the colour of the tarpaulin cover in comparison to the leather edging. Both the officer in the 250 and the one on the bonnet wear despatch riders overcoats.

INSET PICTURE: Note the two (of four) bolts that attach the armoured cover over the ceramic isolator and aerial base plus a connections box. The plate that holds the aerial equipment is bolted to the top plate that runs around the inside of the top edge of the armour and is entirely separate from the armoured cover.

Vehicles of the 2nd Company, 12th Reconnaissance Battalion (12th Panzer Division) operating in the Orel / Gomel area in the autumn of 1943. The camouflage of dunkelgelb or 1942 yellow has been applied directly onto the panzer grey producing unusual patterns to nearly all of the vehicles.

The picture on this and the following 6 pages are all taken from one film with virtually concurrent numbers and thus raises a few questions about camouflage, basic vehicle colours and the timing of changes. Quite how long the overlap was after the order to change from plain panzer grey to dunkelgelb we'll never know, but it is interesting to have all three phases in one set of pictures within one particular unit. The order went out in May 1943 for front line units to re-spray their vehicles.

At Kursk, virtually every front-line unit involved wore the new colour scheme and camouflage combinations, yet in this set and others in this book, there are anomalies that defy convention. Rear echelon vehicles and supply columns were generally the last to receive the new colours, but in these pictures the Reconnaissance Battalion of a Panzer Division are still waiting for supplies to reach their front-line.

A platoon of six 250's move out for another patrol. Note how the crew of the lead 250/3 have carefully avoided losing the front number plate, but the crews of the 250's behind have been less fussy and over-painted the entire front nose plate. In the patch top left of the nose plate it is just possible to see the divisional symbol of a circle with the "Y" in the centre rubbed out from the *dunkelgelb* over spray.

Note how the crew have completely over-painted the number plates on the vehicle and carries no visible markings apart from the *balkenkreuz*. The camouflage pattern does not follow any official guidelines but like the other vehicles in the unit the painter has created this curious broad stripes and dots of colour pattern being very careful to leave dots of grey amongst the over-spray of sand or *dunkelgelb*. Of the four vehicles here, (there is a fourth in the dust cloud in front of and in between the two in the mid-distance) the lead pair of 250's retain there overall coat of grey with no secondary colour.

Note the grenade case slung over the rear of the amour on the 250 closest to the camera.

With 002 painted on to the *dunkelgelb*, which is partially covering the white *Balkenkreuz*, this is the commander's vehicle of the 2nd Company of the Reconnaissance Battalion. Note how they avoided over-spraying the inscription *"werkzeugkasten"* on the exterior toolbox, the workshop made stowage locker on the track guard, the condition of the front mudguard and that the semaphore indicator has come adrift.

208

As units return back from a patrol, a newly delivered 250 *'Neu'* is receiving its unit and tactical symbols from a paintbrush-wielding crewmember at the front. This is one of the early models with the small running lights mounted on the front mudguards and the Notek driving light, and no provision to store tools on the upper plate of the bonnet.

Note the difference in colour of the previous years yellow on the 'Alt' in the distance and the new *dunkelgelb* of the Neu. It is interesting that it is equipped with an *MG34* and not an *MG42*, but if you look closely the shield is in grey and lifted off an *'Alt'* to use on this *'Neu'*. The cradle behind the shield will take both mounts for both machine guns but it would appear that this unit only used *MG34's* and even though the replacement vehicle would be most welcome, it came supplied with the *MG42* gun mount in the shield.

Note that the door for the exterior locker door is missing on the 250/10 in the distance but still has all of the wooden drawer units.

209

OPPOSITE TOP: In the winter of 1943/44 the 5th Panzer Division were involved in heavy fighting north of Pripjet pulling back to Wlodawa to counterattack towards Kowel, remaining south of the City until May 1944. The German Army were on the defensive and a general order was issued to destroy whatever could not be taken with them. Of the four-man squad, note the soldier on the right who is carrying a mine detector. The 250 appears to be from the 13th or 14th Panzergrenadier Regiment of the Division. Note the black rectangle used to highlight the markings and the new style of *Balkenkreuz.*

OPPOSITE BOTTOM: On very close inspection of this picture there is the faint outline on the right for the tactical sign for an Armoured Car Company on the nose plate of this 250/1, which is followed by a 250/9. The date given in the archives states Tarnopol, November 1943.

ABOVE: A late production 250 Type 2 'somewhere in Russia'. The divisional symbol on the left of the nose cannot be clearly ascertained. It looks like a derivation of the bison symbol of 7th Panzer Regiment (10th Panzer Division), but this is not clear as the 'Y' symbol is missing from the nose plate but it could appear on the rear plate?

It is not easy to put a date to this picture. Almost certainly taken in autumn, the camouflage colours are interesting and a bit of a mystery. If it is a grey vehicle why are the divisional and tactical symbols plus the registration plate surrounded by a paler colour? If this 250 wears a *dunkelgelb* base coat then what colour is the darker shade and is it in fact paint? The

real drawback of a plain *dunkelgelb* vehicle (once the weather has turned in the late autumn or after the spring thaw) is that they stand out against the leafless trees and lack of ground colour.

Tonally the darker colour could be mud, which has been applied to lessen the 250's visibility, as it seems to be the same shade as the front wheel and the tracks. This could explain why the colour changes above the front visors, on the exhaust cover (behind the front wheel) and on the soft metal sheet below the nose because it is being worn away through use and the inclement weather.

The other possibilty, or possible scenario that could have led to its camouflage arrangement is that it is a grey vehicle which has received an over spray of yellow and at the same time they have re-applied the registration plate on a fresh patch of paint. The divisional and tactical markings could have been wiped into the wet paint to form the appropriate symbols.

149

150

Units of the 2nd Reconnaissance Battalion / 2nd Panzer Division cross the Dnieper River. Of the 9 250's at least 5 are 250/9s. The closest is a 250/5 (Light reconnaissance vehicle, not to be confused with the 250/5 for the artillery) and the rest are mainly 250/1's with perhaps another 250/3 or 5 in the far distance. Records show that the 250/9 armed with the 20mm *KwK38* cannon is featured in the *Beladenplane* for *Leichter Shutzenpanzerwagen* dated 15.1.43. However it is the prototype vehicle based on an old Sd Kfz 253 or Sd Kfz 250 built using the early body-style. Full production began in March 1943 and were generally issued to Type 'C' reconnaissance companies.

It is always difficult to tell grey from dunkelgelb in winter conditions because all colours appear darker against the white of the snow. The two 250/9s closest to the camera appear to be *dunkelgelb* with an overspray of green yet the 250/3 appears to be darker and therefore possibly still in its original grey.

Note the exterior locker on the 250/5 has door lock assemblies like an Sd Kfz 251 Ausf D and a rack on the rear for extra jerry cans. The crew have hung the windscreen inserts box that would usually be placed on the rear of the co-driver's seat, to free up a little more interior space.

Having suffered heavy casualties in defensive fighting east of the Dnieper River at Gomel, the Division was withdrawn from front-line duties at the turn of 1943/1944. What is not clear here is whether these units are advancing up to the front line in October or November, or withdrawing to assembly points for onward transfer to France in December or January?

Because it does not have a front shield this vehicle would appear to be a 250/7 equipped with the heavy mortar (S.GR. W.34). It has the mounting rack for the base plate on the rear armour (that is shared between this and the heavy MG version of the 250/1) from which hang two 'Teller' mines and a bucket. The 'Jerry can' is placed to the left because of the rack.

Once again within the same set of pictures there is a question over the colour of the vehicles. If the trident symbol is white and the teller mine on the right is sand then what two colours are we seeing on this 250?

It would appear that whoever applied the second coat (if the lighter colour is the second coat) that they went to the trouble of avoiding the divisional symbol and the *Balkenkreuz* in the process. This would lead us to think that this is a (now) dirty *dunkelgelb* over the grey base coat, which has faded with time and usage. However if the other teller mine is green and the jerry can is grey this could make the camouflage colours green over a dirty *dunkelgelb* base coat! In the colour chapter this picture has been portrayed with a base colour of grey with *dunkelgelb* or sand over-spray.

Four

BA1011-578-1946-25

BA1011-578-1946-26

TOP LEFT: In late January 1944 two German Army Corps (XI and XXXXII) became trapped just west of the Dnieper River by a powerful Soviet encirclement operation. An initial attempt by the battle-fatigued 11th and 13th Panzer Divisions to break through to the embattled defenders of the 'Tscherkassy pocket' broke down in the face of determined resistance, and both Divisions were subsequently forced onto the defensive as the Red army attempted to further the distance between German relief forces and those caught inside. Here, elements of the 13th Panzer participate in the air evacuation of wounded. It is not clear whether these casualties are escapees from the 'pocket' or troops from the 13th Panzer. Note the animal skin rugs draped over the side of the 250 and the two wounded in beds on the horse-drawn cart in front.

OPPOSITE BOTTOM: The tactical sign is for a medium Reconnaissance Company above the divisional symbol for the 13th Panzer Division (which looks similar to the old *Kradschuetzen* symbol).

ABOVE: This 250 appears on the right of the photograph on the following page. The individual being transferred to the stretcher is hanging on to a crewmember in some discomfort. The object sticking up above him is the unsecured end of a tarpaulin hoop. The wounded have been transported under cover and the tarpaulin has been hastily removed just before this photograph was taken. Note the wounded wrapped in a blanket in the 250 to the left. Visible in the distance is another 250/1 'Neu' and a 250/9 'Alt' with its grenade shields folded open.

FOLLOWING PAGE TOP: The *Junkers 52* transport plane is probably from Generalleutnant Seidemann's VIII Air corps. This corps had a two-fold task: to lift supplies into and retrieve wounded from the pocket, and support the relieving forces, whose own supply lines were floundering due to the poor conditions. Utilising temporary, often waterlogged airfields, over 800 *JU 52*'s formed an 'air bridge' for their beleaguered compatriots. Braving enemy action and often atrocious weather conditions, some 113 of these 'workhorses' were lost in the Tcherkassy operation. The crew of this *JU 52* have taken some care to ensure that the (now worn) whitewash coat has not covered any aircraft identification areas, including the yellow 'eastern front stripe'.

FOLLOWING PAGE BOTTOM: The wounded await loading in a queue stretching around to the right side of the aircraft. It is not apparent where the beds came from! The winter of 1943/44 was regarded as one of the mildest in living memory. In early February a sudden thaw resulted in a half-meter layer of snow melting into the ground and causing chaos to both sides alike. The front track wheel of the 'Neu' on the right now looks like a flat dish because of the mud. The 250/1 'Neu' in the centre is marked 'K83' behind the Balkenkreuz and the bridging plate is visible on the forward part of the exterior locker. On the rear panel, the field workshop has fashioned a 'Jerry can' holder, note the stretcher straddling the top. The Neu on the far left is armed with an *MG13*.

BA101I-708-0298-23

Two views of the same 250/3 of the 1st Panzer Army in preparation for the breakout from the Kamenets – Podolsk pocket in March of 1944 with either late Pz Kpfw IV Ausf G or Hs in attendance. It seems as if literally everything received a coat of whitewash when applied, as the wooden box, all the helmets and the wooden jack block have a faded coat of extra paint. Note how the paint has worn away on the top edge of the superstructure in the main picture above. The crew are either erecting or stowing the tarpaulin support hoops and the canvas cover can just be seen on the extreme right of the picture.

BA101I-708-0298-36A

ABOVE: Oberst (later Generalleutnant) Hyazinth Graf Strachwitz, formally of the Panzer Regiment Grossdeutschland, visiting troops on the Narwa front in 1944. He appears to be holding a walking stick; no surprise when one considers he was wounded no less than fourteen times, including a nasty accident during the 'Kursk offensive' when the recoil of his tanks cannon hit him. Note the *PAK 40* tucked into the tree line and a second 250 in the distance. Contrary to the evidence of the crates (for 75mm anti-tank rounds), it is doubtful if this vehicle is an Sd Kfz 250/6 ammunition carrier. Given how

high up the crewmember is in the vehicle, it would appear that he is standing on the seat box of an Sd Kfz 250/1. This example has a *dunkelgelb* base coat with a worn whitewash finish.

BELOW: With the winter snow gone and the battlefield turning to mud with the spring weather the last thing you would want is a plain *dunkelgelb* 250 Neu with remnants of the winter whitewash still on the vehicle. In the background there are the remains of at least three T34/76 tanks.

BA1011-667-7130-33

BA1011-667-7130-31

165

BA1011-575-1818-24

ABOVE: This rather tired looking Type 2 Sd Kfz 250/3 has received the same level of hand-painted finish as the one seen on page 112. On the top edge of this front mudguard, someone has welded an eyelet on a small piece of metal. The 'Jerry can' has been jammed in between the width indicator and the *Notek* front light and then fastened with a webbing strap. Behind this is a neat row of all too easily lost track blocks.

The conduit from the rear Notek is fastened with a clip to the track guard. It eventually disappears under the rear bodywork and through a hole in the rear door threshold plate. The registration plate is painted onto the track guard (which has lost it's half-round beading on the edge,) and is unusual in that it retains the symmetrical pattern of metal number plates. This particular 250 was originally finished in 'dark grey' and has been over painted.

OPPOSITE: A 250/5 radio operator listens intently to incoming messages through his *Doppel-Fernhoerer.b* headphone set. The rubber pads were intended to cut down the background noise levels in an armoured fighting vehicle, but here he keeps 'one ear open' for verbal orders from outside. He uses a munitions box (thought to be for 8cm mortar shells) as a portable writing table and times messages with a civilian watch. The two radio sets visible are the *Fu 8* which, is an *Mw.E.c* and *30 W.S.a* sited in the lower rack. To the right of the top radio will be the *Fu 4* set, a single *Mw.E.c* receiver.

Although published before, this photograph is presented in a large format image to reveal all of the detail. it was taken in the spring of 1944 in the Ukraine and the 250 is returning from the front as a platoon of infantry wait to move forwards.

On the front nose plate of this early model 250/3 'Neu' there is the tactical sign for a headquarters unit of an armoured Reconnaissance Battalion. The first versions of the 'Neu' were equipped with *Notek* front lights and a few, like this one, also had small running lights on the front wings. Note the two different pattern treads, the *gelande* (cross country) pattern (as normally seen on the 'Alt') on the left and the alternative 'Neu' type on the right. There are no clasps for either a spade or a pittock on the engine deck.

171

A photograph of what are thought to be elements of the 29th Panzergrenadier Division, taken at the Anzio-Nettuno beachhead sometime after the Allied landings in March 1944.

The 250 is an early Type 2, with the beadless mud and track gaurds. It has probably seen service for two and a half years hence the worn paintwork on what was once a 'dark grey' 250. Compare the factory *dunkelgelb* coat on the 251/1 Ausf D to the slightly paler coat on the 250. Is the tree looking war torn through shelling, or the efforts of the troops to camouflage their vehicles?

LEFT: Somewhere behind the front line in Normandy 1944, the engine of this interesting 250 has received a bit of attention. The nose is now being replaced under the watchful gaze of two officers and an NCO.

Unfortunately, because of the branches on the vehicle it is not possible to tell exactly if the 20mm cannon support is welded in this position or whether it is lying there waiting to be re-mounted. Given the length of the *KwK 38* cannon and mount (which forms the basis of this field modification), it is quite possible that this is the correct position for the support post. With such a small vehicle, it is unlikely that the cannon was mounted on a pedestal within the interior. If it were mounted on the driver's roof, it would be of more use for anti-aircraft defence (one of the more overriding concerns during the summer months of 1944), but makes it possibly too high up for ground target use.

BA101I-495-3436-22

BA101I-495-3436-17

LEFT: This picture was possibly taken in Bourgetheroulde, southwest of Rouen in September 1944. Even though it has been seen before, I have included it because of the state of the vehicle itself. Note the conditions of the mudguards; there are no tools, headlamps or *Notek* driving light. Both air vents are badly crushed, as is the toolbox. The MG shield has either gone or is stowed inside the 250. The canvas cover is not a simple sheet but tailor made in 5 pieces with double stitched and hemmed seams to make it watertight. It has a faded two-colour camouflage scheme over a *dunkelgelb* base coat.

BELOW: This second 250 is in a similar condition. The individual standing in the back is wearing a SS M44 camouflaged tunic, introduced in March 1944 and intended to be worn for both combat and work duties. This assumes that this is a SS vehicle, but with no front plate to verify this and an army tunic being worn in the vehicle behind (see above), who knows? Such confusion was common at this time. Having suffered near catastrophic losses in the 'Falaise gap', by September, it was expedient for the shattered German forces to retreat back across the Seine River.

BA1011-300-1951-17

BELOW: Still armed with an *MG34*, this is another set of pictures taken in France after the invasion of Europe in 1944. Note how the camouflage paint has covered over part of the *Balkenkreuz*, the aerial position is correct for later versions of the Type 2, and the contrast in colour between the canvas material and the leather edging.

ABOVE: With the pair of vehicles so close together, perhaps the lead 250 is towing the other? With the proof of Allied air superiority all too obvious in this picture, camouflage was a necessity as these two crews risk their lives as they pass through the Normandy countryside in broad daylight.

BA1011-493-3358-37A

OPPOSITE PAGE & RIGHT: A new 14th Panzer Division was formed in France in the summer of 1943 and soon found its way back to Russia. The new Reconnaissance Battalion was renumbered 14, and in the inset picture it is possible to read the markings 'Pz. AA 14'. Underneath is the tactical symbol for the HQ Company. This photograph was taken much later in the war, perhaps when the Division was participating in the summer retreats of 1944.

The individual wearing the goggles around his neck wants to show off his 'armoured status' and has pinned a skull on his cap. He is wearing a M42 tunic with standard collar insignia. The *Stabsgefreiter* 'B' displays the wound badge in black, Panzer assault award and the arm patch of a signaller above the rank chevrons of his M40 tunic. Note the black side caps and that 'C' wears either a woollen or herringbone 'StuG' tunic with attached Panzer patches and skulls.

BELOW: Even when viewed enlarged, it is difficult to know exactly what is going on here. This appears to be a workshop unit working on a gearbox or differential (on the table and part covered with a sheet or rags) from one of the 250's. However, at the rear of the left 250 it looks like an animal is being cut up, suggesting that there are elements of a butchery company using the same premises. Certainly a lot of personal equipment has been unloaded from both of the Type 2 250's with the standard rear door and lock without the rear vision visor port, but retains the earlier style of track guards. Note also the sustained fire mount for the MG34 which is protected by its canvas cover and the pale caps, possibly ex-Afrika Korps members now serving in Italy.

WF

Somewhere in Italy in the summer of 1944 a 250/8 'Neu' trundles into town. Even though the 250/8 was listed in manuals pre-dating the introduction of the 'Neu' version, there are (as yet) no known pictures of this gun mount ever being used in conjunction with the 250 'Alt'. As increasing numbers of 75mm L/24 guns became available (from up-armed Pz Kpfw III's and IV's), the Army developed the *75mm K51 (Sf)*, gun mount for the roof of both the 250 and 251. Used to equip the heavy weapons company of Reconnaissance Battalions, these were made in limited numbers before their planned deletion in favour of the more useful 251.

This is the later production version with the *Bosch* headlight on the front left wing. The co-driver's position has been removed and the visor is now a simple welded piece of armour plate. The driver's visor is the standard unit. Look carefully into the back of the truck car on the right to see a soldier happily sitting in the semi-shade under the tree branches. The vehicle in the middle of the picture is a bit of a mystery. If any reader knows the identity of this, we would be grateful for any further information.

Taken in Romania in July 1944, this 250/3 from an unidentified unit has many interesting and unique features. It has to be a 250/3 because there is no way the individual sitting on the edge on the left could be there if the vehicle was equipped with the steady arm for the 'scissor' optical scopes.

The rear post and 'mushroom' locking cap are still in place even though the arm for the anti-aircraft boom is missing. The crew have used a canvas sheet (not the tarpaulin roof) to protect the radios from dust and heat. It appears that they have utilised a Sd Kfz 251 2 -metre aerial and base instead of the usual *Fu. sprech. f* 1.4 metre aerial (mounted on the roof just above the co-drivers head), and sits at this angle because it was designed for a 251 and not this 250.

Despite having exterior lockers, the crew have built themselves a wooden bin on the right hand side upper armour, possibly from where the side meets the rear armour up to the roof over the driver's compartment. The only way they have been able to attach the tree branches is to jam them behind the rear *Notek* convoy light. Note how the 'jerry can' rack overhangs to the right. Just visible on the top right above the can, there is extra tubing that extends up to meet the armour. The entire frame is welded to the body. There is only one vehicle registration plate, on the left, and the rear reflector is missing. The individuals crowding around the barrier appear to be engineers preparing the bridge for demolition.

213

A *Hauptmann* waits for further news from this 250/3 'Neu'. He is wearing a motorcyclist's overcoat (one only has to browse through the pages of this book to see that this item was an obviously popular choice for officers), and carries a despatch/ map case and field binoculars. There is a second 250/3 'Neu' parked up and waiting in the background. It is just possible to make out its *Sternantenne D* above the heads of the crew inside the closer 250.

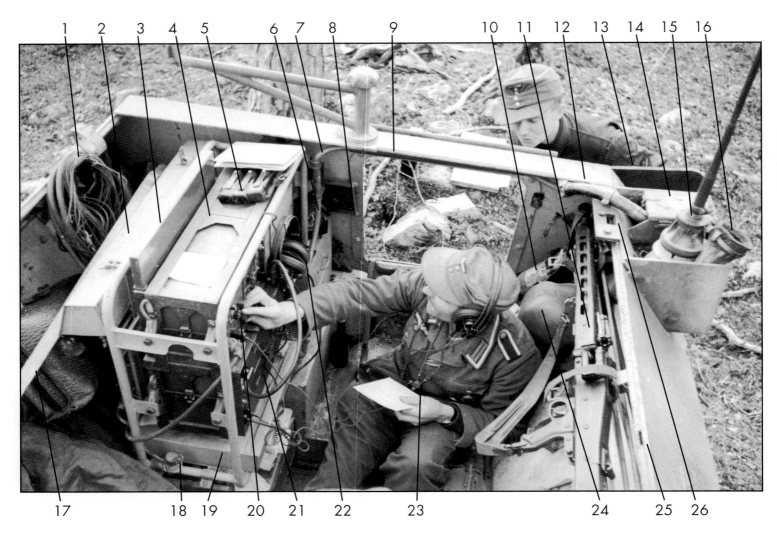

1. Spare field-telephone cables.

2. Rain cover over the 3 *Umformers* (transformers) that convert the power from the vehicle power supply.

3. *30 W.s.a* metal cover (in its slot).

4. *P 10 USE* twin radio rack.

5. MP 40 ammo pouch.

6. *Keinzle* clock for timing messages.

7. Retaining tube and bracket welded to the main frame to guide the aerial cable.

8. M.w E.c front cover.

9. Secondary retaining tube for the aerial cable.

10. *Tetra* fire extinguisher.

11. MG 42.

12. Pre-formed aerial tube.

13. Armoured cover to aerial base.

14. Box with lid for the electrical connections (dependant upon radios used) and ceramic isolator base for the *Sternanteene D* aerial.

15. Antenne base Nr. 1.

16. Antenne base cover with spring fastening.

17. Tarpaulin hoop.

18. Power socket.

19. Metal drawer.

20. *10 watt Mw. E.c* receiver.

21. 30 W.s.a Sender unit.

22. *Doppelfernhoerer B.*

23. Larynx microphone.

24. *M42 Stalhelm.*

25. Slot for the tarpaulin hoop. (Three each side)

26. Slot for the tarpaulin hoop through the aerial box mount.

All posed pictures (because they cannot see much as a forward observer in a forest) but probably the best set of 250/5 'Neu' pictures taken. Note that the interior of the rear door has received the same camouflage as the exterior. In the photo top right they have put the windscreen inserts box on the back of the driver's seat and not the co-drivers seat which he is using as a table whilst he sits on top of the gearbox cover. Note the radio operator's seat folded up to the left of the rear door.

BA101I-111-1800-08

BA101I-111-1800-04

This picture was probably taken in the late autumn of 1944 and shows a command post for an unidentified *Gebirgsjaeger* unit (note the edelweiss insignia on the officer's arm and the Feldmuetze of the man to the extreme right). The officer is actually a *Sonderfuehrer*, one of many specialists attached to combat units in an advisory role. He bears the temporary rank of *Leutnant* and wears the early war cord shoulder straps.

The individual to the left is wearing the winter suit printed in the 'reverse splinter' pattern, while at least two motorcyclist's overcoats can be seen, a popular choice for officers. Note the greatcoat wearer in the 250/1 and the aerial set for the *Torn. Fu. f.* on the right.

Apparently on an anti-partisan sweep somewhere in the mountains of southeast Europe, these *Gebirgsjaeger* troops find that a bridge has been demolished. They now need to locate another route across. Seen here are two 250 'Neu', a 1-ton prime mover towing a *PaK 40*, a mule train and what appears to be a struggling *Kuebelwagen*.

OPPOSITE PAGE: Note the rack for the 'jerry cans' on the 250/1 and the *MG42* main armament. Having successfully forded the stream, the 250/3 has already moved up and established point duty on the corner of the road.

BA101I-204-1719-26

215

The *Notek* front light indicates that this is one of the early versions of the 250 *'Neu'*. This particular vehicle does not have the track tensioning information plates seen on other examples. See how the rear convoy light cable runs down the outside of the mudguard and under the rear of the bodywork overhang where it enters the vehicle.

Like the *'Alt'*, it has the articulated red reflector disc bolted onto the chassis/body flange at the rear left only. Note the two different variations of 20-litre fuel cans in the rack.

Someone is determined to slow this unit down. Having cleared one barrier of rocks, they now start on a second further up the road. Are there partisans somewhere close by observing them? In these confined conditions, a close quarter ambush would be devastating.

Note the slightly different design of the jerry can rack and the damage to the rear right exterior locker. The tow hook is twisted round to lay horizontal facing to the left.

215

Six

D 672/9

Zum Einlegen in das Gerät!

Leichter Schützenpanzerwagen

(Sd Kfz 250)

Beladepläne

Vom 15. 1. 43

LOADING PLAN

D672/9

To be left in the vehicle!

Light Riflemen's Armoured Vehicle

(SD KFZ 250)

Loading Plans

From 15.1.43

Contents

Preliminary Remarks

1. For the stocklist, the item count and for the proof of the relevant sets of equipment as well as single items, only the equipment list of the unit is acceptable.

Tempory deviations between loading plan and equipment entries in the equipment list are sufficient.

2. All items are to be fitted into the intended holders which are intended for the purpose, all other items to be stored with the heaviest at the lowest level. Each item must be stored firmly, with packaging if required. Take special care with fragile equipment, protect from pressure and shock.

3. Direction notices (front, right etc.) are meant in direction of travel.

4. Abbreviation of vehicle type: Light Riflemans Armoured Vehicle Sd.Kfz250.

5. This type includes the Loading Plans to accommodate the fitting sets as below:

a) Sd.Kfz250/1
   1. 1 Light MG crew or
   2. 1 Heavy MG crew
b) Sd.Kfz250/2 Light Communication Armoured Vehicle
c) Sd.Kfz250/3 Light Radio Armoured Vehicle
d) Sd.Kfz250/4 (designation follows later)
e) Sd.Kfz250/5 Light Observation Armoured Vehicle
f) 1. Sd.Kfz250/6 Light Ammunition Armoured Vehicle (for 7.5 Stu. Gun) (short type A)
   2. Sd.Kfz250/6 Light Ammunition Armoured Vehicle (for 7.5 Stu. Cannon 40) (type B)
h) Sd.Kfz250/7 Light Riflemans Armoured Vehicle (troop vehicle)
i) Sd.Kfz250/8 (designation follows later)
j) Sd.Kfz250/9 Light Riflemans Armoured Vehicle (2cm)
k) Sd.Kfz250/10 Light Riflemans Armoured Vehicle (3.7 PAK)
l) Sd.Kfz250/11 Light Riflemans Armoured Vehicle (heavy tank gun 41)
m) Sd.Kfz250/12 Light Survey Armoured Vehicle

6. The equipment outlined in the 'Loading Plan' of the base vehicle as 'fitted items', also are part of the inventory of all the following above listed 'Loading Plans'.

7. Regards to additional holders for individual loading requirements, see D672/8, spare parts list for building-up base fittings and supplements.

LIGHT RIFLEMEN'S ARMOURED VEHICLE (Sd Kfz 250)
Loading Plan No. 1
FOR EQUIPMENT BELONGING TO THE BASE BUILD UP OF VEHICLE
Pictures: 1, 2, 2a, 3 and 4

Number and name of item:	Where to Stow
I. Externally:	
3 tool boxes (drawers)	a. In tool case between R/H mudguard
LEFT	
1 vehicle jack, winder rod and support block	b. on mudguard
1 starting handle	d. on mudguard
1 crowbar	e. on mudguard
1 tow rope	f. on mudguard
1 spade	g. on mudguard
1 wire cutters (large)	h. on mudguard
RIGHT	
1 accessories case	i. on mudguard
1 axe (hand)	j. on mudguard
1 pick axe	k. on mudguard
1 fire extinguisher	l. on mudguard
1 axe (large)	i.i in accessories case on mudguard
II. Internally:	
Observation items:	
2 long protective windows	n. in box on co-drivers seat
1 short protective window	n. in box on co-drivers seat
2 protective glass panes (70 x 270 x 54)	o. on left sidewall
2 protective glass panes (70 x 150 x 54)	p. on right sidewall
Signalling Equipment:	
1 rod (baton) to give signs with (ommited during war)	q. on right near co-driver
Other Equipment items:	
4 spare track links	r. under floor
1 extinguisher	r.i rear left sidewall
1 torch	s. right sidewall in front of co-driver
carrier for torch out of use	t. right on sidewall
1 first aid kit	u. inside rear door
2 sets of keys for padlocks on vehicle equipment of which 1 set in reserve	decided by leader of unit or driver
2 handles for flaps (21E 8999-1)	

1

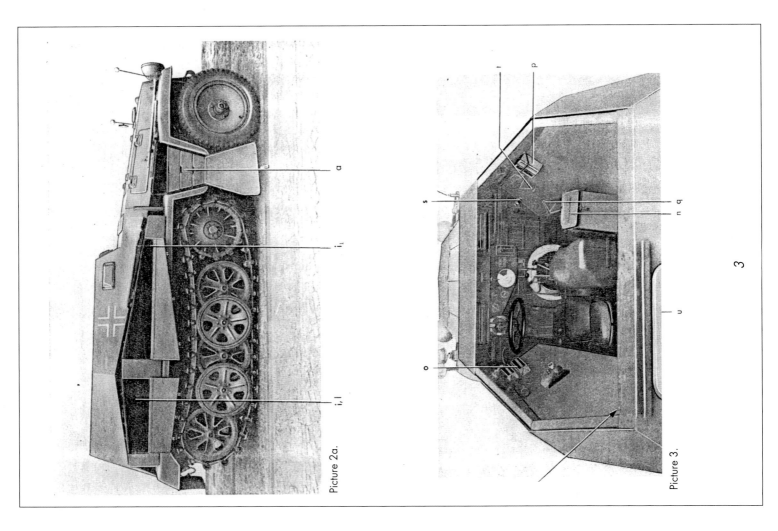

Picture 2a.

Picture 3.

3

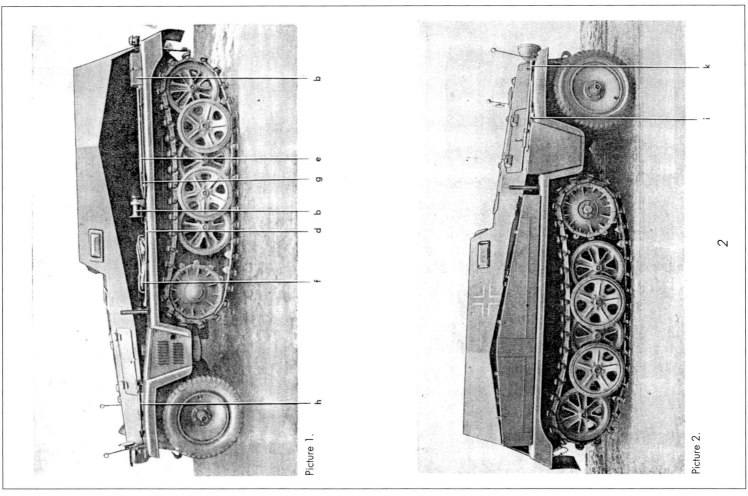

Picture 1.

Picture 2.

2

220

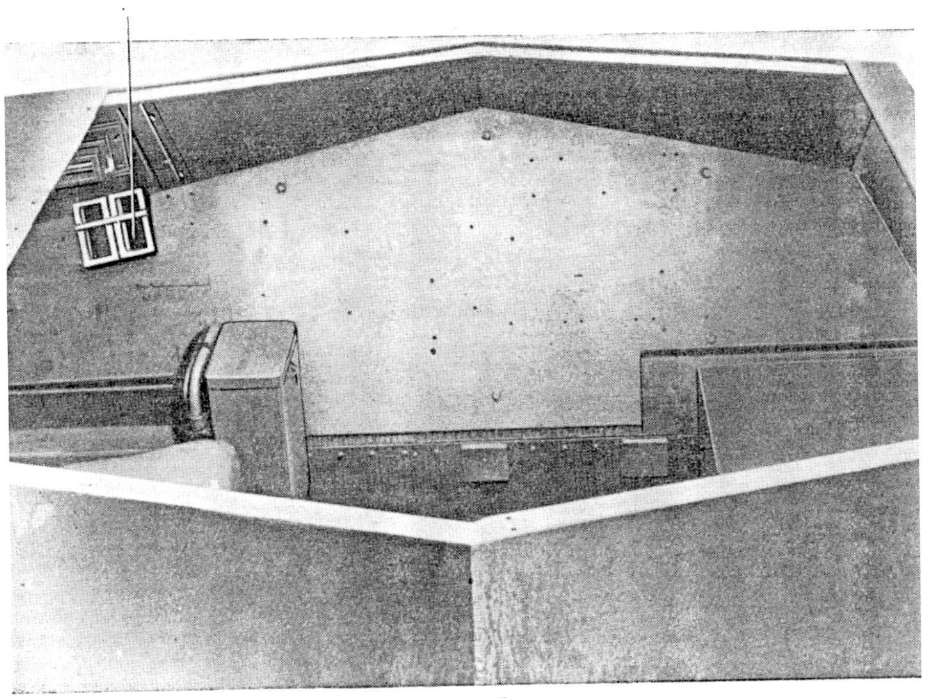

Picture 4.

4

Sd Kfz (Sonder Kraft Fahrzeug) SPECIAL POWER VEHICLE LOADING PLAN

Sd Kfz 250/1 - for a group with 2 light machine guns
Pictures 5 & 6

Number and name of item:	Where to Stow
II. Internally:	
Armament:	
4 rifles	m. on right sidewall
2 machine guns (M.G. 34)	
of which: 1 static M.G. (mounted)	a. in armoured shield
1 loose M.G.	a1. clipped in right hand wall
2 cartridge sacks 34	
of which: 1 sack 34	f. in ammunition locker
1 sack 34	g. on left sidewall
2 barrel containers 34 + content	
of which: 1 container 34 + content	h. in luggage locker
1 container 34 + content	i. in ammunition locker
2 barrel protectors 34 + content	
of which: 1 protector 34 + content	j. in ammunition locker
1 protector 34 + content	j. in luggage locker
1 M.P. 38 (machine pistol)	l. on right sidewall
1 armoured shield	v. forward on cover plate
1 anti aircraft swing arm	w. rear on cover plate
1 tripod 34	o. on right sidewall
Ammunition:	
4 belt drum carriers 34 with a total of 8 belt drums 34	
of which: 3 belt drum carriers 34	d. in ammunition locker
1 belt drum carrier 34	e. on left sidewall
16 cartridge cases 34	b. under bench seat
of which: 2 oil + petrol containers	
2 stand by cases	c. in ammunitions locker
1 magazine carrier bag with 6 magazines for M.P. 38	l. on right sidewall
Aim and Observation items:	
1 angled hand telescope (f) 8 x 24	
or	y. in luggage locker
1 binocular hand telescope 10x (teleplast)	
Signalling items:	
1 vary pistol	p. on right sidewall
12 Shots of illumination and signal ammunition in box	p. on right sidewall
Other equipment items:	
6 clothing bags	n. in luggage locker
1 gas mask 34 with breathing hose	u. forward left next to driver
1 top cover	r. at ammunition locker
1 cover window	s. at bench seat
1 set of cover struts	t. on left sidewall

5

Loading Plan No: 3

For Sd Kfz 250/1 for 2 Heavy MG Crews
Pictures 7 and 7a

Number and Name of Item:	Where to Stow:

II. Internally:
Armament:

4 rifles	l. on right sidewall
2 machine guns 34	
of which:	
1 MG 34 mounted	a. in armour shield
1 MG 34 (heavy MG) 1/ 2/ 3/	a₁. on right sidewall
1 MG mounting frame 1/ 2/ 3/	b. on fixing outside vehicle
	b₁. in storage case
2 cartridge bags 34	f. in ammo case
of which: 1 cartridge bag	g. on left sidewall
1 cartridge bag	
2 barrel containers 34 with content	h. in storage case
of which: 1 barrel cont 34 with contents	i. in ammo case
1 barrel cont 34 with contents	j. in ammo case
2 barrel protectors 34 with contents	j₁. in storage case
of which: 1 barrel protector	k on right sidewall
1 barrel protector	t. front on cover plate
	u. at rear on cover plate
1 MP38	
1 armoured shield	
1 anti aircraft swing arm	

NOTES:
I 1. Should the lock container, (fastened to the left frame section of mounting frame), be inconvenient when loading, fix on left hand rear brace instead, to prevent it hindering removal of MG lock.

II The following refers to: 4. (heavy) unit of light riflemans company (armoured) on SD.KFZ 250

2. The leading vehicle has no heavy MG with accessories etc.

3. 1.2 (heavy MG) group: group leader vehicle has no heavy MG etc.

Ammunition:

4 belt drum carriers 34	d. in ammo locker
with a total of 8 belt drums 34	e. on left seat wall
of which: 3 belt drum carrier 34	c. under seat bench
1 belt drum carrier 34	
16 cartridge cases 34	ci. in ammo locker
of which: 2 oil and paraffin container	
2 supplement cases	
1 magazine carrying pocket with	k. on right sidewall
6 magazines for MP 38	

Aiming and Observation Equipment:

1 hand angled telescope (f) 8 x 24	w. in luggage locker
or	
1 twin binocular periscope	
10x (teleplast)	

7

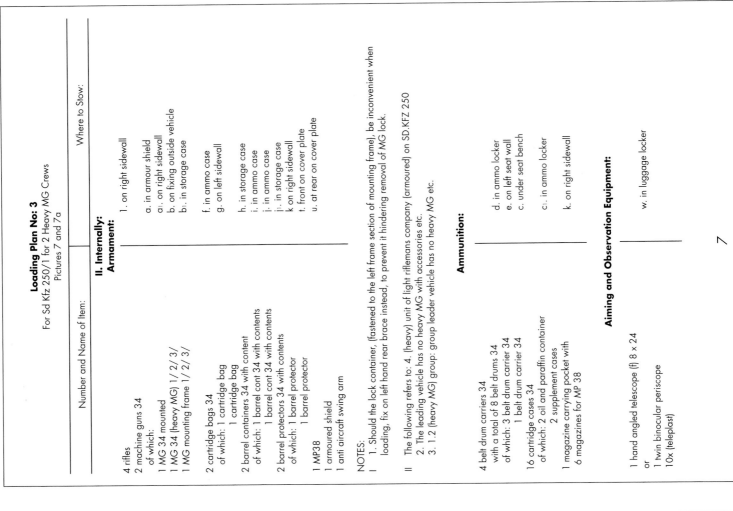

Picture 5.

⟵ Front

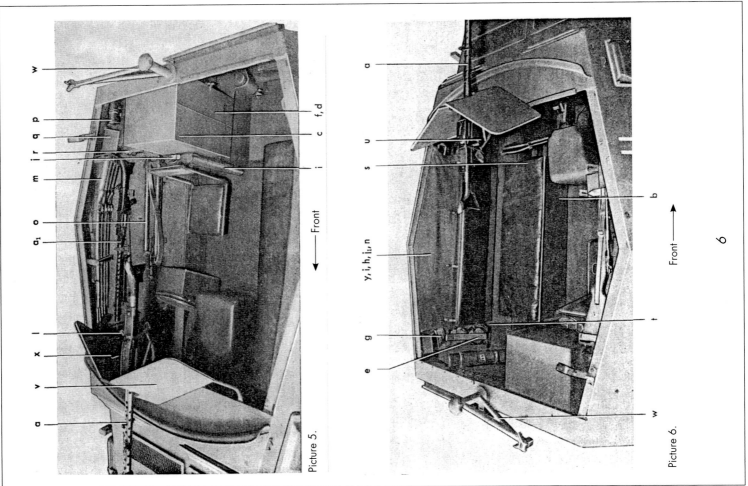

Picture 6.

Front ⟶

6

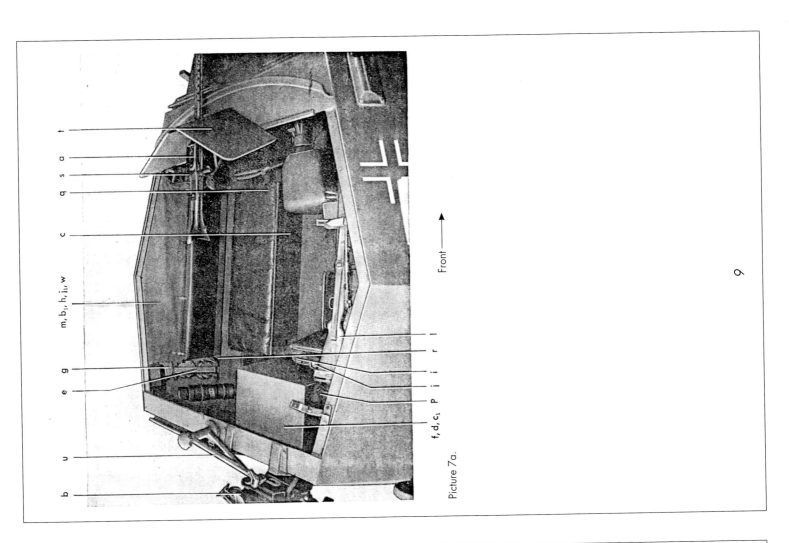

Picture 7a.

Front ⟶

9

Number and Name of Item:	Where to Stow:

**Wireless Equipment V[4]
Signalling Equipment:**

1 vary pistol
12 rounds of vary pistol in signalling
ammo in container

n. on right sidewall
o. on right sidewall

Other Items of Equipment:

6 clothing bags
1 gas mask 34 with breathing hose
1 vehicle cover
1 cover window
1 set of cover poles (supports)

m. in luggage locker
s. front left, next to driver seat
p. at ammo locker
q. at seat bench
r. on left sidewall

NOTES:
4. The wireless equipment of the vehicle is subject to guidelines of the unit, with additions by the A.N. Heer.

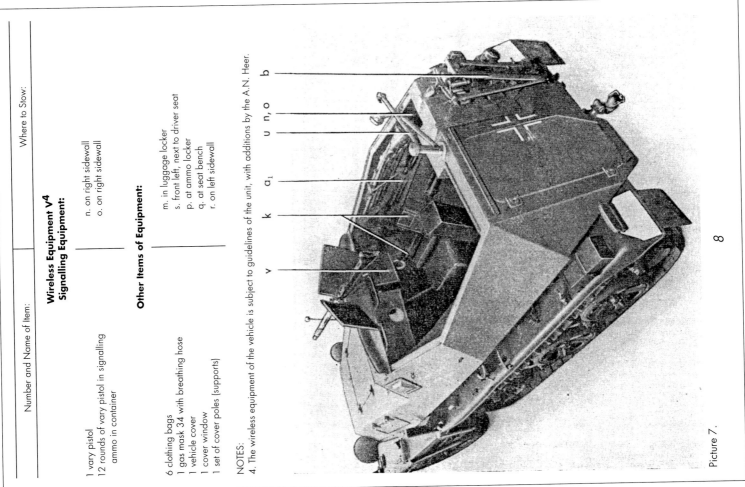

Picture 7.

8

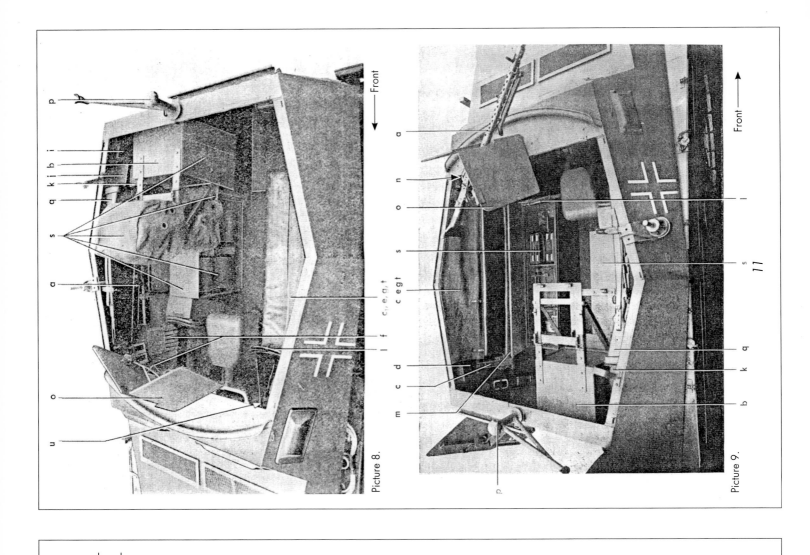

Picture 8.

Picture 9.

Loading Plan No: 4

For Sd Kfz 250/2 Light Communications Armoured Vehicle

Pictures 8, 9, 10 and 10a

Number and name of item:	Where to Stow:
4 rifles	q. on right sidewall
1 light M.G. 34 (fixed MG)	a. in armour shield, when in transit stow on R/H sidewall
1 cartridge sack 34	d. on L/H sidewall
1 barrel protector 34 with contents	e. in luggage locker
1 M.P. 38	f. on R/H sidewall
1 armour shield	o. front on cover plate
1 anti-aircraft swing arm	p. rear on cover plate

Ammunitions:

2 belt drum carriers 34 with total of 4 belt drums 34	c. on L/H sidewall
of which: 1 belt drum carrier 34	c_i. in luggage locker
1 belt drum carrier 34	b. in locker
4 cartridge boxes 34	
of which: 1 supplement box	f. on R/H sidewall
1 oil and paraffin container	
1 magazine carrying bag with 6 magazines for MP 38	

Aiming and Observation Equipment:

1 binocular hand (twin) periscope 10x (Teleplast) or 1 hand (angled) telescope (f) 8 x 24	t. in luggage locker

Communication Equipment:

1 set of communication equip. for light communication troop (motorised)"1	s. fitted according to regulation D/701/2.

NOTES:

1. To this a previous certificate for equipment for small communication troop is required (motorised) as D/701/2.

Wireless Equipment: 1.

1 vary pistol	i. on R/H sidewall
12 rounds vary - signal ammo	j. on R/H sidewall

Other pieces of Equipment:

4 clothing bags	g. in luggage locker
1 gasmask 34+breathing hose	n. front L/H side next to driver seat
1 vehicle cover	k. st ammo locker
1 cover window	l. at seat bench
1 set cover poles (supports)	m. on L/H sidewall

NOTES:

1. The wireless equipment is subject to guidlines of the unit, with additions by the 'A.N. Heer'.

10

Loading Plan No: 5
For Sd Kfz 250/3 Light Radio Arm Car
Pictures 11, 12 and 13

Number and name of item:	Where to Stow:

II Internally
Armament:

3 rifles
1 light MG34 (standing MG)
1 cartridge bag 34
1 barrel protector 34 with content
2 MP (machine pistol) 38
of which 1 MP
of which 1 MP

i. on right sidewall
a. in the armoured shield
d. on left sidewall
e. in the luggage case

j. front right on sidewall
Next to man (for Kp. Troop leader)

Ammunition:

2 belt drum carriers 34 with total of
4 belt drums 34
of which: 1 belt drum carrier 34
d.o 1 belt drum carrier 34
4 cartridge boxes 34
of which: 1 supplement box
d.o. 1 oil and paraffin container
2 magazine carrying bags with
each containing 6 mags for MP 38

c. on left side wall
c.. under seating bench
b. under seating bench

j. front right side wall
1 next to man (Kp Troop leader)

Aiming and observation equipment:

1 binocular hand (twin) periscope
10x (Teleplast)
or
1 hand (angled) telescope (f) 8 × 24

s. in luggage case (locker)

Radio Equipment: q. r1
Signalling Items:

1 vary pistol
12 rounds of vary pistol
and signalling ammo
in container

f. on right sidewall
g. on right sidewall

Other Items of equipment:

4 clothing bags
1 gas mask 34 with breathing
hose
1 case for 5 smoke candles
1 hood (roof cover)
1 set hood supports
1 hood window

m. in packing case
l. front left next to driver

k. under seat bench
m. behind radio rack
o. on left sidewall
p. on seat bench

13

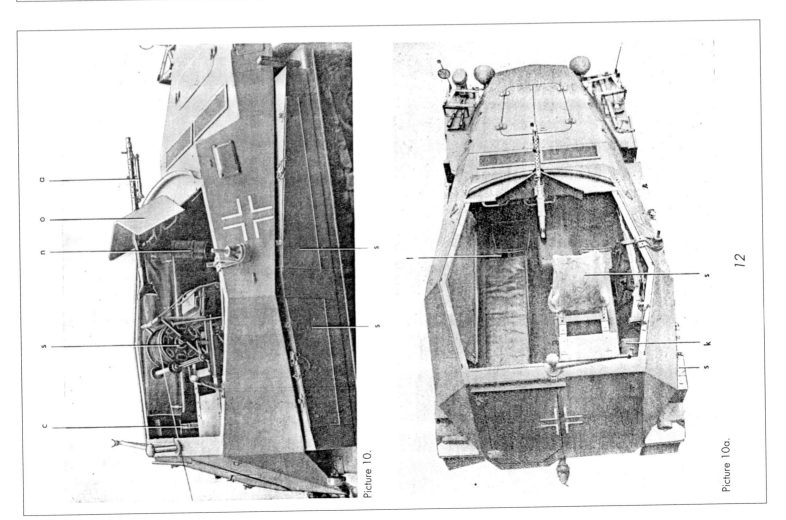

Picture 10.

Picture 10a.

12

m, s, e

d c

p

c., k, b

Front →

o

n

Picture 13.

15

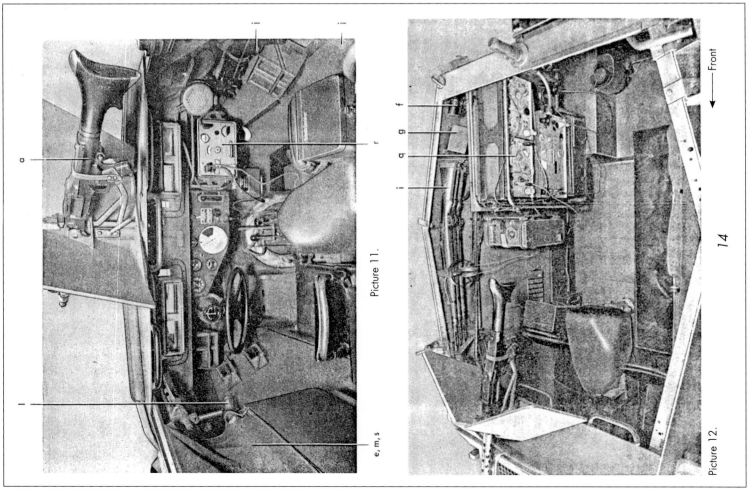

a

i

i

r

e, m, s

Picture 11.

f

g

q

i

← Front

Picture 12.

14

226

Picture 14.

Picture 15.

Loading Plan No: 7

For Sd Kfz 250/5 Light Observation Armoured Car

Pictures 14, 15, 16 and 17

Number and name of item:	Where to Stow:
II Internally Armament:	
6 hand grenades	h. on right sidewall
1 MG (MG 34 mounted)	a. in armoured shield
1 cartridge bag 34	d. behind radio stand
1 barrel protector 34 with contents	e. on RH sidewall
2 MP38 (Machine Pistols)	g. front on right and rear on left sidewall
1 anti aircraft swing arm	s. at rear on cover plate
Ammunition:	
2 belt drum carriers 34 with a total of 4 belt drums 34	c. on right behind co-drivers seat
4 cartridge cases 34	b. on right behind co-drivers seat
of which: 1 oil and petrol container	
1 spare case	
2 magazine carrying bag with	
6 magazines for MP 38 each	g. front on right, and rear on left sidewall
Aiming and Observation Equipment:	
1 binocular hand (Twin) periscope 10x (Teleplast)	z. behind radio stand
or	
1 hand angled telescope (f) 8 x 24	n. on right sidewall (twin periscope only on turntable during use)
1 case with twin periscope 14 Z Q1 with content	
Radio Equipment: p, p.1, z, q.2 Signalling Items:	
1 vary pistol and 10 rounds	l. on right sidewall
illumination and signal ammo in container	m. on right side wall
3 signalling flags	w. on left sidewall
Direction Equipment:	
1 large frame 40 with cap holder for direction ring	x. on left sidewall
1 case for direction ring 40 with content	o. on left sidewall
Other Items of Equipment:	
4 clothing bags	y. behind radio stand or with man
4 field water bottles	k. on left sidewall
of which: 1 water bottle	k.. on right sidewall
3 water bottles	
4 gas masks	i. on left sidewall
of which: 2 gas masks	ii. on right sidewall
1 gas mask	i.2 forward, to left of driver seat
1 gas mask 34 with breathing hose	
4 mess tins	j. on left sidewall
of which: 3 mess tins	ji. on right sidewall
1 mess tin	t. on right behind radio set
1 top cover sheet	u. behind driver seat
1 cover window	v. on left sidewall
1 set of cover supports	

16

17

Loading Plan No: 8

For Sd Kfz 250/6 Light Ammunition Armoured Vehicle
For 7.5cm STU. Kanone (Assault Gun) Type A (short)
Pictures 18, 19 and 20

Number and name of item:	Where to Stow:

II Internally Armament:

1 machine gun 34	a. in armour shield, during transit on right sidewall
1 cartridge bag 34	d. on left sidewall
1 barrel protector 34 with content	e. on let sidewall
1 MP38 (machine pistol)	g. on right sidewall
1 anti aircraft swinging arm	o. at rear on cover plate
1 armoured shield	p. at front on cover plate

Ammunition:

2 belt drum carriers 34 with a total of 4 belt drums 34	c. on left side behind cartridge case
4 cartridge cases 34 of which:	b. in pack case on right behind ammo rack
1 supplement box	
1 oil and petrol container	
1 magazine carrying bag with 6 magazines for MP 38	g. on right sidewall
70 rounds in 35 cartridge cases for 7.5cm assault gun (short)	n. in ammunition rack

Aiming and Observation Equipment:

1 binocular hand (twin) periscope 10x (Teleplast)	
1 hand angled telescope (f) 8 x 24	t. in packing case

Radio Equipment m, m.1, m.2.1 Signalling Items:

1 vary pistol	i. on right sidewall
20 rounds of vary pistol and signalling ammo	i. on right sidewall

Other Items of Equipment:

2 clothing bags	l. on right behind cartridge cases
1 unit lantern with accessories and carbide container	k. on right behind cartridge cases
2 field water bottles	u. behind ammunition racks
1 gas mask 34 with breathing hose	h. front left next to driver
1 gas mask 34	h. rear left on sidewall
2 mess tins and utensils	v. behind ammunition racks
1 hood (roof cover)	q. between ammo. racks
1 set hood supports	r. in spares case on right mudguard
1 hood window	s. at the drivers seat

19

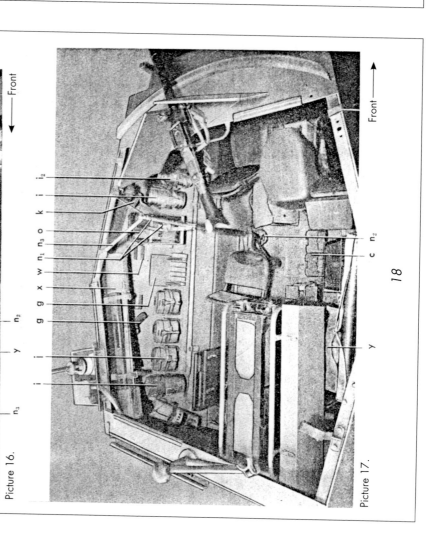

Picture 16.

Front

Picture 17.

Front

18

228

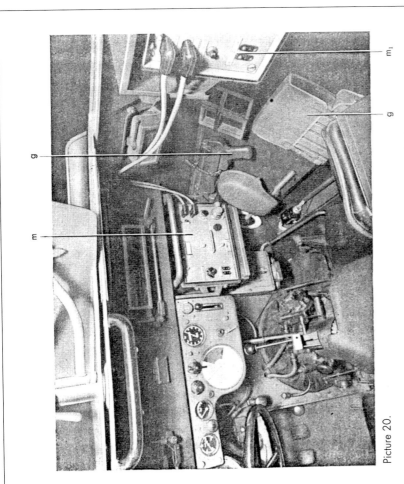

Picture 20.

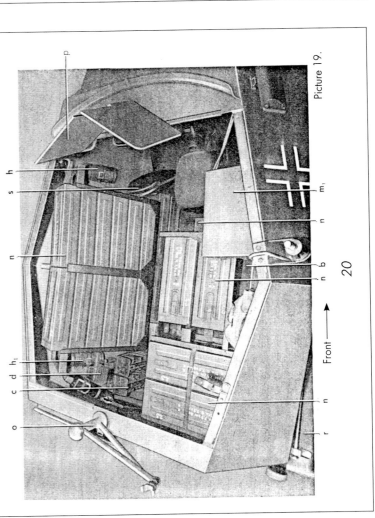

Picture 18.

Picture 19.

21

20

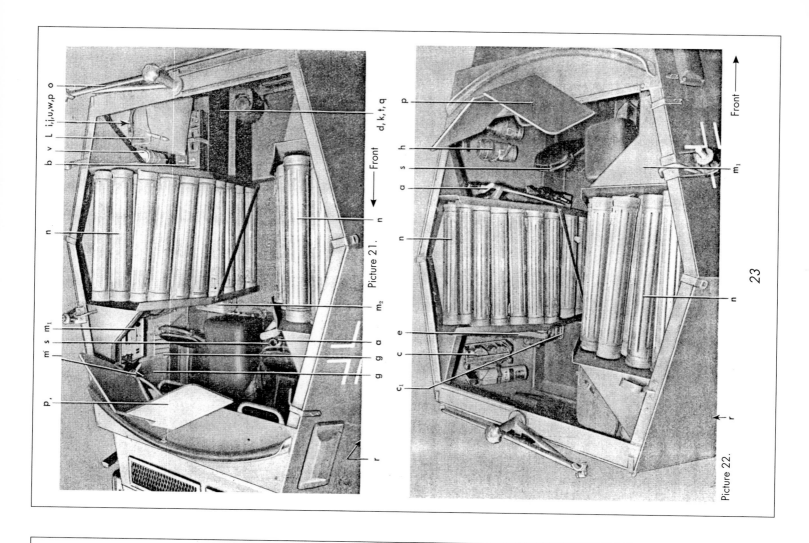

Front →

Picture 21.

23

Front →

Picture 22.

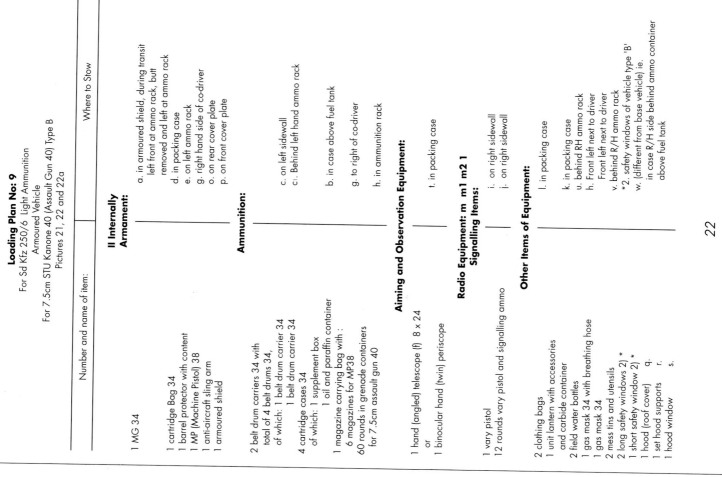

Loading Plan No: 9

For Sd Kfz 250/6 Light Ammunition
Armoured Vehicle
For 7.5cm STU Kanone 40 (Assault Gun 40) Type B
Pictures 21, 22 and 22a

Number and name of item:	Where to Stow
II Internally Armament:	
1 MG 34	a. in armoured shield, during transit left front at ammo rack, butt removed and left at ammo rack
1 cartridge Bag 34	d. in packing case
1 barrel protector with content	e. on left ammo rack
1 MP (Machine Pistol) 38	g. right hand side of co-driver
1 anti-aircraft sling arm	o. on rear cover plate
1 armoured shield	p. on front cover plate
Ammunition:	
2 belt drum carriers 34 with total of 4 belt drums 34,	c. on left sidewall
of which: 1 belt drum carrier 34	c₁. Behind left hand ammo rack
1 belt drum carrier 34	
4 cartridge cases 34	
of which: 1 supplement box	
1 oil and paraffin container	b. in case above fuel tank
1 magazine carrying bag with :	
6 magazines for MP38	g. to right of co-driver
60 rounds in grenade containers for 7.5cm assault gun 40	h. in ammunition rack
Aiming and Observation Equipment:	
1 hand (angled) telescope (f) 8 × 24	t. in packing case
or	
1 binocular hand (twin) periscope	
Radio Equipment: m m1 m2 1 Signalling Items:	
1 vary pistol	i. on right sidewall
12 rounds vary pistol and signalling ammo	j. on right sidewall
Other Items of Equipment:	
2 clothing bags	l. in packing case
1 unit lantern with accessories and carbide container	k. in packing case
2 field water bottles	u. behind RH ammo rack
1 gas mask 34 with breathing hose	h. Front left next to driver
1 gas mask 34	Front left next to driver
2 mess fins and utensils	v. behind R/H ammo rack
2 long safety windows 2) *	*2. safety windows of vehicle type 'B'
1 short safety window 2) *	w. (different from base vehicle) ie.
1 hood (roof cover) q.	in case R/H side behind ammo container above fuel tank
1 set hood supports r.	
1 hood window s.	

22

230

Loading Plan No: 10

For Sd Kfz 250/7 Mortar Troop
Pictures 23, 24, 25, 26 and 27

Number and name of item:	Where to Stow:

II Internally Armament:

3 rifles	r. on right side wall
1 fixing mechanism for base plate of heavy mortar (S.GR.W.) 34	a. outside on rear of vehicle
	outside on rear of vehicle
1 base plate with carrying gear	l. outside on rear of vehicle
1 barrel with cover and carrier	j+i. inside vehicle R/H pack case
1 special base plate	M. on floor of vehicle
1 "two leg" support with carrier	k. at the barrel
1 grease pot	q. in packing case
1 loading mechanism	p. in packing case
1 small artificer's tool box	
for MG 34 with contents as in appendix : J 3401	i. in left hand packing base
1 MG 34 (mounted MG)	a. in arm shield or sling arm in transit on R/H sidewall
1 anti-aircraft swing arm	a₂. at rear on cover plate
1 armoured shield	a₁. at front on cover plate
1 cartridge bag 34	d. at rear on L/H sidewall
1 barrel protector 34 and content	e. in R/H packing case
2 MP 38's	h. front R/H sidewall and next to man

Ammunition:

1 cartridge case 34 for oil and equipment (for heavy mortar)	D. in front of fuel tank
1 ammunition case with carrier	n. on right on ammo cases
21 ammo cases	
of which: 10 cases	o. in ammo frame (rack) above fuel tank
6 cases	o₁. on left at rear of vehicle
5 cases	o₂. in rack at rear of gearbox
2 belt drum carriers 34 with total of 4 belt drums 34	c. at rear on left sidewall
of which: 1 belt drum carrier 34	
1 belt drum carrier 34	c₁. In left hand packing case
4 cartridge cases 34	
of which: 1 supplement, case	b. in packing case on right
1 oil and paraffin container	
2 magazine carrying bags with 6 magazines each for MP 38	h. front R/H sidewall and at man's side

Aiming and Observation Equipment:

1 binocular hand (twin) periscope 10x (Teleplast)	B. in packing case
1 hand (angled) telescope (f) 8 x 24	

Radio Equipment (t8)
Telecom Equipment:

1 set of (small) telecom equipment (field telephone) K.A.N Army "N" 1979	C. in left hand pack case

25

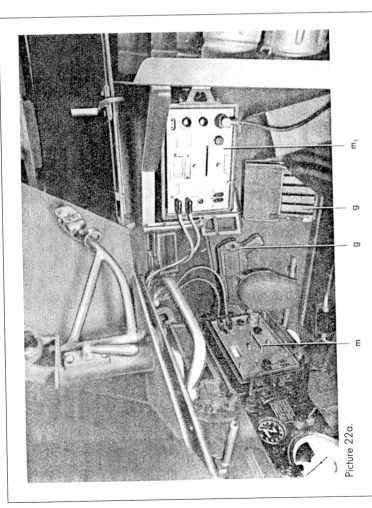

Picture 22a.

24

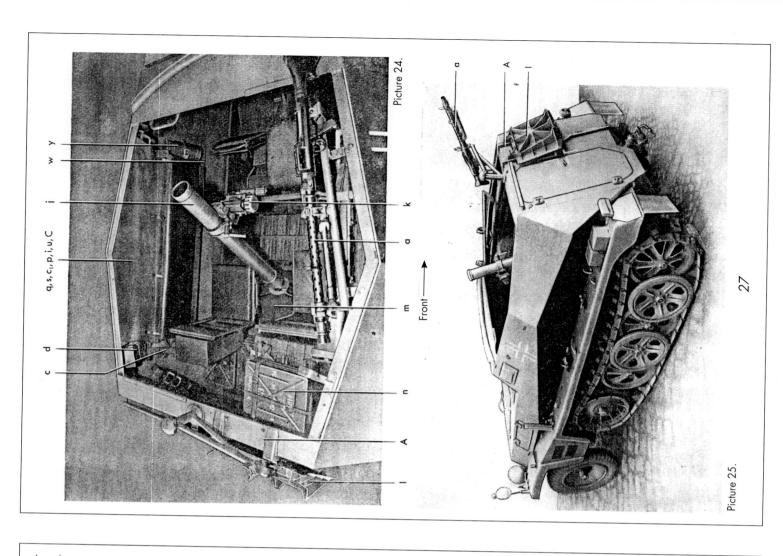

q, s, c₁, p, i, u, C

Front →

Picture 24.

Picture 25.

27

Number and name of item:	Where to Stow:
Signalling Equipment:	
1 vary pistol	Z_1. in left hand pack case
12 rounds vary and signalling ammo	Z_2. in left hand pack case
Direction Equipment:	
1 range finder, accord to "J 2741" (only in vehicles without heavy mortar)	Z. In left hand pack case
Other Items of Equipment:	
4 clothing bags	s. in pack cases and behind ammo rack and under right hand seat
1 unit lantern with accessories box and container for carbide	u. in left hand pack case
1 gas mask 34 with breathing hose	y. front left foreward near drivers seat
1 Protective window + 1 cover hood	v. righthand behind ammo rack
1 set of hood supports	w. on lefthand sidewall
1 hood window	x. behind driver's seat

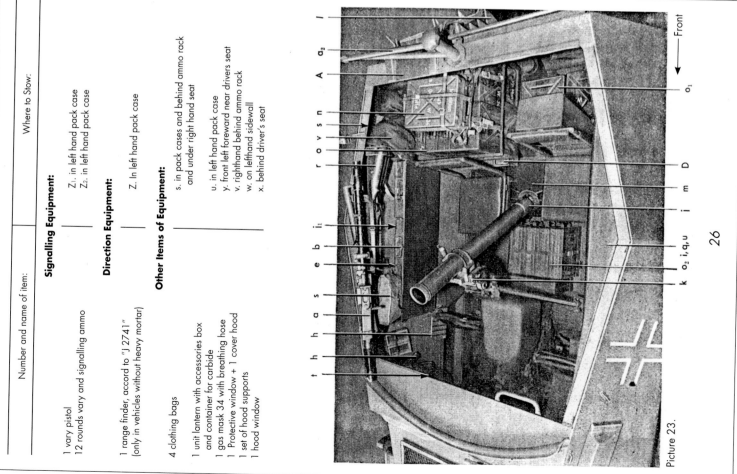

Front →

26

Picture 23.

Loading Plan No: 12
For Sd Kfz 250/9 Light Riflemens
Armoured Vehicle (2cm)
Pictures 28, 29, 30, 31, 32, 33 and 34

Number and Name of Item:	Where to Stow:

II Internally:
Armament:

1 MG 34 — n. mounted gun carriage
1 butt for MG 34 — s. on R/H sidewall in leather sling
1 barrel container for 2 spare barrels — r. on L/H sidewall
1 tool bag for M Gun — t. on L/H side near door
1 oil and spares case or MG 34 — u. in container R/H side
1 "two leg" stand for M Gun — m. on R/H side
1 canon KW K38 (20mm) — v. on mounted gun carriage
1 cleaning case 2cm — z. on R/H mudguard
1 muzzle protector for KE K38 — y. on the barrel
1 accessory bag for 2cm — x. on turn table base
1 cover hood and protective cover
for 2cm and M Gun — d. outside on L/H mudguard
1 machine pistol 38 — D. at front L/H sidewall
8 "Egg" hand grenades — H. in case on L/H sidewall
4 explosives — f. on R/H mudguard
3 complete fuse cords for explosives — k. in case outside door

Ammunition:

6 belt cases for MG 34 — o. on R/H sidewall
2 belt cases for MG 34 — p. on turn table carriage
6 belt cases for MG 34 — q. on L/H side
1 magazine case 20mm (2cm) — A. on turn table carriage
1 magazine case 20mm — B. at co-driver position
of which: 2 magazine cases
1 magazine case — C. on the container
1 magazine carrying bag with — C. above the container
6 magazines and filler for MP 38 — E. on L/H sidewall

Aiming and Observation Items:

1 binocular hand (twin) Periscope
10 x (Teleplast) — L. as required on co-driver's seat
or
1 prismatic hand monocular telescope (f) 8 x 24 — - on the 2cm (20mm) weapon only
1 Tower telescopic sight TZF3a

Radio equipment 1, J2:
Signalling Equipment:

1 Vary pistol — F. on left sidewall in holder
12 rounds of illumination and signalling ammunition — G. in case, left or right forward

Other items of equipment:

1 starting handle — a. on the right mudguard
1 petrol canister (20 litres) — m. in special fitting outside rear

29

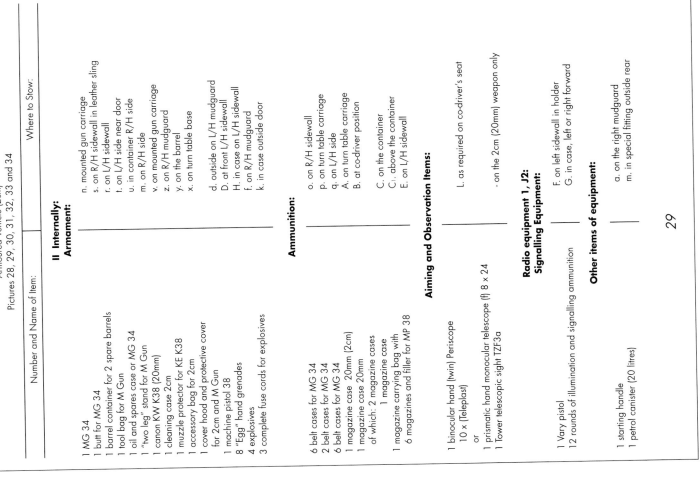

Picture 26.

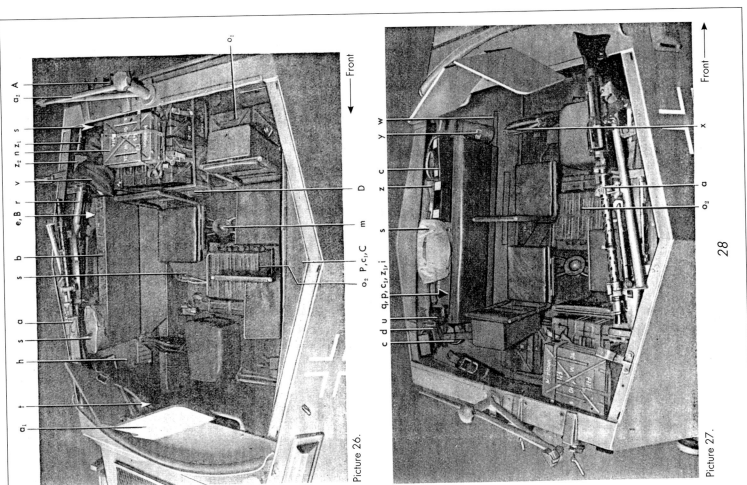

Picture 27.

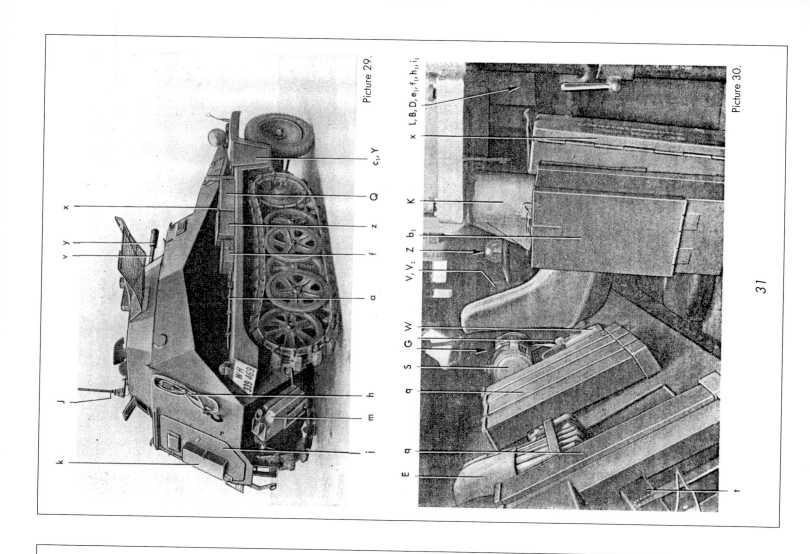

Picture 29.

Picture 30.

31

Number and Name of Item:	Where to Stow:
3 bread bags	
of which: 1 bread bags	T. forward on right hand side
2 bread bags	T_1. at rear right, over container
1 fill up funnel	U. forward on shelf in engine-housing
1 large wire cutter	B. on left mudguard
3 field water bottles	
of which: 1 bottle	W. on left sidewall behind driver
2 bottles	W_1. on left side behind door
2 gasmasks	
of which: 1 gasmask	k_1. on right hand sidewall
1 gasmask	k_2. on left hand sidewall
1 gasmask 34 with breathing hose	S. forward left next to driver
1 hand lantern	Y. in toolbox on right mudguard
1 hand searcher (torch)	Z. with driver above dashboard
1 hand grease can	a_1. on shelf in engine housing
1 map board	b_1. at the turn base
5 track links	i_1. under the pack pockets in co-drivers seat
2 climbing spikes	c_1. in tool box
3 mess tins	
of which: 1 mess tin	d_1. on right sidewall
2 mess tins	d_2. on left sidewall
1 pick axe	l. above left mudguard on outer wall
3 overcoats	e_1. in the co-drivers position
1 oil canister	g_1. under the engine cover
3 packing bags	h_1. in the co-drivers position
2 long protective windows	V. to left of driver
1 short protective window	V_1. to left of driver
1 steel wire rope	g. in front on engine
1 steel wire rope	h. on rear of vehicle
1 store case for iron ration	Q. on the right mudguard
1 tool case, built in	K. on the turn base
3 waterproof covers	f_1. in the co-driver's position

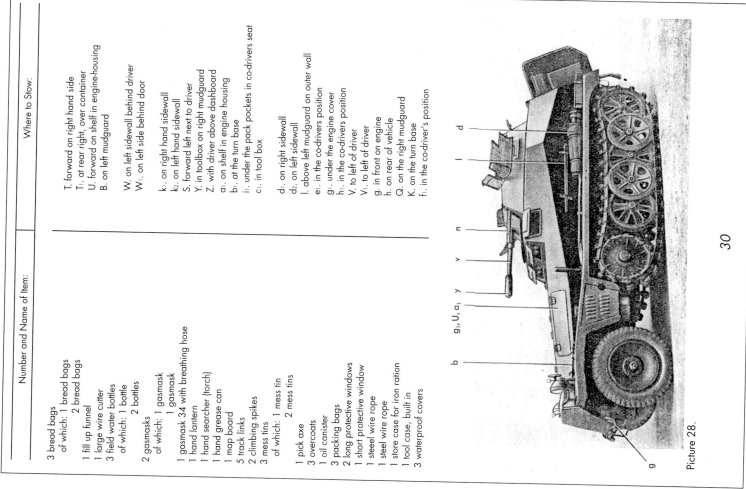

Picture 28.

30

Picture 33.

33

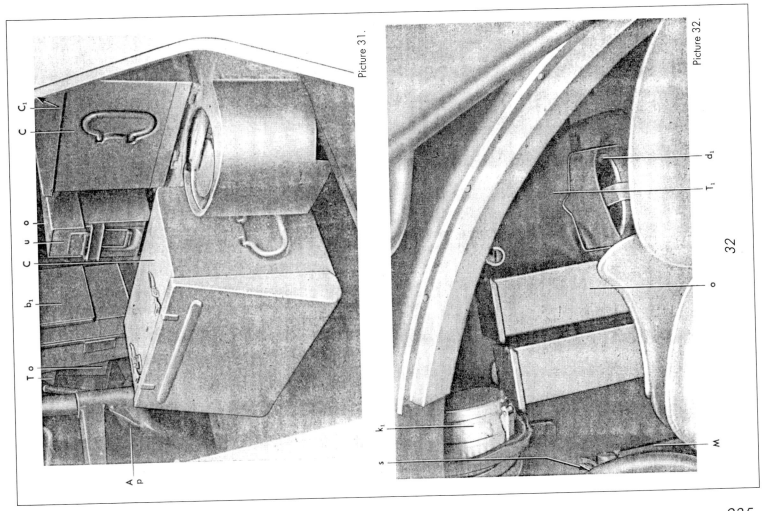

Picture 31.

Picture 32.

32

235

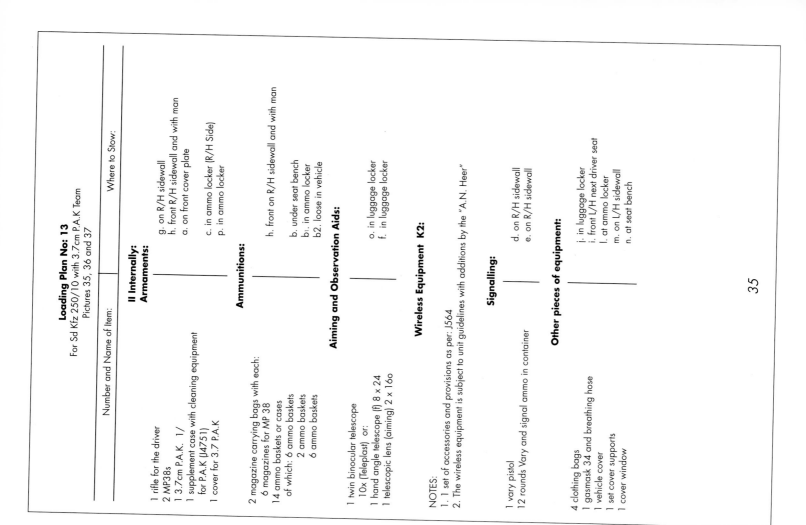

Loading Plan No: 13
For Sd Kfz 250/10 with 3.7cm P.A.K Team
Pictures 35, 36 and 37

Number and Name of Item:	Where to Stow:
II Internally:	
Armaments:	
1 rifle for the driver	g. on R/H sidewall
2 MP38s	h. front R/H sidewall and with man
1 3.7cm P.A.K. 1/	a. on front cover plate
1 supplement case with cleaning equipment for P.A.K (J4751)	c. in ammo locker (R/H Side)
1 cover for 3.7 P.A.K	p. in ammo locker
Ammunitions:	
2 magazine carrying bags with each:	h. front on R/H sidewall and with man
6 magazines for MP 38	
14 ammo baskets or cases	b. under seat bench
of which: 6 ammo baskets	b. in ammo locker
2 ammo baskets	b2. loose in vehicle
6 ammo baskets	
Aiming and Observation Aids:	
1 twin binocular telescope 10x (Teleplast) or:	o. in luggage locker
1 hand angle telescope (f) 8 x 24	f. in luggage locker
1 telescopic lens (aiming) 2 x 16o	
Wireless Equipment K2:	
NOTES:	
1. 1 set of accessories and provisions as per: J564	
2. The wireless equipment is subject to unit guidelines with additions by the "A.N. Heer"	
Signalling:	
1 vary pistol	d. on R/H sidewall
12 rounds Vary and signal ammo in container	e. on R/H sidewall
Other pieces of equipment:	
4 clothing bags	j. in luggage locker
1 gasmask 34 and breathing hose	i. front L/H next driver seat
1 vehicle cover	l. at ammo locker
1 set cover supports	m. on L/H sidewall
1 cover window	n. at seat bench

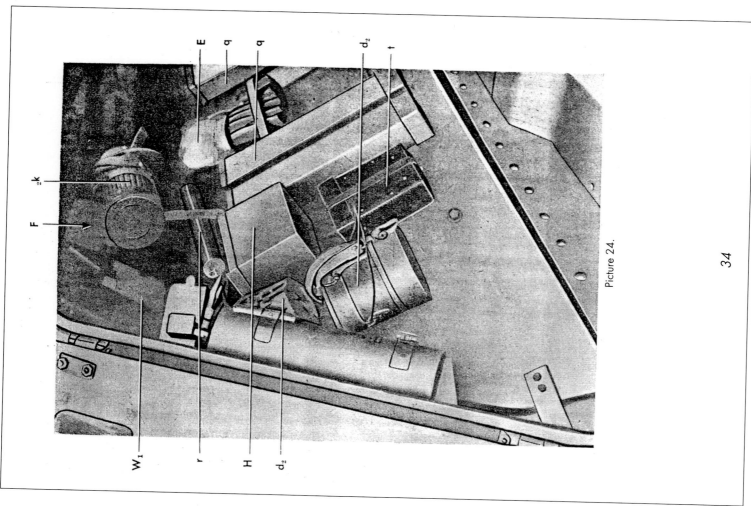

Picture 24.

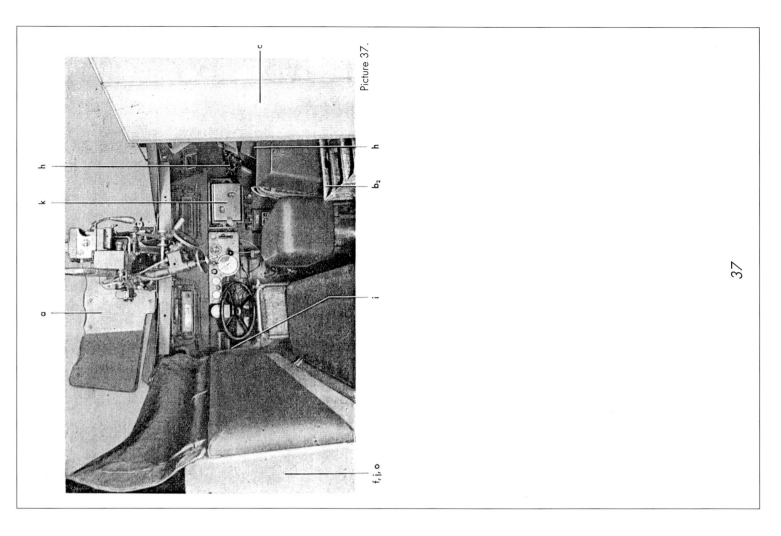

Picture 37.

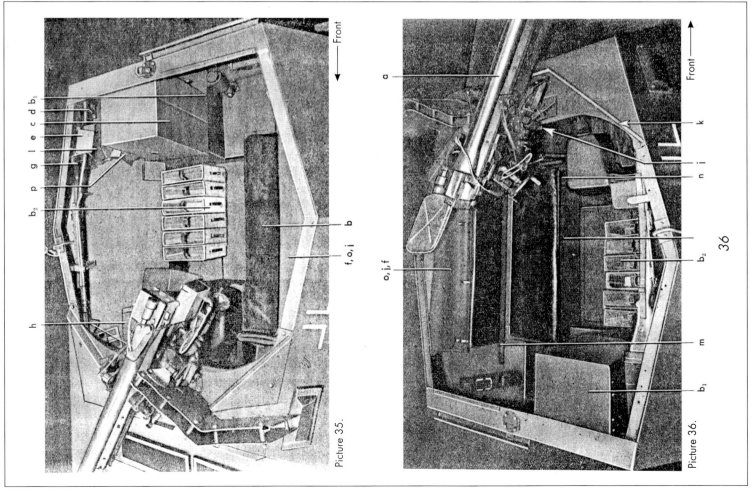

Picture 35.

Front

Picture 36.

36

37

237

Loading Plan No: 14

For Sd Kfz 250/11 with Heavy Anti Tank Gun 41
Pictures 38, 39, 40 and 40a

Number and Name of Item:	Where to Stow:

II Internally
Armament:

3 rifles — m. on R/H sidewall
2 MP38 (Machine pistols) — n. front R/H sidewall and with man
1 MG34 (light machine gun) mounted — a. in anti-aircraft swinging arm (in transit R/H sidewall)

1 anti aircraft swinging arm — t. at rear on cover plate
1 cartridge bag 34 — d. on L/H sidewall
1 barrel protector 34 with content — e. in packing case
1 heavy anti tank gun 41 — h. at front on cover plate
1 spares case and cleaning gear 41 — j. in packing case
1 field gun carriage for 41 with spike — l. outside, rear of vehicle
1 cover for gun 41 — k. in packing case

Ammunition:

2 magazine carrying bags with each: — n. front R/H sidewall and with man
  6 magazines for MP 38
2 belt drum carriers 34 with
total of: 4 belt drums 34
  of which: 1 belt drum carrier 34 — c. on L/H sidewall
  1 belt drum carrier 34 — Cl. in packing case
  — b. in ammo locker
4 cartridge cases, anti tank gun 41
  of which: 10 cartridge cases — i. under seat bench
  3 cartridge cases — ii. in ammo locker
  1 cartridge case — i.2 under R/H seat or inside vehicle area

Aiming and Observation items:

1 twin binocular telescope — y. in luggage locker
10x (teleplast)
or
1 hand angle telescope (f.) 8x24

Wireless Equipment S2:
Signalling:

1 vary pistol — o. on R/H sidewall
12 rounds vary and signal ammo in container — p. on R/H sidewall

Other pieces of equipment:

4 clothes bags — r. in luggage locker
1 unit lantern with accessory box and container — q. in luggage locker
for carbide
1 vehicle cover — x. front L/H next driver seat
1 gasmask 34 and breathing hose — u. at ammo locker
1 set of cover supports — v. at seat bench
1 cover window

38

Picture 38.

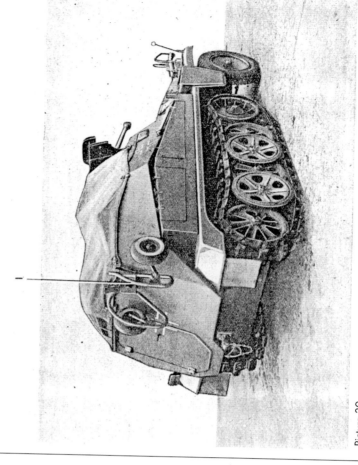

Picture 39.

39

238

Loading Plan No: 15

For Sd Kfz 250/12 as Light Survey Troop Armoured Vehicle
Pictures 41, 42, 43 and 44

Number and Name of Item:	Where to Stow:

II Internally
Armaments:

4 rifles — f. on R/H sidewall
1 MP38 — f. front on R/H sidewall
1 MG34 (light machine gun) fixed — a. in armour shield - in transit, store on R/H sidewall
1 cartridge sack 34 — d. on L\H sidewall
1 barrel protector 34 and contents — e. in luggage case
1 armour shield — m. 1 front or rear on cover plate

Ammunitions:

1 magazine carrying bag with
6 magazines for MP 38 — f. front R/H sidewall
2 belt drum carriers 34 with
4 belt drums 34 — c. on L/H sidewall
of which: 1 belt drum carrier 34
1 belt drum carrier 34
4 cartridge cases 34 — c. in luggage case
of which: 1 supplementary case — b. under seat bench
1 oil and paraffin container

Aiming and Observation Items:

1 twin binocular telescope — n. in luggage locker
10x (Teleplast)
1 hand angle telescope (f) 8 × 24

Wireless Equipment: m.4
Signalling Items:

1 vary pistol 3/ — h. on R/H sidewall
12 rounds vary and signal ammo 3/ — h. on R/H sidewall

Other items of equipment:

clothing bags 2/ — g. in luggage locker
1 gas mask 34 and breathing hose — l. front next to driver
1 special equipment 1/ — l.
1 vehicle cover — i. Behind radio rack
1 cover window — j. at seat bench
1 set of cover poles (supports) — k. on L/H sidewall

Berlin, on 15/1/43
High Command Of The Army
Army Office of Armament
Dept Group For Development and Tests
By Order of:
Holzhauer

NOTES:
1. To this belongs the 'Loading Plan for special equipment of the light survey troop armoured vehicle re: D298/41
2. Number accord. to D298/41.
3. Further Very pistols and set of Very and signal ammo re: D298/41.
4. The wireless equipment of the vehicle is subject to guidelines of the unit with additions by the 'A.N. Heer' further refer to guidelines in SD.KFZ - D9020/12.

41

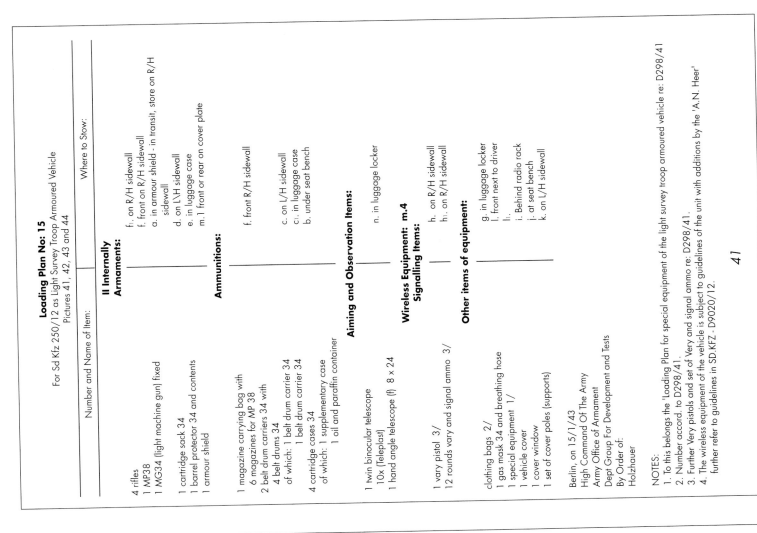

Picture 40.

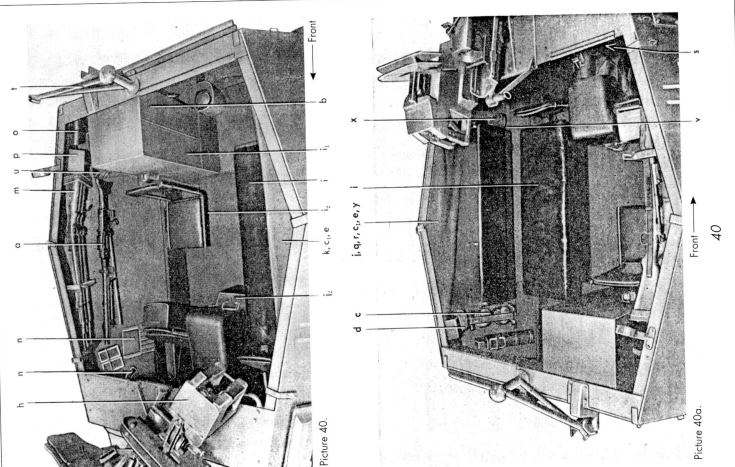

Picture 40a.

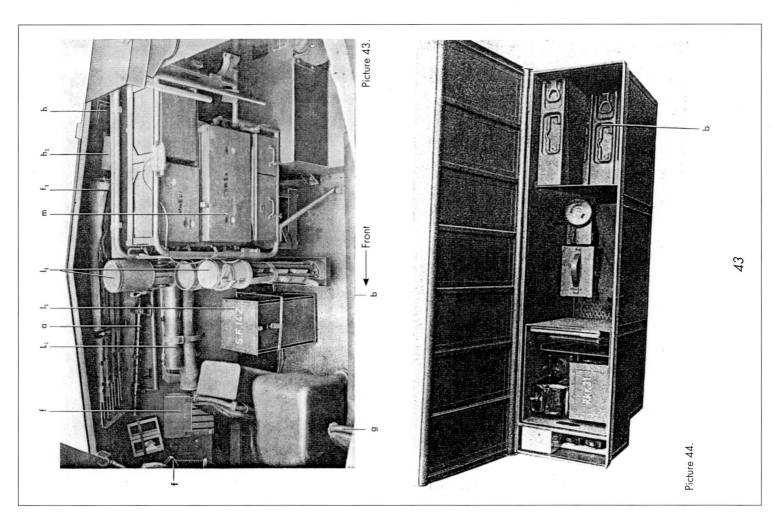

Picture 43.

Picture 44.

43

Picture 41.

Picture 42.

42

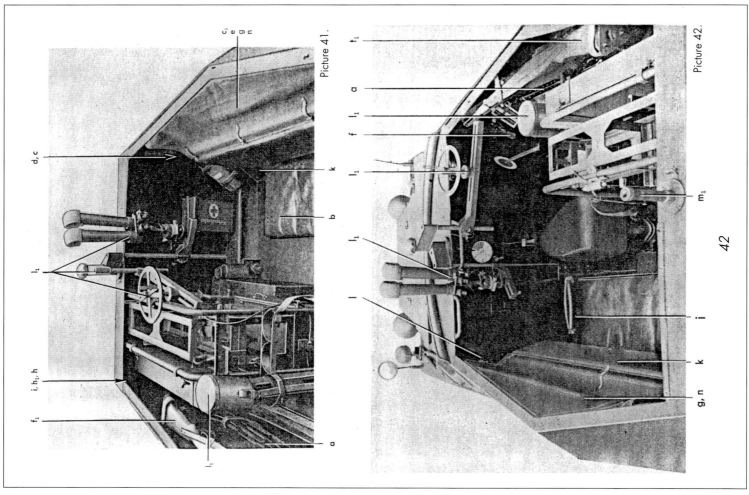

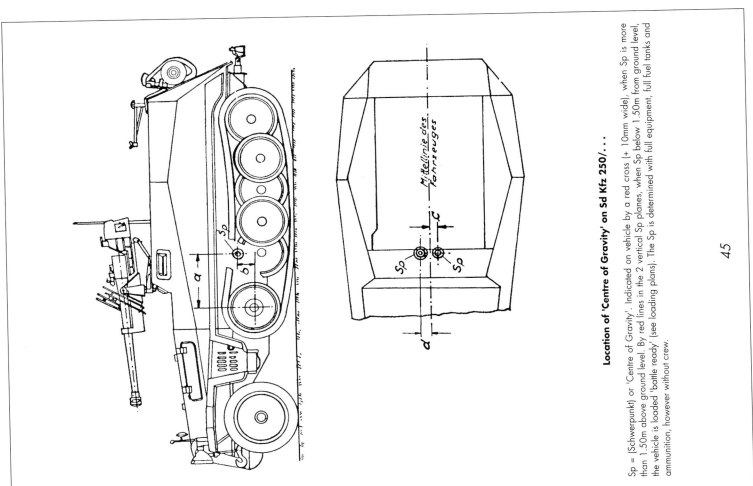

Location of 'Centre of Gravity' on Sd Kfz 250/...

Sp = (Schwerpunkt) or 'Centre of Gravity'. Indicated on vehicle by a red cross (+ 10mm wide), when Sp is more than 1.50m above ground level. By red lines in the 2 vertical Sp planes, when Sp below 1.50m from ground level, the vehicle is loaded 'battle ready' (see loading plans). The Sp is determined with full equipment, full fuel tanks and ammunition, however without crew.

45

Supplement

44

BIBLIOGRAPHY - SOURCES - REFERENCE

GENERAL

Ausgabe für den Schützen der schützenkompanie. W. Reibert. Berlin. 1941

The German army 1939-45. A. Seaton. Weidenfeld & Nicolson Ltd. 1982

The German army 1933-45. M. Cooper. Macdonald & Jane's publishing Ltd. 1978

Handbook on German military forces. Louisiana state university press. 1990

Panzers and artillery in World War II. G.F. Nafziger. Greenhill books. 1999

Panzer battles. F.W. Von Mellenthin. Cassell & Co. Ltd. 1955

Panzer grenadier, motorcycle & panzer reconnaissance units 1935-45. H. Scheibert. Schiffer publishing Ltd. 1991

Panzertaktik. W. Schneider. J.J. Fedorowicz publishing. 2000

Panzertruppen 1943-45 (volume 1 & 2). T.L. Jentz. Schiffer publishing Ltd. 1996

Scorched earth. P. Carell. G. G. Harrap & co. 1970

Army group South - The Wehrmacht in Russia. Werner Haupt. Schiffer Military History. 1998

7th Panzer Division. Hasso von Manteuffel Schiffer Military History. 2000

The 10th Panzer Division. J. Restayn & H. Moller J.J. Fedorowicz publishing. 2003

UNIFORMS AND EQUIPMENT

Badges and insignia of the third Reich. B.L. Davis. Blanford books Ltd. 1983

Camouflaged uniforms of the German Wehrmacht. W. Palinckx. Schiffer publishing. 2002

Camouflaged uniforms of the Wehrmacht. J. Borsarello & D. Lassus. ISO publications. 1988

Field uniforms of German Army Panzer forces in World War 2. M.H. Pruett & R.J. Edwards
J.J. Fedorowicz publishing Inc. 1993

Field uniforms of Germany's Panzer elite. R.J. Edwards & M.H. Pruett. J.J. Fedorowicz publishing Inc. 1998

The German army handbook 1939-45. A. Buchner. Schiffer publishing. 1992

German army uniforms and insignia 1933-45. B.L. Davis. L.Leventhal Ltd. 1971

German combat equipments 1939-45. G. Rottman. Osprey publishing. 1991

Uniforms and traditions of the German army 1933-45, (volumes 1 & 3). J.R. Angolia & A. Schlicht
R.J. Bender publishing. 1984/1987

Wehrmacht camouflage uniforms D. Peterson. Windrow & Greene Ltd. 1995

Die Deutschen Funknachrichtenanlagen bis 1945. Band 3 Hans - Joachim Ellison. Telefunken Systemtechnik GMBH

VEHICLES

Encyclopaedia of German tanks of WW2 P. Chamberlain & H.L. Doyle. Arms & armour press. 1978

Schützenpanzer B. Culver & U. Feist. Ryton publications. 1996

Panzer Colours 1 - 3 Bruce Culver Squadron/signal publications 1978

Kraftfahrzeuge und Panzer Werner Oswald. Motor buch Verlag. 1982

German Military Transport of WW II John Milsom Arms & Armour Press 1975

Wheeled vehicles of the Wehrmacht Chris Ellis Avocet/Crystal 1988

Germany's First Ally Charles K. Klement & Bretislav Nakladai. Schiffer Military History 1997

WEAPONS

Guns of the Reich. G. Markham. Arms & armour press. 1991

MG34-MG42. German universal machine guns F. Myrvang. Collector's grade publications Inc. 2002

Small arms of the World (edition 10) W.H.B. Smith/ J.E. Smith. Stackpole books. 1973

OTHER BOOKS IN THIS SERIES FROM TOTAL DETAIL PUBLICATIONS

To complement this **Archive** - Part 2 book, other titles in this series from 'Total Detail' featuring the **Sd Kfz 250** include an **Archive** - Part 1 book, a **Living History** book and a comprehensive **Technical** book.

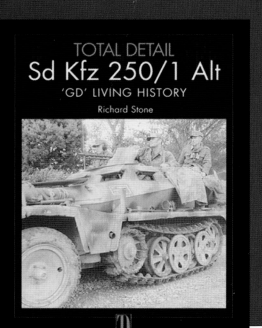

VOLUME ONE - Sd Kfz 250/1 Alt.
'GD' Living History - Available now

Highlights include:
- Oversize A4 - 320 Pages
- Over 250 black and white photographs
- Over 450 colour photographs
- Original Sd Kfz 250/1 Alt
- Original Sd Kfz 251/1 ausf D
- Original Kubelwagen and Schwimmwagen
- The best 'GD' living history group
- Uniforms & full infantry kit in colour
- Ordnance section in colour
- Translated Soldbuch pages
- Rare and unusual items of interest
- Detailed maps and archive pictures

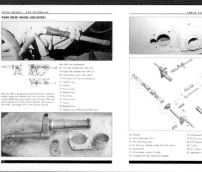

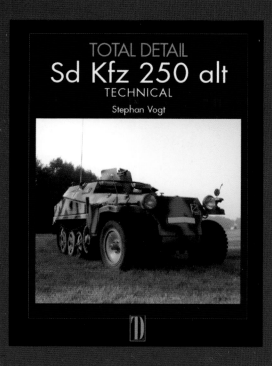

VOLUME TWO
Technical (Spring 2005)

Highlights include:
- Oversize A4
- 300 Pages (approx.)
- 140 pages of technical drawings and detail pictures
- 1:10 and 1:35 scale line drawings
- Complete engine & gearbox details
- Complete chassis and full bodywork drawings
- Full interior details and equipment
- 80 pages of translated original German manuals
- 70 colour pages of all of the existing 250's
- Camouflage schemes
- 3D colour cut away illustrations
- Restoration pictures
- Archive pictures